UNDERSTANDING
Culture's
Influence *ON*
BEHAVIOR

RICHARD BRISLIN

East-West Center
Honolulu, Hawaii

Harcourt Brace Jovanovich College Publishers

Fort Worth   Philadelphia   San Diego   New York   Orlando   Austin   San Antonio
Toronto   Montreal   London   Sydney   Tokyo

To my daughter, Cheryl, who will be
starting college the year this book appears.

Ted Buchholz	PUBLISHER
Eve Howard	ACQUISITIONS EDITOR
Mark Hobbs	PROJECT EDITOR
Debra Jenkin	PRODUCTION MANAGER
Beverly Baker	DESIGNER
Debra J. Wilson	ILLUSTRATIONS
Gary Logan	COVER PHOTOGRAPH

Library of Congress Catalogue Number: 92–072695
ISBN: 0–03–075897–1

Address for editorial correspondence:
Harcourt Brace Jovanovich College Publishers,
301 Commerce Street, Suite 3700, Fort Worth, TX 76102

Address for orders:
Harcourt Brace Jovanovich, Publishers,
6277 Sea Harbor Drive, Orlando, FL 32887.
1–800–782–4479, or 1–800–433–0001 (in Florida)

PRINTED IN THE UNITED STATES OF AMERICA
2 3 4 5 039 9 8 7 6 5 4 3 2 1

CONTENTS IN BRIEF

PREFACE

This text, written for college juniors and seniors enrolled in courses dealing with culture's impact on human behavior, was written with two very basic assumptions. The first is that people, all over the world, will continue to increase their contact with members of diverse cultures. The second is that research in cross-cultural studies can provide very helpful guidelines for people as they interact in a fast-changing world marked by increasing intercultural contact. Given progress in cross-cultural and intercultural studies, texts can be written and courses offered that can stimulate students to understand better their own culture, the cultures of others, and how culture influences human behavior. Often, such a course will be offered out of a psychology department and will have the title "Cross-Cultural Psychology," and this text was written with this course in mind. Given the interest of many other professors in cross-cultural and intercultural studies, however, this text may also prove useful in courses such as intercultural communication, multicultural education, international human resources development, and international management. Given that many professors feel that students should be introduced to issues of cultural diversity as soon as possible, the text may also prove useful for students taking a first course in the study of human behavior.

The reasons for the increase in intercultural contacts are many. People continue to seek opportunities to better themselves by making the decision to emigrate. Students take advantage of educational opportunities in other parts of the world. Jet travel allows easy travel across the globe. As part of their vacations, it is becoming popular for people to actively seek out opportunities to learn about other cultures. Businesspeople in any one country cannot dictate international trade policies. More and more, people from different countries must communicate effectively to establish joint manufacturing agreements and international marketing plans. As more and more countries seek political independence (e.g., within the former U.S.S.R.), growing numbers of highly trained people will be needed to establish workable diplomatic contacts.

Other reasons involve the interaction of people from culturally diverse groups within the same country. In many parts of the world, members of minority groups are refusing to become part of a homogenous melting pot. Instead, they are insisting that their culture be respected and that professionals in various fields be knowledgeable enough to take cultural differences into account. For example, parents want teachers to know about and understand cultural differences that might affect their children's progress in school. Members of minority groups seeking medical help demand that physicians and nurses be sensitive to and knowledgeable about culturally influenced behaviors that affect health care delivery. When people seek jobs or places to live, legal requirements in many countries prohibit discrimination on the basis of gender, ethnicity, race, or religion. In some cases, this means that people who might once have been members of a powerful majority group will be interacting with culturally different others even if they view these interactions as undesirable. Another of the themes of this book is that such people will do well to change their ethnocentric outlook. People will experience far less stress, and may even reap the benefits of being challenged and stimulated by cultural differences, if they accept the reality of increased intercultural contact.

Given that increased intercultural interactions will surely be a reality, many of today's college students can become better prepared through their choice of courses. They can take courses in cross-cultural psychology, intercultural communication, multicultural education, international business, human resource development, and so forth. For some students, however, the study of culture and cultural differences can be an especially difficult task. Even when they know that intercultural contact will be part of their *futures*, they may have had little *previous* experience with cultural differences. They may have grown up in neighborhoods where people were from very homogenous backgrounds. Even if they attended schools with a culturally diverse student body, social norms may have dictated that "different people shouldn't mix" and that "people should stick to their own." In addition, they may rarely have had opportunities to examine the influence of their own culture on their own lives, since such thinking is a rather abstract exercise in the absence of experiences with people from different cultures.

In preparing this text, I have tried to keep in mind that it can be a difficult task to introduce culture and cultural differences. One approach that should help is to ask students to read and analyze various critical incidents, and I have written several for each chapter that should help clarify important concepts. Critical incidents present readers with real situations with which they can empathize: People in the incidents are making decisions about their romantic relationships, about their jobs, about their educations, and about behaviors that can prevent later health problems. All the incidents involve the influence of culture and demand an understanding of cultural differences. People from different cultures are trying to interact and to understand each other, but something goes wrong! Why were the results of the interaction so disappointing? All of the critical incidents involve cultural differences, and all introduce concepts developed by cross-cultural researchers that help in analyzing and understanding the differences. Students can be introduced to the importance of understanding the concepts developed by cross-cultural researchers by seeing the important role the concepts play in various critical incidents similar to some that happen in their own lives. With this introduction as background, the concepts are then more fully explained through discussions of various cross-cultural research studies, the basic "building blocks" of our knowledge about culture's influence on human behavior. The combination of concepts useful in thinking about one's own behavior and the analysis of research studies assists in fulfilling two goals. Many professors who teach courses in the behavioral and social sciences encourage students to gain new insights into their own lives and become exposed to sophisticated research studies at the same time.

Another way of introducing the importance of culture and cultural differences, adopted in this text, is through the selection of research areas with which students already have some familiarity, given their participation in their own culture. For example, all readers have some memories of their own socialization experiences, during which they may have made mistakes but learned about their culture's norms as a result (Chapter 4). All have gone to school (Chapter 5), have been tempted to act in a prejudicial manner and/or have been the target of discrimination (Chapter 6), and have been expected to interact with others who are different, perhaps in terms of social status within their culture (Chapter 7). Most readers will have worked for wages and either are holding down jobs now or will be doing so in the near future (Chapter 8). All readers have had interactions with members of the opposite sex and have undoubtedly wondered about differences among the males and females whom they have known (Chapter 9). All readers desire the benefits of good health and are concerned with behaviors that can prevent health problems (Chapter 10). By starting with their existing knowledge of and interest in these topic areas, information on how culture affects people's socialization, formal education, choices about work, and so forth, can be integrated into the discussions. Ideally, students will gain further insights into their own culture by comparing their experiences with those that are common among people in other countries.

When terms are used carefully, researchers often distinguish between two types of studies. "Cross-cultural research" is the broadest term, and it refers to studies dealing with how culture influences human behavior. One approach to cross-cultural research is to carry out parallel studies, that is, studies of similar concepts in different cultures. For example (and discussed more fully in Chapter 5), Tobin, Wu, and Davidson (1989) studied preschools in Taiwan, Japan, and the United States, with special attention given to how very young children are expected to change as a result of preschool experiences. The documentation of differing expectations yields important and interesting findings. For example, American children are expected to learn to speak up for themselves; the Taiwanese and Japanese children are expected to fit into a group and to downplay individual demands. "Intercultural research" refers to studies of people from different cultures coming into contact and interacting frequently, often in face-to-face relationships. If American children were living in Japan and were attending preschools there (a few case studies of this were discussed by Tobin and his colleagues), then investigators have the opportunity to formulate an intercultural research project. They might examine, for instance, the behaviors of Japanese teachers who are unaccustomed to American children who, in their own country, would be expected to make individual choices about preferred school activities. Studies of intercultural contact make the role of culture especially clear since, often, people are behaving very appropriately from the point of view of norms *in their own culture*. When well-meaning people have difficulties interacting in intercultural settings, examinations of the cultural backgrounds of the people involved often lead to good explanations for the reasons. Both cross-cultural and intercultural research studies will be discussed in this text. In my own teaching, I have found that students often find intercultural studies most interesting since they can often imagine themselves as participants in the types of interaction studied. For example, they can imagine themselves as school children faced with very different cultural expectations. With their interest stimulated, they then enjoy reading the cross-cultural studies that have investigated the role cultural factors play in decisions about important topics such as schooling, mate choice, work, and health.

Many people offered assistance by reviewing chapters, suggesting important research studies for inclusion, testing out chapters in their own teaching, suggesting ideas for how material might best be presented, and offering encouragement when stumbling blocks were encountered. These people include John Adamopoulous, Deborah Best, D.P.S. Bhawuk, Michael Bond, Ayse Carden, Ge Gao, Sharon Gorman, Geert Hofstede, Eve Howard, Shari Koga, Walt Lonner, Roy Malpass, Steven Moles, Janek Pandey, Anita Rosenfield, Karen Schmidt, Larry Smith, Pirong-rong Ramasoota, Ted Singelis, Harry Triandis, Kim Turner, Tu Wei-ming, and Tomoko Yoshida. First drafts of several chapters were written while I held a visiting appointment at Arizona State University, and I am grateful for the support of faculty and staff there. Daniel Romano conceived the drawings that were later developed into the sketches and figures found throughout the text. All of these people greeted this text writing project with enthusiasm, and I hope that our shared excitement about the study of culture's influence on behavior will be conveyed to readers.

CONTENTS

4 SOCIALIZATION

CONCEPTUALIZING CULTURE AND ITS IMPACT

Stan was first attracted to Rogelia when he heard her tell a joke about Imelda Marcos's shoes. Rogelia had never met anyone with the confidence and "take charge" attitude that Stan possessed.

Stan was 23 years old, having moved to the Philippines after completing his education in Ohio. He hadn't traveled very much prior to accepting a job in the Philippines as an agricultural specialist, and most of his friends had been from the same American middle-class background as himself. He had taken courses in tropical agriculture and wanted to see for himself if the recommendations made in the books could be put to use. Rogelia was from a rural village. She moved from the village to Manila, where she met Stan, because of scholarships for academic achievement at the secondary school level. She finished her degree program at the University of the Philippines and was now teaching at a good private school.

Stan and Rogelia started dating and their emotional feelings toward each other intensified. After about six months, however, problems began to occur in the relationship. Rogelia's parents were not happy that she was dating an American. Stan felt that Rogelia's friends disapproved of the relationship and that they were not particularly friendly toward him. Stan and Rogelia then agreed to stop dating, realizing the romantic relationship was not working.

A few weeks after this agreement, Stan called Rogelia and asked her to go to a movie. Stan mentioned that he wanted to continue the friendship. Puzzled by the call, Rogelia refused, letting it be known that she didn't want to see Stan again under any circumstances. Stan was quite puzzled and was very hurt by Rogelia's coolness.

This anecdote involves behaviors that are influenced by people's cultures. The culture in which Rogelia has grown up has given her guidance on specific behaviors: People who were once in a romantic relationship rarely have any contact after that relationship ends. Filipinos believe that maintaining friendly relationships causes jealousy among the persons' eventual marriage partners and interferes with the loyalty expected toward the extended families of the married couple. The culture in which Stan has grown up does not give such explicit guidance. Stan, rather, is in the realm of individual differences. Some Americans maintain close relationships with former romantic partners and some do not. Some want to keep up friendly relationships, and their current spouses even encourage this. Others feel that maintaining such relationships will be too emotionally painful and that it is best to cease contact. Some Americans decide one way and some the other: There is no widely shared set of guidelines, and it is the concept of "widely shared" that is central to an understanding of culture. This point will be reiterated throughout this chapter.

A major difficulty in discussions of culture is that people rarely have the opportunity to examine the influence of their own cultural background on their behavior. Stan and Rogelia, for example, have no way of knowing how the other is interpreting the reasons for their misunderstandings. Coming from backgrounds (Ohio and the rural Philippines) where most people were similar to them, they have never been stimulated to examine culturally based reasons for problems. They are forced to think about such possibilities only because their cultures have come into contact.

As with all of the examples to be discussed throughout this book, many of the issues raised will, hopefully, encourage readers to think about the influence of culture on their own lives. In this example, the behaviors are not unique to Filipino or to Filipino–Americans. The issue of maintaining contact with former romantic partners will be controversial in any culture that emphasizes the importance of the extended family and maintains norms that encourage people to frown upon divorce. Within the United States, for example, Hispanics (Marin & Marin, 1991) who maintain the traditional value of close family ties will be able to identify with Rogelia's preferences. They will not be as comfortable as Anglo–Americans about maintaining close ties with former romantic partners. Note that the term *traditional* is being used. If people move away from the part of the world in which they were socialized (to be discussed more fully in Chapter 4), they will be exposed to cultural differences that challenge their attitudes and values. Many challenges stem from people's desires to move from rural areas of the world to highly industrialized cities. Such moves force people to make adjustments in their lives, and one potential change is that traditional family ties become less strong as people are exposed to the impersonal norms of the big city (Yang, 1988). Some Hispanics have made such a move, have been exposed to values that challenge their traditions, and have decided that they prefer the more modern values. Examples are people from Mexico who have moved to big cities in the United States and who consequently come in day-to-day contact with Anglo–American culture. These Hispanics will be more likely to identify with Stan's preferences. They will agree that relationships with past romantic behaviors can be maintained and that these continuing friendships do not necessarily pose a threat to current romances. In the case of Hispanics, then, it is important to know the amount of exposure that they have had to nontraditional values since both culture *and* culture contact can have an impact on their behavior.

Such contact will become more frequent all around the world, and it will be one of the major influences on life in the twenty-first century. Businesspeople will continue to accept international assignments. Investments across national boundaries will bring additional business-oriented contact (Adler, 1991). The increasing desire for democracy in Eastern Europe and Asia will bring visits by political experts who give instruction in such modern democratic practices as appealing to the electorate through the mass media (Warner, 1990). High-quality advanced education will continue to be a product that students will seek out even if it is in countries other than their own (Paige, 1990). Within large countries, minority groups (e.g., Blacks, Hispanics, and Native Americans in the United States) are refusing to become part of a melting pot and each is demanding that their cultural background be respected. Neighborhoods, schools, businesses, and the delivery of social services will all see the increased effects of legal demands that ensure the rights of previously rejected ethnic groups (Cushner, 1990). All of these facts demand sensitivity to the nature of people's cultures and to cultural differences. Given its complexity, the concept *culture* needs to be the focus of a detailed examination.

CULTURE: PINNING DOWN AN AMORPHOUS CONCEPT

- When doing business with the Japanese, Americans must keep in mind that there are cultural differences in how meetings are carried out and in the way in which contracts are negotiated.
- Don't just go to well-trod tourist spots! Mix with the people and experience their culture.
- The students you will teach will probably not have the same middle-class background as you. They will likely be from different cultures. When preparing lesson plans and making decisions concerning how best to present material to students, this important fact must constantly be remembered.

These statements, typically found in magazines for businesspeople, in tourist guides, and in texts for teacher trainees (respectively), are all correct but contain a potential stumbling block. The concepts *culture* and *cultural differences* are used in ways that may not be very helpful. The danger in the frequent use of the term "culture" is that it contains so much information about values, ideals, concepts, and expected behaviors that the term is not terribly useful in analyzing any one specific aspect. It is the specific aspects of culture that are helpful in analyzing human behavior. In the examples above, the specific aspects of Japanese business practices nontourist activities, and children's expectations about what will happen during the schoolday will guide decisions about behavior. In the example of Rogelia's behavior toward Stan, it is the *specific* guidance concerning continuing relationships with former romantic partners.

To pin down the amorphous concept "culture," it is useful to examine a list of its features in checklist form. These features can then be examined with a possible aspect of one's own culture in mind. Put another way, various "candidates" can be put forward, with consideration focusing on whether or not they are part of one's culture. For example, a candidate for consideration might be "continuing relationships with past romantic partners." To preview a conclusion I will make after this list is considered, the more checklist features a candidate for "an important aspect of my life" has, the more likely it is to actually be culturally influenced. Readers might list a few values, ideals, and assumptions about life that they consider personally important. Examples might be "standing on one's own two feet," "education as a way of advancing oneself in life," "respect for elders," "the right to own handguns," or "respect for the rights of women." Then the list of features of culture can be consulted. The more points on the checklist the candidate passes, in the judgment of a reader, the more likely the candidate is to be part of the reader's culture. If the candidate passes only a few of the checklist-generated questions, then it is probably determined by factors other than culture, such as people's personalities or their idiosyncratic preferences that are not widely enough shared to be considered part of culture. The checklist starts with widely shared views concerning how life should be lived.

ASSUMPTIONS ABOUT LIFE. Culture consists of ideals, values, and assumptions about life that are widely shared among people and that guide specific behaviors. Immediately, we are faced with an element of invisibility. Assumptions and ideals are not immediately obvious. Rather they are stored in people's minds and consequently are hard for outsiders to see. Since the component of ideals and values is part of almost all anthropological definitions of culture (Kroeber & Kluckhohn, 1952), it is important to consider it carefully. Assumptions and values are stored in people's minds and can be called upon when necessary for their usefulness in guiding specific behaviors. The value of "personal cleanliness" guides widely practiced behaviors such as taking a daily bath or shower. Often, when a value is not threatened, there will be no behaviors visible that cause people to think about the value. People don't think much about "cleanliness" if everyone they know is careful about their personal hygiene. But when the value comes into question in some way, behaviors to protect it can be expected if the value is culturally determined. I was once a member of a club that had not held an election of officers in fifty years. Instead, a committee would present a slate of candidates to the membership, and the club members would approve the slate by voice vote. One year, a group of newcomers nominated a candidate for president after the chair of the committee presented the suggested slate. Without blinking an eye, the committee chairperson asked each candidate to give a short speech outlining goals for the club, and also called for pieces of paper so that members could vote. The vote took place. The committee's candidate happened to win, but the new candidate won two years later. The point for consideration here is that the committee chair possessed the cultural value, "election through the democratic process," even though relevant behaviors hadn't been called upon in fifty years. Because of his long-term participation in organizations within his culture outside of this one club, he could call upon behaviors associated with the value *democracy*. He called for speeches and for pieces of paper so that club members could vote by secret ballot. The value of democracy, shared by all club members, was retained. This value was invisible at first since it was contained in members' brains, outside the view of outsiders who might have visited the club that election day. But when called upon, that important value led to visible behaviors.

THE PERSON-MADE PART OF THE ENVIRONMENT. Another key aspect of culture is that it is created by people. Whenever a candidate for a cultural value is considered, aspects that are clearly formulated by people should come to mind. First emphasized by Herskovits (1948), the "person-made" aspects of culture can be contrasted with the environmental givens that people face. Are typhoons in Hawaii part of its culture? Is the cold weather during Minnesota winters part of the culture to which people are exposed? Should the hot and humid weather commonly experienced during summers be considered part of the culture that influences the lives of children born and raised in Alabama or Mississippi? The best answer is "no." These aspects of climate are part of the environment that people face and are not person-made. However, people's *responses* to the environment that surrounds them *are* part of their culture. In many Pacific Island societies, houses are made of inexpensive and readily available materials so that they can be replaced at minimal cost should a typhoon destroy them. In Minnesota, person-made norms about the proper response to snow are so widely known that they are part of psychological personality tests to measure well-socialized individuals. The California Personality Inventory (Gough, 1969) contains the item, "Every family owes it to the city to keep its lawn mowed in summer and sidewalks shoveled in winter." If people answer "agree," this contributes to their score on a scale that measures the internalization of a cultural norm that involves concern for others. Norms for proper behavior are excellent examples of person-made aspects of people's environment, in short, their culture.

There are interesting examples of how person-made responses to their environment influence a variety of other human behaviors. Writing in the *Encyclopedia of Southern Culture*, Arsenault (1989) argues that the introduction of air conditioning had an impact on the cultural value of "Southern hospitality." Prior to about 1950, people would respond to hot and humid summers by sitting out on their porches and chatting with neighbors and passersby on the sidewalk. After the introduction of air conditioning and its widespread adoption in the mid and late 1950s (a good example of a person-made intervention to make life more comfortable), people would sit in their own living rooms and read, watch television, or chat with immediate family members. The sense of a wider community and knowledge about the goings-on in the lives of one's neighbors became noticeably diminished. Person-made interventions (air conditioning and also television) had an impact on a cultural value.

TRANSMISSION GENERATION TO GENERATION. Cultural values exist for long periods of time in a society. Examples of these values can be found in the oral or written literatures of a culture. To look at the point from the opposite direction, cultural values cannot be introduced quickly. It usually takes years for people to become familiar enough with a new value or ideal for it to be considered part of their culture.

     If there are values considered central to a society that have existed for many years, these must be transmitted from one generation to another. Children must learn the values from various elders who have the responsibility to make sure that the children grow up to be acceptable members of the community. These elders include the children's parents, teachers, noteworthy community figures such as politicians and physicians, religious

The time spent watching television can substitute for the sense of

leaders, and so forth. Interestingly, there are often adults in a community who can be considered negative models who do not behave according to the culture's values. These are the adults who have not made the transition from childhood to acceptable and respected members of the community. Examples are criminals, derelicts, the habitually unemployed, and harmless but odd figures sometimes known as "village idiots."

Parents often point to successful adults as the types of people that children can become if they adopt culturally acceptable behaviors, whether these be doing one's homework in the United States or helping adults with the cultivation of crops in a Pacific Island society. Examples of successful adults are lawyers, college professors, and physicians in the United States and chiefs in Pacific Island societies. Approaching their responsibility in another way, adults often point to negative models to convey feelings about unacceptable behaviors, such as laziness or a lack of success in career development. When my father was young, there was a man in the community who wore a hook on his deformed arm. His family name was Jackson, and "Hook" Jackson had the job of cleaning up after horse-drawn carriages that passed through the streets. Teachers and parents would all use Hook as a negative model: "If you don't do your homework [or stop

community that results from frequent conversations with friends.

fighting, or help out around the house with your chores], you'll end up just like Hook Jackson!" Hook passed into a better life by the time of my own childhood, but his activities became part of my family's oral tradition. By telling me stories about Hook and other community characters, my father clearly communicated his thoughts concerning acceptable and unacceptable career choices and the proper preparation (during childhood) for adult responsibilities. Guidance about behavior considered proper in a culture is often contained in stories that elders share with children (Howard, 1991).

EXPERIENCES DURING CHILDHOOD. If cultural values and ideals are transmitted generation to generation, then there must be childhood experiences that lead to the learning and eventual internalization of the values. Put another way, if people write down a candidate for a cultural value, they should be able to think of experiences during their childhood that helped them to learn that value.

Most readers socialized in North America and Europe will agree with the ideal that "it is wise to develop good public speaking skills" because they are so important in a variety of careers. Given this ideal, there must be childhood experiences relating to the development of good public speaking skills. Most people remember childhood experiences (often uncomfortable) surrounding their first public speaking endeavors. They will remember their nervousness, their stumblings, and their anxieties. Often, they will remember physical symptoms, such as excessive sweating, an increased heart rate, and nausea. It takes a great deal of time and practice to develop good public speaking skills, and people become truly comfortable with their supervisor's request to "prepare a speech" only after a number of formal courses in high school and college.

At times, the memorable childhood experiences can lead to specific behaviors associated with public speaking that people practice as adults. When I was 13 or 14, I was in charge of preparations for a Boy Scout hike through a national forest. Later, I was asked to talk about the hike in front of the church group that sponsored the Boy Scout troop. I described everything that went wrong: inadequate food, inadequate cold-weather gear, and problems associated with transportation to and from the national forest where the hike started and ended. My father was in the audience and later took me aside. He said, "Richard, don't ever make excuses when you give a public presentation. People don't want to hear about all these troubles. If there are problems, discuss the positive lessons learned and make jokes about the difficulties." My father was not being overly critical or unkind. He was carefully grooming me to become an adequate public speaker, realizing that this skill is useful in many adult careers.

Interestingly, I later learned that there are clear cultural differences in what is considered to be good public speaking. In Japan and many other Asian countries, speakers often begin with apologies. "Thank you for taking the time and trouble to come. Please forgive this inadequate speech and please forgive me for preparing it so poorly. You know much more about the subject matter than I do." This difference has led to a cross-cultural joke that people, knowledgeable about both styles, frequently share. The role of humor in public presentations was mentioned as part of my father's advice. A Japanese businessperson was visiting a Fortune 500 company in New York. He was asked to give a speech. He began, "I realize that Americans often begin by making a joke. In Japan, we frequently begin with an apology. I'll compromise by apologizing for not having a joke."

CULTURE IS NOT WIDELY DISCUSSED. Readers might engage in a short exercise. Assume that immigrants to their community (from either Mexico, Southeast Asia, or the states formerly comprising the U.S.S.R.) asked the question, "What is there about your culture that I should know so that we can understand each other better?" Readers might list three answers to the question.

My guess is that this will prove to be a difficult exercise. One reason is that people do not frequently ask this or a similar question when they find themselves in the company of others who share the *same* culture. In other words, people do not frequently talk about their own culture or the influence that culture has on their behavior. These mildly non-common-sense assertions may sound strange. On the one hand, I am writing an entire book about the importance of culture in people's lives. On the other hand, I am arguing that people don't talk about it very much.

The explanation of this seeming contradiction is based on the fact that culture is widely shared. Since cultural values and ideals are widely known within a society, people do not have to talk about them very much. If everybody knows and shares a set of ideals and values, there is little need to discuss them. Most North Americans and many Europeans will agree that "voting in a democratic manner" is a cultural value. Yet adults who were socialized into familiarity with the value do not find the need to discuss it with any frequency or in much detail. The value *is* discussed in countries where democracy is a developing value (Romania, Nepal, states of the former U.S.S.R.), and where political activists are demanding it (China, Cuba). Arguments pro and con are lengthy and intense because not all people in these countries are familiar with all aspects of democracy. In North America, with a long tradition of democratic political processes, extensive discussions of democracy itself are unnecessary.

Returning to the example of good public speaking, I have been on selection committees for college and university faculty members. As part of the interview process, candidates frequently give a public presentation. When considering the merits of the various candidates, public speaking skills are not extensively discussed. Committee members are very familiar with the need for these skills, and they have recently seen demonstrations of either their presence or their absence. Consequently, they do not have to spend a great deal of time discussing the quality of candidates' speaking skills. To add to the complexity, public speaking skills can play an important role in the committee members' recommendations. When cultural values and ideals are involved, the length of discussion time devoted to an issue does not necessarily indicate its importance.

There are other important implications stemming from the fact that culture is not frequently discussed. One is that people are poorly prepared to discuss their culture with interested visitors and with people wishing to learn from each other's experiences. To return to the example of voting in democratic elections, many well-educated Americans will not be able to give terribly helpful answers to Russians, Romanians, and Chinese dissidents who ask basic questions about democracy. After a few generalizations such as "voting on the first Tuesday in November" and "candidates selected by two and sometimes a few more major political parties," people become inarticulate. The reason is that democracy in America is taken for granted and consequently people don't have to discuss it as a cultural value. As a result, people *don't have practice* discussing the nature of democracy such that they can explain it to interested outsiders. What they *do have practice* discussing are issues on which there is disagreement within their own culture. Examples are the qualities of different well-known candidates seeking elected office (in contrast to the value of the democratic elections themselves), and the best ways to encourage unregistered voters to become interested in voting (in contrast to the importance of voting as central to democracy). Other examples are the controversial issues about which people in a culture disagree, such as women's right to an abortion, the wisdom of owning handguns kept in one's home, and the right of very old and ill people to enlist the assistance of others if they want to take their own lives. Put another way, these controversial issues are not those on which people in a culture have a widely shared view. As previously discussed, the concept of culture as "widely shared" in a society or community is central to its understanding.

WELL-MEANING CLASHES. Another set of issues that people are poorly prepared to discuss and to interpret are the well-meaning clashes that occur when people from different cultural backgrounds come together and interact in face-to-face encounters. "Well-meaning clashes" is a term that describes encounters in which people are behaving properly and in a socially skilled manner *according to the norms in their own culture*. If the people were interacting with others in their own culture, there would likely be few problems since the people involved share many of the same values and can even remember similar childhood experiences that led to the development of their good manners. But in an interaction with someone who does not share the same cultural background, a clash can develop if the behaviors considered proper and socially skilled in one culture are considered improper or even inappropriate in the other. The term *well-meaning* is used because no one in these interactions is trying to be difficult or unpleasant. All the people involved are trying to be well-mannered and polite. But since the different cultural backgrounds of people lead them to different behaviors considered "well-mannered," clashes often develop. These clashes are difficult to untangle in discussions and explanations because the people involved have had little experience investigating their culture's guidance concerning polite behavior. By the time people reach adulthood, they are supposed to know what good manners are. Why should people discuss them all the time? Given their inexperience, however, explanations to smooth over well-meaning clashes are frequently so poorly done that ill-feelings remain among the people involved.

Well-meaning clashes are impactful and memorable. If there are opportunities to examine the reasons for clashes, some of the most effective learning about the importance of culture can take place. Since the clashes are personally impactful, people want to know why they happened. When they hear that an understanding of *their own* culture is needed for good interpretation, they become interested in their own cultural background, perhaps for the first time. Realizing the possibility that an interpretation of cultural clashes can be a good educational approach, Brislin, Cushner, Cherrie, and Yong (1986) created 100 short incidents that described problematic interactions among people from different cultural backgrounds. Readers are asked to give explanations of the difficulties that the people encountered. Here is one of the 100 incidents, called "Informal gatherings of people."

> After a year in the United States, Fumio, from Japan, seemed to be adjusting well to his graduate-level studies. He had cordial relations with his professors, interacted frequently with other graduate students at mid-day coffee breaks, and was content with his housing arrangements in the graduate student dormitory. Fumio's statistical knowledge was so good that professors recommended that certain American students should consult him for help in this area. He seemed to be excluded, however, from at least one type of activity in which many of the American graduate students participated. This was the informal gathering of students at the local pub (bar) at about 5:00 PM on Friday afternoons. People did not stop and invite him to these gatherings. Since he was not invited, Fumio felt uncomfortable about simply showing up at the pub. Fumio wondered if the lack of an invitation should be interpreted as a sign that he was offending the American students in some way.

What is a good analysis of the situation involving the lack of invitations to the pub gatherings (Brislin, et al., 1986, pp. 203–204)? Readers are then asked to make choices among a variety of alternative explanations, more than one of which can contribute to an understanding of the clash. Here are several possibilities:

1. The Americans were rude in not inviting Fumio, a guest in their country.

2. The pub gatherings are meant to be an activity in which people who are very familiar with each other can relax on an informal basis.

3. Japanese rarely drink beer. Realizing this, the Americans did not invite Fumio.

4. The Americans resented the fact that Fumio knew more statistics than they did and this made the Americans feel inferior because they had to ask Fumio for help.

5. Pub gatherings on Friday afternoons like this one, are largely based on pairings of specific males with specific females. Since Fumio had no girlfriend, he was not invited (adapted from Brislin, et al., 1986, p. 204).

Analysis of this well-meaning clash can be carried out in terms of what is considered well-mannered behavior toward guests. Fumio was acting from his socialization into Japanese culture, which includes the guideline that guests should be invited places. American businesspeople in Japan frequently comment on the number of social gatherings to which they are invited (Ramsey & Birk, 1983). In fact, the social gatherings are so frequent that they can become a drain on the American's energy. "They expect me to go to three nightclubs on a Wednesday night, staying out until 2:00 AM, and then be fresh for an 8:30 AM meeting the next day. And I'm still jet lagged from my trip. How do they do it night after night?" One explanation for this Japanese pattern of after-work socializing is that it is a substitute for lawyers. Americans ask lawyers to protect their interests in business negotiations. The Japanese ask Americans to social gatherings to see if their potential business partners are honest, reliable, and socially sensitive people who can be trusted if agreements to cooperate are signed. There may be greater cost effectiveness in the Japanese approach. It is less expensive to entertain potential partners (even at Tokyo's exorbitant costs at bars and restaurants) than to pay lawyers their $150-plus per hour.

This rather long explanation is necessary to introduce Fumio's point of view. He is accustomed to the practice of *inviting* visitors to social gatherings. Consequently, he quite reasonably expects that if Americans want him to attend a gathering in their country, they will invite him. The Americans, on the other hand, are unconsciously making very fine distinctions within the category, "types of social gatherings." In the case of the Friday afternoon pub gatherings, a key word is "informality." People who work in the organization just show up! There are rarely written invitations or even carefully worded oral reminders concerning the gatherings. After drinks are ordered at the pub, people sit around telling humorous stories and complaining about their superiors. In so doing they let off steam, relaxing with people whom they know well. Since everybody knows each other, time and energy do not have to be spent on introductions of newcomers, making good first impressions, and searches for topics of conversation to which everyone can contribute.

Fumio is at several disadvantages with respect to this type of social gathering. He doesn't know the custom of simply showing up at a pub whether one is invited or not. If he does show up, he may feel uncomfortable since he cannot participate smoothly in the telling of jokes (more about this point, below). He may sense that he is a damper on the merrymaking if people do not try to find conversational topics to which he can contribute. Or, he may find that the people try *so hard* to find topics they are obviously straining themselves and are thus detracting from their own enjoyment. (Further discussions of interactions across cultural boundaries will take place in Chapters 6 and 7; see also Stephan, 1985.)

The clash, then, is between two sets of expectations that people have brought from their cultural backgrounds: "guests are invited" versus "people just show up." Is the clash well-meaning? Were the people involved trying to be decent according to the guidelines of their culture? Here, the behavior of the Americans should come under scrutiny. Were they being rude (alternative explanation number one, above), thus demonstrating an absence of well-meaningness? As with the analysis of many intercultural encounters, the answer lies in fine distinctions (Foa & Chemers, 1967). Are the Americans being rude? insensitive? unthinking? A case can be made for the latter. Returning to the point that culture becomes taken for granted and not discussed, the Americans might not have thought much about the necessity of issuing an invitation to Fumio. They might have unthinkingly felt that if Fumio wants to come, he will just show up. One of the very difficult issues in the analysis of behaviors influenced by culture is that since they are so accepted and taken for granted, people don't think about the need to explain the behavior to outsiders.

The incident involving Fumio and the American students also allows me to review a difficult point introduced earlier in the analysis of Rogelia and Stan's difficulty. The distinction between cultural variables and individual differences is not an easy one to make, yet it is critical in the study of culture and behavior. Recall that one of the alternatives that might be helpful in analyzing Fumio's difficulties (number 4, above) centered on the possibility of jealousy. The Americans may have resented Fumio's superior knowledge of statistics and may have avoided him due to their jealousy. This alternative is an example of an "individual differences" explanation. There are undoubtedly a few individuals who would be jealous if a colleague like Fumio came to their organization. On the other hand, there are other individuals who will be happy to have Fumio around since they can ask him for help on difficult problems. The certainty of a jealous reaction is not so widespread that it can be considered part of American culture. Rather, a few people might be jealous, a few might be happy to know a person who can help them, a few might be proud of Fumio since he brings positive attention to the organization as a whole, and a few will dislike statistics so much that they don't care one way or the other. People react in a variety of ways, a clear case of individual differences. Knowledge about or participation in after-work-hours gatherings, on the other hand, is widely enough shared to be considered part of American culture. The *exact place* where the gatherings take place differs according to people's occupations: bars serving a great deal of beer for laborers, colorful but mildly seedy pubs near college campuses for graduate students, and cocktail lounges for young urban professionals. The similarity is that all are after-hours gatherings at which people "just show up," and this is an aspect of the people's culture.

CULTURE ALLOWS PEOPLE TO FILL IN THE BLANKS. If values and behaviors are culturally influenced, people should be able to expand on the issues involved when given a short sketch that captures a few key elements (Higgins & Bargh, 1987). Consider the example of Fumio again. Alternative explanation number 5 suggests that these Friday afternoon gatherings are based on pairings of specific males and specific females. Knowledgeable people discount this explanation for the reasons already discussed: People just show up after work hours, and Friday is a workday. But if later asked, "What if the gathering was on a Saturday night? Is it *more likely* that attendance would involve pairings of specific males and specific females?", many Americans will answer "yes." To use the language introduced here, they will be able to fill in the blanks when given a description of some basic social encounters that are influenced by culture. To return to the example involving the club that had not held elections in 50 years, most people whose culture includes a long history of democratic participation could predict what the chairperson would do when faced with an unexpected nomination from the floor. Given this basic sketch, people can predict that there will be speeches, passing out of ballots, secret voting, counting of ballots, announcement of the winner, and a gracious acceptance speech by the winner.

Another example may be helpful. I might tell others, "We have a distinguished visitor who will give a talk to our organization at 3:00 PM, and there will be a short reception at 4:00 PM. We expect twenty people. Can someone plan a reception for a budget of $100?" If a person is familiar with American culture, he or she can "fill in the blanks" and plan a decent reception. Will there be vintage French wines and caviar? Not on a $100 budget! Filling in the blanks here means that the person will probably reserve a room that can hold thirty comfortably (in case a few more than expected show up), will make sure that a high-status executive is present who can give a short speech thanking the visitor, and will order pastries, coffee, and a fruit punch.

When considering the "filling in the blanks" test of a candidate for a cultural value or practice, it is wise to place oneself in the position of an outsider to one's culture. To use the three examples, will an outsider (someone socialized in another culture) know the distinction between

Friday and Saturday night gatherings, know how to proceed according to democratic election practices, and know what is reasonable to do for $100 at a reception? The answer is clearly "no." The detailed knowledge that people can bring to a short sketch of behaviors influenced by culture can be startling when considered carefully. To reiterate a point, such knowledge is taken for granted among people within a culture, and they find little need to talk about it in great detail. This leaves people ill-prepared to present the detailed knowledge to others, for instance, to a newly arrived colleague from India who volunteers to organize the reception.

This discussion of details associated with cultural practices allows me to fulfill a promise that I made earlier: I will discuss the place of humor. As implied in the discussion of well-meaning clashes, one of the best ways to gain insights into one's own culture is to talk with outsiders who are trying to adapt to and understand it. Once a friendly relationship is established with long-term visitors to a culture (e.g., foreign students obtaining degrees on overseas-study grants, businesspeople setting up international joint ventures), good conversations can be held concerning cultural differences. The question, "What do you find puzzling or difficult in this country [or community, or organization]?" frequently yields interesting answers. One often-heard response is that long-term visitors (sometimes called sojourners) find it difficult to participate in at least one major type of informal interaction with people in the host culture. These are the interactions that involve the sharing of jokes and funny stories. It must be kept in mind that such interactions are frequent: during coffee breaks in one's organization, at informal lunches with co-workers, during the after-work-hours gatherings already discussed, as part of weekend social activities, and so forth. Sojourners complain that they don't understand the jokes and can't tell any that others will find funny. As a result, the sojourners feel out of place and also conclude that they are a damper on the other people's good times.

One reason why the jokes are hard to understand is that there is often extensive detail that people have to understand and combine to "get" the joke. Much humor is based on two categories coming together and being "twisted" into one another. Ordinarily, the two categories are not combined in everyday thinking and talking. The discovery of how the two categories are being combined in a unique manner is the basis of "getting the point" of the joke. Jay Leno tells his audience that there was a rat discovered living in the basement of the United States Senate. However, the senators won't be bringing in an exterminator because they always look after their own. The reason why this story is humorous is that rarely combined categories, what rodent exterminators do and what United States Senators do, are twisted into one another. Discovering the point behind the twisting is intellectually satisfying and pleasurable and the discovery is one reason for the resulting laughter people express. People must know the content (sometimes extensive) of the categories. In this example, people must know about the long history of wheelings and dealings, some venturing into the unethical and dishonest, in which United States Senators engage. Outsiders might be unaware of American's traditional ambivalence between respect and distrust regarding its elected officials.

Another example of a humorous story, this time involving even more detailed knowledge of the categories involved, may make this presentation clearer. A man wanting a career as a nightclub entertainer taught a dog how to talk. The man and his dog went to a prestigious booking agent who asked the man to put on a demonstration of the dog's skills. The man asked the dog: "What's the top of a house called?"

DOG: Roof!
MAN: What's the texture of sandpaper?
DOG: Rough!
MAN: What do you do for the home team at the football game?
DOG: Root!
MAN: Who was the greatest baseball player ever?
DOG: Ruth!

At this point the booking agent threw the man and his dog out of his office. Outside, on the street, the dog told the man, "I told you that the best baseball player was Joe DiMaggio!"

Imagine the predicament of sojourners from Germany who hear this story at the water cooler during an informal break where they work. They have to know an incredible amount of knowledge: the onomatopoeic quality of the words, "rough," "root," and a dog's barking sound. In other languages, just as an aside, the word for a dog's bark is *another* but quite different approximation of what *they* hear as the barking sound. Sojourners have to know that there are real arguments among baseball fans concerning who was the better player, given that they both had immense talent: George Herman "Babe" Ruth or Joe DiMaggio. Then, the sojourners have to see how the categories "similar sounds to a dog's bark" and "great baseball players" are twisted together. It is little wonder that they find informal gatherings that involve the telling of humorous stories so troublesome. The major point for discussions of culture's influences on behavior is to reiterate the conclusion that culture presents detailed knowledge and this knowledge is taken for granted. Outsiders, not socialized into familiarity with American baseball and familiarity with a collection of disparate words, will be unable to participate fully in cultural practices that demand detailed knowledge. The sojourners will be unable to "fill in the blanks" when given the basic sketches that are the core of most humorous stories.

CULTURAL VALUES REMAIN DESPITE COMPROMISES AND SLIP-UPS. If a value is strongly influenced by culture, it remains in force even when obvious compromises, blunders, exceptions, and slip-ups come quickly to mind. Let's look at another candidate for a cultural value in the United States: a free press whose members can pursue the truth (and later report openly in the newspapers or on television) as they see fit. I believe that most readers will agree that this is a cultural value. Some who have had courses in journalism will be able to make arguments that a free and vigorous press, even though it is often bothersome and even abrasive, is preferable to alternatives such as government-controlled media. But are there compromises and slip-ups in the practices of a free press? There certainly are! The press is far more likely to pursue stories with an obvious visual or attention-grabbing aspect. It is more "newsworthy" to cover the one embezzler being carted off to jail (with his hat in front of his face) than it is to cover the 1000 people in the same organization who show up at work day after day. It is easier to research stories about powerless people (e.g., the homeless, victims at the scene of airplane accidents) than about the powerful, who have layers of assistants and secretaries well trained in the art of saying "no" graciously. When deciding on which stories to pursue, reporters too often have to take into account possible repercussions stemming from coverage of the rich or powerful. Most reporters with whom I have talked point to stories that were "killed" by their editors because there were negative consequences (loss in advertising revenue, loss of political support for upcoming planned mergers with other newspapers or TV stations) that the editors wanted to avoid. On the other hand, reporters are sometimes so vigorous in their quest for news that they blow minor stories out of proportion and/or taint the reputations of honest people somehow peripherally associated with the story.

Despite these admitted difficulties and blunders, does the cultural value of a "free press" remain? I believe that the answer is "yes." Even though large numbers of exceptions can be named, people are likely to conclude that the value remains part of American culture. In Japan, a candidate for a cultural value might be "respect for people who teach our country's 5- to 18-year-olds." Are there exceptions? Certainly! There are incompetent teachers in Japan as there are in all professions. Some parents quietly and secretly maneuver so that their children are not assigned to those teachers toward whom they have little respect. These exceptions, however, do not interfere with the basic Japanese value of respect toward teachers (Stevenson, Azuma, & Hakuta, 1986).

The concept that values remain despite compromises can also be addressed by looking at examples that probably do not "pass the test." One has already been introduced. Is "respect for teachers of our 5- to 18-year-olds" a cultural value *in the United States*? I believe that there are too many slip-ups, and consequently, a "yes" answer is inappropriate. There are too many mothers and fathers who tell their brightest sons and daughters, "You can do so much better than to become a high school teacher!" There are too many college professors and physicians who quickly move on to others at a cocktail party when they find the person next to them is an elementary school teacher. We *could* point to ideals and argue (rightly, in my opinion) that there are few professions more important than the one that guides and educates our young citizens, but there are too many everyday challenges to this ideal for it to be part of American culture. Is "equal rights for women" a cultural value? It may be in the future, but there are too many exceptions for a "yes" answer today. There are too many marriages where women contribute to the household income *and* do far more than 50 percent of the housework (Biernat & Wortman, 1991). There are too many careers that women have to "put on hold" given the demands of childbirth and child-rearing for which American business, industry, and academia show little concern. In the cases of respect for teaching and equal rights for women, the test of "remains despite slip-ups" yields the conclusion that these are *not* part of American culture.

EMOTIONAL REACTIONS WHEN OBSERVING VIOLATIONS. People find violations of culturally influenced values and practices emotionally arousing. They do not respond, "Oh, isn't that an interesting exception to what our culture practices!" Rather, they respond in a much more emotional manner. They might become obviously angry or upset if the social setting permits such reactions. If they have to mask their feelings for one reason or another, there will be less visible emotional reactions such as increased heart rate, sweating, heavier breathing, increased blood pressure, and churning of the stomach. For example, even if people raised in a Christian religion have not seen the inside of a church for a long time, they will become upset if religious objects are the targets of disrespect. The value of "respect for the religion of my childhood" yields an emotional reaction if they see others use a Bible to press leaves or to prop up their feet. Returning to other examples introduced in this chapter, there will be emotional reactions if the president of a club does *not* hold democratic elections for his or her successor if such procedures are requested by a sizable percentage of the membership. Despite widespread disappointment and even disgust with the efforts of television and newspaper reporters, the vast majority of Americans would become visibly upset if the government placed restrictions on a free press. Some of the candidates for cultural values do not pass this "makes people react emotionally" test. I don't believe that most readers would become visibly upset if they overheard one college student try to persuade another to abandon plans for a career in elementary school education.

ACCEPTANCE AND REJECTION OVER TIME. People can reject a cultural value at one point in their lives and accept it at other times. The clearest example may be participation in democratic elections. Less than 50 percent of eligible voters participate on any one election day. At first glance, this would seem to indicate that democratic elections are not widespread enough to be considered cultural. The key point here is that the non-voters can participate on *another* election day at a future point in their lives. If compelling candidates are competing for the same office, or if important issues are under consideration, people may leave their homes and become participants in the electoral process. In addition to giving up their right to participate in elections, some young people seem to reject the values of their culture altogether. They abandon contact with their families, join communes, protest intensely against government policies, dress in a manner likely to offend a society's well-mannered citizens, and so forth. These same rebellious people, however, have been exposed to the values of their culture and have participated in the sorts of childhood experiences that educate them about their culture. At a later point in their adulthood they can reenter their culture, put on attractive workclothes, wash their hair, and seek employment. Most readers probably know a few people who were extremely rebellious during their youth but who now are vice-presidents of large organizations or who are full professors at our fine colleges and universities.

Another example that is interesting to consider is "the right to a trial before a jury, with a set of rights guaranteed by the Constitution." It is extremely easy to become irritated and disgusted with this set of values when society's sleazeballs who are clearly guilty "get off" because the evidence against them was gathered through unconstitutional means. These same values, however, become important and cherished when people's loved ones (or the people themselves) are accused of a crime.

THE DIFFICULTY OF FAST CHANGE. When changes in cultural values are considered, there is likely to be the reaction that "this will be extremely difficult and time consuming." This reaction will apply both to existing cultural values that might be changed, or existing values that we may want to become part of our culture. We may decide that we want to encourage our best and brightest students to enter the teaching profession so that they can educate our 5- to 18-year-olds. This goal demands that our culture begins to give teachers more status and respect. Will greater respect for the teaching profession become part of American culture in the near future? I don't believe so. Assuming that our culture's leaders decide to make it a value (itself a problematic step in the process), it will take several generations for the value to be considered widespread. Salaries will have to be increased. Career counselors will have to recommend the teaching profession. Obviously bright and able people will have to enter the profession and become positive role models for the next generation. None of these steps will happen quickly or easily.

American society has seen the challenging of cultural assumptions during the twentieth century, but these challenges have involved incredible amounts of effort. Looking back on America's history, it is a fair conclusion that there was a value placed on the separation of races. As late as the 1920's and 1930's, most Americans agreed with the sentiment that "it is best to keep the Black and White races as distinct from each other as possible." This value was clearly visible in society's segregated schools, churches, and neighborhoods (Brophy, 1989). It was seen in the designation of occupations that were considered suitable for Whites and Blacks. It was seen in laws ("Jim Crow") that set firm standards of who could and who could not use public accommodations, such as swimming pools, restrooms, and restaurants. Cultural values have certainly been challenged since the 1940's in the set of efforts collectively called the civil rights movement (Williams, 1987). But simply pointing out that the efforts have been undertaken "since the 1940's" is a reminder of how long it takes to change cultural values and how much effort has been invested. Many readers will be able to make convincing arguments that the value of racial equality is *still* not part of American culture after over 50 years of intense effort (e.g., Gaertner & Dovidio, 1986). There are still too many exceptions (violent racial incidents, de facto neighborhood segregation, less-than-adequate housing and inner-city schools) for "racial equality" to be considered part of American culture.

SUMMARIZABLE IN SHARP CONTRASTS. Some cultural differences can be summarized in sharp contrasts that differentiate behavior in one society compared to another. Some of the most important and early analyses on the difficulties of understanding cultures other than one's own were written by Edward Hall (1959, 1966, 1976). One of the reasons his contributions are widely cited is his great skill at pointing out sharp contrasts that summarize large numbers of specific behaviors that are puzzling to people. Three of his analyses (covered in the three books cited above, respectively) are people's use of time, the spatial orientation they adopt when interacting with others, and the distinction between high and low context.

Punctuality is probably the clearest example involving the dimension of time. When meetings are scheduled to start at 10:00 AM in a North American organization, attendees can expect the meeting to start either promptly or at 10:10 AM at the latest. At 10:12 AM, it is considered quite proper for someone to say, "Perhaps we should start. Some people have eleven o'clock appointments." This sort of scheduling is not possible in other parts of the world, notably Latin America and many Asian countries. Meetings scheduled for 10:00 AM may start by 11:15 AM, but then again they may not. Complaints about the lack of punctuality and the difficulties of keeping an efficient schedule are common in the "war stories" of North American businesspeople who travel to South America. There are many reasons for this cultural difference in the importance of punctuality. One is the priority people put on the requests for their time. In North America, businesspeople on their way to a meeting at 11:00 AM may be interrupted by a co-worker needing help on a stock market analysis. In such cases it is proper to say, "I have an 11 o'clock. Can we chat about it after lunch, say 1:30?" In other parts of the world, the needs of the person making the last-minute request for assistance are *as important* as the needs of the person waiting for the previously scheduled meeting. Given the cultural appropriateness of treating the two individuals equally at the moment, the businesspeople try to help both by giving assistance to one immediately, realizing that the other will "understand" and will be willing to wait. The preference to offer immediate help reflects a concern with "event time" in contrast to "clock time." Events take a certain amount of time. When one event is completed (e.g., helping someone) the next event can start (e.g., keeping the appointment). "Clock time" involves greater attention to the formal appointment. Many Hispanic–Americans and Filipino–Americans retain a preference for event time and consequently are sometimes labeled as "not punctual."

The spatial orientation people choose when interacting with each other is also the subject matter of "war stories." In North America, how close together do two people stand if they meet each other at an informal reception? The answer is approximately the length of a tall man's arm: three feet. If the distance is closer than three feet, then one or both of the two people may become uncomfortable. If one person is male and the other female, the conclusion may be that sexual advances are involved. If the people are of the same gender, sexual advances are still a possibility, and another is that one of the people will be judged as "pushy." In other parts of the world, including Latin America, the distance new acquaintances adopt is closer: two to two-and-a-half feet is more appropriate. The possibility of intercultural difficulties should be immediately clear. If an attractive North American male meets an attractive Latin American female, the distance they adopt might be two feet from each other. The female might say to herself, "This is a prim and proper distance with which I am comfortable." The male might conclude, "She is interested in me personally. Perhaps I can ask her out for a date!"

Conclusions about people's intentions can also be made if the distance is *more* than people find comfortable. In North America, if people adopt a distance of four feet or more, it is easy to conclude that they have cool feelings toward each other. Sometimes this conclusion is correct, but there can be exceptions. Specialists who work with the deaf, upon hearing a presentation on cultural differences in the spatial orientation of people, sometimes apply the concepts to a problem they have observed. When hearing individuals interact with a deaf individual who uses American sign language, the deaf person seems to prefer a distance of about four feet. The hearing individual often concludes that the deaf individual does not want to have much future interaction: the adopted distance is interpreted as a polite signal that further development of an interpersonal relationship is not desired. The deaf person, however, has adopted the distance with which she or he is comfortable. Deaf people need a four-foot distance to express themselves using their sign language. Some signs involve movements of the hands away from the body. If they stood closer than four feet, they would sometimes strike the other person with their hands! A major theme to be covered and reviewed throughout this book is that if these cultural factors are understood, people from very different backgrounds will make fewer negative judgments about each other.

A third sharp contrast involves behavior in cultures called "high context" and "low context." In high-context cultures, the rules, norms, and guidelines for various types of social encounters are very clear. Everyone well-socialized into the culture knows exactly how to behave in a variety of situations. At meetings in an organization, who is the first to speak? When meeting people for the first time, how do people know when they have introduced a topic of conversation that someone does not want to pursue? How do people indicate a need for privacy? Who takes credit for successful outcomes accomplished through team effort? In high-context cultures, everyone knows the answers. In low-context cultures, all these questions lead to negotiations of one sort or another. Since there are no rules, people have to invest a great deal of time and energy in formulating ad-hoc solutions. A good example of the difference can be seen during a large organization's meetings in Japan compared to those held in the United States (Christopher, 1983). How does a person best introduce a new plan for future business ventures? In Japan, people know the rules. The person goes around to the offices of all the individuals who might be affected by the proposal. After these one-on-one meetings, the concerns of others are integrated into a final draft. This is also "cleared" with the people affected. Then, during a formal meeting of company executives, the new proposal is put on the table. In actuality, this step is a formality because by this time everyone present knows a great deal about the proposal. The proposal is then approved by consensus, with a formal voice vote rarely taken. This is high-context behavior: Everyone knows what to do!

Compared to Japan, the United States is considered a low-context culture. There are many ways to accomplish one's goals, and Americans feel constrained if there are too many rules (Hofstede, 1980). For example, there are a number of ways to introduce a proposal in one's organization. A person can follow the typically Japanese route as outlined. Or, the person can introduce the proposal at a meeting even if the people present have not heard about the ideas involved. Or, the person can ask a highly respected executive to introduce the proposal, and in so doing communicate a willingness to share the credit for any eventual successes. There are other, clever ways if the person desirous of introducing the proposal feels that there will be a set of negative reactions that might kill efforts at early stages of the planning. The person might "leak" the proposal to a newspaper reporter. The story appears in the press, the sources of and reasons for negative reactions become clear, and the person then addresses those people and their reactions in future efforts (Brislin, 1991). The important point for the present discussion is that the exact guidelines for behavior are not clear: the behavior is low context.

Another example that may make the distinction clear involves a cultural change within the United States (and many other highly industrialized nations) over the past 60 or 70 years. During the early part of this century, marriage was high context. People knew what to do: The male would be the breadwinner, and the woman would stay home, raise the children, and have dinner on the table when the man came home. People didn't have to spend time and energy on such questions as How will we arrange for day-care? Where will we live? Who makes the major decisions involving the family? The answers, respectively, were that day-care is a strange concept because the woman stays home with the children, the family lives where the man obtains the best job possible, and the man makes the decisions. When there were problems, my mother tells me, the support groups for all the people involved had one basic message: Keep the marriage together! Everybody knew these facts; it was high context. Currently, the answers and the goals are not as clear. To experience challenges and positive self-identities, many women seek work that takes place outside the home. If a couple decides to have children, day-care becomes a topic for consideration. Couples have to negotiate where they will live. Will it be where the man or the woman gets the best job? Decisions about important issues are reached after discussion and negotiation. If there are problems, there are a number of available and acceptable solutions, and keeping the marriage together is one of many. The answers to questions and guidelines for behavior are not at all clear—marriage is low context. The absence of guidelines and widely accepted norms is undoubtedly one reason for the high divorce rate in the world's most industrialized nations.

REVIEWING THE CHECKLIST OF CULTURE'S FEATURES

When people ask themselves whether or not certain ideals or expected behaviors are part of their culture, they can consider these possibilities as "candidates" for the status of culturally influenced. Then, they can proceed down the checklist and ask whether or not the candidate passes the test implied in each checklist entry. The more entries that are "passed," the higher the probability that the candidate is part of culture.

To review, the features of culture to be considered are as follows:

1. Culture consists of ideals, values, and assumptions about life that guide specific behaviors.

2. Culture consists of those aspects of the environment that people make.

3. Culture is transmitted generation to generation, with the responsibility given to parents, teachers, religious leaders, and other respected elders in a community.

4. The fact summarized in point number 3 means that there will be childhood experiences that many people in a community remember happening to them.

5. Aspects of one's culture are not frequently discussed by adults. Since culture is widely shared and accepted, there is little reason to discuss it frequently.

6. Culture can become clearest in well-meaning clashes. This term refers to interactions among people from very different backgrounds. They may behave in proper ways according to their socialization, but there is a clash when the people from different cultures interact.

7. Culture allows people to "fill in the blanks" when presented with a basic sketch of familiar behaviors.

8. Cultural values remain despite compromises and slip-ups. Even though people can list exceptions, the cultural value is seen as a constant that continues to guide specific behaviors.

9. There are emotional reactions when cultural values are violated or when a culture's expected behaviors are ignored.

10. There can be acceptance and rejection of a culture's values at different times in a person's life. Common examples involve rebellious adolescents and young adults who accept a culture's expectations after having children of their own.

11. When changes in cultural values are contemplated, the reaction that "this will be difficult and time consuming" is likely.

12. When comparing proper and expected behavior across cultures, some observations are summarizable in sharp contrasts. Examples are the treatment of time, the spatial orientations that people adopt, and the clarity (versus lack thereof) of the rules and norms for certain complex behaviors.

EXAMPLE OF A CANDIDATE: THE DIFFUSION OF POWER

One important use of the checklist of cultural features is that it can encourage examination of behaviors that people have not thought about very much. Point number 5, above, suggests that culture is widely accepted and taken for granted. If it is taken for granted, people do not have the opportunity to examine very basic aspects of their lives. One such important but rarely examined value, in my opinion, is the diffusion of power in the United States. No one person or group of people has a monopoly on power. Rather, power is spread throughout diffuse and sometimes competing groups. Further, without thinking about it too much, Americans are happy with this state of affairs (Brislin, 1991). Consider the candidate "diffusion of power" in light of the twelve-point checklist.

The cultural value that power should be diffuse affects a large number of specific behaviors. Consider the introduction and possible acceptance of proposals for new legislation. The number of people who become involved is massive (Smith, 1988): members of the legislative branch of government, the country or state's chief executive, lobby groups, the press, influential community leaders, possibly the judiciary, and so forth. Yes, the fact that so many people have to give their input is frustrating to those who want to see a certain piece of legislation implemented quickly. The inefficiency and time demands, however, are a protection against tyrants (Crick, 1982). If the system to implement legislation was so efficient that new laws could be passed and enforced quickly, then tyrants could use the system to introduce their own venal agenda. The quick passage of housing legislation to help the homeless seems desirable. The quick passage of legislation to dictate a set of politically oriented books that all schoolchildren must read is not. To protect against megalomaniacs who would abuse a system that allows quick passage of laws, the cultural value of power diffusion has been widely accepted (if not frequently examined in detail).

The specific behaviors that diffusion of power guides, then, are the involvement of many people who must invest a great deal of time pursuing their goals (feature number 1 in the checklist). Many specific "person-made aspects" stemming from power's diffuseness have been incorporated into American culture (feature number 2). Just one is the important role of people who can form coalitions among members of competing factions. Such people are able to communicate effectively with all factions *and* be trusted by large numbers of people within each group. Such people are extremely valuable to the workings of a democracy: Without them factions would dissipate their energies complaining about each other. Governments in newly developing democracies in Eastern Europe and the former U.S.S.R. will be dependent upon people able to communicate with feisty individuals from the multiple parties that have been created since the rejection of communism.

There is transmission of information from generation to generation (feature 3). Respected leaders pass their wisdom on to younger people in a process commonly called "mentoring." Much of the mentoring process involves what might be called the "unwritten rules of power" or how people *really* use selected strategies to maneuver around competing factions (Kipnis, 1984). Childhood experiences are impactful (feature 4). On entering into major life transitions such as going away to college, many parents tell their children, "Don't make enemies today because these people won't be around to help you tomorrow." Updated with application to achieving goals in one's organization, the advice is "Don't reject or ignore people who you think might be enemies today. If people become enemies, they are not available to contribute their talents to coalitions tomorrow."

Once it is assumed that people *should* know about power diffusion and the necessity of maneuvering among factions, then this aspect of American culture is not frequently discussed (feature 5). I have seen attractive and intelligent 30-year-olds kept out of powerful decision-making groups because they make too many enemies. The leaders realize that the young adults will hurt the group more than help it if they irritate others who might be able to assist the group attain its goals. But because the 30-year-olds *should* know this aspect of their culture, nobody tells them why they are not invited to important meetings of the group.

Differing approaches to power lead to impactful clashes (feature 6). Consider the case of people from a culture where there has long been only one political party and one type of government that can be discussed. If these people travel to a country where there are many political parties and open debate about the best form of government, they are completely unprepared to defend their political views. They have never had the experience of participating in a vigorous discussion involving the serious consideration of alternative views. They become upset and even emotionally distraught (feature 9) when asked very simple questions about possible shortcomings in their government's approach to the use of power.

Examples of "filling in the blanks" (feature 7) can be the exact behaviors necessary to deal with power's diffuseness. If the phrase "form coalitions" is mentioned, sophisticated people can fill in exact steps (Brislin, 1991). For example, people should identify the interests of various factions to determine if there are similarities around which a coalition can form. Once goals are established, it is wise to ask, "What powerful people will be helped and hurt by the proposals formulated to achieve these goals." Then, the assistance of those who will be helped can be enlisted and modifications to the proposals can be made to satisfy or at least to neutralize the opposition. The important point to consider here is that explicit instruction concerning the necessity of such steps is unnecessary among sophisticated people. Given the basic sketch concerning the necessity to form coalitions among members of competing factions, sophisticated people can fill in the blanks and engage in the necessary specific behaviors.

There are many compromises and slip-ups in the use of power. Occasionally people try to monopolize power and are unwilling to share decision making with others. They do not form coalitions. Rather, they try to dictate their whims. If they have money, or a high position within their organization, or the ability to punish others who do not do their bidding, they can be successful *for a time*. But eventually, they are likely to lose power and to become uninfluential and sometimes pathetic figures within their society. A few moments of thought should bring to mind people in national politics who fit this description: the members of Richard Nixon's inner circle are prime examples. Readers can probably think of others who worked in smaller scale arenas such as universities, business organizations, or local government bureaucracies. The temporary successes of these people are "slip-ups" to the cultural value that power should be diffuse. The slip-ups and compromises do not damage the value.

Acceptance and rejection over time (feature 10) is common when power is considered. Many young adults complain that power's necessities such as coalition formation lead to practices such as backroom deals. Later, they find that they can't think of an alternative. If they want certain proposals to become implemented, they will need help. In return for the help, powerful people will expect favors to be returned. In forging coalitions, if there is an alternative to the maxim that "if you scratch my back I'll scratch yours," I am unaware of it. Yet it takes a great deal of time for people to learn the necessary behaviors that accompany a democracy's diffuseness of power (feature 11). As mentioned above, it will take countries in Eastern Europe a great deal of time to develop leaders who are comfortable with democracy. Part of power's diffuseness is that an electorate can remove powerholders from office. This means that leaders have to remain attractive to voters, a fact not necessary to consider under previous totalitarian governments. Amusing stories will continue to be written (e.g., Warner, 1990) about Eastern European leaders who are learning to make political television commercials, talk in 10-second sound bytes, and stage attractive media events to call attention to themselves. Such behaviors, of course, are in sharp contrast (feature 12) to the "we dictate, you accept" relation of government leaders to their citizenry.

I believe that the value that power should be diffuse "passes" the test: When the 12 features are considered, the indications are that the value is part of American culture. At this point, the concept of cultural values should be becoming clear. There are widely accepted ideals of how a society *should* work that guide the choice of specific behaviors. Another way to examine how culture works is to consider a number of theoretical developments that social and behavioral scientists (educators, psychologists, communication researchers, anthropologists, etc.) have contributed. These theoretical ideas are very helpful in answering the question: What are some of the major ways in which cultures differ? Some of these ideas involve sharp contrasts (feature 12) and consequently can be understood if behaviors commonly found in one's own culture are compared with behaviors in other cultures that differ in significant ways. Some of the theoretical contributions may seem overly abstract and unhelpful at first glance, but if care is devoted to their understanding rich dividends will be paid. A number of such theoretical contributions, useful in understanding the arguments made in the remainder of this book, are covered in Chapter 2.

2

THEORETICAL CONCEPTS THAT ASSIST IN THE UNDERSTANDING OF CULTURE

The analysis of culture's influence on behavior is not an easy task. Just one reason is that there are so many specific cultural differences found around the world that the challenge of understanding even a small percentage of the differences seems impossible. One approach to the problem is to set aside (but not ignore) the quest for specific details and instead to aim at the discovery of concepts that *underlie* specific differences. In Chapter 1, for instance, cultural differences regarding the proper way to behave at business meetings were discussed. Many specific differences could have been listed, but these would soon tax the patience and memories of readers. The approach chosen was to discuss a concept at a higher level of generalization that should put specific differences in a helpful perspective. That more general concept was high versus low context: well-accepted rules versus ad-hoc negotiations among individuals.

I believe that there are a number of such general concepts that, if understood, assist in the analysis of many behaviors in many areas of life: school, workplace, family, and so forth. Indeed, these places where many important behaviors occur will be the subject of later chapters. To meet the joint goals of (a) continuing the discussion of culture and cultural differences and (b) introducing concepts that will be used in future chapters, I would like to discuss five topics in this chapter. These are

1. the changes that can be expected as a result of good education and training programs that introduce people to culture and cultural differences;

2. ethnocentrism;

3. attributions, or people's judgments about the causes of behaviors that they observe;

4. people's disconfirmed expectancies during their intercultural interactions;

5. individualism versus collectivism in people's cultural background.

DOCUMENTED OUTCOMES OF TRAINING AND EDUCATION PROGRAMS

Formal programs that have the goal of educating and training people to better understand culture and cultural differences will be reviewed in chapters 6 and 7. The goals of these programs are to prepare people to live and work effectively with individuals from other cultural backgrounds and to increase people's understanding of culture and cultural differences (Landis & Brislin, 1983). Research on the *outcomes* of successful programs can be profitably reviewed here since the accumulated findings of various studies pin down the meaning of "greater sophistication concerning culture and cultural differences." Put in a slightly different way, the outcomes of good education and training programs pinpoint the types of sophistication that people can be expected to develop. The outcomes can be conveniently grouped in three categories: changes in people's thinking, changes in people's emotions, and changes in people's behaviors. This list represents a compilation of findings from a large number of studies (e.g., Brislin, Landis, & Brandt, 1983; Befus, 1988; Hammer, 1989; Cushner, 1989; Cui & Van Den Berg, 1991).

CHANGES IN PEOPLE'S THINKING. Developments toward greater sophistication in people's thinking involve movement toward complexity. In movements from simple to complex thinking, people are not satisfied with quick, facile, and inadequate explanations of behavior that they observe or read about. Instead, they search for a more complex picture that involves multiple points of view and multiple possible explanations. In reading about developments in Eastern Europe or the former U.S.S.R., for example, they want to know about political factors, economic factors, possible changes in people's everyday lives, implications for the movement of people across national borders, the role of rarely discussed differences among various factions *within* countries, the possible roles that can be played by world powers such as the United States, the European Common Market, Japan, and so forth.

Given this ability to think in complex terms, people are less willing to use stereotypes when discussing other cultures. Stereotypes are generalizations about a group or class of people that have no place for individual differences. Examples can be heard in everyday conversation: "Blacks want...."; " Republicans can never ..."; "People in Russia are moving toward democracy because..." These generalizations ignore real and important differences among the positions taken by Blacks, Republicans, and citizens of Russia. Based on their knowledge that good education and training programs dealing with culture can lead to less stereotyping, some researchers have adopted an interesting measure in their evaluation studies. They have presented the graduates of their programs with a list of groups (e.g., Hispanics, Poles) and have asked people to match the groups with various descriptive adjectives be (e.g., ambitious, aloof, fun-loving). If graduates *refuse* to carry out the task and instead scrawl "this is a silly test that does nothing more than stereotype the groups," then the researchers conclude that their education and training programs have had a positive outcome.

When people become more complex in their thinking and refuse to stereotype, this usually leads to appreciation from members of *other* cultures. Individuals do not want to be stereotyped—they appreciate the fact that others are taking the time and energy to learn their culture's complexities so that fine distinctions can be made. Another outcome of good education and training programs is that people can accurately explain the reasons for complex problems and dilemmas that are found in other cultures. Further, they can explain the reasons in terms and arguments that are considered acceptable *from the point of view of people in the other culture* (Triandis, 1977). If they can make arguments in this manner, people are not imposing positions that are familiar only in their own culture. Rather, the people are taking the trouble to explain issues using analyses considered sophisticated by members of the other culture.

Given this increased sophistication, people become more skilled at interpreting and responding to the sorts of problematic intercultural encounters that have been discussed so far in this book. Recall in Chapter 1 that various well-meaning clashes were discussed: breakups of relationships, feeling left out of social gatherings, irritation when a scheduled meeting does not start on time, and so forth. Skilled people are able to identify the sources of the problems and to suggest reasonable ways of dealing with the difficulties (Cushner, 1989). One term for this skill is *means–ends thinking*. People can imagine reasonable endpoints, such as increased understanding or the ability to interpret difficulties in cultural terms when appropriate. They are also able to identify effective means to reach the ends, such as well-timed private conversations with the individuals involved in the difficulties. Skilled persons can also identify the reasons for difficulties in their *own* lives. When asked to examine puzzling episodes that involve others from quite different backgrounds, the people are able to analyze the encounters with increased sensitivity, understanding, and knowledge about cultural differences.

CHANGES IN PEOPLE'S EMOTIONS. A number of factors cause the study of culture and cultural differences to be emotionally impactful. People put a great deal of time and effort into becoming well-socialized members of their own culture. They develop a view of the world that makes sense to them. When they discover that members of other cultures have a different view, some of their fundamental assumptions about life are challenged. Most Americans believe that it is best if they choose their own spouse after a period of dating various people. It is quite disconcerting for them to study the tradition of arranged marriages that is common in many

Asian countries. They are further upset upon learning that there are good arguments for arranged marriages. Parents often know many of the eligible candidates for marriage within their own and neighboring communities. They certainly know their own children and are deeply concerned about their welfare. They also know what it takes to keep a marriage going after the fun and exuberance of the honeymoon period. They know the challenges of life after people reach their 30th and 40th birthdays. Why shouldn't they choose spouses for their children?

A related point to constantly consider is that intercultural interactions are anxiety arousing. When intercultural interactions are discussed, the meaning is precise: face-to-face encounters among people from different cultural backgrounds. Examples are meetings between international students and host-country citizens on a university campus, or business negotiations between delegations from mainland China and the United States. Various researchers have argued that *any* intercultural interaction can cause anxiety (Weldon, et al., 1975; Barna, 1983). Assume a student from Korea enters the room of an American professor of Caucasian ancestry. Compared with interactions among similar people (Korean student with Korean professor, Caucasian American student with the American professor), there will be more anxiety. If the participants' physiological responses could be monitored, the intercultural interactions would lead to increased heart rates, increased sweating, elevated blood pressure, and perhaps churnings of the stomach. One reason for anxiety is that the participants don't have clear guidelines concerning how to behave. What is a proper request of a college professor? What sorts of things might this student ask that I can't handle? These thoughts are *more likely* to run through people's minds if they are from different cultural backgrounds (Chick, 1990).

Good education and training programs that deal with culture and cultural differences lead to decreases in anxiety. People become more comfortable with the cultural differences they might have to confront, and they experience a decrease in the feelings of uncertainty that so commonly lead to anxiety (Gudykunst & Hammer, 1988). Other emotions, more commonly called "feelings" in everyday life, switch from burdens to pleasures. People begin to enjoy interacting with culturally different others both in the workplace and during their voluntary free time. They look forward to the challenges that intercultural contact can bring, such as expansions of preconceived views and alternative ways of looking at complex issues. They also begin to view others as different from a mass of stereotyped others vaguely known as "them" or "those people over there" (Amir, 1969). The others become known as individuals with names, goals, and problems much like everyone else: worries about the future of one's children, coping with the cost of living, and frustration with the traffic! It is far more difficult to feel negatively about individual people whom one has met in positive circumstances (such as a good educational program) than to feel negatively about a "bunch" of others one has never seen.

With this set of positive feelings toward people previously considered as "those others," a deep understanding of cultural relativity is possible (Broaddus, 1986). Cultural relativity refers to an awareness that different cultures have different ways of meeting life's demands. Different cultures have various guidelines regarding important decisions such as choosing a marriage partner (as discussed above), raising children, taking care of the infirm elderly, and so forth. If people are able to consider these guidelines in terms of the *other* culture's values, they are practicing cultural relativity in their thinking. The opposite of cultural relativity, of course, is the imposition of one's *own* values learned in one's own community. If arranged marriages are frowned upon simply because they seem unfamiliar to the point of bizarreness, then such a judgment is an imposition rather than an example of culture-relative analysis.

Many students become acquainted with the concept of cultural relativity in their studies of psychology, anthropology, education, and other disciplines. The better students learn the concept well enough to write a short essay on mid-term and final exams such that they receive a good grade. The difference between this type of learning and a *deep* understanding of cultural relativity involves people's emotions. People who understand cultural relativity realize the importance of culture and how seemingly strange behaviors can be analyzed only if they understand many other aspects of the culture. They are unwilling to make judgments based on the one set of values they know from their own cultural background. Further, they become emotionally upset if they *do* make such non-culturally relative judgments (Devine, Monteith, Zuwerink, & Elliot, 1991).

A related emotional reaction is that sophisticated people are able to admit to themselves that they are not yet ready to understand unfamiliar behaviors. Upon encountering difficulties in other cultures for which they are unprepared, they are willing to suspend their judgment and to await further information. The exact term for this desirable reaction is "tolerance for ambiguity." People *do* feel emotional arousal due to their inability to engage in appropriate behaviors. They know that they are in a state of ambiguity: they do not understand the unfamiliar behaviors around them and do not know how to behave appropriately themselves. But they can tolerate this emotional arousal, knowing that if they suspend judgment and search for additional information, they will be able to engage in culturally appropriate thinking and behavior.

CHANGES IN PEOPLE'S BEHAVIORS. When people think about or have emotional reactions toward other cultures, the results are often invisible to observers. In contrast, behaviors are visible. Some of the most memorable difficulties in intercultural encounters are caused by contradictions between people's thinking, emotions, and behaviors. People might *say* that they can engage in culturally relative thinking and will not become emotionally upset when faced with challenges to their preconceived views.

However, they might become obviously uncomfortable when faced with such difficulties, and they might engage in such visible behaviors as angry outbursts, sullenness, or withdrawal from conversations (Crosby, Bromley, & Saxe, 1980).

Good intercultural training and education programs decrease the number of such negative behaviors. Rather, people engage in behaviors much more indicative of positive interpersonal relationships, and these behaviors are clearly visible to outside observers. For example, people do not tense their bodies when culturally different others approach them. Rather, they are relaxed and can engage in the informal, pleasant banter that is part of the workday at all organizations known as "a good place to work." People report that they feel comfortable interacting with hosts and feel that they are successful in encouraging a positive tone in the workplace.

It is very important to note that these reports are not just the product of overactive imaginations. Hosts also report that the people in question are engaging in positive behaviors. For instance, if the training or educational program is meant to prepare Whites to interact more effectively with Blacks in the workplace (Randolph, Landis, & Tseng, 1977), Blacks have positive reactions about the behavior of Whites. Blacks report greater ease in everyday communication, sense that the Whites have respect for the behaviors exhibited by Blacks, and feel that all the people in the workplace are willing to help each other. The distinction between Whites reporting positive behaviors and Blacks having the same reaction is important. Everyone has met individuals who *feel* that they are positive influences in the workplace but are, in reality, very much disliked. With good training and education programs, the reports of positive behaviors are mutual.

In studies of intercultural education and training, there is an interesting and important finding that has been documented several times (Weldon et al., 1975; O'Brien & Plooj, 1977). The finding combines information from the previous discussion of anxiety in this chapter with this current discussion of behavior. One way to measure changes in behavior is to have graduates of education and training programs interact with people from very difficult cultures. After the training program ends, graduates are invited to a reception and are told that culturally diverse people will be in attendance. In addition to the graduates a second group, consisting of people who have *not* participated in education and training programs are also in attendance. For convenience, let's call the people "graduates" and "non-graduates." Finally, a number of culturally diverse people (from countries other than those of the graduates) also attend the reception. They take on the task of rating the intercultural sophistication of the attendees at the reception. These raters are unaware of who is a graduate and who is not, and consequently their ratings are not influenced by knowledge of who went through a program. The raters keep in mind such factors as which people seem at ease interacting with culturally different others, who is good at keeping up conversations on topics of mutual interest, who shows respect for people from other cultures, who avoids stereotyping people, and so forth. The results of various studies (Weldon, et al., 1975; O'Brien & Plooj, 1977; Landis, et al., 1985) have shown that non-graduates are rated as more interculturally sensitive and sophisticated than graduates.

The last sentence is not a misprint, and at first glance it might seem a disappointing finding that hardly stands as a beacon in the dark for the creation of education and training programs. The key (as introduced above) is that there is a relation between anxiety and behavior. The receptions with culturally diverse people were held immediately after the programs ended. The anxiety of graduates had increased since, probably for the first time, they became aware that their behavior can have an impact on culturally different others. A point made in every good program is that behaviors appropriate in one culture are sometimes inappropriate in another (leading to the sorts of well-meaning clashes discussed in Chapter 1). Consider the plight of the graduates, then, at the post-program reception. They are thinking to themselves, "I have learned about cultural sensitivity and how my behavior can be misinterpreted by well-meaning people from other cultures. I'll have to be careful about how I behave at the reception." When interacting with the culturally diverse others, then, they are tense, anxious, and ill at ease. Or, they may try so hard to be culturally sensitive that their efforts come across as clumsy. The culturally diverse raters will sense these difficulties and will have to report to the researchers that the graduates, at best, stumbled through the reception. On the other hand, the non-graduates are blissfully unaware of the impact of their own cultural background on their behavior. They undoubtedly interact with the culturally diverse raters in their normal style. While not especially culturally sensitive, the non-graduates are more pleasant to be with than the uptight graduates.

There is a positive side to this interesting set of research findings. After a period of time during which graduates can calm themselves, they are rated as more sophisticated by the culturally diverse people at the reception. For instance, if the reception was held the day after the program ended, graduates interact well with the people from different cultures. Graduates need a period of time during which they can think about their new knowledge concerning the importance of culture and cultural differences. They need time to recover from the anxiety caused by the awareness that their behavior has an impact on culturally diverse others. After they calm down and have a chance to demonstrate their cultural sensitivity at a reception, they are rated as more sophisticated than non-graduates. These findings have led to a recommendation for education and training programs. Administrators should schedule time at the end of programs to allow participants to work through their anxiety. A session of about two hours during which the nature of anxiety is openly discussed, and during which people are given time to practice recommended behaviors, is very valuable.

Once the initial anxiety that stems from increased cultural awareness has dissipated, people can engage in the sorts of behaviors recommended during their program. Some behaviors have already been discussed in Chapter 1: sensitivity to the spatial orientation one adopts when interacting with others; making a point to include visitors in informal social gatherings; and engaging in modest versus forthright introductory remarks during one's public lectures. Research has shown (O'Brien, Fiedler, & Hewlett, 1971) that good programs can increase job performance *when* job-related behaviors are both teachable *and* are central to good performance in other cultures. The combination of the highlighted words, "when" plus "and," are important to consider since it is all too easy to overpromise the positive effects of good programs. The research project which led to the conclusion about teachable and performance-related behaviors is an interesting one to review.

The research (O'Brien, et al., 1971) involved young American volunteers involved in health-related projects in Honduras. One of the projects contained the job requirement that volunteers give inoculations to Honduran citizens so that diseases might be prevented. A culturally based difficulty, however, is that Honduras has values centering on respect for elders, and most Americans are not familiar with these values. In the United States, a young person can have expertise in an area and can use it during interactions with elders. As part of these interactions, young people can direct the behavior of elders in situations where the expertise is relevant. For example, 25-year-old X-ray technicians can tell 75-year-old patients where to go, what clothes to remove, how to stand or lie down for the X-rays, and so forth. Such behaviors are expected and even encouraged in American culture.

In Honduras, elders expect much more deference from younger people. Elders direct the efforts of the young and do not react comfortably when a community's youth tells them what do do. So how do young American volunteers give inoculations to older people in Honduras? There may be a number of answers, but the one chosen centered on the *manner* in which the inoculations were given. As part of their training, the volunteers were instructed to give the inoculations in a calm and respectful manner, and to combine this with a demeanor indicating that they have been giving inoculations for years and years. This calm, respectful, and confident attitude did not allow opportunities for the elders to conclude that cultural values were being violated. If the volunteers had been slow and nervous, on the other hand, the elders would have had reason to think about possible violations of cultural practices. There are often signals in the well-meaning clashes already discussed than *can lead to* negative conclusions. Examples are non-verbal signs that a person is upset, changes in voice tone, slip-ups when trying to pronounce easy words, and so forth. The communication of calmness, confidence, knowledge, and respect (Chaika, 1989) gives people little reason to think about anything but receiving the inoculation and returning to their daily activities.

Medical volunteers who successfully graduated from a cultural-orientation program performed more effectively during their assignment in Honduras. They were more productive in their jobs, as shown by records of the number of inoculations they were able to administer. Note that the behaviors involved, a respectful and confident demeanor in the presence of adults, have a cultural component and are teachable. As part of their training, volunteers could practice these behaviors. A good recommendation for the sorts of programs under consideration in this chapter is to search out such teachable behaviors. On an anecdotal level, I was once the beneficiary of this type of behavior-based education. I was about to travel to Japan for a lecture tour. A good friend, who was very knowledgeable about Japan, took the time to rehearse me in a number of very specific behaviors. These included having business cards printed, giving them out during initial encounters shortly after shaking hands or bowing, preparing physically for the multiple and long evenings out that hosts will offer as part of their normal hospitality, giving modest initial remarks during one's lecture, thanking people for taking the trouble to come to a lecture which could be better given by audience members, and welcoming attendees to the reception that followed the lecture. Without this preparation that involved teachable behaviors relevant to my task and considered important in the other culture, I hesitate to think of the total failure the lecture tour would have been.

SUMMARY: THE BENEFITS. I believe that the list of benefits that can stem from good education and training programs is impressive. The changes in people's thinking include the willingness to entertain more complex points of view, the rejection of stereotypes, and the ability to understand problematic encounters in a manner similar to individuals in *other* cultures. The changes in people's emotions include decreases in anxiety brought on by intercultural encounters, an acceptance of the fact that observed differences cannot be interpreted in isolation and solely from one's own viewpoint (i.e., cultural relativity), and a willingness to tolerate ambiguity while searching for good explanations of observed differences. Changes in people's behavior include greater ease when interacting with culturally diverse others, positive responses from *the others* concerning people's anxiety-free and respectful interactions, and the ability to engage in specific culturally sensitive behaviors that can be introduced and rehearsed during good programs.

CONCEPTS CENTRAL
TO GOOD PROGRAMS

These benefits, then, are the endpoints of efforts to increase people's sophistication about culture and cultural differences. What is good content for education and training programs so that these benefits might be obtained? I believe that the answer to this question is the same as the answer to another: What are important concepts that permeate virtually all attempts to understand culture and cultural differences as they apply to people's everyday lives? Certain concepts are covered in good educational programs and assist greatly in understanding the role of culture in more focused discussions concerned with specific social settings. These settings will be discussed in future chapters: the home, school, workplace, and so forth. Covering a few central concepts in this chapter, then, allows me to continue the discussion of education and training programs as well as to introduce material that is central to later chapters. The concepts to be discussed are ethnocentrism, attribution, disconfirmed expectancies, and individualism–collectivism. The links among these four concepts, which probably seem like a random collection at the moment, will be made clear toward the end of this chapter. Understanding these four theoretical concepts allows very practical insights into everyday human behavior, and I will try to point out these applications.

ETHNOCENTRISM. The opposite of cultural relativism is ethnocentrism. When people make ethnocentric judgments about culturally diverse others, they are imposing the standards with which they are familiar given their own socialization (Allport, 1954; Adler, 1991). The roots of the word give other insights into its meaning. "Centrism" refers to the center of one's judgments, and "ethno" refers to one's own ethnic or cultural group. Ethnocentric judgments, then, are based on feelings that one's own group is the *center* of what is reasonable and proper in life. Further, the term implies that others can be judged according to one, central set of standards. An implication of the judgments is that one group is clearly better, even superior, than the other since its members practice proper and correct behaviors. As might be expected, the group considered better or superior is the one to which the person making the ethnocentric judgments belongs.

There are other overly dogmatic and overly focused views about life that also have the suffix "ism" attached to them. In fact, these views are sometimes called "the isms." They include racism, sexism, and less frequently, classism and ageism. The commonality with ethnocentrism is that all these views about life have a strong component that put people into favored and inferior categories (more on these topics will be presented in Chapter 6, this volume). Once people are put into an inferior category, disparaging remarks about them are easy to make. Further, the group that considers itself superior can think of justifications when it denies opportunities to the other group. Examples of racism abound in most societies. In the United States, the White majority has justified and protected its privileged position by viewing the Black minority as inferior. If Blacks are considered inferior, then substandard schools and inadequate job training programs can be defended. The view is, "They can't benefit from anything better." Similar arguments are brought forward when members of one gender (most often males) deny opportunities to the other. For years, women were denied entrance to medical school because they were not considered "up" to the demands of the profession. Another argument was that if they were given medical training, they would eventually leave the profession to have families and a lot of money would be wasted. When similar arguments are made to deny opportunities to people from a less privileged social class background, or to people who have reached a certain age, the vile practice of "decisions according to isms" is continued. Children of working-class parents might be denied opportunities for executive-level training programs because they are seen as having inadequate communication skills compared to age peers from the middle and upper class. People who have reached 60 or 65 years of age might be automatically retired from their jobs in favor of younger people. In all these cases people from one favored group, whether it is based on skin color, gender, class background, or age, are viewing another group as inferior and as unworthy of equal treatment.

Discussions of ethnocentrism are made more complex when its admitted advantages are considered (Damen, 1987). If people view their own group as central to their lives and as possessing proper standards of behavior, they are likely to come to the aid of other group members when there are troubles. In times of war, the rallying of ethnocentric feelings makes a country's military forces more dedicated to the defeat of the (inferior) enemy. There have undoubtedly been times in the historical past when ethnocentric feelings did not play a great part in people's everyday lives. People might not travel 50 miles from where they were born. Given natural barriers such as mountains and rivers, they might never meet others who were clearly different in terms of skin color, language, and customs. If they did, their natural ethnocentric viewpoints and lack of familiarity with culturally different others must have combined to make interactions defensive and often hostile.

People's natural ethnocentric feelings, which include the positive feature of looking after one's own and protecting against what *might* be hostile outsiders, do not suit us well in today's world. Many reasons combine to challenge the usefulness that ethnocentrism might once have yielded. Some of these reasons were reviewed in Chapter 1: air travel, international investments, the spread of democracy, the movement of students across national boundaries, and the insistence of culturally diverse people that they not become indistinguishable contributions to a melting pot. How can people overcome the natural tendencies of ethnocentrism and begin to think in broader, culturally relative terms? The answer is to call upon the skill that separates us from other primates: We can think about and reflect upon our own behavior. We can become aware of the disadvantages of ethnocentric thinking, intercept ourselves when putting culturally diverse others at a disadvantage, and switch to a more tolerant and culturally relative position (Schneider, 1991). An important conceptual tool for this switch in thinking is an understanding of how people make attributions about behavior.

ATTRIBUTION. When people observe behaviors that are different from what they expect in their normal, everyday routines, they make judgments and draw conclusions so that they can make sense out of their observations. Attributions refer to judgments about the *causes* of behavior (Jones, 1979; Ehrenhaus, 1983; Gudykunst & Nishida, 1989). Questions center on *Why* people are behaving as they do? *What* reasons do they have for their choices? *Who* might be influencing them? *How* did they come to the point at which they made certain choices about their behavior? and so forth. Consider the most basic case: Two people meet and the interaction clearly does not go well. The people strain to find something to talk about, stumble in their attempts to put each other at ease, and leave the interaction in a clumsy manner. This is what might have happened if Stan and Rogelia, whose romance was discussed in Chapter 1, accidentally met each other during intermission at a concert they were both attending with others. It is important to note that there will be at least four types of attributions made:

*There are four types of attributions possible when two people interact.
Each person makes attributions about the other (1 and 2), and
they make attributions about themselves (3 and 4).*

1. Stan will make attributions about Rogelia's behavior;
2. Rogelia will make attributions about Stan's behavior;
3. Stan will make attributions about his own behavior;
4. Rogelia will make attributions about her own behavior.

The types of attributions summarized as 3 and 4 are sometimes ignored. They should not be since people clearly think about *their own* behavior. "How am I doing? Am I behaving in a confident manner? Am I doing something that can be easily misinterpreted?" An important issue in intercultural interaction, I believe (Brislin, 1981), is that there are at least two reasons why people's attributions risk being more problematic than if the people were from very similar cultural backgrounds. One is the increased level of people's anxiety, as previously discussed. When anxious, people are not as careful and clear in their thinking. In the example, Stan and Rogelia are not in good positions to reflect clearly, especially concerning their own behavior (attributions 3 and 4). The other reason is that people are less familiar with the other culture than they are with their own. Consequently, they have less access to the reasons that the *other* person is using in making attributions. In the example under consideration, Stan may not know that Rogelia is unfamiliar with the possibility that former romantic partners might maintain warm friendships. Not knowing that this possibility is part of Stan's thinking, Rogelia may think that Stan is being extraordinarily ill-mannered and rude in pursuing any sort of interaction.

Stan and Rogelia, then, are making quite different attributions. Neither person disagrees about the *behaviors* involved (that Stan continues to seek out Rogelia's company), but they do disagree about the attributions concerning these behaviors. Stan feels that he is friendly and that Rogelia has withdrawn her friendship. Rogelia feels that she is behaving properly according to her upbringing and that Stan is being rude. A major intervention into problems like these is to search for opportunities to make isomorphic attributions (Triandis, 1977, 1990). This somewhat technical term is frequently heard in discussions among specialists in cross-cultural research (e.g., Gudykunst & Nishida, 1989; Bhawuk, 1990). It refers to the ability to make the *same* attribution as the *other* person in the interaction. Isomorphic attributions *can* be a goal in any interaction, as all readers have surely been in conversations where they were badly misunderstood by someone well known to them. Readers have surely thought, "I wish that other person could see the issue from *my* point of view!" And this is the key to isomorphic attributions: to understand the *other* person's judgments about the causes of problematic interactions. Making isomorphic attributions does not necessarily involve *agreeing* with the other person's judgments, but it does involve understanding the basis for his or her views.

Making isomorphic attributions concerning the behaviors of others that people know well is difficult enough. Complexity is added in intercultural encounters because people are unaware of how cultural factors may be influencing people's behaviors. Whenever there is a misunderstanding, there is a strong tendency for people to interpret it in personal terms: "The other is making decisions that deal with *me* and that are specifically targeted at *my* feelings" (Brislin, et al., 1986). Without the types of educational programs discussed earlier or extensive intercultural experiences during which people work through large numbers of problematic encounters, this tendency to interpret problems in personal terms continues. Often, the quest to make isomorphic attributions will move the analysis of problems away from personally directed reasons to explanations involving culture and cultural differences. If Stan and Rogelia have the opportunity to learn about each other's culture, they will be more likely to make isomorphic attributions. Stan will learn that Rogelia is unfamiliar with the maintenance of past romantic relationships. Rogelia will learn that Stan simply wants to maintain the friendship and is not being rude according to the values of his culture. Neither Stan nor Rogelia has to *agree* that the other has a reasonable point of view. Recall from the discussion of culture's features in Chapter 1 that familiar values and behaviors cause emotional reactions when they are violated. Stan and Rogelia will not quickly become comfortable with the other's point of view. But they can learn to understand the other's attributions and in so doing become more tolerant of behaviors that once seemed strange and ill-mannered.

One of my friends is a member of an intercultural marriage. (This type of marriage is discussed in Romano, 1988.) He was socialized in Palestine and his wife was socialized in Wisconsin. One of the reasons for the success of the marriage, he feels, is that he and his wife can call upon cultural differences when there are misunderstandings and disagreements. In one disagreement, my friend sided with his father in a family argument about where to send his children (and his father's grandchildren) to school. He later confided to his wife, "I agree with you, but I sided with my father." His wife said, "How could you do that?" My friend replied, "He's an old man and, as you know, has a terminal cancer. He won't be with us much longer. My cultural background says that I should respect him and honor his wisdom. I also have to make his last years comfortable. That's why I sided with him." His wife might not agree with this point of view, but she can learn to understand how culture gives guidance for such behaviors.

A few reasons for the *greater* likelihood of making incorrect attributions in intercultural encounters have been mentioned. They are anxiety arousing; many encounters will be unfamiliar and consequently will demand explanations; so much about the other culture is unknown that people will try out explanations of observed behaviors simply to fill the uncomfortable void that uncertainty and ambiguity always bring. Another feature of intercultural encounters is that they are often very memorable, impactful, and sometimes very vivid. People have a strong tendency to overinterpret the effect of vivid and impactful events in which they are directly involved (Sherman, Judd, & Park, 1989). These events overwhelm other, often less colorful, evidence that might assist in making isomorphic attributions. An example should make this point clear.

Assume that a highly respected book exists that gives information on overseas job opportunities. Interested in gaining international experience, Jack consults the guide and discovers that there are many opportunities in Japan. The guide reports that based on a survey of 300 Americans living in large cities, the respondents feel that well-qualified Americans who have good job-searching and interviewing skills will be able to find employment. This is especially true for Americans able to accept positions as English language teachers in Japan's schools or in the training divisions of Japanese companies. Jack is impressed, applies for a passport and visa, and tells his friends of his plans. One friend, Sharon, expresses surprise. "My cousin went to Japan looking for work. He couldn't find a job and was very disappointed. He spent all his savings traveling and living there for a while, and he had to come back to America when his money ran out. Are you sure you want to go to Japan?"

What will Jack do? The strong tendency is to put a great deal of weight on Sharon's comments. Her comments were undoubtedly delivered in a memorable, impactful manner. Her recollections of her cousin's experiences were probably presented in vivid, emotional language. Jack undoubtedly became deeply involved in the conversation with Sharon and began to sympathize with the cousin's plight. Sharon's comments are much more attention-grabbing than the information presented in the guidebook that Jack has read. From the standpoint of careful decision making, Jack should be examining 301 pieces of information: the reports by the people surveyed that are collected in the guidebook, and the experiences of Sharon's cousin (Kahneman & Tversky, 1984). But because Sharon's report is so much more colorful than the rather dull information in the guide, it will likely be given far more weight than it deserves. The strong tendency is to accept the personalized report and to ignore the survey results from the 300 people. This tendency is so strong that Jack might not even think very much about why Sharon's cousin is an exception. Maybe the cousin interviews very poorly, perhaps he was able to show little respect for the Japanese he met (discussed in Chapter 8), and so forth.

The only way to stop making attributions based on limited or faulty information is to become aware of the underlying reasons for why we think the way we do. Then, we can stop and ask ourselves, "Am I making an attribution based on easily available, personalized, and colorful information? Is there other, perhaps duller information that I might seek out before coming to any conclusions?" This same search for additional information is the recommended action for the other factors leading to potentially faulty attributions in intercultural encounters (Adler, 1991). "Am I too anxious, too upset to make good attributions? Is there so much

new going on in my life that I am being tempted to make more attributions than I should? Are there aspects of the other people's cultural
background of which I am unaware that, if better understood, would help
me to make better attributions?" If people ask themselves these questions
and behave according to the answers, they are likely to have more success
in their intercultural interactions.

DISCONFIRMED EXPECTANCIES. If people make attributions that
eventually prove incorrect, they may behave in ways that are also
incorrect *before* they find out that their attributions are wrong. Put
another way, people might find themselves in a puzzling intercultural
encounter. They make an attribution, follow up their thinking with
seemingly appropriate behaviors, and only later discover that both the
attribution and behaviors were faulty. This discovery brings with it an
added set of emotional reactions.

The additional emotional reactions stem from disconfirmed expectancies. Such reactions are a *guaranteed* part of any extensive intercultural
interactions (Brislin et al., 1986). People make decisions about what they
expect when crossing cultural boundaries, and they also (with every good
intention) make decisions about their behavior. A major reason for
people's decisions about their behavior is that they feel that it will bring
positive results, such as a good impression on others (Bandura, 1986).
When they find that their expectations are disconfirmed they become
very upset.

Most often, the degree of emotional upset is based on the *difference*
between expectation and reality. Readers may find the following mental
exercise helpful. Think of an event in the past that was upsetting and that
brought with it an intense emotional reaction. With the benefit of hind-
sight, was it the event that caused the upset or was it the *difference* between
the event and what was expected in the social situation where the event
occurred? I believe that many readers will conclude that, in retrospect, the
event was not all that bad and was not all that difficult to handle. The
intense emotional reaction was due to the fact that the event differed so
much from expectations. If expectations had been more accurate, the
difference between reality and expectation would have been smaller, and
consequently there would have been less emotional trauma. Many educational programs that prepare people to live and work in other cultures
cover the issue of disconfirmed expectancies. One specific exercise is to ask
participants to list their expectations. Often, people list goals that are
unrealistic (Katz, 1977), such as making ten or twelve friends in the other
culture within three months. The program leader can then engage the
participants in discussions that lead to the reformulation of expectations
more likely to be in line with reality.

Disconfirmed expectancies are certain in intercultural encounters.
Colleagues and I had an interesting experience. We prepared a set of
educational materials designed to help prepare people to live in other

cultures and/or to work extensively with culturally diverse people in their own country (Brislin, Cushner, Cherrie, & Yong, 1986). We organized the materials around 18 thematic areas that should assist people in interpreting any *specific* intercultural experience they will later encounter. Some of the 18 themes have been integrated into this book (e.g., attributions, ethnocentrism) and others will be covered later in this chapter (e.g., individualism–collectivism) or in other chapters. To best present the 18 themes, we decided to make them part of 100 critical incidents or short vignettes of the type already presented (Stan and Rogelia's difficulties with their relationship; Fumio's feelings that he is being ignored). We felt that these short vignettes would "bring life to" the 18 themes since the stories involve the sorts of problems and issues with which readers can sympathize. One of these 18 themes is disconfirmed expectancies. After the book containing the 18 themes and 100 critical incidents was published, we were asked to give workshops for people anticipating extensive intercultural interactions: overseas businesspeople, university professors wishing to internationalize the curriculum at their schools, counselors working with a culturally diverse clientele, adolescents about to spend a year attending high school in another country, and so forth. We found that people appreciated talking about disconfirmed expectancies as one of the 18 themes or concepts that would help them understand their upcoming interactions. But we also found that disconfirmed expectations permeated virtually all of the 100 critical incidents that we prepared (a point also made by Bhawuk, 1990). Put another way, it is extremely difficult to write incidents that capture experiences people are likely to have *without* disconfirmed expectancies being part of the reason for the difficulties reported in the incidents. To borrow from research on abilities as studied by psychologists (e.g., Anastasi, 1988), disconfirmed expectancies is a general factor found in large numbers of situations. Just as many psychologists argue that intelligence has a general component that can be found in performance on large numbers of specific tasks (e.g., arithmetic, vocabulary learning, writing) disconfirmed expectancies seem to be a component of virtually all memorable and impactful intercultural experiences.

If this is true, then people should have a set of tools that are useful when they find that their expectations have been disconfirmed. As with their growing insight into the ways people make attributions, the tools will involve bringing in more sophisticated thought processes. A good tool is to "talk down" the disconfirmed expectancies (Meichenbaum, 1977; Seligman, 1989) that people encounter during one or more of their intercultural experiences. Talking down means putting the experience into a proper perspective such that it does not permeate all of one's thinking. Rather than interpreting the experience as a sign of failure, which can eventually lead to a sense of helplessness and to depression, talking down involves focusing on the experience and moving beyond it only after very careful thought. Assume the experience involves a clearly unsuccessful job interview in another country. There are three steps in the talking down process.

1. Make one's thinking specific. Rather than interpreting the incident in global, general terms such as "I am making a terrible adjustment in this country," thinking should be focused on the specifics. Further, care should be taken not to move beyond the specifics except after extensive thought. A more specific focus would be, "I didn't do very well in this interview, but this doesn't mean I'll do poorly in all interviews." Focusing on specifics makes change possible, since it is far easier to change specific behaviors (e.g., interviewing style) than highly general behaviors that suggest few opportunities for direct intervention (e.g., adjustment to another culture). Indeed, change is central to the second step in the thinking-down process.

2. Make the issue involved changeable. If step number 1 is taken, then people have a specific issue or behavior on which they can focus. The next step is to focus on those aspects of the issue that are changeable. For the issue of the unsuccessful job interview, changeable aspects on which the disappointed candidate might focus could include manner of dress, how to keep up a conversation with a Japanese interviewer, or methods of showing respect for others during the conversation. One possible cultural difference (Pascale & Athos, 1981) is that American job candidates might be anxious to communicate their qualifications. Consequently, they might discuss their education and job experience during the first 15 minutes of their interview. This might be quite proper behavior if they were interviewing in a big city within the United States. But the Japanese interviewer may prefer casual conversation on seemingly unimportant matters— what Americans call "small talk." The interviewer wants to obtain a "feel" for candidates: Are they trustworthy? Are they respectful? Do they seem to have the social skills needed to fit into the Japanese organization and to cooperate with others? If candidates begin to talk about themselves too quickly, they may be seen as boorish. The key to the discussion here is that American candidates have a specific focus that they can view as changeable. They can change their behavior and can engage in the pleasant, friendly small talk that the Japanese prefer.

3. Focus on possible external aspects. When people experience failure in a social situation, there is the possibility that they will conclude that "It is my fault! There is something wrong with me personally!" When people think in this way (Carson, 1989; Seligman, 1989), they are focusing on possible internal aspects of their experiences. They are focusing on aspects that involve their abilities, their social skills, or their personalities. In reality, there are often external aspects that have little to do with the people experiencing failure. In the example we have been considering, a 5-minute glance at any good book in industrial psychology (e.g., Landy, 1989) will reveal that interviews are a notoriously unreliable method of selecting people for jobs in an organization. There are so many factors *external* to the job applicant, such as the number of openings at any one time or the idiosyncrasies of the interviewer, that a focus on internal factors can be both incorrect and damaging. Another external reason, very common according to my observations, is that the organization has already committed the job opening to someone but has to go through the charade of multiple interviews to satisfy legal requirements. A better reaction than a knee-jerk focus on internal factors is to say (to oneself) something like, "I didn't get this job offer but there are a lot of reasons for this that have nothing to do with me. I'll just keep scheduling interviews until I get a good mix of genuine job openings and an interviewer who appreciates what I have to offer."

There is a danger to an overemphasis on external thinking because it can take attention away from internal factors that should be addressed. If the job candidate is not showing respect for the Japanese or is not engaging in the small talk called for in the interview, a total focus on external factors will mean that appropriate modifications in the candidate's behavior will not be forthcoming. The recommendation to consider external factors is meant to help people broaden their thinking so that they are not overwhelmed by the internal thought that "it's *all* my fault!"

When the three steps are followed, people are less likely to feel helpless and to become depressed (Seligman, 1989). Rather, they find themselves able to think about ways to move from their temporary failure into new situations (or new mental views of their situations) that can lead to greater chances of success. Part of this thinking in people's intercultural encounters should include the self-directed question, "Is there anything in the cultural background of the other people that I should be considering?" As discussed in Chapter 1, this can be a difficult question since many people are unaccustomed to thinking in terms of culture and cultural differences. One approach to making one's thinking more sophisticated is to examine the conceptual tools that cross-cultural researchers have developed to summarize and to organize cultural differences they have studied. One such tool centers on the individualistic contrasted with the collectivistic background of people in different cultures. This distinction helps in the understanding of many specific cultural differences and is a helpful tool in understanding intercultural interactions.

INDIVIDUALISM AND COLLECTIVISM. A number of researchers have argued that one of the most important factors in a culture is the relative emphasis placed on individualism and collectivism (Hofstede, 1980; Triandis, 1990; Triandis, Brislin, & Hui, 1988). While there is no culture that totally ignores individualistic or collectivistic goals, there are important differences in which of these factors is considered more important. In individualistic cultures, people set and work toward their own goals. In situations where there is a conflict between an individual's own goals and those of a valued group (e.g., family, co-workers), consideration of the individuals' goals is of major importance. Given this emphasis on a person's own goals, the words *individual* and *individualized* are constantly used. We hear the terms in elementary schools ("the individual learning style of each child"), in the workplace ("the individual's career development"), and in the family ("each child develops an individual identity"). Aphorisms and advice related to individualism are frequently heard: "Stand on your own two feet," "Learn to blow your own horn since no one will do it for you," and "Take the initiative—don't wait for someone else to throw something your way." Other signs of individualism include parental beliefs that part of their task is to prepare children to leave the home (perhaps at age 18 when they go to college) so that they can have their own separate and successful lives. Many parents in individualistic cultures are proud to say that they will have enough financial resources at age 65 or 70 such that they do not have to depend on their adult children.

In collectivist cultures, people are more likely to downplay their own goals in favor of goals set by a valued group. That group is most often one's extended family, but it can also be one's organization or one's religion. People obtain much of their identity as members of their collective. When asked to complete statements that start with the phrase "I am . . . ," members of collective cultures (hereafter called collectivists) are much more likely than individualists to list membership in a group (Triandis, Brislin, & Hui, 1988). They might list membership in a family, a religion, or an organization. Individualists, on the other hand, are much more likely to list trait labels that imply how they are distinct from other people. Individualists are likely to list aspects of their personalities such as "hard-working," "intelligent," or "athletic." Generalizations concerning where individualism and collectivism are found must be cautiously made since there will always be exceptions, but a few remarks may be helpful. Individualism is commonly found in North America and Western Europe, and countries strongly influenced by these areas, such as Australia and New Zealand. Collectivism is common in Asia, Africa, Central and South America, and in small Pacific Island societies. As might be expected, in a worldwide survey of work related values in 40 countries, the United States is the most individualistic nation (Hofstede, 1980).

The differences in the way that people describe themselves has implications for everyday behaviors. In Japan, a collectivist country, people have to mention the organization to which they belong when talking to someone else who is not already well known. The organization is mentioned first: "Hello, this is Mitsubishi company's Fumio Yoshida. May I please talk to . . . ?" When I first went to Japan, an experienced colleague wisely advised: "Have business cards printed with your organization prominently indicated. If you don't people will not know who you are!" This advice means that people often have two sets of cards, one for Japan and one for their own country. In the United States, people often have cards that emphasize individual features such as books written, unique talents, and hobbies. The organization for which they work is sometimes not mentioned.

A few of the key differences between individualists can be summarized in pictorial form. With both individualists and collectivists, there is a sense of self separate from others. Every adult knows that they have a face that they cannot see except in a mirror, learns (sometimes to their horror) that the voice quality they hear when they speak is not what others hear, and comes to realize that there are certain steps in life that only the self can take (e.g., feeding oneself, entering a marriage). The differences between individualists and collectivists involve the amount of psychological distance from, or the importance of emotional closeness with, other people.

Moving from the bottom to the top of Figure 1, individualists and collectivists do not differ in terms of closeness to members of the nuclear family: spouse, parents, children. The caveat has to be added, however, that this statement is true only when members of the nuclear family are getting along well. Surely all readers have known nuclear families whose members have engaged in bitter, hostile actions against each other. The differences between individualists and collectivists emerge in relations with people beyond the nuclear family.

For individualists, there is a comfortable psychological or emotional distance between themselves and members of other groups. With the extended family, they have good relations with some uncles and cousins but merely cordial (sometimes called "Christmas Card") relations with other kinfolk. For collectivists, there is a much closer relation between the self and another collective, often the extended family. The collective becomes the place in which people find their identity as human beings. Collectivists identify themselves as better depicted in the bottom diagram in Figure 1. Or, they identify with a modification of the picture that has the self surrounded by a group. Collectivists feel comfortable with this

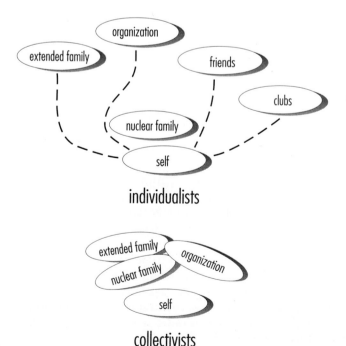

FIGURE 1. The Relation of the Self to Others in Individualistic and Collectivist Cultures.

constant psychological presence of their group. Individualists report they would feel stifled if they were surrounded by others. There would be too many people whose opinions would have to be considered before an individualist could act in the pursuit of his or her goals. Individualists find that clearing one's plans with others interferes too much with their desire "to do their own thing."

Placing an individualist and a collectivist in a similar dilemma may make some key differences clearer. Assume that a 40-year-old woman lives in the same city as her 78-year-old mother. The two live in separate houses, but the daughter can check in on her mother two or three times a week. The daughter is an only child, and her father has passed away. The mother is in reasonably good health for a 78-year-old, but is beginning to experience the problems that many elderly people face: mild arthritis, poor vision, slowness in recovery from respiratory infections, and so forth. The mother has an active social life in her church, in a bridge club, and as part of volunteer work at the local hospital. The daughter receives a job offer in a city 1000 miles away. It is exactly the sort of job she has long desired: good salary, challenging work, excellent working conditions, intelligent and pleasant co-workers, and good opportunities for future promotions. What will the daughter do: stay near her mother to take care of her, or move 1000 miles away to take the job?

A collectivist is more likely to turn the job down and stay with her mother. Her identity as a human being is much more closely tied to her family, and she is likely to feel responsible for her mother's happiness during her old age. When turning the job down, she is demonstrating the key value of a collectivist: downplaying her own goals (i.e., her own ambitions) in favor of the group's goals (i.e., her mother's happiness). An individualist is more likely to take the job in the city 1000 miles away. Her sense of identity is more closely linked to the pursuit of her own goals, her own ambitions, her own preferences. She is more likely to follow through in her desire for a better job, leaving the care of her mother to others (e.g., nursing home or a retirement community). Even some possible compromises involve downplaying the mother's preferences. If the daughter takes the mother with her to the new city, the mother has to leave her friends and active social life behind.

It is important to note that these generalizations will not fit all cases. In collectivist societies, some people will make the move to the new city; in individualist societies, some people will stay and take care of their mothers. The generalizations about individualists and collectivists (this one and others to be made in later paragraphs) refer to trends over large numbers of people. If 100 cases were studied in collectivist and individualist societies, more collectivists would behave in a manner that emphasized their group's goals, and more individualists would behave in a manner that emphasized their own personal goals. This concept concerning "trends over large numbers of people" is important to keep in mind whenever culture and cultural differences are discussed.

Understanding some basic arguments about individualism and collectivism allows insights into seemingly unrelated behaviors. Three will be discussed here: social skills, the distribution of rewards for group effort, and advice for people moving from one culture to another (more details can be found in Triandis, et al., 1988; Hsu, 1981).

1. Social skills. A consideration of effective social skills allows a review of the concept "ethnocentrism." Judgments about "effective" and "proper" behaviors can only be made if people have detailed knowledge about culture and cultural differences. If people judge those from another culture as "lacking in social skills," they are undoubtedly making an ethnocentric judgment based on their own culture's standards.

Proper social skills for individualists and collectivists follow from the length of the lines (see Figure 1) linking the self to others. Take the case of individualists and their relation to organizations that might offer them employment. Who is expected to make the move along the line from the self to the organization? The answer, of course, is that the individualists themselves are expected to make this move. The individualists cannot expect to have others *assure* them of entry to organizations with good jobs. Instead, they have to depend on themselves. In doing so, they must call upon a set of behaviors known as social skills (Singleton, Spurgeon, & Stammers, 1980), although a more proper label is "social skills useful in individualist cultures." These include meeting people quickly, putting them at ease, finding topics of conversation which others can readily discuss, being interesting so that the others will have memories of any interactions six months later, and so forth. These skills are useful since they allow people to obtain information from others central to the pursuit of individual goals (Brislin, 1991). For instance, assume that individualists are at an informal party. If they can meet others quickly and put them at ease, they may find that someone has a good link to an organization at which employment is sought. The other person may be able to share the names and phone numbers of the key people involved in hiring decisions. The same social skills of quickly meeting others and finding interesting topics of conversation are also useful if a job interview is scheduled. Public speaking is an example of another important social skill. If a person can give a dynamic, interesting, and memorable speech at a public gathering, audience members may later remember the speaker if they are asked to recommend people that can fill job openings in their organizations. As discussed in Chapter 1, my father realized the importance of good public speaking skills and encouraged me to develop them.

Similar social skills aid in the movement from the self to other groups: to clubs, to churches, to opportunities to make new friends. This movement is especially important in a highly mobile society such as the United States where large numbers of people move to new communities each year. They must call upon their social skills in establishing new interpersonal relationships that lead to various benefits: information about the best jobs, opportunities for deep friendships, possible romantic partners, and so forth.

Social skills that put a premium on movement away from the self to others are not as important in collective societies. Consider the bottom part of Figure 1. When the person labeled "self" needs a job, who arranges opportunities to meet potential employers? The answer is "a high-status member of the collective." If a person is desirous of an accounting job in a large organization, then someone in the collective who is a member of that organization is called upon for help. Alternatively, someone who *knows* an influential executive in the organization takes the responsibility for identifying job possibilities. Other than letting members of the collective know employment is desired, the job seeker is not expected to take as active a role as the individualist described previously. One collectivist from India explained to me, "The person seeking the job is rather like a member of the audience watching a play in which others talk about a person. The strange part [to an individualist] is that the person being talked about is *me!*"

Social skills that allow people to meet strangers quickly and to put others at their ease are not as important in collective societies. Important *collective* social skills are loyalty to the group, cooperation, contributing to the group without the expectation of immediate reciprocity, and public modesty about one's abilities (Triandis, 1989). Loyalty and cooperation are expected since these qualities ensure the survival and effectiveness of the collective. Loyalty is *eventually* repaid when a given person needs the assistance of the collective, as in the example of the search for employment. Modesty is needed for a number of reasons. One is so that the person can defer to the high-status members of the collective who have the most favors to grant. In exchange for deference, thereby having their high status reinforced, influential members of the collective share their resources. Another reason is that too much immodesty can interfere with the smooth functioning of the collective. If people "blow their own horns" concerning their abilities, this can cause envy, jealousy, and strain on the collective. If people who are obviously self-confident about their abilities constantly put themselves forward (as they do in individualist societies), then they are investing their energies into self-promotion rather than into the welfare of the collective. Many collective societies have a saying (or its equivalent) that "the nail that sticks up gets hammered down" (Damen, 1987).

2. Distributing Rewards for Group Efforts. When people work together on a group project, it is sometimes difficult to decide how the benefits of the work will be distributed. Assume that there are four people who worked on a joint project within their organization. Two of the four clearly did more work than the others. They worked overtime, did more reading on topics related to the project, and so forth. As a result of the group's success, the organization's president decides to present the group members with a $10,000 bonus, above and beyond their salaries. How is the money to be distributed among the four people?

There are a number of distribution patterns. In the pattern known as "equality," each person receives the same amount of money: $2500. In the pattern known as "equity," each person receives an amount corresponding to his or her contributions (Leung & Iwawaki, 1988; Fiske, 1991). Assume that an outside observer studies the contributions of the four people in the group (A, B, C, and D) and makes conclusions about their efforts. Assume further that the conclusions (accepted by the four people) are that A contributed 35 percent to the effort, B contributed 30 percent, C contributed 25 percent, and D contributed 10 percent. Under an equitable distribution, the four people would receive $3500, $3000, $2500, and $1000 respectively.

An equitable distribution of rewards is preferred in individualistic societies. People who invest time and effort in a project want their contributions to be recognized and rewarded. The goal is to reward the efforts of *individuals* in the group rather than to ensure that the group will survive into the future. The quest for individual rewards often leads to a great deal of tension when benefits are to be distributed. People disagree concerning the relative contributions of group members and feel ill-treated if they do not receive as much as expected. They may become upset if co-workers who put in less time and effort receive a large percentage of the benefits. This concern with individual rewards and recognition often leads to difficulties in forming work groups in the first place. Many readers have undoubtedly had experiences similar to those in the following example. A professor wants to introduce the importance of cooperative team effort to her American students. She asks the students to form groups of three, each group to do a team project. One grade will be given for the final report each group submits. Some individualist students will surely say, "What happens if I end up doing more than one-third of the work, or if the others don't follow through on their promises? If I work harder, how will this be recognized? I'm trying to get into a prestigious law school and can't afford a 'C' grade."

Collectivists, on the other hand, prefer an equal distribution of rewards. The goal is to keep the collective intact, and it must be constantly remembered that collectivists obtain their identity from their group membership more than from the pursuit of individual goals. Collectivists feel that if the benefits were distributed unequally, even if some people put in more effort, then ill feelings would result and the group's existence would be threatened. Given that the *group's* well-being is important, people downplay their desires for individual recognition. If one person feels upset, he or she might say, "Some of the people did not work very hard on this group task, but they may work harder on the *next* one that the group undertakes."

3. Advice When Moving from One Culture to Another. If individualism and collectivism are understood, some specific pieces of advice for moving across cultural boundaries can be suggested. Different pieces of advice are applicable to individualists moving to a collective society (e.g., the USA to Japan), and to collectivists moving to an individualist society (e.g., Argentina to Great Britain) (Triandis, et al., 1988; Bhawuk, 1989, 1990).

Recall the discussion of social skills. Individualists are well-advised to work through a collective in obtaining such goals as introductions to prestigious people or interviews for good jobs. They should contribute to the well-being of a collective and only later ask for benefits that the collective might offer. If they pursue their own goals as they would in their own society, they will be seen as pushy, ill-mannered, and disrespectful. In general, people should remember that members of the other culture obtain a great deal of their identity from membership in a collective. Nothing should be done or said that might be interpreted as an insult to the collective or to one of its members. If a person does something positive for a member of a collective, he or she can rest assured that the other members will hear about it. Members of a collective share information among themselves far more frequently than individualists share information with their friends and acquaintances.

Once people start contributing to a collective, they should expect that rewards will be distributed equally rather than on the basis of equity. In fact, the people can interpret this as a complement. When distributing rewards equally the collective is saying, "We realize you value your group membership and we value your presence and your contributions. Since you are putting the collective's well-being foremost, we know that you will want to accept this equal distribution of rewards." Individualists are also well-advised to be modest in describing their abilities and accomplishments and to defer to high-status people in the collective. If the individualists contribute to the group, *others* in the collective will accept the task of praising the people's abilities.

Different pieces of advice should be helpful to collectivists moving to individualist cultures. Most collectivists will not be traveling with their group: foreign students, overseas businesspeople, and emigrants almost always leave some members of their collective in the home country. Consequently, they cannot depend on their collective to provide them with key information and opportunities that are useful for goal attainment. They must adopt the sorts of behavior that individualists display, such as meeting people graciously and finding conversational topics of mutual interest. They must develop what individualists call a "network," that is, a circle of acquaintances who give each other assistance. Members of a network are different from close friends. The latter type of people give emotional support; people in a network trade favors. For instance, one person in a network has the phone number of a clever accountant knowledgeable about income tax deductions when people live in more than one country during a given year. If a person shares this phone number, he or she can expect to have the favor returned at a later date. If people don't return favors, they are often dropped from network membership.

When preparing a set of materials useful in helping people move across cultural boundaries, colleagues and I (Brislin, Cushner, Cherrie, & Yong, 1986) found that collectivists frequently complained about the difficulties of setting up a network. They are not accustomed to meeting people whom they have never seen before and behaving so as to be memorable. When told by individualists (correctly) that parties and other informal social gatherings are good places to meet people, they are confused by the informal rules. At parties, people are expected to "circulate," to speak with many others who are present. If a person spends too much time with a specific individual, he or she is said to "monopolize" the time of the other and also risks the reputation of being a bore. In contrast to the rule that people should circulate, collectivists would rather spend one or two hours with a few people so that participants in the interactions become well known to each other. They feel that the movement from person to person at an individualist party leads to superficial interactions, and they are *very* uncomfortable with the practice. Recall Figure 1: the top diagram suggests greater comfort with movement from person to person at parties. The bottom diagram suggests greater comfort with long conversations among two or three people.

Collectivists also have to learn to communicate their abilities and accomplishments so that individualists will know what their contributions to projects can be. Again, they will not have their group to perform this task for them. They should not brag, of course, but they must learn to talk about themselves so that they become part of other people's memories. Recall the saying common in collectivist societies: The nail that sticks up gets hammered down. Collectivists have to put this saying aside when in individualist societies. Business people have to speak up at meetings and communicate their ideas; foreign students in graduate school have to present their research in seminars; immigrants have to present themselves at employment agencies and present their qualifications and job experiences. Explicit attention to public speaking skills (as defined by individualists) should be helpful in any of these tasks that involve putting the self forward.

Once collectivists realize that they do not have a group that demands the loyalty and deference to which they are accustomed, they will become more comfortable with the equitable rather than the equal distribution of rewards. Since greater emphasis is placed on individual accomplishments and recognition than on group solidarity, they will realize that rewards often follow the level of individual contributions.

4. Balancing Individualism and Collectivism. Perhaps some personal observations about the balance of individualism and collectivism will be helpful at this point. Many developments in the late twentieth century will encourage greater individualism: movement across cultural boundaries, movement from rural areas to cities within various countries, greater dependence upon technology, the desire of women to gain personal identity from employment rather than (or in addition to) homemaking (discussed further in Chapter 9), the worldwide demand for democratic governments, and so forth. But individualism has its price: Other people who might lend support in times of trouble may not be present. The lack of a supportive collective is undoubtedly one reason for difficulties found in the world's most individualistic nation, the United States. There is a very high divorce rate because concerned others are not always present when

One criticism of highly individualistic societies is that citizens have too little concern for the intense difficulties faced by others.

a married couple needs help. Stress-related problems, such as heart disease, are common (Ilola, 1990), and one reason is that supportive others are not always available to help people cope with difficulties (Bond, 1991). Members of culturally diverse groups sometimes find themselves in contradictions. Black Americans may be willing to compete and to develop the social skills necessary for success in an individualistic society, but they may find that their goals are thwarted because of prejudice and discrimination. The resulting stress is one reason for high blood pressure and anxiety disorders among Black Americans (Neal & Turner, 1991). Social problems such as homelessness and inner-city poverty are embarrassments to a great nation, but one reason these are present is that individualism does not necessarily include a concern for (and the willingness to invest resources in) the unfortunate. People's happiness in the most individualistic societies, I believe, will be dependent upon their ability to shift their thinking from the single-minded pursuit of their own goals to a greater concern for the welfare of others in their communities.

CHAPTER SUMMARY

The material in this chapter was selected and organized to answer the question, "What are some useful concepts helpful in understanding virtually any treatment of culture's influence on behavior?" These concepts can then be applied to various analyses of culture's importance that will be presented in future chapters on such topics as socialization, gender, health, and the workplace. Five broad concepts were selected. The first dealt with how people develop an understanding of culture's impact, as shown by the results of effective education and training programs. As people become more sophisticated, they will be better able to work with culturally diverse people in the sorts of settings to be discussed in future chapters: schools, hospitals, business and industry, and so forth. The four other concepts dealt with various challenges people will face as they (a) participate in good orientation and training programs and/or (b) experience challenges during their own everyday intercultural interactions. These concepts deal with overcoming one's ethnocentric attitudes, understanding how people make attributions about others' behavior as well as their own, the inevitability of disconfirmed expectancies, and understanding different behaviors familiar to people from individualist versus collectivist backgrounds.

As people develop a greater sophistication about culture's influence on behavior, changes occur in their thinking, attitudes, and behavior. Changes in their thinking include an ability to take a more complex view of issues, decreased use of oversimplified stereotypes, and a greater understanding of culturally diverse others *from the viewpoint of those other people*. Changes in their attitudes include a deeper understanding of the meaning of cultural relativity, the willingness to admit to themselves that they do not understand certain cultural differences and to withhold judgment about them, and decreases in the anxiety brought on by intercultural interactions. Changes in people's behavior include more ease and comfort when interacting with culturally diverse others and the willingness to engage in specific behaviors when they are considered appropriate by members of other cultures.

Along the route to these desirable changes, people will confront a number of important concepts. They will experience challenges to their ethnocentric feelings, or the tendency to judge others based on the standards with which they are familiar from their own socialization. One reason for the challenges is that they find the attributions they are making about culturally diverse others simply are not working: They are not helping people achieve their goals. Attributions refer to judgments about the causes of behavior. Judgments based solely on one's own familiar standards are likely to be inappropriate. As people become more sophisticated they are able to make more isomorphic attributions, that is, attributions that agree with interpretations of behavior that *the other people make about themselves*.

In addition to making more accurate attributions as they become less ethnocentric, people will also have fewer disconfirmed expectancies. Many times, the reason for people's stress is not due solely to the difficult experiences with which they have to cope. Rather, the stress is due to the difference between what was expected and what was experienced. As people have more and more intercultural encounters, they will likely develop a more realistic set of expectations concerning what is likely to happen to them. One set of differing expectations is brought about by people's socialization in individualistic or collectivist cultures. In individualistic cultures, people learn to place a great deal of emphasis on their own, personal goals. They will make mistakes in other cultures if they do not give attention to the goals of the collectives in which they are given membership. In collectivist cultures, people are willing to place less priority on their own goals and to defer to those of a collective, whether it be their extended family, organization, or religious affiliation. Collectivists who find themselves in individualistic cultures have to develop various skills not previously needed. These include skills related to effective public speaking, describing one's abilities and accomplishments, and developing a network of people whose members exchange favors.

In applying any of these concepts, attention must be paid to the viewpoint of people in other cultures. A theme found throughout this chapter is that the reasons for others' behaviors can be understood only if people avoid imposing their preexisting views. This central concern is also part of any good research methodology that allows the careful study of culture and cultural differences. The topic of research methods and approaches is the focus of the next chapter.

3

SOME METHODOLOGICAL CONCERNS IN INTERCULTURAL AND CROSS-CULTURAL RESEARCH

People's intercultural interactions can be frustrating or exciting, depending upon the point of view that they bring to their encounters with culturally diverse others. The well-meaning clashes described in Chapter 1 can cause anxiety, but they can also stimulate examinations of the cultural influences on *one's own* behavior. If people move beyond the ethnocentric reaction that "we are right and they are wrong," they may be willing to analyze their own behavior when they are misunderstood or when they cannot communicate effectively with others. These miscommunications are *guaranteed* to occur during extensive intercultural encounters. When people make attributions about the reasons for unfamiliar behaviors, they will surely make errors. This *could* cause people to cease seeking out intercultural interactions and, instead, to stick with others much like themselves so that there will be a greater chance of mutual understanding. On the other hand, people might think about their mistakes when making attributions and use these as opportunities to examine the normal thought processes of human beings. The same thought processes called upon in making attributions about culturally different others are also used when people think about a wide variety of important events in their lives. Psychologists have attempted to help people cope with various problems (e.g., depression, weight control, marital difficulties) by guiding individuals toward more effective and realistic thought processes (e.g., Bandura, 1989; Seligman, 1989). People familiar with these thought processes through examinations of their intercultural encounters will have an advantage in benefiting from such interventions.

Frustration and excitement are also possible reactions among researchers who engage in cross-cultural and intercultural studies (Triandis & Berry, 1980; Lonner & Berry, 1986). Consider researchers in such fields as psychology, education, or communication who are deciding among various interesting and important topics to which to attach their analytical skills. Several possibilities might present themselves, and one could involve the career development of young executives in the researchers' hometown. Another might involve the adjustment of some of those same executives who decide to accept international assignments at the branch offices of their organizations. If the researchers decide to attach their talents to the second study area, they (hopefully after careful thought) are accepting a set of burdens above and beyond those of the first study. They will not have easy access to the young executives given their assignments in other countries. The researchers will probably have to deal with translation issues if they include the important step (discussed in Chapter 2) of assessing *host* feelings toward the contributions of young executives. Hosts in some countries may have little familiarity with being interviewed or being questioned about their reactions to colleagues, in contrast to executives in other countries who may have participated in 15 or 20 research studies during their high school and college years. When carrying out research in countries other than one's own, people often have to trust mail and communication systems with which they are not intimately familiar. These systems seem to be especially prone to error exactly when the most important steps of the research process are to take place (Johnson & Tuttle, 1989).

So why do researchers accept the additional burdens that cross-cultural research demands? One set of related reasons revolves around a set of clear advantages that cross-cultural research brings to the investigation of important topics. This set of advantages, in the view of many researchers who have devoted their careers to cross-cultural efforts, offsets the admitted difficulties introduced above.

SOME ADVANTAGES OF CROSS-CULTURAL RESEARCH

Virtually all cross-cultural researchers (see Triandis, Lambert, Berry, Lonner, Heron, Brislin, & Draguns, 1980; Segall, Dasen, Berry, & Poortinga, 1990) argue that the development of concepts and theories dealing with human behavior demands that behavior in all parts of the world be investigated. This seemingly common-sense proposition is at odds with an alternative position that there is so much commonality in human behavior that researchers can investigate it in one place (e.g., the United States, Western Europe) and then generalize to behavior everywhere. If the first position is accepted, then cross-cultural research brings a set of benefits that are almost impossible to achieve in research carried out *within* any one country.

INCREASING THE RANGE OF VARIABLES. Research involves the study of how one variable (what has been more frequently called a concept) relates to others. However, it is difficult to study the effects of one variable on another if there is little range in a variable or little difference in the behavior of the people who participate in the study. For instance, can we study the effects of having a television set in the home on student achievement in school if we carry out the study in the United States? The answer is most likely "no" because almost all homes in the United States contain a television set. We would have a terribly difficult time finding homes without TV so that we could compare students living there with students from TV-owning homes. To study the effects of owning a television set, we have to carry out research in other cultures where television is being introduced for the first time (e.g., rural Arctic villages in Canada and Alaska: Lonner, 1985). With most introductions of new technology (Rogers, 1989), some people in a community adopt innovations quickly and others take a "wait-and-see" approach. We could study early purchasers of television sets with persons who delay their decision. To use the language of research methodology, a person can observe a *range* in the variable of television ownership (yes or no) only by working in certain countries.

Another example may make this important point concerning the range of variables clear. In the United States, could a study be carried out to investigate the effects of divorce on the attitudes of children? Specifically, could we study the attitudes toward marriage among 12-year-olds as a result of their familiarity with a divorce among married couples that they have known. I believe the answer is "no." Virtually all 12-year-olds know of marriages that have ended in divorce. It would be extremely difficult to find adolescents who do not know of a divorce within their extended family or within their communities. We would have to carry out the research in other countries (e.g., the Philippines) where divorce is far less common to obtain a range (in this case, knowledge of divorces contrasted with no knowledge) within the variable or concept that we wish to study.

Important work using the advantage of expanded range has taken place within the study of personality (Miller, 1984; Schweder & Bourn, 1984; Pepitone, 1987). In the United States and Western Europe, an extremely active research tradition involves the study of personality as defined by combinations of trait labels. When people in these parts of the world describe themselves and others, they are likely to use labels that bring to mind permanent traits, such as "friendly," "dominant," "achievement oriented," "shy," and so forth. Most readers have probably taken personality tests and have received the results presented in the form of these trait labels. This manner in which personality is described may not be universal, however. Perhaps the fondness for trait labels that summarize a great deal of information is a convenient aid in fast-moving, individualistic societies. As pointed out in Chapter 2, individualists often move from community to community throughout their lives. They meet others and must make quick judgments about whether or not to seek out further interaction with their new acquaintances. The use of trait labels (other examples are "hardworking" or "gracious") can be of tremendous help in making these important judgments.

Persons in collective societies, on the other hand, are much more likely to have known each other for long periods of time. Especially in rural areas, collectivists have many years to become very familiar with the behavior of various family members, neighbors, and community leaders. In addition, it must be constantly remembered that collectivists obtain much more of their identity from their relationships with other people than do individualists (as discussed in Chapter 2). As a result of their greater concern with others, collectivists are likely to be much more attentive to subtle differences in the behaviors that they observe. One set of subtle differences involves different behaviors in different social situations. A person may be very kind to his or her spouse, but not to subordinates in the workplace. Another person may be hardworking in school, but rather lazy and unproductive upon taking a job after graduating with a college degree. These observations about behavior involve a *trait in a social setting*. They involve more complex analysis than the simple use of a general trait, such as "kind" or "hardworking." Research has shown that collectivists make these complex sorts of personality judgments more frequently than individualists (Shweder & Bourn, 1984; Miller, 1984; Schweder, 1991). Collectivists are more sensitive to differences in people's traits when those people interact in various settings.

The advantage of cross-cultural research is that range has been added to the concepts under study. If only individualists were studied, we would run the risk of concluding that people think about their own personalities and the personalities of others in terms of traits. But the range of people participating in the study places limits on our conclusions. Individualists move so frequently within their society that the easy summary labels represented by traits provide useful shortcuts when they meet new people and decide whether or not to seek out more interactions in the future. The danger in the study of personality, however, is that these useful shortcuts might be mistaken for a universal description of how people think about themselves and others. If cross-cultural research is carried out that includes the participation of collectivists, then range is being added to the study. The increased range is the length of time people know each other and their expectations that they will have interactions with each other well into the future. Given this greater familiarity and longer time perspective, they are more sensitive to differences among people in different social settings.

Interestingly, personality theorists in *individualistic* societies have begun to investigate the study of personality-in-social settings (Magnusson & Endler, 1977; Funder & Colvin, 1991). They have found that they are able to make more accurate predictions about behavior when they have information about people's personalities *and* the social situations in which they participate. In adopting this approach, they are thinking about human behavior in a way similar to that of collectivists. This is another benefit of cross-cultural research: examining how people in other cultures behave on an everyday basis and using some of *their* insights to improve theories about human behavior.

The distinction between describing people's traits as a general summary of their personalities, in contrast to describing people's traits in social settings, may become clearer if an example is discussed that readers have probably experienced. Consider the traits of people with whom one might form a romantic attachment. What might come to mind? "Considerate," "good-looking," "fun to be with," and "exciting" could all be desirable characteristics. Note that these terms describe the sorts of traits that people use to describe their own and others' personalities. But are these the best ways to think about potential romantic partners? Aren't there differences in social settings that should also be taken into account? For instance, most readers have probably had exciting first dates with people, but later dates were disappointing. One reason is that "the early stages of the dating relationship" and "later stages" involve different social settings. Different traits are given careful consideration at the two stages. For instance, people are impressed with others who are "exciting" and "physically attractive" when they consider going out with them on a first date. As relationships develop and people decide whether or not to become committed to each other, different traits are given attention. "Considerate," "hardworking" (so that people can hold down good jobs), and "likes children" will undoubtedly be given greater prominence in people's thinking. If the people are sensitive to the fact that they consider different traits at different stages of their relationships, they are showing an understanding of personality-in-social settings that is very common among collectivists. One reason for the practice of arranged marriages in some collective societies is that 50- and 60-year-old adults know about these differences. Consequently, they can choose a person who will be a good spouse over the entire span of the marriage, not just the "honeymoon" phase.

Many times, individualists have to learn from "the school of hard knocks" that different traits are important in different social settings. Most readers have undoubtedly heard complaints (from their own lips or those of their friends) that someone they know was exciting in early stages of a relationship but showed himself or herself to be a "real jerk" in later stages. I remember a counseling session where a colleague and I were trying to help a faltering marriage. The man complained that his wife never cooked meals and never cleaned the house. My colleague asked, "What attracted you to your wife before you were married?" The man answered, "She was fun to be with and was always ready to go to parties." The counselor then asked, "Aren't you now changing the rules? You dated because of a fun-loving personality, and now you want someone who can cook and keep house. These are very different traits!" Encouraging people to become more sophisticated in their thinking is central to various interventions meant to help them cope with life's stressors (Seligman, 1989).

UNCONFOUNDING VARIABLES. Another, and very intriguing, use of cross-cultural research is that variables which occur together in one culture can sometimes be separated when studies are carried out in other cultures. When researchers identify two or more important variables or concepts that have an impact on human behavior, they often want to identify the relative importance of the variables. If the study was concerned with people's preferences in marital partners, for example (Buss, et al., 1990), the researchers want to make statements about the relative importance of such variables as "dependable character," "good looks," and "similar political background." If variables always occur together, however, they are said to be "confounded." If the variables occur together in the same people, it is very difficult to separate out their relative impact on human behavior. At times, the variables can be unconfounded or separated if cultures can be found where they do not occur together within the personalities or life experiences of the same people.

A classic example from the work of Malinowski (1927) carried out in the Trobriand Islands is worth retelling (example also reviewed by Campbell, 1964, and Guthrie & Lonner, 1986). Malinowski had read the work of Sigmund Freud, who proposed a concept called the oedipal complex. According to Freud, young boys have an inevitably difficult relationship with their fathers because they are jealous of the father's role as the mother's lover. Malinowski observed that there is a problem in Freud's work due to confounded variables. Other variables occur *together* with the father's role as mother's lover. One is that he is also the son's disciplinarian, and he might be the target of his son's negative emotions because he administers punishment for misbehaviors. Based on Freud's observations in Vienna, Austria, we cannot say which reason for the son's negative emotions is the stronger. The variables of "mother's lover" and "son's disciplinarian" are confounded.

Are there cultures in which the roles are separate or unconfounded, that is, where *different* people have the roles of mother's lover and boy's disciplinarian? The answer is "yes." In many Pacific Island societies, including the Trobriands, the mother's oldest brother is responsible for disciplining his nephew when necessary. The father continues to have normal marital relations with his wife but is expected to play a less important role in the disciplining of his sons. Who is the target of the boy's negative emotions? The answer is that the boy is more likely to dislike his uncle than his father. This important work cast doubt on Freud's assumption that the oedipal complex and its inevitable son–father tension was a universal to be found in all parts of the world.

The important role of the mother's brother in some Pacific Island societies has led to another cross-cultural joke (one was discussed in Chapter 1, p. 8). Teachers from the United States were asked to accept two-year contracts in various Pacific Island schools, sometimes arranged through the Peace Corps. They naturally began by introducing ideas with which they were familiar, such as parent–teacher associations (PTAs). They were disappointed with the attendance, especially from the children's fathers. After a few months, they discovered the important point already introduced: The maternal uncle is responsible for the socialization of the child, and this includes looking after the child's progress in school. When the American teachers started an organization more like a UTA (Uncle–Teacher Association), they had more success.

Research on health and medicine often looks to cross-cultural research to unconfound variables (Ilola, 1990; also Chapter 10, this volume). Two sets of variables that are often confounded are (a) the biological heritage of people in a culture and (b) their dietary habits. If research is carried out within a culture where people have the same biological heritage and similar dietary practices, it is difficult to assess the relative importance of the two types of variables. These variables can be unconfounded when people from the same biological heritage accept the dietary habits of the *different* cultures to which they move. In investigating the relative importance of biological and cultural factors on alcohol use, Sue, Zane, and Ito (1979) studied people whose biological heritage was Japanese. However, different Japanese people within their study had lived in the United States for varying lengths of time. If biological factors were of prime importance, all people of Japanese heritage should have a very similar pattern of alcohol use. If cultural factors were more important, people should have differing patterns of alcohol use depending upon their exposure to and active participation in American society. Sue and his colleagues argue that the latter factor is more important. People's pattern of alcohol use was predicted by the length of time they had been in America. Similar results have been shown for the effects of diet. The longer people of Japanese ancestry have been exposed to a typical American diet (more meat, more fat, fewer vegetables, more calories than in Japan), the more likely they are to have health problems typical of Americans (e.g., coronary diseases) (Reed, et al., 1982).

INCREASED SENSITIVITY TO CONTEXT. One of the basic principles in many theories within the behavioral and social sciences is that behavior is a function of the person and the situation. To understand behavior, we must have extensive knowledge about the people (e.g., their personalities, their attitudes, their values) and the situations in which they find themselves. Aspects of the situation (Argyle, Furnham, & Graham, 1981; Detweiler, Brislin, & McCormack, 1983; Funder & Colvin, 1991) include the formal and informal rules, types of challenges, public versus private, and amount of structure. For example, consider behavior at a funeral. To predict behavior, we need to know about the people who will attend and the social situation summarized by the term *funeral*. If the funeral is *highly structured* and has the *rule* that people behave in a very solemn way, then most observations will involve people's quiet, attentive behavior. In this case, aspects of the people involved (e.g., their sense of humor, their extroversion vs. introversion) will be overwhelmed by the social situation. But imagine that the funeral is an Irish wake. Here, the social situation is more like a party, and the acceptable rules allow a greater variety of behaviors.

Parties have "rules" that allow some people to be very loud and energetic and others to be quieter. Some people can drink large amounts of alcohol and others will sip ginger ale. Some will talk to five or six others over the course of the party, and others will circulate and have a few words with all others who are in attendance. Behavior at an Irish wake, then, will be more variable than at a solemn funeral. Given that there are rules that allow a wider variety of behaviors, knowledge of people's personalities (e.g., extraversion vs. introversion) and their attitudes toward alcohol use will be predictive of how they act.

The important point that behavior is determined by both aspects of people and the situation should constantly be kept in mind. It appears in arguments that are central to many different academic disciplines. In linguistics, for example, the point appears as part of the competence–performance distinction. This distinction refers to the fact that people should not automatically diagnose the competencies of others from their performance in a specific situation. Very often, aspects of the situation are such that they do not allow underlying competencies to be expressed. Readers have undoubtedly experienced a problem stemming from this competence–performance distinction. Haven't we all performed poorly on a test such that our underlying competencies were called to question? But in thinking back on the test, weren't there problems with the testing situation such that we felt it unfair and unreasonable that our competencies were being judged? The test may have been administered in a threatening situation, may have had amgibuous questions, or may have been taken on a day when we were ill. All of these features of the situation interfered with a fair assessment of our underlying competencies.

In an article with the interesting title, "Some Issues on which Linguists Can Agree," Hudson (1981, p. 336) presented the following summary of the competence–performance distinction:

> A child's poor performance in formal, threatening, or un-
> familiar situations cannot be taken as evidence of impoverished
> linguistic competence, but may be due to other factors such as
> low motivation for speaking in that situation, or unfamiliarity
> with the conventions for use of language in such situations.

Problems with mistaking competence from performance, and in-sensitivity to the situational factors to which people respond, are common despite Hudson's important arguments. People, including behavioral and social scientists who should know better, continue to make judgments about competencies from analyses of performance. One reason is that most people (as discussed in Chapter 1) have had extensive experience in only one culture: the one in which they were socialized. In the one culture, they are often insensitive to the social situations in which behavior takes place because the situations are so familiar. The social situations in which they find themselves, such as those at their schools, churches, workplaces, and homes, become taken for granted (Chapter 1, pp. 8–10). Given this degree of familiarity, there is rarely any reason to examine the reasons for behavior that situational factors might bring.

When behavioral and social scientists carry out research within their own society, they are going to have the same difficulty analyzing the effects of situational factors because these are so familiar. It is difficult to take a step back and to objectively look at the differing contributions of people and situations since the researchers themselves are people who live in the situations on an everyday basis. To use a common metaphor, it is difficult for them to separate the forest (the total number of factors that influence behavior) from the trees (various people in society).

This long introduction has been necessary to provide the background for an argument about an advantage of cross-cultural studies. Researchers may have an easier task separating the contributions of people and the contributions of situational variables on the behavior that they observe. When doing research in other cultures, many situations will be new, unfamiliar, and fresh to their eyes. Since the situations will not be so familiar as to be taken for granted, it should be easier for researchers to examine the social settings they observe and to make suggestions about their possible impact. They can then combine these observations with analyses of person-centered concepts (some of which may also be unfamiliar and thus easier to perceive) to make more accurate predictions about behavior. Many times, the identification of person-centered *and* situational variables will be facilitated if the performance–competence distinction is kept in mind.

An actual incident may make all these arguments clearer (only names have been changed to protect people's privacy). Wiladluk was a teenager from one of the rural provinces in Thailand that was quite distant from any large city. She had learned many skills necessary for making a living in her village, such as farming, homemaking, and even some native healing practices. She had learned these skills by working closely with adults who were respected in her community: her father for farming skills, her mother for cooking and sewing, and the native healer for the use of herbs to treat various illnesses. She was clearly what her neighbors called "a clever girl," and she was also very friendly with others. These were the two reasons why the native healer took a liking to her and shared knowledge of select herbs.

Wiladluk's formal schooling was spotty. Educated teachers from the big cities such as Bangkok got bored living in the provinces and either maneuvered their way out of their contracts or put minimum effort into their teaching. Still, Wiladluk was able to learn reading and writing skills, and because she was clearly the brightest person in her classes, she received the greatest amount of attention from her teachers. When Wiladluk was 16, an especially concerned teacher came to the village. He recommended that Wiladluk take the national exams for entry to Thailand's universities. He worked side by side with Wiladluk helping her to improve her academic skills so that she would do well on the formal exams (similar to the Scholastic Aptitude Test with which many Americans are familiar). Wiladluk did well on the tests, won a scholarship that was to pay all her expenses, and went away to a good university in one of Thailand's big cities.

At the university, Wiladluk did not do well. Her professors did not give her good grades on her essay tests, complaining that Wiladluk did not make her points clear to people who might read her essays. Wiladluk was very disappointed and was afraid that she would have to return to her village with a reputation as a failure. She felt that she would bring disgrace to her family since she was not able to take advantage of the tremendous opportunity that had been offered to her. What might be done to help Wiladluk?

There are many reasons for Wiladluk's difficulties, and researchers from countries other than Thailand may have a clearer view of several. Since the researchers themselves are undoubtedly experiencing adjustment difficulties brought on by movement from their home countries to Thailand, they may be able to empathize with Wiladluk's plight. Just as it is difficult to move from country to country, it is stressful to move from rural areas to big cities within a country (Brislin, 1981). Friends and family are left behind in the village, difficulties have to be overcome in the search for housing, and life in big cities is almost always experienced as more impersonal than life in villages (Berry, 1990). If the researchers are individualists (Chapter 2), they may have a clearer view of the special problems faced by collectivists. Thai researchers, probably having been socialized as collectivist themselves, may take the expectations faced by collectivists for granted and may see Wiladluk's problems less clearly. In this case, Wiladluk is faced with a problem brought on by a basic aspect of the collective person. Identity is obtained by reference to a group, and the group's relationship to her is central to her view of herself. If she does poorly at the university, she is not the only one who will be seen as a failure. She perceives that her entire collective will be disappointed, and this brings additional stress into her life. Note the importance of keeping the competence–performance distinction in mind. Wiladluk clearly has many of the necessary competencies, as shown by her achievements in her village. But situational factors in the big city, such as the more impersonal lifestyle and *lack* of day-to-day contact with her supportive collective, put such stress on her that competencies cannot be expressed in effective performance.

MORE ON CONTEXTUAL FACTORS: LEARNING IN AND OUT OF CONTEXT

Since sensitivity to the context of human behavior cannot be overemphasized in cross-cultural research, it is useful to analyze Wiladluk's difficulties from another viewpoint that also involves contextual factors. In analyzing how people best learn new facts, attitudes, and skills, an important distinction is whether the new ideas are presented "in context" versus "out of context" (Cushner, 1990). If people learn in context, this means that they learn new ideas in the same situation where they are actually applied. So when Wiladluk learns farming skills while working side by side with her father, and learns the uses of various herbs when sitting next to the healer (in the setting where the healer meets her patients), Wiladluk is said to be learning "in context." There are immediate links made in Wiladluk's mind between the new ideas and possible practical applications of the ideas. Further, Wiladluk's teachers can observe the development of Wiladluk's skills and can make adjustments as they present new ideas to her or decide to go over ideas already presented (a process analyzed by Rogoff, 1990). Even Wiladluk's tutor who prepares her for the university exams is working in context. He is working side by side with his student, and he can make adjustments in the material he presents. Further, this new learning has a clear application in the near future: performance on the university entrance exams.

In contrast to the type of learning to which Wiladluk is accustomed, the presentation of new ideas and material to be mastered at the university level is out of context. Wiladluk is assigned material from texts and is expected to learn material presented by professors in a lecture format. She does not work side by side with a teacher. Rather, she reads her texts by herself and takes notes on her professor's lectures as one of hundreds of students in a lecture hall. The learning may *or may not be* useful and applicable in the future. The material might be useful in taking an exam in the not-so-clear future, but Wiladluk cannot be sure. The learning may be useful if she returns to her village, but it might also be forgotten and remain in her old, dust-gathering former textbooks.

In addition to the stress of adjusting to a new lifestyle at the university, then, another reason for Wiladluk's difficulties is her unfamiliarity with a different style of learning. Returning to the distinction already introduced, her underlying competencies are difficult to express since she is expected to *perform* as a participant in an unfamiliar teacher–student learning style. As pointed out in Chapter 1, observations of cross-cultural differences as well as one's own intercultural encounters can stimulate examinations of one's own socialization. This point can be combined with the argument being made here: Observers in Thailand who are from other cultures might be able to diagnose Wiladluk's difficulties more readily than Thai nationals. The observers may be more able to distinguish Wiladluk's abilities from the context in which she is expected to display her abilities. Since many Thai nationals were socialized in a culture where the link between abilities and context was experienced together, they may have a difficult time separating the two. For example, it is only after a study of these cultural differences that I can see the importance of out-of-context learning in the American school system. When thought about carefully, out-of-context learning is rather odd.

Children go to school and learn material that they *might* apply someday. In high school, students take geometry and may use it someday as they figure out how many square yards of carpet to buy for their newly acquired first home. Such out-of-context learning is probably a relatively recent phenomenon brought about by industrialization and the rise of cities. In the past, certainly before the printing press and the norm of literacy in technologically developed societies, most learning was in context. Children learned the knowledge, attitudes, and skills necessary for survival in their culture by observing adult behavior in the context where the new learning could be applied. Given the presence of books and the need to instruct children apart from their parents who go off to jobs in the businessworld, out-of-context learning becomes the preferred style in the place we call "the school."

In addition to realizing the importance of this style, cross-cultural comparisons and personal intercultural encounters have also led to an awareness of how some of my socialization experiences have led to a preparation for out-of-context learning. Put another way, some of my own socialization experiences led to *less* of a distinction between home and school than that experienced by Wiladluk. For instance, my mother tells me I used to put puzzles together by myself, sitting in a corner of our home and deciding how the puzzle pieces go together to make a complete picture. She would read books to me when I was 3 and 4 years old, but then I could thumb through them on my own. On finding a picture in a book that I did not understand, I could *initiate* conversations with my parents by asking them about the picture's content. All of these childhood experiences (recall the importance of these from Chapter 1, pp. 7–8) led to positive outcomes. The skills I learned before I entered school—working alone on intellectual tasks, gathering information from books, and initiating conversations with adults—were very useful in my adjustment to kindergarten and the first grade. People who never had the opportunity to develop these skills will likely experience more stress in their first extensive out-of-home encounters with a new setting and with unfamiliar adults: the school and its teachers (Heath, 1983). The point for the present discussion is that I would be unable to make the distinction between skills at home and skills in school unless I had observed schoolchildren in other cultures. My own development of a set of person variables (skills) applicable to various settings (home and school) occurred together, and are difficult to separate in any analysis of person–situation interactions. Given my analyses of how people use skills in different settings as part of their life in other cultures, I can then look back on my own life and apply the concepts stimulated by the cross-cultural observations. This ability to look with fresher eyes on one's own socialization into a culture is one of the benefits of cross-cultural research and of one's own intercultural experiences.

GUIDANCE IN MAKING CROSS-CULTURAL OBSERVATIONS: EMICS AND ETICS

In their quest for the benefits of cross-cultural studies and analysis, researchers have developed a set of conceptual tools that are useful in making decisions about their research methodology. One is to make a distinction between culture-common and culture-specific concepts. Culture-common concepts are those that can be found among people all over the world. Many culture-common concepts will have a basis in the demands that people face in their own desire for survival and the survival of their community. Some examples have already been discussed: socializing children to become responsible members of society; maintaining harmony among people so that disagreements do not result in violence; and the stresses encountered when cultures come into contact. Other examples are placing controls on people's sexual appetites and looking after the needs of elderly people who can no longer contribute their labors to the community (Aberle, Cohen, Davis, Levy, & Sutton, 1950; Lonner, 1980).

Culture-specific concepts are found in some but not other societies. These concepts represent a culture's unique adaptations to the demands it faces. Often, culture-specific concepts represent *additions to* or *variants on* culture-general concepts with which all people are familiar. Some examples that have been already covered include the maintenance versus severance of relations with past romantic partners, differences in responsibility for the disciplining of children (the children's father vs. uncle), and the prevalence of in-context versus out-of-context learning. Note that these culture-specific concepts represent different ways that people deal with culture-general demands: bringing people together for consideration as marriage partners; socializing children to be responsible adults; and educating children in the skills needed for survival in a culture. Very often, cross-cultural research focuses on this combination of culture-general and culture-specific concepts, both of which are necessary for an understanding of culture and cultural differences.

Cross-cultural researchers frequently use a shorthand pair of descriptors to summarize their arguments about their studies. Culture-general concepts are frequently called "etics" and culture-specific concepts are frequently called "emics." The emic–etic distinction has encouraged a rich and extensive literature and has sharpened the thinking of cross-cultural researchers (Berry, 1969; Brislin, 1980, 1983; Poortinga & Malpass, 1986; Headland, Pike, & Harris, 1990). I will attempt to make some basic points that (a) explain key aspects of the distinction and that (b) introduce the longer treatments of emics and etics referenced above. While not all these scholars agree with these explanations and emphases, I believe that the following presentation provides a basis for further discussions among people who hold differing views.

The basis of the terms is interesting, and it also provides another way of explaining culture-general and culture-specific concepts. The term *etic* comes from phonetic analysis as carried out by linguists. In a phonetic analysis, an attempt is made to develop a system that includes all meaningful sounds in all the world's language. A meaningful sound is one that makes a difference in communication between speaker and listener, and in a phonetic analysis sounds have to make a difference in at least one of the world's languages. For instance, some languages have a glottal click sound, some have an initial "ng" sound, and some have a trilled "r" sound. People have to make these sounds clearly to be understood and to be considered a good speaker of the language. If a sound makes a difference in any of the world's languages, it should be part of a phonetic analysis.

The shorthand term *emic* is borrowed from a phonemic analysis in linguistics. In this type of analysis, linguists document the meaningful sounds *within* any one language. If a language does not have a sound that speakers have to make to be understood, then that sound would not be part of a phonemic analysis. Does the English language have an initial "ng" sound? No, it does not. Does English have a glottal stop (in contrast to a glottal click)? After quick consideration people might answer "no," but after a more lengthy analysis an example would be found. If people are suddenly surprised at something that might bring them negative outcomes, they might say, "Oh-oh! This is going to be difficult!" The sound between the two "ohs" is a glottal stop, and it is one of the phonemes in the English language. People must be able to articulate phonemes to be considered good speakers of a language. For example, people must be able to make the initial "th" sound (the symbol is θ) in the words *these*, *think*, and *through*. Some languages (and even dialects within English) do not have this sound, and so people might say something like, "I dink I will go to the baseball game tomorrow." This shows that they do not know the phonemes of standard English. Incidentally, this (θ) sound is one about which non-native speakers frequently complain when they study the English language. The best-known distinction, given that it forms the basis of ethnic jokes, is the initial "l" versus the initial "r" sound. There is a difference in the sentences, "I have a lock" and "I have a rock." People have to make this phonemic distinction to be considered good speakers of English. There is no distinction between the initial "r" and initial "l" sounds in the Japanese language. Native speakers of Japanese have to put extra effort into making this "l–r" distinction in their speech.

Borrowing from phonetic and phonemic analysis, the term *etic* is used to refer to concepts and ideas that are common across cultures. In the best research, theoretical ideas are put forward that explain how various concepts relate to one another in people's thoughts, emotions, and behaviors. Examples include guiding children to a responsible adulthood and dealing with the inevitable conflicts that arise as different people interfere with each other's pursuit of their goals (Leung & Wu, 1990). Emics refer to culture-specific concepts found in some societies but not others. Often, emics are the culturally specific ways that cultures deal with etic concepts. For example, some cultures stress strict obedience in socializing children since the society is dependent upon people working together and following well-known rules. Traditional agricultural societies are examples: People have to follow strict rules concerning when to plant crops, when to harvest them, and how to store food to protect against a future crop failure. People cannot behave any way they want: They have to be socialized to follow rules. In contrast, hunting societies emphasize more independence in their socialization. Hunters usually work in small groups since too many people would make so much noise that game would be scared away. They have to be flexible in their behavior, changing their plans and even the site of their communities as game in a certain area becomes scarce. They have to live a more independent lifestyle than agricultural peoples, and their social-ization of children emphasizes independence training (Berry, 1979). The etic, then, is that children should be able to contribute to the economy of their communities. The emics are the differing child-rearing practices that adults emphasize. A combination of etics and emics is necessary for understanding the socialization of children in agricultural and hunting societies.

When reviewing phonemic analysis, examples were given of sounds that non-native speakers of a language have difficulty reproducing. This aspect of "difficult to learn and to understand" is also an aspect of emics. It is the *emics* of another culture that are hard to understand. The etics are easier to grasp since, by definition, they are common to people in all cultures. When living in another culture, then, people can relate to the etic of "developing relationships that may lead to marriage." The emics of another culture, however, will be unfamiliar because they are not ex-perienced in one's own culture. Learning emics is similar to Japanese speakers learning the "l–r" distinction, or English speakers learning the "r-trilled r" distinction if they study Russian. Time and effort has to be invested; behaviors will seem strange at first; and it will take time before the emics seem natural and everyday in their occurrence. It will take time before people from collective societies are able to maintain friendly rela-tions with previous romantic partners, and before people from individual-istic societies recognize and understand the reasons why the maintenance of friendly relationships is problematic.

A common error in both cross-cultural research *and* people's every-day thinking is to believe that one's own etic–emic combination is true for all cultures. When such thinking takes place, the problem of ethno-centrism is being broached. If the etic–emic combination involves raising responsible children (etic) together with the goal of encouraging inde-pendent thinking (emic), it is incorrect to apply this combination to all cultures. The etic part may be reasonable, but believing that one's own emics are *part of* the culture-common etic is problematic. When people think and behave in this way, they are said to be imposing an etic (Berry, 1969). They are forcing a point of view (as assumed etic) on another culture without being willing to look for emic aspects. Further, they are viewing their own emics as part of a complex concept that they are imposing on others. Knowing about emics and etics has practical applications. American teachers are most often socialized in a middle-class background where one *emic* in parent-to-child behaviors is encouraging independent thinking. Children from this type of background often do well in school because teachers expect and reward independent thinking (Cushner, 1990; Hamilton, Blumenfeld, Akoh, & Miura, 1991). Examples are the students' own choice of topics for their term papers or their own choice of books for free-reading period. If teachers impose this *emic* aspect of their own socialization on their expectations for student behaviors, they will not be as effective with children socialized according to other emics (e.g., obedience and deference to authority, as described above).

EMICS AND ETICS: AN EXAMPLE. Complex problems involving extensive culture contact can often be analyzed using etics and emics as a starting point. Clear failures often involve a misunderstanding of another culture's emics.

In a foreign-aid project meant to assist the economy of a developing nation in East Africa, a highly industrialized nation (the United States) attempted to improve the rangelands where cattle graze (case analyzed by Talbot, 1972). Members of the East African tribes had small herds of cattle because their rangelands had little grass. Natural events such as fires and droughts kept the rangelands relatively barren. Each herder, however, tried to have as many cattle as possible as this was a sign of status and wealth. Multiple cattle also allowed more food for a herder's family in the form of milk and blood (a source of protein).

The members of the development team attempted to improve the tribe's economy by instituting water-irrigation projects. They were "successful" in the sense that they did indeed introduce projects that delivered more water. Grass on the rangeland became more plentiful. After a period of time, however, disaster struck and the tribe was faced with starvation. The increased availability of water led to increases in the amount of land where good pastures could be established. With increased food for their cattle, the tribesmen allowed their herds to multiply. Eventually, the larger number of cattle overgrazed to the extent that grass was no longer available. Cattle died and members of the tribe were faced with starvation.

Analysis of this case study can be aided with explicit attention to emics and etics. As discussed previously, complex concepts are often combinations of a common etic core *plus* culture-specific emics. This combination is sometimes called the etic core with its emic coloring. What must be avoided is to view one's own etic–emic combination as universal and impose it on others. If this is done, the extremely important step of examining the other culture's emics is forgotten.

The analysis of the rangeland development project centers on the viewpoints of the technical assistance advisers from the United States and the herdsmen from the East African tribe. There are some etics that are, by definition, shared by the two groups of people. Examples are that cattle demand a great deal of care; cattle can be used as a source of protein (meat for Americans, blood for the herdsmen); and the knowledge that the improved delivery of water will increase the land available for pastures. In addition to these etics, however, there are some emics that are the sources of the difficulties. I will number them since each emic in one culture can be presented in a way that contrasts with the emics of the other group.

In the United States, (1) there are many sources of wealth and status other than cattle. People can make a great deal of money selling stocks and bonds, for instance, and they can demonstrate their status by owning an expensive car or wearing trendy clothes. There is (2) a long history of conservation of resources. Most American science texts have units on the conservation of our natural resources, and children who join the Girl Scouts or Boy Scouts can earn several merit badges dealing with conservation (I was once a merit badge counselor for the "soil and water conservation" award). Another possible emic (3) is that big projects bring more attention to people, and are more useful in their career development, than small but efficient projects. Somehow, spending tens of millions of dollars on an irrigation project is more attention-grabbing than a smaller project that helps herders raise healthier animals within their small herds.

Among the East African herders, (1) cattle are the prime source of wealth and prestige. Consequently, opportunities to increase the number of cattle in one's herd are welcome. However, (2) there is not a great deal of experience with activities summarized by the term *conservation*. Before the irrigation project, a number of factors limited the size of herds and so tribesmen rarely were faced with the issue of having too many cattle. Fires and drought would limit the amount of grass available for grazing, and disease would occasionally decrease the size of herds. When ample water and grasslands became available, the herdsmen had far fewer limits placed on the number of cattle for which they could provide adequate care. Without a history of conservation, and its important component that animals must be sacrificed now to plan for a productive future, herders allowed their cattle to reproduce until large numbers overgrazed the grasslands. There were undoubtedly small increases each year, but (3) small increases noticeably improve the herdsmen's economic status. An American dairyman might have to add 100 cows to his herd to warrant comment from neighbors (recall the American emic of big projects bringing attention). For the East African tribesman, an increase of three or four animals per year would bring positive comments from others. But if many tribesmen increase their herds in this slow but sure manner, there will eventually be too many cattle for the available grasslands.

The difficulties stemmed in part, then, from an unwillingness or inability to understand another culture's emics. The American etic–emic combination (e.g., delivery of water *combined with* a history of conservation activities) was imposed on the herders. The East African herders admittedly shared some etics with the Americans, for example, water delivery and the importance of good care for one's animals. However, there is a *danger* with etics: The similarities in *some* aspects of a complex concept can lead to a false sense of security that *all* aspects of the concept are the same. When this is done, people miss the emics present in the other culture.

A final example may be helpful, especially since virtually all readers will be familiar with some aspects of it. In considering the concept "intelligence" across cultures, there are some etic aspects. Solving problems, the exact form of which has not been seen before, is one etic. Intelligent people can be confronted with unfamiliar problems and suggest workable solutions. In many parts of the world, an *emic* aspect of intelligence is "quickness." The most intelligent people not only solve problems, but they do so quickly. This is an emic aspect with which virtually all readers have had experience. Surely they have taken *timed* intelligence tests (e.g., the Scholastic Aptitude Test is a variant), and all have said to themselves, "If I only had more time, I could have answered a lot more questions!" This emic aspect of intelligence is not universal. A number of psychologists (Wober, 1974; Serpell, 1982; Dasen, 1984) have analyzed the emics in other cultures. Among the Baganda people of Uganda, for example, intelligence is associated with slow, careful, and deliberate thought (Wober, 1974). It is much more important to carefully consider a large number of potential solutions to problems, slowly examining one's memory to see how these solutions worked in other problematic situations, before sharing one's thoughts with others. As Lonner (1990) points out, if leaders of the Baganda attended a supercharged, hour-long decision-making meeting among executives in North America or Western Europe, the meeting would be over before the leaders might make their contributions. A grave mistake would be made if the executives made judgments about the Baganda leaders based on their own etic–emic combination: problem solving with an emphasis on time. Not all children presenting themselves in North American and Western European classrooms have this "quickness" emphasis. I probably did. When I presented completed puzzles to my mother (discussed earlier, p. 70), she probably said, "Oh, Richard, it's wonderful that you did them so quickly!" This made me better prepared to benefit from the expectations of my elementary school teachers. But quickness is not universally valued, and it is not in the background of all schoolchildren in a culturally diverse country such as the United States or Canada. The wise teacher realizes that quickness is not universal and will make efforts to *gradually* introduce students to the emphasis on time that they will face during their lives.

EQUIVALENCE OF CONCEPTS

The discussion of emics and etics leads directly to another major concern with which investigators must deal when making decisions about research methodology. The concern is the equivalence of concepts across the cultures that are included in the researcher's study. In general terms, questions about equivalence are put in the form, "Do the concepts being investigated, and especially the way the concepts are being measured, have the same meaning in the different cultures?" In more specific terms, reference has to be made to the topic under investigation in a specific study. For example, a given researcher might be interested in studying the concept, "disciplining young men to control their aggressiveness," and a study might be carried out in several cultures (this topic has been investigated by Goldstein & Segall, 1983). Questions about equivalence must be raised when a concept such as "aggressiveness" is used. Is the concept equivalent in the cultures under study? Assume that children are on a playground, and a young boy has been playing with his ball for a half-hour. A slightly older and heavier boy comes along and takes the ball away. The "equivalence" issue arises when considering possible responses that the younger boy might make. When is behavior considered "aggressive"? If the younger boy forces his ball away from the older boy, shoving him slightly in the process, is this aggressiveness or sticking up for one's rights? Different cultures have different guidelines for labeling behavior as aggressive. To make the matter more complex, there are differences within a complex society such as the United States. One of the graduate students with whom I have worked remembers when he was 10-years-old. His mother (who happened to be a well-known member of the school board) and father met with his teacher for a discussion about his progress. The teacher said, "His schoolwork is fine, but I wish he would be more aggressive about asserting himself on the playground and in the classroom when other students take advantage of him." His parents replied, "We're Quakers, we are trying to raise him according to Quaker values, and so we are happy to hear that his behavior is pacifist." The rest of the parent–teacher conference proceeded in a clumsy manner after this exchange of views.

Other research examples that must be examined with the equivalence issue in mind have been introduced in this chapter. The concept "intelligent behavior" is certainly not equivalent in the United States and among the Baganda of East Africa if part of the meaning involves quickness in one culture and slow, deliberate thought in the other. The concept "making judgments about the personalities of others" will demand a careful analysis of equivalence issues. If people in individualist societies make judgments about traits that supposedly generalize across situations (recall the discussion, pp. 61–63), and if people in collectivist societies make judgments based on traits *in* situations, direct comparisons of the judgments will be difficult to make.

A number of approaches to dealing with the equivalence issue have been developed (Hui & Triandis, 1985; Malpass & Poortinga, 1986). Three will be discussed here: translation equivalence, conceptual equivalence, and metric equivalence. Some researchers prefer to use the terms "culture common" and "culture specific" instead of etics and emics in discussions of equivalence. To prepare people for further reading of the material cited throughout this book, I will use culture common/etic and culture specific/emic interchangeably.

TRANSLATION EQUIVALENCE. A good start at identifying problems involving equivalence is to examine descriptions and measures of concepts as they are translated across languages. If concepts can be easily expressed in the languages of the different cultures being studied, then researchers are making a first step in dealing with equivalence issues. If concepts do not translate well, researchers *should not* throw up their hands in frustration. Material that does not translate well can indicate emic aspects that allow researchers to identify the meaning of concepts in different cultures. It must be kept in mind that the emics of other cultures are likely to be unfamiliar to outsiders, and these "outsiders" include researchers from other countries. Unfamiliar aspects of a concept might be difficult to translate because (a) there may not be readily available terms to capture those aspects, and/or (b) translators working across the various languages might be unfamiliar with the emic aspects. Rather than discard the seemingly unsuccessful attempts to translate concepts, researchers should collect and analyze them for insights into behavior in the other cultures. These general points may become clearer if an example is presented.

The back-translation procedure is a good place to start examinations of the equivalence issue. In this procedure, material in an original language is carefully prepared. In research projects, for example, the material might be a questionnaire asking about child-rearing practices. A bilingual then translates the material to the target language, and a second bilingual (unfamiliar with the efforts of the first bilingual) translates the material back to English. The two English versions can then be examined to determine what "comes through" clearly, and the assumption (not yet proven) can be entertained that the target-language version is adequate if the two English versions are equivalent (more about back-translation can be found in Brislin, 1980, 1986).

By studying the back-translated original-language version, researchers can gain insights into what, and what cannot, be easily expressed in the target language. In research carried out in Guam, where the native language is Chamorro, I was interested in the personality variable called "desire for social approval." If people have this desire, then they want to express themselves to others in a manner such that they gain approval. To do so, they often flatter themselves, deny their faults, and say positive things about themselves even when these are not strictly true. To measure this concept, Crowne and Marlowe (1964) wrote statements that identified mildly negative behaviors in which almost all people engage. If people who respond to the statements *deny* engaging in these behaviors, they are said to be desirous of social approval.

One of the statements is, "I like to gossip at times." The assumption behind using statements like this is that if people were totally honest with themselves, they would answer "yes." In a study carried out in Guam, where the native language is Chamorro (Brislin, 1970, 1986), back-translation was used. One bilingual translated this and other statements into Chamorro, and another independently back-translated to English. Changes were made in an effort to make a *second* English version more easily translatable, and this was given to a third bilingual. The process continued for three rounds, and it can be summarized in a diagram:

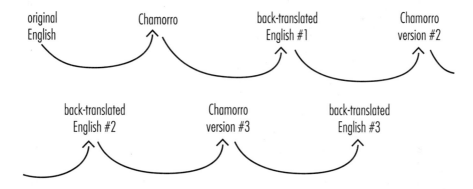

The assumption is that if the English-language materials could "survive" this procedure (called "decentering"), then the concepts that remain in the back-translated English version #3 must be readily expressible in Chamorro. In addition, an assumption is that the Chamorro #3 version and the English #3 version could be "translation equivalent," and that further cross-cultural research efforts are warranted. Note that the procedure is much like the game called "rumor." Ten or more people form a circle, and one person whispers a sentence into a second person's ear. The whispered communication continues around the circle, and the last person tells the entire group what she or he heard. Often, a great deal of the original sentence is lost or changed. The material that comes through, however, is often very clear, memorable, and easily expressible (e.g., "The temperature was over 100 degrees").

In the study involving the Chamorro language, the item "I like to gossip at times" ended up as "Sometimes I like to talk about other people's business" in the third English back-translation. Results like these then stimulate discussions with the translators, and some of the most important findings emerge from this important step. The bilinguals told me that there is no one word for "a gossip". The Chamorro language demands that the speakers indicate whether they are referring to a male or to a female gossip. There were readily available words, on the other hand, to render a good translation of "talk about other people's business." There was a better equivalent for "sometimes" in contrast to "at times," and consequently the former was favored. In subsequent research efforts, the *modified* version of the original item was used (i.e., the "talk about business" rather than the original "gossip" version) since the latter is translation-equivalent according to this procedure.

The results of seeking translation equivalence for other items sometimes demand smaller, but no-less-important, changes. Another of the original items is, "I have never intensely disliked anyone." The third back-translated version was, "I have never really disliked anyone." The bilinguals told me that it was difficult to translate "intensely," and this is an example of the general point (Brislin, 1986, p. 146) that adverbs frequently cause trouble in translation. There was a better equivalent for "anyone" than "someone." Again, the modified version based on the third back-translation, and the third Chamorro version, were used to measure the need for social approval among English and Chamorro speakers.

This multiple-translation procedure is more suitable in identifying culture-common aspects of a concept then in determining possible culture-specific (emic) aspects. If wording survives the multiple translations into and back from another language, then both the original and target languages are likely to have frequently used terms and phrases to describe the ideas contained in the material. If aspects of the concept cannot be readily translated (as with "gossip," above), then these aspects *will not* be found in the back-translated versions. If aspects are either dropped or *added* by translators who follow instructions to "communicate these ideas as best you can in the target language," they may be emics. For instance, when I found that "gossip" was not to be found in the back-translations, I suggested to myself that there may be an emic involved. I was correct: Conversations with translators led to the realization that a distinction must be made between male and female gossips. This an emic aspect of the Chamorro language. The recommendation for working with etics and emics in translation is to *not* become frustrated when material does not translate exactly such that there are perfect equivalents in the back-translations. Instead, a careful record should be kept of what is dropped and what is added by the translators so that the identification of etic and emic aspects of concepts can be suggested. Searching for emic aspects of concepts can be very exciting because it is intriguing to consider unfamiliar aspects of human behavior. It must be kept in mind that emic aspects are going to be unfamiliar to people: If the aspects were similar, they would be shared across the cultures under consideration and would be readily expressible in the various languages that are indigenous to the cultures.

At times, findings will be very dramatic. Phillips (1960, p. 32) was interested in studying family relations and chose a sentence-completion task as a method suitable for comparing responses in the United States and Thailand. He reported difficulty, however, in having the following sentence stem translated into Thai: "Sometimes a good quarrel is necessary because ... " Phillips responded to difficulties in the translation efforts by viewing it as an opportunity to have a conversation with his translators. After comparing notes, and hearing Phillips' analysis of why this item is readily understandable to native speakers of English, the Thai translators developed an important insight which helped Phillips with his study. The translators concluded that whereas Americans might find it conceivable that a good quarrel would have some kind of cathartic effect, this aspect of the more general concept (husband–wife disagreements) is incomprehensible to Thais. Returning to the major point, difficulties in the translation procedure should not be viewed as an opportunity to throw one's hands in the air and to use foul language. The procedures should be viewed as an opportunity to determine culture-common aspects (based on materials that translate easily) and culture-specific aspects (based on materials dropped or added during translation).

CONCEPTUAL EQUIVALENCE. The results of a multiple back-translation procedure, then, can yield insights into culture-common and culture-specific concepts. The material that proceeds smoothly through the multiple steps is said to be translation equivalent. Material that does not translate well, or that is added by translators, is set aside for its possible usefulness in identifying culture-specific aspects of concepts.

The type of equivalence known as "conceptual" begins with the assumption that there will most likely be *different* aspects of a concept that serve the same purpose in different cultures. An analysis that has the goal of conceptual equivalence often identifies etic aspects, and then further identifies the emic aspects that are related to the etic in the various cultures under study. As with many general points, arguments become clearer when specifics are examined. A few examples already introduced can be called upon here. If an etic aspect of intelligence is "solving problems," there are various emic aspects that are related to this goal, and they are different in various cultures. In the United States and Western Europe, one emic is "quickness." Among the Baganda of Uganda, one emic is slow and careful thought. Among the Chi-Chewa of Zambia (Serpell, 1982), one emic is responsibility to the community, which involves getting along well with others. All of these emics are "conceptually equivalent" in that they are part of the definition of intelligence as employed by respected adults in the different cultures. Quickness, deliberate thought, and social responsibility are equivalent in the three cultures since they are used by adults who are asked the question, "Which young people in your community are considered intelligent?"

Important research involving conceptual equivalence has investigated the concepts of privacy and crowdedness. There are undoubtedly cultural differences in the amount of time during which privacy is desired. Since people in collective societies obtain much of their identity from their relations with others (Chapter 2; Triandis, 1989), they are probably more likely than individualists to seek the company of ingroup members. Since individualists obtain much of their own identity from their unique interests, many of which can be carried out when alone, they may be interested in greater amounts of privacy than collectivists. Still, privacy and the company of others undoubtedly involves a dynamic process in which some mix of the two is desired, and too much of one will lead to discomfort. Some people will demand more than others, but an interest in privacy is probably universal. The *way* in which people seek and maintain privacy, however, may involve differences from culture to culture (Altman & Chemers, 1980).

The possible universality of privacy and perceived crowding, with attention to possible cultural differences in the manifestation of the desire for privacy and the desire to avoid crowdedness, was investigated by Nagar and Paulus (1988; see also Pandey, 1990). Based on work carried out in the United States and India, and combined with observations in Colombia, Peru, and Mexico, four universal aspects that may determine perception of crowding were identified:

1. Spaciousness, or the perceived amount of space possible in which a person can move freely.

2. Positive or supportive relationships, or the number of people in a social setting that a person enjoys having present.

3. Negative or disruptive relationships, or the number of individuals in a social setting that a person does *not* enjoy having present. This aspect also includes the presence of one or a few people that actively disrupt a person's behavior in a social setting.

4. Uncontrolled disturbances, or irritants that a person cannot eliminate. These include noise, the presence of disruptive people, pollution, a stress-causing superior, and so forth.

These four aspects or factors work together, and positive aspects of one can ameliorate the negative aspects of another. There may be little spaciousness on a crowded bus or airplane (aspect 1), but if there is a pleasant and attractive companion who is a good conversationalist (aspect 2), the social setting may be experienced as pleasant. Likewise, negative aspects can overwhelm positive features. A person might find himself or herself in a large, attractive, beautifully furnished room, but if there is one disliked person present, the setting might be experienced as both crowded and unpleasant. The various aspects have differing influences on a wide range of people's attitudes and behaviors. Reported psychological problems, such as stress, were most closely associated with the uncontrolled disturbance aspect. People seem less affected by a clear difficulty in a setting if they feel that they can control it. A *lack of control* over the difficulty is more impactful than the presence of the difficulty itself. For example, an obnoxious person at a party will not necessarily cause stress; an inability to avoid this person is the more likely cause. The best predictors of a general sense of psychological well-being were a satisfaction with the amount of space and the absence of negative relationships. There can be cultural differences in the *amount* of space considered necessary and the exact reasons people label a relationship as negative. In Japan, for example, homes are much smaller than in the United States and less space is required for a person's judgment of "comfortable." In the United States, a person might be labeled as "disruptive" if he or she does not follow through on commitments to complete a task in an agreed upon period of time. In Latin America, that same person might be labeled as cooperative if reasons for not completing the task centered on assisting members of the ingroup on *their* tasks.

Returning to the concept of conceptual equivalence, there are different ways that people seek to reduce the feeling of crowdedness and to seek the experience of privacy. In the United States and many other highly industrialized nations, people build fences around their homes. The need to be with others is satisfied through invitations to others who then join people inside their homes. As mentioned above, Japanese homes are small. A frequent conceptual equivalent to entertaining in the home is to entertain guests at a restaurant. Put another way, Americans in Japan might ask themselves, "How do I know when I am being accepted by the Japanese?" If they wait for a behavior with which they are familiar, invitations into the others' homes, they may wait a very long time because such behavior is uncommon. The equivalent to the American home visit is an invitation to a restaurant where the Japanese act as hosts and pick up the bill for dinner.

There are various conceptually equivalent ways to achieve privacy. Given the large homes in which many Americans live, people can go off to a room and be alone. When they appear in a room used by many people, such as the living room, they are signaling to others that they are available for social interaction. Pandey (1990) analyzed conceptually equivalent behavior among people crowded into Mexican slums. When people retreated to their small homes, this was a widely accepted signal in the community that those persons wanted privacy. Respecting this norm, others did not "drop in." The need for social interaction was satisfied by simply leaving one's house. The slums are so crowded that people will surely run into each other in the common areas outside the homes. These extensive opportunities for social interaction served the need to be with others, and any sense of psychological overload due to crowded conditions could be alleviated by retreats into one's home.

Conceptual equivalence will always be an important issue in crosscultural research and in the analysis of people's intercultural encounters. Returning to the discussion of ethnocentrism in Chapter 2, a knowledge of conceptual equivalence assists in the understanding of odd and different behaviors that people observe in other cultures. These different behaviors will often represent conceptually equivalent ways of obtaining widely understood goals. Given the sophistication needed for a good analysis of conceptual equivalence, the imposition, simplicity, and judgmentalness involved in ethnocentrism have to disappear. Occasional periods of privacy are a universal need, as is the desire for interaction with others. The varying uses of one's home to balance these two needs represent conceptual equivalents. If understood, they reduce the ethnocentric feeling that "this is strange" and help people behave in appropriate ways when they find themselves involved in extensive intercultural interactions.

METRIC EQUIVALENCE. There is a sharp contrast between conceptual equivalence and metric equivalence. Conceptual equivalence centers on the analysis of different behaviors serving the same general concept. The example of quick versus slow thought serving the analysis of intelligent behavior in different cultures has been used several times. Metric equivalence centers on the analysis of the same concepts across cultures, and its analysis assumes that the same scale (after proper translation procedures) can be used to measure the concept. Since all readers have undoubtedly taken a version of an intelligence test, let's use that as an example. Assume that an American woman takes a test, and the conclusion is that her IQ is 120. A woman in Chile takes a carefully translated version of the same test and also scores 120. If metric equivalence is assumed, the conclusion is that the two women have equal intelligence. The assumption is that the scale, or metric, is measuring exactly the same concept (intelligence) in the two countries, and that a score in one country can be directly compared with a score in another.

Explanations of metric equivalence are clearest in their *misuse*. People often assume metric equivalence, even when they do not use that term, rather than think about the complexities of emics, etics, and conceptual equivalencies that have been analyzed in this chapter. Assume that high school counselors are deciding whom they might encourage to take an advanced mathematics course during their senior year. If an American male has an IQ score of 130 in his folder, he might receive such encouragement. Assume that the counselors also have the file of a student who was born in Mexico and has lived in the United States for the last 5 years. His native language is Spanish, and he has learned English well enough to receive good grades and to occasionally find his name on the school honor roll. His folder says that his IQ score is 115. If the counselors do not encourage him to take the advanced math course, they are assuming metric equivalence of IQ scores. They are assuming that an IQ of 130 as achieved by the American student (whose native language is English) is better than the score of 115. No analysis has been made of the social problems faced by the native speaker of Spanish. No consideration is given to the fact that he took the IQ test in a less familiar language, and a score of 115 under these circumstances might indicate *more* intelligence than the score of 130. If counselors assume metric equivalence, they are saying that the IQ test measures the same abilities of the two students, and that 130 is better than 115. Readers may find it instructive to recall a time in their lives when they were put at a disadvantage given someone's assumption of metric equivalence. Many people have been treated badly because a *number* had been attached to them, and that someone else with a higher number was given privileges or opportunities denied to them. But given their current understanding of the complexities of research methods discussed in this chapter, people can now see there were problems in the assignment of such numbers that led to unfair treatment.

Occasionally, people may *deny* metric equivalence when it should be considered. Continuing the example of school counselors and their recommendations about mathematics, assume a female student has achieved an IQ score of 130. If counselors fail to recommend that she take the mathematics course, perhaps believing the myth (analyzed by Hyde, Fennema, & Lamon, 1990) that women do noticeably less well in advanced mathematics, they are denying the possibility of metric equivalence. They are calling on their own mistaken myths rather than studying the research literature and finding that men and women with ability levels represented by IQ scores of 130 can rise to the expectations of good science and mathematics teachers. Given proper support and encouragement, *both* men and women do well in advanced mathematics courses.

In good cross-cultural research, claims of metric equivalence will be just one part of a scholar's claims that he or she has identified cultural differences in behavior. For example, John Berry (1979; also introduced on p. 73 of this chapter) carried out research to determine if people in cultures whose economy is based on agriculture are more conforming than people whose economy is based on hunting. The argument is that agricultural people are more conforming since they have many rules to follow: when to plant, when to harvest, how to store food to be prepared against the possibility of poor crops in the future, and how to prevent raiding the storehouses whenever people wish. In contrast, hunters have to be more independent. They have to try different ways to attract game animals, must be willing to work alone or in small groups (too many hunters would scare game away), and must be willing to abandon current hunting areas for others when game is scarce.

To test this prediction, Berry showed people diagrams such as Figure 2. He or his research assistants asked, "Which line is the same as line A?"

FIGURE 2. Task Presented to Assess
Conformity or Independence.

The questioner also mentioned that many people who already participated in the project answered that line 4 is the same. This is clearly wrong. The dependent variable in the study was the number of agriculturalists and hunters who *ignored* the suggested answers of others and who answered in their own independent manner that line 5 is the same.

As predicted, hunters (Eskimos in northern Canada) were more independent in their judgments than were agriculturalists (the Temne of Africa). The agriculturalists were more likely to conform to the suggestion that others had reported that line 4 matched the standard line. In making his claim, Berry is assuming metric equivalence. He is assuming that if people in one culture report that line 4 is the same as the standard, that this has the same meaning in the other culture. He is assuming that the "measure of conformity and independence" can be used to assess the same concepts in the two cultures. A key point is that Berry brought in a great deal of additional information to bolster his case. He presented the results of other measures that can be predicted from an independent versus conforming orientation; he presented details on the child-rearing practices in the two cultures; and he analyzed the agricultural and hunting tasks faced by adults in the two cultures. His total set of arguments were consistent, and they also agreed with the independent work of others (e.g., Barry, Bacon, & Child, 1957). His findings based on an assumption about metric equivalence fit into a large set of arguments supporting his prediction concerning independence and conformity.

I believe that metric equivalence will often play this sort of limited but still important role. At times, a concept (or aspects of a concept) will be so similar in different cultures that the quest for a metrically equivalent scale will be worthwhile. More frequently, however, the facts that (a) human behavior in any one culture is complex and that (b) complexity is added when behavior in different cultures is studied, will lead to the conclusion that the assumptions behind metric equivalence are unwarranted. Instead, researchers will often return to conceptual equivalence, searching for different behaviors that serve similar functions in different societies. Various examples of conceptual equivalence will be covered in future chapters: different approaches to assuring that society has well-educated adults (Chapter 4), different expectations about what good superiors do for their subordinates (Chapter 8), and different approaches to interventions when people encounter stresses in their lives (Chapter 10). The realization that different behaviors serve similar goals, and that differences can be interpreted only in relation to the pursuit of those goals in different cultures, is one of the most important contributions that cross-cultural research has made.

CHAPTER SUMMARY

Cross-cultural researchers take on an additional set of burdens when they decide to carry out studies in cultures other than their own. They often have to work in an unfamiliar language and among people suspicious of the presence of outsiders asking questions about human behavior. If researchers travel to other countries, they must leave most of their support group behind and must experience the stresses of adjustment that all people face when residing in another culture. Many researchers feel, on the other hand, that there are benefits that outweigh these difficulties. The range of variables can be increased by comparisons across cultures, for example, the number of people any one individual feels should be consulted about important decisions. This number is usually much larger in collective than in individualist cultures (Chapter 2). Variables can sometimes be unconfounded, or taken apart, to determine the relative contributions of each. As Ilola (1990) points out, if people in a certain culture consume similar foods, the variables of the people's genetic propensity for certain diseases is confounded with their diet in terms of the possibilities for research. If people from such a culture become *immigrants* to another, the variables can be taken apart if the immigrants acquire the dietary habits of the new culture.

Another benefit is that researchers can often analyze the contributions of the social context when they carry out research in other cultures. Much behavior is made suitable for the context in which people find themselves: solemn at a Catholic funeral service, light-hearted and joking at an informal party, and sympathetic when listening to friends describe their current problems. Since researchers grew up in their own culture, however, they experienced combinations of behaviors-appropriate-to-situations as they grew from children to adults. It is often difficult to analyze the influence of the social context because people within any one culture take it for granted. When observing behavior in other cultures, on the other hand, the influence of the social context is sometimes easier to analyze since it is fresher, less familiar, and clearer to outsiders.

An ability to analyze the contributions of social context can be helpful in many different attempts to understand human behavior. The experiences of schoolchildren are good examples. Much of the learning in school is "out of context." Children learn material from the teachers' presentations and from books, and this new learning *might* be useful at some later date. In many parts of the world, most learning is "in context": children learn agricultural, hunting, and domestic skills by working next to their parents and other respected elders. Further, clear uses of the new learning are introduced, and the children can apply the new learning almost immediately. One type of learning is not better than the other— they are simply different. When children accustomed to in-context learning enter formal schools, however, stresses are added to their lives because of unfamiliarity with out-of-context instruction.

Another important conceptual tool for cross-cultural research is a sensitivity to etics and emics. An "etic" is a shorthand term to describe a concept that is common across cultures. Many concepts common to cultures will be based on the demands with which people all over the world must deal: ensuring a food supply, controlling people's sexual appetites, socializing children to be responsible adults, and so forth. "Emics" refer to culturally specific aspects of complex concepts, for instance, the manner in which different cultures socialize children. Emics often cause intercultural misunderstandings since, by definition, they are widely accepted by people in one culture but are unfamiliar and consequently "seem strange" to people in another. In the United States, for example, naughty children are punished by being confined to their homes. This interfers with their desire to play with friends in different parts of their neighborhood. In Japan, naughty children are punished by being kept out of the home, forcing them to spend time in their neighborhood until their punishment is over. This interferes with their desire to become part of the close collective represented by their families (Stevenson, Azuma, & Hakuta, 1986). The etic aspect of the two examples is that children are punished when they displease their parents. The emic aspects are the specific ways this is accomplished in the different cultures under study. One culture's emics will seem odd to people from another, and the analysis of difficulties in intercultural interaction often involves the analysis of emic differences (Gudykunst & Kim, 1984). The meaning of a concept for any one culture will be a combination of the etic core (here, punishment for misdeeds, parental disapproval) and the emic coloring (the place where children are sent).

Discussions of emics and etics are closely related to treatments of the equivalence of meaning across cultures. The starting point for most analyses of complex concepts is that there will *not* be perfect equivalence. Rather, there will be aspects of concepts that may be similar, but that analyses of translation, conceptual, and metric equivalence must be carried out in the cultures under study.

In the analysis of translation equivalence, researchers study what is readily expressible in the various cultures under study. In the back-translation procedure, one bilingual translates a set of original materials from one language to another, and a second bilingual translates *that* version back to the first language. The two original-language versions can then be compared. Material that is not easily expressible will often be dropped and not appear in the second original-language version. Researchers should then consider the possibility that the dropped material is emic to the language of the first culture. At times, some material will translate smoothly but will not necessarily be equivalent. The English term *friend* will readily translate into the Spanish *amigo*, but is the meaning of the two words equivalent? For example, are the same behaviors expected of a "friend" as an "amigo"? To answer this question, an analysis of conceptual equivalence is necessary.

When carrying out an analysis of conceptual equivalence, researchers attempt to discover different behaviors that relate to the same complex concept. Intelligence is a concept that relates to the solving of unfamiliar problems, but different behaviors serve this concept in different cultures. In some cultures, intelligence involves quick thinking and an emphasis on time. In others, intelligence involves slow and deliberate thought. The aspects of quickness versus deliberateness are conceptually equivalent in that they guide people into answers to the question, "Which people are considered intelligent in this culture?" The identification of conceptually equivalent behaviors is one of the most exciting possibilities in cross-cultural research. It assists the goal of reducing ethnocentric thinking because an analysis of conceptual equivalence forces people to think about complex behaviors in a very different manner. If people can observe unfamiliar behaviors in other cultures, and can determine that they relate to complex concepts in ways that make sense in the other cultures, then they are avoiding ethnocentric thinking. They are avoiding the imposition of thinking that is familiar in their own culture and are instead attempting to understand culturally diverse people *from the point of view of those people*.

Metric equivalence will be uncommon, but understanding it assists in the conduct of research since it is a type of equivalence that has very clear assumptions. If metric equivalence is claimed, then researchers are asserting that like numbers on a scale represent like values. A clear example is body temperature: A reading of 100 degrees Fahrenheit indicates a slight fever. If researchers assume that this number has the same meaning of "slight fever" in all parts of the world, they are assuming metric equivalence. Given that human behavior is so complex, and given the frequency of conceptually equivalent rather than exactly equivalent behaviors when cultures are compared, arguments for metric equivalence should be made only when researchers have extensive evidence to support their claims.

A central feature in all of the approaches to cross-cultural studies discussed in this chapter is that good researchers make intensive efforts to understand behavior from the point of view of people in other cultures. They are not imposing their own viewpoints. In the language of this chapter, they are not imposing their own emics by assuming that they are etic, and they are not assuming that their own understanding of complex concepts are universally equivalent. This sensitivity to others, and the quest to understand the cultural background of seemingly strange behaviors, are good goals for all people who deal with cultural diversity. Many insights into people's cultural background can be gained through the study of how children are socialized to become productive members of their society. This is the topic of the next chapter.

ADDENDUM: THE ANALYSIS OF METHODS IN A CROSS-CULTURAL INVESTIGATION

Another way to introduce some key methodological concerns in cross-cultural research is to review their use in a specific study. This discussion introduces concepts that are covered in book-length treatments of cross-cultural research (Brislin, Lonner, & Thorndike, 1973; Triandis & Berry, 1980; Lonner & Berry, 1986); and in standard methodology texts applicable to various types of research within the behavioral sciences (e.g., Nachmas & Nachmas, 1987; Dane, 1990; Miller, 1991). Consequently, the arguments presented in this addendum will be clearest to readers who are familiar with one or more of these books, or whose professors have covered important concepts presented in these sources.

The study to be reviewed was carried out by Kleinhesselink and Rosa (1991) and was concerned with the perception of risks, especially their harmful effects, in the United States and Japan.

THE FORMULATION OF RESEARCH QUESTIONS. The increased impact of modern technology has brought comforts to many people, such as air-conditioned homes and offices, affordable automobiles, and medications (drugs) to combat disease. However, all of these technological innovations include risks that can harm people: air conditioning demands electricity, and this requires the presence of power plants where accidents are possible. Automobiles demand gasoline, and the use of gasoline leads to harmful air pollution. Medications can prolong life, but there are risks (often called side effects) associated with the use of virtually all powerful drugs, and there are risks when two or more drugs are concurrently used by the same person against advice. Since the United States and Japan are two of the world's most highly industrialized nations, it is important to determine what people think of these risks and how they organize information about risks in their minds. If health-care workers and accident-prevention specialists know how people organize information about risks, they have a greater chance of formulating recommendations for risk prevention (discussed in Chapter 10) that people will follow.

CULTURE-COMMON AND CULTURE-SPECIFIC FACTORS. Kleinhesselink and Rosa (1991) integrated their research ideas with the existing published literature by starting with the list of 81 risks and hazards developed and standardized by Slovic, Fischhoff, and Lichtenstein (1985). Examples from the list include motorcycles, oral contraceptives, asbestos, commercial aviation, crime, pesticides, fluoridation, and radiation therapy. In adapting this list that had been used previously among respondents in the United States, the authors made a number of modifications for use in Japan. One was that "newer" risks were added that have achieved more prominence in the mass media and/or people's lives since the development of the original list. These included AIDS, the greenhouse effect, and ozone depletion. Risks that were significantly less familiar to people in Japan were eliminated, such as high school football and coal tar in hair dyes. An alternative procedure would have been to retain these items and to add others that are familiar in Japan but far less familiar in the United States. These could include risks such as overtraining in high school baseball (discussed by Whiting, 1989), overwork in the office, eating blowfish (a little of its toxin leads to euphoria, but too much causes death), and being pushed into subway cars during rush-hour commutes to work. Retaining and creating items familiar in one society but less so in another adds to the possibility of identifying culture-specific concepts. In cross-cultural research, items to which people reply "I don't understand this," are not useless as long as researchers have a purpose in including such items. Here, the purpose is to identify culture-specific concepts as indicated by collections of items, and culture-specific concepts (as discussed previously in this chapter, pp. 73–76) are certain to be unfamiliar to people socialized in a different country.

PARTICIPANTS IN THE STUDY. Decisions concerning the type of participants whom the researchers ask to cooperate should follow directly from the research questions that are formulated. This may seem to be a common-sense assertion, but it is frequently violated. For example, intelligence tests that are standardized in one country are all-too-frequently administered in another without attention to the meaning of this procedure (issues involved analyzed by Lonner, 1990). Why should people in Mexico, or recent Mexican–American immigrants to the United States, be expected to demonstrate the abstract quality "intelligence" when administered tests standardized on middle-class Caucasian Americans? Too many researchers and users of standardized tests give insufficient attention to this question.

The responses (e.g., opinions, behaviors, statements about personality) gathered from participants should allow the researchers to perform straightforward analyses that allow clear answers to their research questions. In research investigating the role of people's self-interest on their attitudes toward government-directed interracial interaction, for example, Sears and Funk (1991) reviewed studies where self-interest was a possible factor for some participants but a remote factor for others. For example, one type of government-directed interracial interaction is forced busing in which children from a certain neighborhood are bussed to another school whose administrators are trying to achieve a racial balance. Some participants in the research studies had children in public schools, and the possibility existed that their children would be bussed. Other respondents were childless or had the funds to send their children to private schools. Comparing the attitudes of the two groups allowed a test of the role that people's self-interest plays. Results of this and similar studies indicates that a broader assessment of people's racial tolerance or intolerance (analyzed more fully in Chapter 6 and Chapter 7) is a better predictor of government policies than is the assessment of people's short-term self-interest. Further, Sears and Funk (1991) argue that bussing is not the only government policy where racial attitudes play a stronger role than self-interest. They argue that racial tolerance or intolerance plays a strong role in the acceptance or rejection of policies toward neighborhood integration, affirmative action, health insurance for the poor, and bilingual education.

Returning to the study of risks, the researchers chose samples of college students in both the United States and Japan. Student samples are much-maligned since they often represent a choice based on convenience to the researchers rather than the possibility of answering carefully formulated questions. The researchers thought about these issues and carefully defended their choice of participants.

> [M]any of the risks being assessed are the result of recent developments in science or high technology. Proper assessment of these risks, then, requires some awareness on the part of respondents, and this is more assured with college students who are generally more informed on such matters. . . .
>
> Colleges and universities are likely [to be] one setting where the impacts of changing values and attitudes are first experienced. This means, in turn, that we would expect college student samples from two advanced societies, ceteris paribus, to be more similar than samples drawn from other settings. The net effect of the expectation is a more conservative, and therefore more rigorous test, of cultural differences (Kleinhesselink & Rosa, 1991, p. 17).

The argument about conservativeness in research is important. If researchers carry out tests called conservative, it means that they are accepting the fact that it will be harder to discover differences, in this case, between respondents in the United States and Japan. College students in the two countries have some similarities: their ages are similar, they attend classes, read newspaper stories about technological breakthroughs, worry about the dangers associated with premarital sex, and so forth. If differences are found among respondents in the two countries *despite* these similarities, then the researchers can claim strong support for the answers they provide to the original research questions that they posed.

TRANSLATION. The researchers used the back-translation procedure in a manner similar to the recommendations made earlier in this chapter (pp. 78–81). The English original was translated into Japanese, and this version was then back-translated into English. After revisions, the procedure continued until the meanings of the English version, Japanese version, and back-translated version were equivalent as judged by (a) comparisons of the two English versions and (b) an independent review of the Japanese version by two bilinguals.

RESULTS. Separate analyses of data gathered in the two countries indicated that there are two culture-common factors that people use in organizing their perceptions of risks. One is the degree to which a risk is known or unknown, and the second is the amount of dread people feel toward the risk. Cultural differences occurred in the degree to which these factors played a role in the thinking of Americans and Japanese when they considered a given risk. For example, the risks associated with nuclear power (war, weapons testing, waste disposal) were rated as more "known" to the Japanese, and the items clustered together more for the Japanese than for the Americans. One reason, of course, is that the Japanese have firsthand experience with widespread nuclear destruction as a result of atomic bombs dropped on Hiroshima and Nagasaki in 1945. There were no results that could be considered culture-specific or emic, that is, factors that guided the thinking of people in one country but not the other. One reason, as discussed previously, is that the researchers did not include individual items that identified risks in one country that might be far less familiar in the other.

FUTURE RESEARCH. One indicator of a good research study is that it stimulates important follow-up work. Less-important studies can find their way into print, but they may become ignored by others who might use the results in the formulation of new and more sophisticated research questions. One of the results of the present study is that the Japanese, compared to the American respondents, feel that the AIDS epidemic is a more familiar risk. This is a surprising finding since the number of reported cases is far lower in Japan (both in absolute numbers and as a percentage of the population) than in the United States. So how can a risk be perceived as more familiar in one country compared to another despite far fewer reported cases? This is an important research question. Possible answers might be found in the educational system in Japan, where high school graduates read the newspapers more often than American high school graduates. Another possibility is that the mass media in Japan has done its job so effectively that the AIDS epidemic is perceived as familiar despite fewer actual cases. More dynamic possibilities include denial among American respondents: In the presence of many cases, people may find comfort in thinking that the epidemic is not so common as to be called "familiar." Still another possibility is the Japanese wariness of elements from outside their culture. The AIDS virus was introduced to Japan by outsiders who had sex, shared needles, or shared contaminated blood with Japanese nationals. The distrust of *any* outside factor is a familiar concept to the Japanese, whether that factor is a new idea in higher education, a new group of immigrant workers, or a new way of marketing consumer products. The fact that the Japanese are familiar with the concept of "wariness toward outside influences" may have become attached to the AIDS epidemic. The key point for consideration here is that such thinking about future research questions could not take place without the results about risk perceptions reported by Kleinhesselink and Rosa (1991).

4

SOCIALIZATION

Children are born into a world, in the classic words of William James (1890), that is little more than a "blooming, buzzing confusion." The total set of experiences in which children participate so that they eventually cease to be totally confused and instead become respected members of a culture is called "socialization." An important point to constantly keep in mind (Child, 1954; Segall, Dasen, Berry, & Poortinga, 1990) is that children are able to behave in many different ways and to engage in many different types of experience. An important part of socialization is that children are guided *away from* this total set of possible behaviors. Instead, they are encouraged to engage in the more limited set of behaviors that are considered acceptable and important within any one culture. The people responsible for the socialization of children are a culture's elders. Parents are universally involved in socialization, but other elders who become involved vary across cultures. In different cultures, elders other than parents will include grandparents, uncles and aunts, teachers, employers (if children engage in work-for-pay or apprenticeships), religious figures, coaches, and so forth. Age peers can also play an important role, especially in cultures where adult males and females work outside the home (Sinha, 1988).

One reason why socialization is often a hard topic for analysis is that we all were socialized into a culture without thinking about it very much. We have been so close to the socialization process in our own lives that it is difficult to take a step back and to analyze it. As with many important aspects of culture that are part of our own lives, the best way to understand a concept is to examine how it influences behavior in other parts of the world. An example of the difference between "total possible behaviors" and the "fewer behaviors acceptable in a culture" is useful in understanding the socialization process. Recall the discussion of individualism and collectivism in Chapter 2, and review Figure 1 on page 49. Assume that you are 14 years old and are at a family gathering with grandparents, aunts, uncles, and cousins in attendance. One of your 8-year-old cousins is rowdy, loud, and keeps running around and bumping into the furniture. What are the *possible* behaviors in which you might engage. You could discipline your cousin through physical punishment. You could shout at your cousin to stop. You could try persuasion. You could call an adult's attention to the problem. Or you could wait for an adult to become irritated enough to take action. The *fewer* acceptable behaviors are learned during socialization, and a 14-year-old who is considered a "responsible young person" in a given culture would be able to behave in accordance with this more limited set of possibilities.

In a collective society, people are socialized to view themselves as part of a group, and the most common group is the extended family. To keep the group functioning well, harmony is a prime value. People are expected to look after each other and to correct each other if there is a problem that can be avoided. In a collective society, a 14-year-old *is* expected to take an active role in the disciplining of 8-year-old cousins. Consequently, the more active behaviors from the list of possibilities (physical punishment, shouting) are considered appropriate. In fact, if they do not discipline their naughty cousins, the 14-year-olds might be chastised by the adults for not behaving properly. By the time children reach their fourteenth birthday, they would have been socialized to take this active role. In contrast, people in individualistic cultures are socialized to be more independent of groups. They are close to a nuclear family, but do not as often identify with their larger extended family. Consequently, adolescents are not expected to take an active role in disciplining their younger cousins. The adolescents would be expected to choose from the more passive set of total behaviors available to them (e.g., calling the problem to the attention of adults or simply waiting for adults to intervene). If they chose a more active behavior such as striking their cousin, they might be punished. Even the intervention of uncles can be unclear at best and inappropriate at worst. When I was a rowdy youngster, it was very unclear whether or not my uncle should intervene or whether he should wait for my father to notice the difficulties I was causing. In individualistic societies, the issue of disciplining children by anyone other than the parents is complex and problematic. We see this in elementary, junior high, and high schools where teachers find it sometimes difficult to keep order and to engage in their main duty (the education of youth!) because of the limitations placed on what they can do with boisterous students.

Various concepts are useful in analyzing how children learn to participate in their culture *and* how they learn to adjust during times of social change. Five conceptual approaches will be discussed in this chapter:

1.   Socialization takes place in a cultural context, and cultures provide settings with which children are expected to become familiar;

2.   The social class into which a child is born affects his or her outlook on life and affects the opportunities in life from which he or she can benefit;

3. Social change can affect how parents interact with their children given that familiar methods of socialization, remembered from the *parents'* own childhood, are no longer appropriate;

4. Children are active participants in their own socialization and affect the behavior of adults and peers as they attempt to learn skills valued in their culture;

5. The parents' acceptance and rejection has major effects on the behavior of children, but the perception of rejection is dependent upon the children's expectations of what sort of discipline they should receive.

SOCIALIZATION INTO A CULTURAL CONTEXT

One of the most important ideas in cross-cultural analysis is that people's behavior can be understood only as it relates to the social context in which people live and work (Cole & Scribner, 1974; Berry, 1984; Super & Harkness, 1986). Consider the example already reviewed. The behavior of the adolescent can be understood only in relation to a social context: whether the family at the gathering is individualist or collectivist. We can consider a given behavior (physical punishment or simply waiting for an adult's intervention) appropriate only if we understand the context in which behavior takes place. It is especially interesting to examine behaviors that are *perfectly appropriate* in a specific setting within one culture but *absolutely rude and boorish* in a similar setting within another culture. Consider the following short example where the social setting consists of an informal dinner party at someone's home.

Kiyoshi, a Japanese executive, was visiting an automobile plant in the American Midwest and was exploring the possibility of a joint venture involving the manufacturing of a new model of car. Hank, an executive at the plant, wanted to show Kiyoshi (who was traveling with his wife) some American hospitality. So he invited Kiyoshi and his wife to dinner at his house. After a prompt arrival at the agreed upon time of 6:00 PM and after some pleasant conversation over soft drinks ("No one drinks hard liquor any more!" Hank thought), dinner was served at 7:00 PM. After cake was served for dessert at about 8:15 PM, Kiyoshi and his wife thanked Hank for his thoughtfulness and walked slowly toward the door. Hank thought something was wrong, either with himself or with Kiyoshi's manners, because he left right after dessert was served. What went wrong?

Hank and Kiyoshi were socialized into different cultures, and these two cultures give guidance in the narrowing of the range from "total possible" to "fewer appropriate" behaviors. In Hank's culture, people spend time with each other and engage in pleasant conversation after dessert. If people leave early, it is taken as an insult: "They only want our food, not our company!'' In Kiyoshi's culture, remaining after dessert is served has a far different purpose. If he stayed, Kiyoshi would be communicating, "We are still hungry." Hank would then have to search his house for more food if he were behaving according to the norms of Kiyoshi's culture. The two behaviors, remaining or leaving, can be understood only in relation to the context in which the behavior takes place. Here, the context is best described as "a social setting at someone's home where food is served." In other settings, the meanings of the behaviors would be quite different. If the setting was a business meeting, and if the Japanese stayed beyond the time when the Americans thought the meeting would end, it can indicate a sign of interest in the negotiations under consideration. The longer period of time might be necessary for the Japanese to understand the proposal thoroughly and to think about ways to communicate the key points both to their superiors and to their subordinates. It is also important for all the Japanese at the meeting to understand the entire proposal, and so some of their time will be spent explaining key points to each other. Americans in such a setting might interpret the extended meeting as a sign of discontentment and might feel that they have to make concessions to maintain interest among the Japanese. For the Americans, it would be far better if they spent the time patiently explaining their proposal to their Japanese colleagues. In so doing, the Americans would be demonstrating their good will and the understanding of Japanese business practices (Tung, 1984).

The key point here is that behavior can be understood only in relation to the social settings or cultural context in which it takes place. The same general behavior in Japan, remaining in the setting, can have quite different meanings depending on the purpose of the gathering. Part of socialization is the learning of such proper behavior–social setting combinations. An interesting result of increasing intercultural contact is that virtually all people, as adults, will have to learn new combinations to interact successfully with people from other cultural backgrounds. In fact, training programs to prepare people to interact effectively in other cultures (Brislin, 1989; Bhawuk, 1990) frequently recommend that people learn to label the various social settings in which they find themselves. Then, they can attach recommended sets of behaviors to these labels. In the above examples, for instance, American businesspeople would say to themselves, "O.K.! I'm in a business setting. If the meeting runs long, this may be a sign of interest rather than a request for concessions. I should patiently go over all the points in the proposal, and they will appreciate this effort."

CULTURES PROVIDE SETTINGS

The concept that behavior can be understood only as it relates to various social settings is of central importance to an understanding of behavior in different cultures. Beatrice Whiting (1980) has pointed out that more attention must be given to understanding the various settings to which children are exposed and within which they develop appropriate behaviors. In fact, she emphasizes that culture affects the way children are socialized by *providing* a collection of settings in which they learn to behave according to the culture's norms. Consequently, understanding the differences in settings to which children are exposed allows insights into cultural influences on behavior. A reasonable generalization is that in all cultures, children are expected to interact side by side with their parents or another elder and to learn gradually some of the skills expected of adults (Greenfield, 1984; Rogoff, 1990). Cultural differences reside in the exact settings and in the skills necessary in those settings. In some cultures, children are exposed to the fields where crops are raised; in others, to the pastures where cattle graze; and in still others to the vast areas outside a village where game might be hunted. Just as with the concept of socialization in general, "settings" are often not thought about since we all have learned appropriate behaviors in many settings while not consciously aware of this fact. Not all settings involve the exotic jungles and elaborate holiday festivities that are pictured in old issues of *National Geographic* magazine. In many cultures, an important setting is the area just outside the home where adolescents are expected to look after their younger siblings while parents earn incomes at various worksites that are distant from their place of residence. In middle-class homes around the world (Lambert, Hamers, & Frasure-Smith, 1979; Cashmore & Goodnow, 1986), the side-by-side tasks in which parents and children are involved center around books and television. Parents read to their children and ask questions about the content of pictures and about the various letters in words. Parents might also watch the same television shows as their children and can then ask questions about the shows' content. When engaging in these activities, parents are guiding their children into behaviors appropriate in settings that the culture defines as important. One of the settings, of course, is "the nuclear family as a center of preparation for school," a concept important in virtually all advice that teachers give to parents interested in a smooth transition from the home to the early years of a child's formal schooling (Lindgren & Suter, 1985).

SOCIAL CLASS AS A PROVIDER OF OPPORTUNITIES

Given that most adults have had at least some interactions with people much more wealthy and with others much poorer than themselves, one of the most effective ways to discuss socialization is to examine the influence of the social class into which people are born (Thurow, 1987; Brislin, 1988; Kagitcibasi & Berry, 1989). A discussion of social class also permits an introduction to some interesting research that has compared the relative influence of social class and culture on the socialization practices of parents. Finally, the discussion allows some speculations to be made about socialization practices around the world given the movement toward democracy that occurred in many nations during the late 1980s and early 1990s and which will undoubtedly continue into the twenty-first century.

Social class refers to the position of people within a society in terms of prestige, power, and influence. Within North America and Western Europe, important markers include people's income, the level of education they have attained, the prestige of the job they hold, and the reputation of the neighborhood in which they live. Across a large and complex society, at least four levels can be found (treatments of social class that describe more levels are based on subdivisions of these basic four). There is a wealthy upper-class whose members can afford items that their culture considers as luxuries; a comfortable middle class whose members can afford the necessities of what their culture considers a pleasant lifestyle; a struggling working class whose members experience uncertainty with respect to job stability and to ownership of necessities; and a frustrated under-class whose members are frequently, if not constantly, faced with unemployment and little hope of positive change. The latter two are sometimes combined and called "the lower class." These markers are useful in initiating efforts to understand social class in all parts of the world, but other indicators (culture-specific factors or emics: See Chapter 3, pp. 71–76) must be added for a more complete analysis. The other markers (which will vary across countries) include the status of a family's name and bloodline, the names of a person's patrons or protectors, religion, the infrequency of physical labor associated with one's job, time available for scholarly pursuits, occupational skills, social skills, and the prestige of the segment of society into which a person is born. Countries with a caste system are probably the clearest examples of the influence of birth into a "segment of society." One aspect of people's culture is the ease versus difficulty of moving beyond one's social status that is present at the time of one's birth. In some cultures (e.g., India: Sinha, 1990), people's caste is a major influence on what they are permitted to do throughout their lives. In other cultures, people can move beyond the low-status level presented to them at birth and have a much wider range of opportunities available to them as long as they have the appropriate income, occupation, education, and skills that they can offer to employers.

In many countries, a family's income is the central influence on class standing and other markers are associated with it in predictable ways. In North America, for example (Gilbert & Kahl, 1982), income is influenced by the level of education people have attained. In turn, income influences how much education parents can offer to their children. Given a certain level and type of education, people can then pursue careers in prestigious occupations, which of course then brings in high levels of income. People's income, in turn, influences the amount of money available to spend on housing in different neighborhoods. The various markers of status are thus interrelated. When there is an inconsistency of some sort, people can become uncomfortable because they don't know how to relate to individuals who exhibit the inconsistency. There are people who make great deals of money for instance, who have little formal education. They may have the income to be considered members of the upper-class, but they may not have the intellectual interests or the social graces that long-time members of the upper-class consider proper. Inconsistencies are also important in analyzing intercultural contact. Many Asian students who study in the United States, Canada, or Western Europe decide to remain in the country where they study rather than return home. This contributes to the problem known as "brain drain," since their skills would be valuable in their home country. A major reason, however, is the inconsistencies they would face should they return home. They may have earned an advanced degree after four years of very hard study, but might foresee a very low paying job awaiting them should they return. Or, they may have been born into a low-status group, and no matter how much education they receive, they will still carry the label of that low-status group. One of my colleagues from India (a full professor at a state university in the United States) was *not* born into the highest caste group. If he returned to India, he would have limitations placed on his career given his modest birth. In the United States, he has faced no such limitations—as many readers will surely agree, few people in the United States care about the caste of intelligent and well-educated Indians whom they meet. Interestingly (and consistent with studies of brain drain: Glaser, 1978), my colleague remained in the United States to give more opportunities to his three children. "Their social mobility is open in the United States, based on their abilities and work. If I returned to India, they'd have the same limitations placed on them as those I would face."

SOCIAL CLASS AND SOCIALIZATION. Based on research with over 4000 respondents, Kohn (1977) argues that parents from different class backgrounds emphasize different values when raising their children. Middle-class parents emphasize self-control, intellectual curiosity, and consideration for others. These considerations can be seen in a typical childhood event that many readers will undoubtedly remember: birthday parties for 5- or 6-year-olds. Self-control can be seen in the arrangement of events. For instance, children learn to wait to open their presents and to dig into their cake until all the guests have arrived, introductions made, and games played. Intellectual curiosity can be seen in typical presents given to children: books, and now that we have reached the latter part of the twentieth century, videotapes. Children at the party are also encouraged to ask questions of adults and to take the party as an opportunity to learn new information (e.g., new party games, new songs, new comic characters depicted in the presents given). Consideration for others is seen in attempts to encourage everyone present to become involved in activities, and in such parental guidance as "Let's wait for everyone to finish their ice cream before opening presents." This description might seem very culture-bound, but to preview a very interesting research finding discussed more fully in the next section, these activities are very similar *among members of the middle class* in various countries. I have attended children's birthday parties organized by parents from a number of different countries (e.g., Japan, Nepal, India, Indonesia), and the structure of the parties is very similar. There are certainly differences in the exact games played, in the sorts of books given as presents, and in the snacks available to children. But the commonalities of children as the center of attention, encouragement to take into account the feelings of others, and control of impulses are striking.

In socializing their children, working-class parents emphasize obedience, neatness, and good manners. One set of activities considered "good manners" is that children are expected to be quiet and almost invisible when adults are present (Gilbert & Kahl, 1982). Rather than interact with adults so that they have opportunities to have questions answered, children are expected to be quiet and to entertain themselves in a room other than the one where the adults are talking. These emphases have implications when children become adults themselves and enter the workforce (Offermann & Gowing, 1990). Children of the working class learn to be comfortable with external standards in contrast to their own, internally set goals. They learn to accept what other people consider to be good manners, and they have limited experience in making suggestions and requests to authority figures. In contrast, on entering the workforce, children of the middle class have certain advantages given their experiences during socialization. They are more comfortable with self-starting, self-instigated behaviors, and are more at ease in asking questions and in making requests of their superiors. The skills they learned as children during interactions with adults (asking questions, making their wishes known) are useful in the work world.

Again looking at the world of work, Kohn (1977) further concludes that middle-class children are better prepared to accept managerial and professional jobs that demand intellectual curiosity and good social skills. For instance, an important social skill that good managers have is that they can understand and empathize with the needs of their subordinates, even if the subordinates are not very clear in communicating their opinions and feelings. Note that this important skill is a result of the empathetic understanding and consideration for others that were encouraged during their middle-class socialization. In contrast, working-class children become prepared to take wage-labor jobs that involve physical effort and that are closely supervised. They accept such jobs partly as a result of less emphasis on intellectual curiosity and partly as a result of their parents concern for external standards and obedience to authority figures. The concern for obedience to parents and adult relatives emphasized during childhood prepares them to be obedient to the external standards set by a visible supervisor in the work world. One way of summarizing these findings is to point out that middle-class children are socialized to earn a good income by using their minds and their interpersonal skills. Working-class children are socialized to earn an income by using their hands and their physical labor.

Are there possible points in the lives of working-class children and adolescents at which interventions can be made to increase the chances of developing skills useful in managerial and professional careers? The answer is "yes," but we have to return to a basic point introduced earlier. Income is the key factor in discussions of social class. Adolescents *can* develop managerial skills through various community activities that take place outside the home. Let's examine what is probably the most common example of such activities: participation in school clubs, teams, and service projects for the community. While participating in these activities, adolescents can learn to set goals, work hard toward their achievement, bring in the points of view of others, work through bureaucratic rules, meet influential people in the community and learn to deal with them (Brislin, 1991), and so forth. Students from the working class, however, participate in fewer such activities than their middle-class peers (Lindgren & Suter, 1985). Family income has its impact: working-class adolescents often have after-school jobs so that they can earn money for family necessities and for basic needs such as acceptable clothes and a reasonable number of social activities. After-school work *might* be a source of possibilities for the managerial skills development under discussion here. However, most jobs available to adolescents are closely supervised and do not involve the choice of activities and the self-directed movement within these activities that encourage the development of managerial skills.

CLASS AND CULTURE. The effects of social class are very strong, and this is a point that has been underemphasized in studies emanating from the United States (a point argued by Brislin, 1988; Kagitcibasi, 1990). One reason for this underemphasis is based on cultural values. As discussed in Chapter 1, culture includes values that people should have (even if they "slip" sometimes in putting those values into practice). One value in the United States is that Americans are members of a classless society. Our Declaration of Independence states that "All men are created equal..." This cultural value includes the feature that given access to universally available education and the possibilities people have to improve themselves through hard work, anybody who tries can move upward within society. The research findings that indicate advantages given to middle-class children are at odds with this value. These findings are uncomfortable for Americans to consider since we have so little experience discussing social class. Recall Chapter 1: If people accept a value (classless society), they don't have to talk about it very much. Recent findings that indicate the effects of social class on career possibilities (Kohn, 1977), achievement in school (Yando, Seitz, & Zigler, 1979), performance on standardized tests (Burg & Belmont, 1990), and health (Belle, 1990) are difficult to discuss.

Another important relationship between class and culture is that the effects of one can be much stronger than the other. In two studies comparing childrearing practices in different countries and among different ethnic groups within Australia (Lambert, et al., 1979; Cashmore & Goodnow, 1986), the researchers were surprised to discover that class differences were stronger than cultural differences. In the Australian study, for example, working-class parents from both Italian and Anglo backgrounds emphasized "being neat," "having good manners," and "being obedient." Any differences that *might* have been attributed to the Italian versus Anglo background of the parents was eliminated or decreased when the parents' educational level was taken into account. Specifically, the less-educated parents from Italian and Anglo backgrounds preferred neatness, manners, and obedience in their children. These findings have an important implication for future research: Studies of cultural differences in the socialization of children will be considered inadequate unless the children's social class background is taken into account.

I am no more comfortable about discussing social class differences than most Americans. Yet I believe more good than harm would come from such discussions. In the absence of an acknowledgment of class differences, people are left with the need to find other reasons for why children from various segments of society are clearly achieving less in school and, once they reach adulthood, in the workplace. If the children have a different skin color, then "race" or "racial differences" are used to explain poor achievement. Of course, this leads to vicious attacks on people and to erroneous conclusions that some people are biologically inferior. If the focus, instead, was on the advantages and disadvantages that class brings, race would enter the discussion far less frequently. Yando, Seitz, and Zigler (1979) are three researchers who have been sensitive to this important point concerning class differences. In a study of 8-year-old Black and White children from different class backgrounds, these researchers found that racial differences meant little. Achievement differences were far more strongly related to social class. Regardless of whether they were Black or White, advantaged children (from homes whose parents had adequate incomes) chose harder problems when asked to make their own choices on a reading task. The advantaged children were also more confident about their abilities. Interestingly, some of the disadvantaged children (from lower-class homes with unpredictable incomes) had good intellectual skills as shown by their scores on intelligence tests. However, the fact of coming from a disadvantaged home had a stronger impact than the children's intellectual abilities. As the researchers summarized, "Indeed, it is striking that even the most capable disadvantaged children showed such low expectations of their abilities" (p. 88).

Even with good intellectual skills then, the disadvantaged children were not confident that they could use their abilities on the reading task. Robert Cialdini (1990) has suggested that there is a metaphor which can help people understand this important issue. Cialdini suggests that middle-class children grow up in surroundings that are like a successful farmer's fruit orchard. The children can look around and see apples, oranges, peaches, and plums growing from trees. They will certainly have to put in some effort to pick the fruit, and will have to learn to use tools, such as ladders, to perform this task, but the *opportunity* to harvest fruit is present. Less-advantaged children, on the other hand, who look at their neighborhoods are more likely to see unhealthy and barren trees. Even if they possess the necessary abilities to harvest fruit and learn to use the necessary tools, they don't see the possibilities of putting their abilities to use. Disadvantaged children are less likely to be socialized into a set of expectations that there are benefits and rewards in society that can be obtained through their efforts.

SOCIALIZATION, FAMILIARITY, AND CHANGE: THE EXPERIENCE OF MODERN INDIA

Earlier, Beatrice Whiting's (1980) insight that culture provides a collection of settings to which children become exposed was discussed. An addition to this insight is that culture encourages children to become familiar with and comfortable in a number of situations so that they know how to achieve their goals. Some children in some cultures become familiar with settings in which agricultural, fishing, hunting, and herding skills are valued. Other children (more in the higher than the lower socioeconomic levels) become comfortable with settings in which they learn from teachers who introduce reading from books, writing on paper, and instruction in how to make effective oral presentations. Young women in some cultures are not encouraged to read and write but instead learn to become comfortable in domestic settings where child-rearing, cooking, cleaning, and husband-nurturing skills are valued.

People are socialized, then, to be quite familiar with a number of social settings so that they can achieve their goals (adequate food supply, academic accomplishments, obedient children) and can be considered valued members of a culture. When there is stability over many years within a culture *and* when people wish no more than to obtain the goals available in these social settings, there is little discontent within a culture. Difficulties emerge in times of social change during which people are *not* familiar with the new or modified settings in which they are expected to participate (Wagner, 1988; Berry, 1990). One reason for increased stress in people's lives is that, given changes in the settings with which they were *once* comfortable, people are unfamiliar with the behaviors necessary to achieve their goals (Moghaddam, Ditto, & Taylor, 1990). People were not socialized into knowledge of the skills necessary in the new and modified social settings brought on by rapid social change. A simple example familiar to virtually all readers should make these points clear. There are many settings in which unmarried males and females might meet: classrooms, laundry rooms, offices, churches, and so forth. Who usually makes the first offer of a date, the male or the female? When I ask this question of students, they complain that today's society doesn't give much guidance. Thirty and forty years ago, in the United States, the answer was clear: The male is expected to make the first move and is socialized to do so from the early teen-age years. With the emphasis on women's rights and gender equality that has occurred over the last 25 years, the common-sense answer is that women should be able to ask a man for a date should they choose to do so. But socialization hasn't caught up with social change—women were not socialized to be comfortable with this task. According to my students, one (probably one of many) solution is that a woman will ask a man to lunch, perhaps to a lunch where four or more people are in attendance. But it is up to the man to figure out that this is a display of the woman's interest, and that it is up to the man to suggest a one-on-one date with more "serious" signals such as a weekend dinner at 8:00 PM, in a nice French restaurant with dim lighting and an expensive wine list.

The distinction between how people were socialized to behave so that they could achieve their goals, and how these socialized behaviors are less useful given recent and rapid social change, is important in analyzing behaviors all over the world. I believe that the world movement toward democratic governments will continue to cause the sorts of changes that will challenge the behaviors people learned in an earlier era (Brislin, 1991). Democracy involves the careful consideration of a number of candidates for leadership positions. This will be uncomfortable for people who were socialized to never disagree publicly with leaders. Democracy involves respect for, or at least tolerance of, people whose opinions are different from one's own. This respect for plurality is not a universal part of people's socialization. Democracy involves respect for the contributions all sorts of people can make, whether they be minorities within a culture, women, immigrants, and so forth. Cultures in which people were socialized to make very clear distinction between classes of people, and to emphasize gender differences in permitting people to obtain such societial benefits as higher education and entry into the professions, will find this aspect of democracy a challenge.

Durganand Sinha (1988) has carried out an analysis of social change in India and the challenges change has brought to familiar behaviors learned during socialization. It is useful to review his research in some detail because I believe these changes and challenges will be seen in other parts of the world during the 1990s and the twenty-first century. Sinha points out that the changes include increases in people's per-capita income, food surpluses in some parts of India in contrast to the famines of past years, increases in the level of education that people achieve, and recent legislation covering property rights, inheritance, the rights of women, marriage and divorce, and minimum wages. These changes have altered traditional relations between powerful landowners and poor peasants, interactions within extended families, and the relative power of the traditional caste structure. Referring to a culture's most important institution in the socialization of children, the family, Sinha (1988, p. 49) points out that "conferring rights on women and making divorce laws easier have dealt a fatal blow to the traditional pattern of joint family [relations] and have even generated familial tensions." The total collection of changes in India are marked by their all-embracing nature, their rapidity, and the fact that they unfold in a non-orderly, unpredictable sequence. In the following discussion, I will draw from Sinha's (1988, 1990) analysis of socialization in India. I will also integrate research and examples from other parts of the world and ask readers to recall some of their own socialization experiences.

MOVE TOWARD NUCLEAR FAMILIES. Families have moved away from a structure in which members of the extended family were in constant communication with one another, shared resources, and were instantly available for emotional support in times of trouble. One reason is the growth of cities and the types of jobs available in industrial economies. Rather than dependence on the extended family, people can move beyond their traditional collective and find employment elsewhere. Once people earn an income through their own efforts that are clearly independent of their extended family, they are likely to become oriented toward self-interest rather than a collective interest. It is important to note that self-interest and "selfishness" do not overlap totally. When applied to the move toward nuclear families, self-interest refers to looking after one's parents (if not married), spouse, and children. The links that become weakened are to members of the extended family such as grandparents, aunts, uncles, and cousins. Durganand Sinha (1989) discusses this move, called *nucleation*, in his own life. As a young man in India, he remembers the presence of uncles and cousins with whom he would spend a great deal of time. In the 1990s, he points out, his family consists of himself and his wife. He moved away from the area where his extended family lived to receive his university education. He accepted employment in a city, again away from his extended family. He had children; they also went to the university and accepted very good jobs in various parts of the world. His grandchildren live with their parents, and so Sinha and his wife see them only during their occasional visits. Sinha, then, has experienced a move toward nucleation within a society where people traditionally experienced close collective ties among extended family members.

When the members of a traditionally collective family are not distant from each other, in contrast to Sinha's case, Kagitcibasi (1988, 1990) points out that there can be collective features in the presence of nucleation. Nuclear families can be the economic unit, but they can still remain emotionally dependent on the extended family. When members of the extended family are ill, want to share joyous events such as weddings or graduations, or need counseling and solace in times of personal difficulties, people beyond the nuclear family frequently become involved. Grand-parents can still be important figures in the socialization of children. Still, the absence of day-to-day contact takes its toll. Recall that socialization involves becoming familiar with various settings. One difficulty brought on by social change is that children need to be socialized into a culture that is (a) different from what their parents experienced and (b) for which socializing events are not yet well developed. Referring to the work of Sanua (1980) on the supportive environment a well-functioning family can provide, Sinha (1988) points out that the traditional Indian family had many people with whom children could interact. If they were having temporary difficulties with a parent, there would be a grandparent, aunt, or uncle to provide support. It is important to point out that the parents were quite aware of and comfortable with the support so provided, remembering times in their own childhoods when the presence of an extended family member was important. Children were not "putting something over" on their parents by seeking out others. With nucleation, however, these other people are not always present for the children. The difficulties that parents and children inevitably experience with each other can intensify into severe problems given the absence of buffers provided by the extended family.

SEGREGATION OF CHILDREN AND ADULTS. The traditional Indian family socialized its children through constant interactions among mem-bers of the extended family, many of whom would be living under the same roof. Through observing the interactions of many adults, including observations of problem-solving behaviors that inevitably occur when people interact in close quarters, children learned the necessary skills to become respected members of their culture. Children were also socialized to view themselves as part of the emotional lives of their extended family members. They were not separated from adults as frequently as children in North America. When guests came to visit a family, for instance, children were not put in a separate room and were not expected to amuse them-selves some place other than where the adults were interacting. Rather, children were integrated into events involving the guests, and they learned about interactions with other types of people by observing and partici-pating in family member–guest relations. With nucleation, children do not have this large number of adults from whom to learn day-to-day lessons. Children are likely to find themselves alone or in the presence of age peers, and consequently become emotionally separated from adults at an earlier age. If the separation occurred when they went to school in years past, it occurs today when adults are no longer in the house during daylight hours. In terms of separation from *large* numbers of adults as represented by the extended family, this independence from others can start at birth given the trend toward nucleation. In terms of separation from an adult whose traditional role involved constant nurturance during infancy and early childhood, this can occur when the mother decides to either join the workforce or to reenter the workforce a short time after delivering her child. If mothers take jobs outside the home, they must become consciously concerned with their children's socialization. Such concern is itself an important change, given that mothers didn't have to think about socialization very much in generations past because of the presence of helpful grandparents and aunts. Another result of mothers entering the workforce is that institutions external to the family must become involved, such as day-care centers. Whatever we think of day-care centers, positive or negative, it is important to note that many mothers have not been socialized themselves to become familiar and comfortable with these institutions.

THE MOVE FROM NURTURANT TO STRICTER CHILDREARING. Traditionally, Indian families indulged their children during the first two or three years of the child's life. Someone was always available to hold, cuddle, and talk to the baby, and body contact between caretaker and child was frequent. Breast-feeding frequently extended into the child's third year, far longer than common in Europe or North America. The extensive body contact provided a great deal of security for the child. Other aspects of childrearing were traditionally nurturant. There were no pressures to toilet train children at any particular age. Children learned to eat, walk, talk, and dress themselves on their own schedule, *without* extended family members comparing notes concerning the age at which this cousin or that neighbor achieved these milestones.

Social change has led to a stricter style of childrearing. Rather than follow the child's preferences concerning times for eating, sleeping, and playing during a given day, events have become more scheduled as directed by adults. More attention has been given to "proper" ages to become weaned from the mother's breast, to be toilet trained, to dress oneself, and so forth. Lists of do's and don't's are presented to children, and children are expected to distinguish acceptable from unacceptable behaviors at an earlier age than in generations past. One reason for these recent pressures is, again, the absence of multiple adult caretakers. If only the parents are present, less stress is generated for them if they encourage strict standards (e.g., food at certain times, rather than at any time the child desires). If both parents are working, they understandably will not have the energy to jump up and down during the evening to meet the unrestrained and unscheduled needs of their children. Another factor to be considered is the presence of persons or institutions external to the family. When neighbors or day-care centers become involved, they will strongly prefer toilet-trained children who can meet a regimented schedule of eating, playing, and napping.

Whenever there is social change, people will disagree concerning whether to behave in traditional ways or to behave according to new practices that they observe. Most readers will have experienced this fact. The traditional practice in many parts of the world is that husbands and wives will live in the same home in the same city. Currently, with both men and women desiring important and influential careers, some dating couples are willing to consider living in different cities and participating in a "commuter" marriage. Other couples find this possibility unacceptable and have to work toward a compromise in the form of a city where they can both work and find acceptable (if not the most advantageous) jobs. Sinha (1988) points out that such disagreements are frequent in India, and they can have impacts on children. With respect to traditionally nurturant compared to more strict childrearing, it is easy to imagine a marriage in which the husband prefers one style and the wife prefers another. When parents disagree, however, their children's adjustments to school and scholastic achievements are affected such that the children have more difficulties (Kakkar, 1970).

INCONSISTENCIES IN RAISING CHILDREN. Parental disagreements about how best to raise children lead to problems that stem from unclear, inconsistent, and sometimes contradictory standards. If the disagreement is between traditional and the still unclear and unfamiliar more "modern" methods, children may be rewarded one day and punished the next when they engage in the same behaviors. One result is that children become anxious because they cannot meet these unclear and inconsistent standards.

The *source* of rewards and punishments is also unclear and inconsistent. Traditionally, an Indian mother was not expected to discipline her children. The person expected to punish children, when necessary, was the father, or elderly aunts and uncles, and sometimes grandparents. The mother was expected to be the source of affection, and consequently children knew where to go when they needed positive attention. Given the absence of extended family members, the mother has to share the disciplinarian role with her husband. Even if she prefers to act in the traditional manner (in India) of offering only love and affection, there will be pressures on the mother to discipline her children on various occasions. The husband may have to work late, may be traveling on business, or may be ill. In such cases, the mother has little choice but to combine the roles of affection giver and disciplinarian, even though she is unfamiliar with ways to manage this combination. Children, then, have to adjust to a mother who offers both rewards and punishments. This becomes confusing for them if they have cousins or friends whose mothers are able to behave in the more traditional manner, and if their mothers are uncomfortable with the task of administering both rewards and punishments.

When both parents work, the problem is made more complex. Parents not only have less time to devote to childrearing, they are also unable to present clear sex-role models to their children. Under traditional norms, the mother took care of domestic tasks and the father worked outside the home. When both parents work, the various duties around the home are more likely to be shared. Further, children quickly learn that the family income is being provided by two persons, not just one. If given only quick consideration, many readers will applaud this state of affairs and will point to the fact that the children have a more complex, potentially more enriched set of role models that they might emulate (Moghaddam, Ditto, & Taylor, 1990). Young girls in India, especially, will have more opportunities for a full life if they are able to move from the traditional expectation that they must be no more than wives and mothers. This may eventually be true, but at present parents are still trying to work out their income-producing and domestic duties given that they are unfamiliar with this combination from their own socialization. When the parents are confused and unclear about their own appropriate behaviors, children become anxious because they do not have consistent rules to follow and models to emulate.

ABSENCE OF ROLE MODELS. In addition to the anxiety that stems from models who are themselves unclear about appropriate behaviors, there are other implications that center around the adults that children *might* emulate. Under the traditional system children had a number of role models whom they might respect and with whom they might identify. If for some reason a young girl did not find her mother to be an acceptable role model, she would have aunts, older cousins, and grandmothers to consider. Currently, given nucleation, these other people are not in day-to-day contact and consequently young girls do not have the constant presence of multiple models. There are still gatherings of the extended family, but there is a difference between these visits among people and the constant presence of people living under the same roof. In addition, there are far fewer individuals available to tell children about mythological figures and to relate the lesson-giving folktales of the culture (Vitz, 1990). Parents are too busy and/or too tired to take on this important task; grandparents used to tell about such historical figures and to relate their tales of heroism, but as has been mentioned a number of times, they are absent from the children's day-to-day lives. The lack of exposure to such folktales and stories about historical figures has its own set of implications. Children do not learn about great figures who behaved in ways that children might emulate or, in the case of villains, make a point of not emulating. Children also become less prepared for the transition to formal schooling. Teachers might expect incoming children to know some of the culture's folktales and to know about some important historical figures. Teachers might be disappointed and label children as "slow" if they lack this knowledge.

THE CHANGING STATUS OF WOMEN. Severe limits were traditionally placed on the roles that women could accept. Wife, mother, and agricultural and domestic laborer covered much of the acceptable range of opportunities. Recently, the government has given attention to the political and legal rights of women. Written statements about these rights can admittedly be formulated more quickly than people's everyday and *comfortable acceptance* of the changes. Even so, more opportunities are available. But as women achieve prominent positions in the various professions, this places pressures on the family where women traditionally accepted a subservient role. When women bring in money to the family, they are naturally going to want their opinions respected concerning how that money is to be used. Men, however, are uncomfortable with this type of change (Kapur, 1970). Men like the fact that their wives are working and bringing in money, but they are uncomfortable with the changes this brings to the traditional manner in which decisions are made in the family. Men may also feel that the women are neglecting their domestic and childrearing duties given their participation in the workforce. Many readers will be familiar with these difficulties either in their own lives or among their married acquaintances. They will also be familiar with the demands that females are expected to be "super women" who can effortlessly hold a job, raise well-behaved children, and attend to the needs of their husbands. The conflicting demands stemming from women's desires to advance in their careers, to maintain domestic harmony, and to be good mothers eventually leads to stress, tension, and anxiety (Sinha, 1988).

If the traditional extended family is no longer a reality in the lives of a married couple, parents must find some alternative to the practice of leaving children with grandparents or elderly aunts. Day-care centers have sprung up, but their use separates children from their parents. Instead of parents who offer settings in which socialization takes place, children turn to their peers. Children share socialization experiences among themselves, and in so doing learn about their culture from each other. With attention given to their peers, children no longer are socialized into the extremely strong ties of the traditional family. This probably leads to greater ease when the children themselves move out into society to seek more education and employment, but it means that the traditional family structure is further weakened. This ease of movement from a conformity-demanding family into society can be looked upon as a positive change by some, but it is the sort of change that causes anxiety and tension until people become comfortable and familiar with its implications. One implication is that children become much more independent if they move away from their traditional neighborhood as they participate in peer group activities. They may become more adept at seeking out opportunities where they can meet adults outside the family, accept new challenges, develop their own opinions concerning a variety of important issues in their communities, and figure out how to solve problems on their own. This independence may be unwelcome, however, if the father accepts the more traditional view that children should conform to his wishes and to his views about important social and political events.

THE EFFECTS OF MIGRATION. Another and quite different change in people's lives has affected relationships within the family. In the search for a better life, nuclear families move from rural to urban areas. While the major reason for migration is the quest for better jobs for the father and (as discussed previously) possibly the mother, children accompany their parents and recently have accounted for 50 percent of migrants. Migration has predictable consequences, and these are seen in many urban areas around the world, not just cities in India. The extended family is left behind in the rural village and all childrearing responsibilities have to be assumed by the parents who have not yet become comfortable raising their children without help from relatives. The nuclear family has to adapt to the unfamiliar lifestyle of the city, with its more impersonal norms for everyday behavior (Yang, 1988), strangers who cannot be called on in times of difficulties, and an unfamiliar bureaucracy to provide needed services such as education for the children and medical care. Given that families do not yet have much money, they cannot afford good housing and often must live in slum areas at best and in public areas (e.g., under bridges) at worst. In such areas, the basic necessities of life such as water, sanitation, and protection during foul weather are frequently absent.

The fact of migration from rural areas to the cities is a frustration for planners, politicians, government officials, and concerned citizens all over Asia. It is easy to wonder why people leave their rural areas and accept the squalor, poor living conditions, and uncertainty of employment in big cities. There are several points to keep in mind. One is that village life should not be romanticized as something that is pleasant and problem-free. Villagers often have to submit to the whims of powerful and uncaring landowners. Land is often poor given the number of years that it has been used and the high cost of fertilizer. The backbreaking work necessary to provide even a minimal standard of living for one's family causes health difficulties and premature aging. When considering the move to a city, sometimes stimulated by news from friends and relatives who left the village in years past, people are not seeking to turn their lives around. Rather, they are seeking to improve their lives by a small but noticeable amount. There are attractions in a city that lead to the *possibility* of a better life. There can be schooling for one's children so that even if the parents are unsuccessful in improving their own lives, there is the possibility that children will do better given that there are more opportunities for formal education. There can be more independence for both men and women who become removed from the presence of landowners and traditional village leaders who often demand unquestioning deference. Despite the problems many migrants will face with chronic underemployment, even part-time work can bring in more money to the family than could be earned back in the village.

While this discussion has focused on developing countries such as India, decisions concerning whether to remain in a rural part of one's country or to move to a big city are faced by people all over the world. Readers might consider this decision as it affects their own lives. Big cities in industrialized nations, such as the United States, have high crime rates, poor air quality, expensive housing, and high taxes. So why do some people choose to live there rather than in small towns? Reasons will vary, but they include prestigious jobs with high salaries, stimulus from cultural events such as operas and symphony orchestras, the excitement that stems from living where important events are happening, and far more choices for leisure-time activities. Some people do not enjoy being reminded of childhood mistakes that occurred during their socialization in small towns, and they escape these memories by welcoming the impersonal norms of big cities.

The general point, then, is that people who move to urban areas expect improvements in their lives. Especially for villagers in less industrialized nations, these changes are often accompanied by potential psychological difficulties. Migrants are forced to adjust to many new norms and values in big cities, and the new challenges they face can overwhelm their resources for coping with difficulties (Peeters, 1986; Golding, Karno, & Rutter, 1990). Many migrants undoubtedly expect much better treatment in the city than they actually receive. They may expect decent housing, ease in finding jobs, and adequate schools for their children. These *expectations* may have been fueled by letters from their relatives who painted an overly positive picture of city life so that they would be seen as resourceful and intelligent by people who remained in the village. The difference between expectations, set up by the letters, and the reality experienced in the city is one cause of stress. Readers might examine this distinction between expectations and reality in their own lives. If people think back about a stressful episode, they might ask themselves, "In retrospect, was the episode as stressful as I thought it was at the time? Or was the resulting stress due to the difference between what I expected and the reality I found?" In the case of migrants to the city, there are few opportunities to intervene into people's lives so that expectations can be brought closer to reality. The result is psychological disturbances, including such psychosomatic difficulties as problems with digestion, sleep, headaches, back pains, and so forth. The difficulties then have negative impacts on the migrants' quest for such goals as employment and the acquisition of housing, compounding the problems set up by the original difference between expectations and reality. City life is stressful for everyone living in less-than-ideal conditions, but it is higher for recent migrants (Thacore, 1973) who have not yet learned the necessary skills to cope with problems they have never encountered before.

To summarize some major points: Social change brings about clear and visible changes in people's lives, such as technological innovations (television, telephones), and greater ease in travel away from the community where they were born. There are also less visible changes within people's lives which can cause anxiety and stress, especially to children who are experiencing the changes themselves and who do not have clear adult role models who can provide guidance. These less visible changes include movement away from the extended family, the segregation of children from adults, stricter norms for childrearing in contrast to the indulgence of children more common in the past, inconsistencies in child-rearing due to disagreements within the family, the absence of role models who are themselves confident how to behave in the face of these multiple changes, the desire of women to seek a wider variety of opportunities than were available in previous generations, and the effects of migration from rural to urban areas. The key to understanding the difficulties that arise is not the changes themselves. Rather, difficulties arise because there are no widely accepted and familiar socialization practices that parents can call on to raise their children to be responsible members of the culture. The parents were socialized into a culture different from the one their children are experiencing today. They remember a culture based on an extended family structure, women who accepted limited roles, nurturant childrearing practices, and so forth. Faced with many social changes, parents are themselves unsure how to raise their children, and this lack of clarity causes anxiety and stress for the children. Interventions to lessen the difficulties brought on by social change have been developed, and they will be reviewed in the next chapter that deals with various informal and formal educational programs.

CHILDREN'S INVOLVEMENT IN THEIR OWN SOCIALIZATION

In this analysis of socialization in India (Sinha, 1988), there were a number of points made that relate to a more general theme that is becoming increasingly important in cross-cultural research. This theme is that children play an active role in their own socialization. Children are not solitary learners, sitting back passively waiting for instruction from a role model and then practicing new behaviors by themselves. Rather, children are active participants in a complex social world in which they are constantly interacting with people and, through their behavior, have an impact on exactly what happens during their interactions with others. In Sinha's analysis this theme was touched upon a number of times. For instance, when children from traditional extended families had difficulties with a parent, they could approach an aunt or grandparent for nuturance. If children are exposed to one set of relatives who behave according to traditional role demands and other relatives who have accepted recent social changes, they have a choice of models they can emulate. This can admittedly cause stress in their lives and their choices can cause conflict within the nuclear family. When children do not have the constant presence of adults in their lives, given that both parents may be working, they do not sit back and wait for the occasional guidance adults might offer. Rather, the children seek out alternative socializing agents and turn to their peer group for participation in new learning experiences.

Barbara Rogoff (1990) has been especially influential in encouraging people to view children as active participants in their socialization rather than as the passive recipients of information. She views socialization in a manner consistent with ideas already presented: Children are exposed to various social settings in which they learn to achieve various goals. The goals *can be* the acquisition of skills such as reading, weaving, or the use of medicinal plants, but they can also be of an emotional nature such as the desire for affection and respect. If the goals are understood, together with the methods by which children and adults interact so that these goals can be obtained, then real progress has been made in understanding the complex question, "How are children socialized to be respected members of a culture?"

Rogoff has been especially concerned with the cognitive development of children, and consequently most of the examples reviewed here will deal with this aspect of socialization. She offers a framework which stresses three factors:

1. Children are active in seeking out and making use of guidance that various people can offer in their efforts to attain goals.

2. Children and adults participate in *arrangements* of activities that are special in the sense that they are uniquely designed to help children attain their goals. Some of these arrangements involve very explicit instruction (*"Never* play with matches!" after a mother comforts children who have burned themselves). A less frequently analyzed set of arrangements involves instruction that is *tacit*. This term refers to settings where adults offer instruction to children without conscious awareness that they are encouraging children to learn and without awareness of exactly how they are modifying their behavior to meet the point where young learners find themselves. Still, the arrangements are routinized since they can be observed in the behaviors of different adults interacting with different children. For example, good adult athletes simplify their instructions to children concerning how to use a baseball bat, tennis racquet, or hockey stick. Even the best adult coaches may not be able to tell others exactly what their thinking is when adjusting to the skill level of the children. The knowledge is tacit, but it is also routinized because different adults present information to children in similar ways.

3. Cultural differences can be found in the goals that adults and children have as they participate in the many activities through which children grow to adulthood. There are also cultural differences in the exact means through which "children achieve a shared understanding with those who serve as their guides and companions through explanation, discussion, provision of expert models, joint participation, active observation, and arrangement of children's roles" (Rogoff, 1990, p. 8). There will be a number of examples taken from studies carried out in various cultures that will be discussed later, but a few remarks here may help

make these concepts clearer. In some cultures, adults explain the steps necessary to complete a task in detail, and children are expected to learn the step-by-step procedures necessary to complete the task. Many readers will remember the specific steps they had to learn before their mathematics teachers allowed them to complete the solutions to complex long-division problems. In other cultures, children observe adults carry out a task as a set of interrelated behaviors that are *not* broken down into steps that are explained in words. When children feel they are ready, they work on the task until they meet a stumbling block, and then the adults intervene with guidance on how to overcome the difficulty. This guidance may involve verbal instruction, the modeling of exact behaviors, or both, depending on the methods commonly accepted in a given culture.

GUIDED PARTICIPATION. A key concept Rogoff employs throughout the analyses that use this three-part framework is called "guided participation." As children learn the tasks necessary to obtain their goals, they participate in activities with people (often adults but sometimes age peers) who know more than they do about a certain area of knowledge or skill. These other people give various types of guidance, adjusting their behavior in various ways to meet the needs of the children who desire to learn from them. The guidance can be tacit or explicit, and either children or adults can accept the responsibility for making arrangements so that learning can take place. Borrowing heavily from the writings of Vygotsky (1987), Rogoff emphasizes that guided participation includes the building of bridges that allow children to move from their present level of skill and understanding to higher levels. It also involves the structuring of various activities so that children can reach these higher levels, with the amount of responsibility that children assume changing over time. An important underlying factor in guided participation is "intersubjectivity," or shared understanding between learners and people who are more expert. This understanding involves such features as the degree of expertise the learner wants to achieve, the skill level at which the learner finds himself or herself in relation to task mastery, and the feelings of shared success among learners and teachers when progress is made. As children interact with different experts in their communities who are able to encourage accomplishments in various skill areas, children increase their understanding of the many problems that have to be solved by well-adjusted adults in their culture.

Children's Involvement in Guided Participation—Examples. As with all aspects of socialization, the *goals* of guided participation should be kept in mind. For example, children must learn what adults consider good manners while eating and proper behaviors related to personal cleanliness. Cultural differences in table manners and personal hygiene have been the basis for many misunderstandings when North Americans and Europeans have traveled to India, Indonesia, Nepal, and other countries in South Asia (Brislin, Cushner, Cherrie, & Yong, 1986). Bob, visiting friends in India who were students with him a few years ago at an American university, wants to express his appreciation for the hospitality he has received. He takes them to a nice restaurant. After ordering their food, the members of the dinner party give Bob a small gift, which he takes in his right hand. When the first plate of food arrives, Bob doesn't bother putting his gift down on the crowded table and accepts the food in his free hand, placing a little on his plate, and then passing it on. From the expressions on their faces, Bob realizes that he has made a mistake, but can't figure out exactly what he did wrong.

The difficulty arises because Indians are socialized to believe that the two hands have very different functions. The right hand is the "clean" one and is for eating. The left hand is "dirty" and is used when eliminating one's solid waste products. People from many other parts of the world do not make this strong distinction and, instead, switch hands for various tasks when convenient.

At what age is this distinction learned? Freed and Freed (1981) observed that children in India are expected to make this distinction regarding use of their hands between 1½–2 years of age. If a child does not learn the difference by observing others and through everyday participation in eating and hygienic behaviors, there would be intervention by the mother or sister. One of these socializing agents would guide the right hand when eating while holding down the left. This intervention would continue until the child behaved in the proper way. Note how guided participation is part of the process by which the child learns the correct way of behaving. If the child learns simply through observation, no physical intervention is necessary in the form of someone guiding and restraining the child's hands. The involvement of a mother or sister continues only as long as necessary. The outcome of the socializing process is impressive. Two-year-olds can tear a piece of chappati (an Indian bread) with their right hands, pick up vegetables with the chappati, and put the combination of foods in their mouths.

As previously discussed, much learning that takes place during socialization is tacit. One aspect of tacitness is that adults encourage the children to learn in situations that the *adults* might not consciously label as good places to master important skills. Baseball coaches, for instance, will almost always point to participation in team sports as an opportunity to learn physical skills. They are not always able, on the other hand, to label participation in team sports as an opportunity to learn important social skills, such as cooperation in the pursuit of commonly accepted goals (Brislin, 1991). The teaching of physical skills is explicit; the teaching of social skills is often tacit. Gaskins and Lucy (1987; analyzed by Rogoff, 1990, pp. 124–126) presented an important analysis of how children learn what is important to know in their communities, not just in their own homes. In the Mayan culture of Guatemala, children can wander about their villages. They are exempt from such social norms as "don't eavesdrop" and "mind your own business." Children can observe adults working, talking, and interacting with each other. If an adult came along and began to observe other adults, social norms dictate that there must be some sort of social interaction between the observer and the observed. In a sense, children are considered "non-persons" whose presence does not need to be acknowledged by adults.

If mothers are confined to their homes because of such domestic duties as cooking or raising infants, they can send their children out to observe village events and to report back later. In this way, mothers keep up with current events and village gossip. The concept of guided participation is part of this process because of the questions the mother asks of her children. Children learn what aspects of social events are important through the content of their mothers' questions. If they can't answer a certain question after an afternoon of wandering around the village, they modify their behaviors on the next venture so that they can answer their mothers' questions the next time. A mother's questions guide her children's behavior. Children learn who in the community is important, the exact places where the most eventful happenings occur, the places that they are "supposed to" avoid but which they should go to nevertheless, and so forth.

INSIGHTS FROM THE WORK OF JEAN PIAGET. Barbara Rogoff (1990) integrated her work on guided participation with the observations of children's cognitive development made by the Swiss psychologist, Jean Piaget (1966, 1970). Space limitations prevent an extensive discussion of his many contributions (for further discussions see Flavell, 1963; Ginsburg & Opper, 1969; Dasen & Heron, 1981; Dasen, 1984), but a few examples provide additional insights into adult–child interactions during guided participation.

The contributions of Jean Piaget are best introduced if the reader imagines himself or herself as a participant in a psychological study that uses one of the most frequently employed tasks designed by Piaget: water conservation. Imagine that a psychologist has a beaker that is about 10 centimeters tall and 10 centimeters in diameter. The beaker is full of water. The psychologist then pours the water into a much taller beaker that is 4 centimeters in diameter. Which beaker has the most water? Adults, of course, have no difficulty answering that the amount of water is the same; it has simply changed its shape (i.e., the amount of water is conserved). Children of about 5 often answer that the tall beaker has more water. Five-year-olds attend to the height that the water reaches and are not able to set aside this visual cue and to focus on the underlying reality that the beakers have the same amount of water. Many 8-year-old children, on the other hand, answer in the same way as adults: The amount of water is the same; it has just changed shape. Eight-year-olds are also impressed with the height of the water in the second beaker, but they have developed

*Five-year-old children think there is more water
when it is seen in a tall container (with a small diameter)
compared to a shorter container with a wide diameter.*

a set of rules that allow them to manipulate concrete ideas (here, the amount of water that they see) in their minds. If readers know children of varying ages (sons, daughters, nieces, nephews), they might try this short experiment. Bowls and tall drinking glasses work well in informal demonstrations if beakers are not readily available.

Five- and 8-year-olds are at different stages of cognitive growth as identified by Piaget and his collaborators. The four stages and approximate ages at which the stages are reached are:

1. Sensory–motor intelligence (birth to about 2 years)—Children learn that there is a physical world that is independent of their own perceptions. They learn, for instance, that an object they are familiar with has an existence even if they can't see it. During these early years, for example, children learn that the book they have been playing with still exists even if a blanket is covering it.

2. Preoperational stage (2 to 7 years)—Children learn that objects and events exist even when they cannot be seen or heard, but they do not possess a set of rules that allow manipulations of these objects and events in their minds. Returning to the water conservation task, they do not have a rule that allows them to judge that the amount of water is the same. Glickman (1983, p. 215) argues that, "In summary, the preoperational child is the prisoner of its own immediate perceptual experience and tends to take appearance for reality." He also provides the interesting example of a magician who entertains a group of 4-year-olds. If the magician pulls a rabbit out of a hat, it does not impress 4-year-olds since, to them, rabbits might be anywhere: a hat, a cage, a zoo, or in the park. The visible evidence of the rabbit is important to 4-year-olds, not the "impossible" place it comes from.

3. Concrete operations stage (7 to 11 years)—Children have developed a system of rules that allow them to manipulate concrete objects, such as water, clay, or even pencilmarks on paper, as they learn to do addition and subtraction in school. So they are accurate on the water conservation task because they can manipulate thoughts about the volume of water in their minds. And, they can be impressed with magicians because they know that the hat that was originally empty should not have a rabbit in it.

4. Formal operations (11 years and older)—Children not only can manipulate ideas about concrete objects but can also manipulate ideas about abstract concepts such as people's intelligence and motivation, ethics, morals, and so forth. For example, children and adolescents are confronted with this problem: A boy tries to help his mother clean the house and accidentally kicks a cupboard door, leading to the breakage of 15 cups. Another boy tries to take some cookies from a container, even though his mother told him not to eat before the big family meal scheduled later in the day. This boy accidentally kicks a cupboard door, leading to the breakage of one cup. Which boy behaved badly and consequently should be punished? Children who have reached the formal operations stage are far more likely to take into account such abstract concepts as "motive" and "intent" and "explanatory factors." Young children often focus on the breakage of 15 cups and say that the boy who caused this extensive damage should be punished. Older children who have reached the formal operations stage focus on the less desirable motives of the boy who broke one cup.

Extensive cross-cultural research (Dasen & Heron, 1981; Segall, Dasen, Berry, & Poortinga, 1990) has led to the conclusion that this sequence of stages is universal among children around the world. The exact age at which the stages are reached can be influenced by the types of stimulation found in one's day-to-day environment. The sons and daughters of potters, for instance (Price-Williams, Gordon, & Ramirez, 1969) sometimes reach the concrete operations stage at a relatively early age because they help their parents knead clay. They become used to the fact that the amount of clay is the same regardless of whether it is in the shape of a round ball or a flat pancake. Children who are exposed to ethical dilemmas in a social studies class or as part of religious study (e.g., Is it acceptable for an adult to steal bread if that is the only way to feed one's starving child?) receive the type of stimulation that allows them to reach the formal operations stage at a relatively early age.

Returning to the discussion of guided participation, adults who have experience working with children undoubtedly modify their behaviors in response to the children's developmental stage. The adults rarely will use Piagetian terms, but they become sensitive to the tasks that a child is capable of carrying out. Price-Williams and colleagues (1969) and Georgie-Hyde (1970) worked with the children of adults who made their living as potters. The children were expected to help their parents, but the exact type of help depended upon their developmental level. Children at the preoperational stage would be expected to help parents prepare clay, but would not be expected to estimate the amount of clay necessary to make a pot "quite a bit smaller than the one we made yesterday." Children at the concrete operations stage might be asked to make this estimate, but they would not be asked to suggest what modifications (never tried before) might be made to make a certain cooking pot more useful. Children at the formal operations might be asked about such modifications, and they might be asked to make suggestions concerning abstract designs that have never been used before but that are consistent with the traditional ways of making pots in a specific culture.

An example of attempted guided participation that failed may make some of these points clear. My 6-year-old son was on a soccer team. One of the coaches, a very concerned man but one who had little experience working with children, brought a chalkboard to practice. He made abstract drawings that indicated the tasks that the players should perform (fullbacks drop back to defend the goal, halfbacks kick ahead of themselves, forwards move up to receive the leading pass, and so forth). The 6-year-olds were supposed to understand the diagrams on the chalkboard and apply the lessons to their play on the soccer field. As might be expected from a review of what children in the preoperational stage can do, coaching based on the use of a chalkboard was unsuccessful. The children were not able to take the abstract arguments about proper strategy and apply them to their actual play. The coach figured this out on his own after two practices, and the chalkboard was not seen again. Instead, the coach made sure that the children learned their tasks while actually practicing them on the playing field. He learned to be an effective teacher in the guided participation process: Teaching must take the existing abilities of children into account.

CHILDREN'S INFLUENCE. An important point is that children can begin to influence their own socialization at a very early age. When the behaviors of children cause their parents or other socializing agents to make responses that affect what the children learn, then all the people involved are contributors to the guided participation process. When our daughters were very young, Susan Braunwald and I kept diaries of their language acquisition (Braunwald & Brislin, 1979a,b). Braunwald was enthusiastic about the concept that children do not simply act as recipients of language who later show what they have learned in the utterances commonly called "baby talk." Rather, children participate in social settings involving guided participation where they learn language *and* other important lessons about their culture. Laura is Susan Braunwald's daughter; Cheryl is mine. All of the events described here took place in either California or Hawaii. When she was 15 months old, Cheryl was with her mother at a bookstore. They were waiting for me to pick them up in our car. Two vagrants who had been drinking heavily were in front of the bookstore.

CHERYL: Hiya! Hiya! Hey, Hiya! (while she waves and looks at the men)
MOTHER: Cheryl, you'd say hello to anyone (At that point, I arrived and all three of us left.)

When she was 18 months old, Laura was in the seat of a shopping cart in the grocery store. She was with her mother.

LAURA: Hi (to a strange man who passes near the cart).
MAN: Hi. How are you?
LAURA: Fine.

Laura repeated this sequence a second time when the man was encountered again in another part of the store. (Both examples from Braunwald & Brislin, 1979b, p. 103.)

Both children were learning the appropriate words to use when greeting people. But they were also learning some social rules: It is all right to greet some people, but not others. The process of guided participation is involved since the children's behavior affects the socializing agent's response. Cheryl begins to learn that it is improper in her culture to speak to vagrants. The response she hears from her mother has a negative tone, and she is taken from the social setting so that she can no longer interact with the two men. In contrast, Laura learns that it is OK to speak to a well-dressed man, who carries himself with a pleasant demeanor, as long as she is in the company of her mother. Note that at 18 months, Laura has learned an important part of an American conversational routine; the exchange continues for several rounds (as seen in Laura's response, "Fine," when asked how she is). Her mother approves of these conversations, as shown by Laura's behavior when the man is encountered again. If the social setting was different, for instance if Laura left her mother and ran up to the man to initiate a conversation, the outcome would have been different. Laura's mother would have guided the participation into the important lesson in American culture: Don't go running up to talk to strangers!

One of the contributions in analyzing guided participation is that it points to learning opportunities that, whether present or absent, are rarely examined by adults so that their implications are explicit. As will be seen in the next chapter on education, some children are guided into activities that allow them to take full advantage of the formal educational system. Other children have *not* been exposed to similar settings where they might have participated in the activities, and consequently they are at a disadvantage on their first day of school. Interventions are possible, but these will be successful only if parents, teachers, and all concerned citizens recognize that socialization involves exposure to settings in which learning takes place. Children who seem "slow" may simply not have had the same exposure as children who appear well prepared.

THE BEHAVIOR OF PARENTS

Research on the socialization of children over the last 20 years has pointed to the need to examine parents' behavior, children's behavior, and the social settings in which they interact. These examinations will involve more complexity than those that attempt to draw conclusions about how children are socialized by looking, for example, only at the behaviors of parents. Many examples have been presented. Parents do not simply demonstrate behaviors that children should imitate. Rather, children often initiate interactions with their parents during which guidance can be offered concerning acceptable behaviors. Parents do not necessarily raise their children in a manner similar to the way they were socialized 20 or 30 years ago. Given rapid social change, the more traditional socialization methods are often impossible to use given the absence of extended family members, the need for day-care if both parents work, and the presence of a child's peer group. Parents do not always tell their children that certain features of their culture are important and thus should be given special attention. Instead, children discover the important aspects through answering the questions their parents raise after the children report on their wanderings about the community.

Another important complexity is that the *expectations* children have about their parents must be taken into account. Pettengill and Rohner (1985) argue that two major dimensions in parental behavior are (a) the degree of acceptance or rejection of children and (b) the degree of strictness or permissiveness in how the children are disciplined. The first dimension (a) involves how much *warmth* parents feel toward their children, and the second dimension (b) refers to the amount of *control* the parents maintain over their children. Rohner (1986) has studied the effects of parental warmth and has documented the severe difficulties that rejection can cause for children.

Rejecting parents often dislike their children and resent the time and effort that the socialization of children entails. They view their children as a burden, and frequently compare them to other, seemingly better-behaved children in their neighborhoods. Important indicators of rejection are parental hostility and aggression, and neglect and indifference concerning the welfare of children. Rohner argues that parental rejection has predictable effects that are universal in nature. That is, parental rejection causes difficulties no matter where in the world it is found. Based on analyses of over 100 societies, Rohner concludes that parental rejection leads to children who become hostile and aggressive in their own lives. Further, they have problems with the management of their antisocial feelings and find themselves unable to control them in schools, among their friends, and with their siblings. The children develop feelings of low self-esteem and view themselves as inadequate compared to age peers. They are emotionally unstable, develop feelings of distrust toward others, and have a difficult time establishing and maintaining close relationships. Close interpersonal relationships, of course, involve emotional investment, and children of rejecting parents are less able to make this commitment to others. They have a negative worldview and are more likely to view their surroundings as the source of difficulties rather than as the source of opportunities. They are more likely to develop psychological problems that demand the intervention of professionals, such as social workers and clinical psychologists.

Returning to the point that socialization involves complex interactions between parents and children, recent research has indicated that *children's expectations* of how their parents should behave must be taken into account (Pettengill & Rohner, 1985; Rohner & Pettengill, 1985; Kagitcibasi & Berry, 1989). Research carried out in Connecticut showed that among American schoolchildren, parental control was seen as a sign of overall hostility and rejection. Children were upset at their parents, and thought of them as rejecting, if the parents imposed large numbers of rules and regulations on the children. In sharp contrast, research in Korea and Japan showed that children looked upon strict discipline as a sign that parents cared a great deal about them. Children in these two countries would be upset if parents did *not* maintain strict disciplinary standards. The key to understanding the difference is to examine the expectations children develop based on the social settings to which they are exposed. American children who view their parents as controlling are likely to have friends and classmates whose parents impose far fewer rules. Based on their interactions with these friends, children of strict parents can develop the view that they are being rejected. In contrast, the norms for strict discipline are more common in Korea and Japan. Children there have far fewer opportunities to encounter social settings in which friends and classmates expose them to standards noticeably less strict. Kagitcibasi and Berry (1989, p. 509) summarized these findings by suggesting that

> In cultural contexts where strict parental discipline is prevalent and therefore perceived as normal by children, it is perceived not as rejection but as parental concern. . . . In contexts where permissive parental behavior is culturally valued, strict parental control is perceived as rejection.

Some of the most rapid social changes that involve important human behaviors occur in the area of children's preferences regarding their parents' behavior. Pettingill and Rohner (1985) asked Korean-American adolescents about their parents' disciplinary practices. In all cases, the parents had been socialized in Korea and were living in the United States as permanent residents or as naturalized citizens. Approximately one-half of the adolescents had been born in Korea, and one-half in the United States. The interesting research issue centered on the expectations of the Korean-American adolescents. Keeping in mind that they are the sons and daughters of immigrants from Korea, would they view behavior more like age peers in Korea (where control is seen as concern for children) or would they view parental parental behavior more like age peers in the United States (where control is seen as rejection)? Readers might like to predict the results of the study. Pettingill and Rohner (1985) found that the Korean-American adolescents viewed their parents in ways similar to those of the American age peers. The rapid change in expectations concerning parental behaviors is striking. "Within a single generation since their parents' immigration, the Korean-American teenagers perceive their parents' behavior, not as adolescents in Korea do, nor perhaps as their parents might expect them to" (p. 248). These changes in expectations undoubtedly cause stress within Korean families. Where do the Korean-American adolescents learn this set of expectations that differ from those of their parents? As was seen in Sinha's analysis of socialization in India, the peer group plays an important role. In addition, the teenagers are exposed to new ideas in the American educational system. For example, American students are often asked to make choices among elective courses and are encouraged to pursue their own individual interests through choices among extracurricular activities. Some teachers expect students to argue and express disagreement with issues raised in the classroom. They are exposed to other socializing experiences that emphasize less strict control over their behavior, such as the honor system while taking exams.

Children's views about the ways their parents are disciplining them cannot be understood without taking the cultural context of behavior into account. If the cultural context emphasizes loyalty to the family and filial piety, one set of expectations will be preferred. If the culture emphasizes individualism and freedom of choice, then children will favor a different set of parental behaviors. Stress within families can occur when a culture's institutions do not have consistent views about the role of children. The Korean and Japanese parents, for instance, may expect deference to the views of the oldest male adult in the house. The school may expect that children formulate their own views and speak out in public, even when these views differ from those of the school's authority figures. A culture's formal educational system has strong effects on the people who participate in its many activities. These effects are discussed in the next chapter.

CHAPTER SUMMARY

Socialization refers to the total set of experiences in which children participate that allows them to become valued members of their culture. A culture's adults are responsible for socializing children. Parents are always involved, and other people become involved depending on the culture in which children are born: teachers, religious figures, grandparents, aunts and uncles, coaches, older siblings, and so forth. Socialization includes activities in which children are *guided away from* certain behaviors and are strongly encouraged to engage in others. When angry, children might shout, hit somebody, plot revenge, or keep their feelings to themselves. Children learn which of these behaviors are appropriate and which are inappropriate, depending on their culture. At times, this guidance leads to behaviors that are considered proper in one culture but rude and boorish in another. For example, interrupting someone may be considered ill-mannered in one culture but a sign of interest in what the person is saying in another culture (Carbaugh, 1990).

Culture affects the way children are socialized by providing social settings with which members are expected to become familiar. These settings can include fields where crops are grown, pastures where cattle are grazed, or birthday parties where social skills are nurtured. Stress can occur when children are expected to move from one setting to another if the behaviors expected in the new settings are quite different. Children who are unaccustomed to seeing books around their homes, for instance, often experience stress when they begin school due to unfamiliarity with the new objects in the new settings. Children who are accustomed to books, and to having books read to them by parents and older siblings, often have a smoother transition to the new setting known as the school.

A major influence on the way children are socialized is the social class into which they are born. Middle-class parents in various parts of the world encourage their children to exercise self-control, to be intellectually curious, and to be considerate of others. If they develop these skills, the children are likely to accept managerial and professional jobs that demand self-initiated behaviors, a respect for new ideas, and the ability to work well with others. Working-class parents are more likely to emphasize obedience, neatness, and good manners. Upon reaching adulthood, children of the working class are more likely to accept wage-labor jobs that involve physical effort and are subject to close supervision. The greater comfort and familiarity with these types of jobs stems partly from the downplaying of intellectual curiosity during socialization and partly because of the concern with obedience. Wage-labor jobs are closely supervised, thus children raised to be obedient are likely to be more comfortable with blue-collar jobs than their middle-class age peers.

Another reason for class differences is the expectations that children develop about the world. If their parents have always brought in a satisfactory income such that the family could afford some luxuries, middle-class children grow up with a positive attitude about life's possibilities. They learn to look on the world as an orchard full of fruit trees. They will have to work hard to harvest the fruit, but the opportunities for life's benefits are visible. If their parents were constantly struggling to keep ahead of bills, on the other hand, less-privileged children are more likely to grow up with a more negative attitude. They may learn to look on the world as a barren orchard where it doesn't make much difference whether they work hard or not. The fact that the social class into which a person was born provides different opportunities for development is difficult to discuss in some countries. In the United States, for example, a value reflected in the Declaration of Independence is that "All men are created equal . . . " Given familiarity with this value, many Americans are uncomfortable with discussions about the advantages and disadvantages brought on by birth into different social classes.

When a culture undergoes extensive social change, it often takes three or four generations for people to become comfortable with the new settings in which children are socialized. Parents may have been socialized in one way, but find that recent social changes prevent them from socializing their own children in similar ways. Durganand Sinha (1988) has pointed to seven types of changes in India that impact on how children are raised, and many of these changes can be seen in other parts of the world.

1. Families have moved toward nucleation. Instead of the extended family of years past, with its collection of other adults to help with the demands of socializing children, the nuclear family of parents and children has become more common.

2. With a nuclear family, children are more likely to be segregated from adults. In the traditional family, children had many opportunities to observe how adults interacted and solved problems when there were difficulties. With fewer people to observe in the nuclear family, children do not have as many opportunities to learn from large numbers of adults.

3. Given that there are no grandparents, aunts, and uncles to help with childrearing, pressures fall upon the parents. In the past there was always someone available to nurture the children. Given the demands placed on parents in more recent years, childrearing has become more strict. Children cannot eat, play, and sleep when they want as in the more nurturant past. Given that parents have limited energy, they have to set schedules for activities such as eating and sleeping, leading to stricter regulations on the child's preferences.

4. *As with any set of social changes, however, some people will prefer the more traditional ways and some will prefer more modern approaches.* The mother and father may disagree about a nurturant versus strict child-rearing style, causing inconsistencies in the way they behave toward their children.

5. *Given nucleation, there are fewer role models from whom children can learn.* There is less chance that a grandparent or elderly aunt, for instance, can tell stories about the important historical and mythical figures in a culture. Visits from relatives become a "special occasion," not a normal, everyday part of socialization.

6. *Social change often includes greater rights, and more opportunities, for women.* If women work outside the home and bring in money, they will want their opinions respected when recommendations are made concerning how the money is to be spent. The demand for respect, however, may interfere with the husbands' expectations that they are the heads of the households and make all important decisions. If both parents work, children often turn to age peers who provide socializing experiences. Children are likely to become independent of their family at an earlier age than in the past if they spend large amounts of time with people outside their families.

7. *Another important result of social change is migration within or across national boundaries in the search for better employment, better housing, and better educational opportunities for children.* Often, the move is from rural to urban areas. Such moves, however, bring additional demands of family members such as adjustment to a different lifestyle and disappointments that reality in a big city did not meet the family's expectations.

All of these changes can lead to stress because parents are struggling to socialize their children into a culture with which *they* themselves are not yet comfortable. The parents are not yet familiar with the new social settings which rapid change has brought. Interventions to ease the stress have been attempted, and a number of these will be reviewed in the next chapter.

Recent research, especially by Barbara Rogoff (1990), has emphasized the point that children are active participants in their own socialization. Children actively explore the world in which they find themselves, and their behavior influences the ways in which adults and peers offer socializing experiences. Much of the learning that takes place is tacit—people are not consciously aware that they are participating in activities that encourage children to learn about their culture. Further, even if adults *are* aware that they are encouraging children to learn, they are unable to explain exactly how they are structuring the tasks they present to children. Still, the adults and children clearly interact in a process known as "guided participation." People who know more about a task or skill adjust their behavior in various ways to guide children in their goals of learning about important aspects of their culture. For example, children in India and other countries in South Asia have to learn that the right hand is for eating and the left hand is for personal hygiene. If children do not learn this through everyday participation in activities in their home, adults or older siblings guide the children's hands. During meals, the "teachers" might hold down the left hand while guiding the right hand toward the food. A key point is that the children's behavior directs the teacher's behavior. If children learn through simple observation, there is no need for the more active intervention of holding down and guiding hands. In some cultures (for instance, the Mayan culture of Guatemala), children are allowed to wander around the village and to observe the behavior of adults. They learn exactly what is important to look for when they are expected to answer their mother's questions about community events and village gossip.

Parents can demonstrate varying degrees of warmth toward their children, and they can exert varying amounts of control over their children's behavior. If parents are perceived as extremely rejecting by their children, research in societies all over the world has documented harmful effects. Children of rejecting parents become aggressive and hostile, are unable to control themselves, are emotionally unstable, and are more likely to develop severe psychological difficulties. Interestingly, a key concept is the type of behavior that children are socialized to expect from their parents. Rohner and Pettengill (1985) demonstrated that with American schoolchildren, parental control was seen as a *sign* of overall hostility and rejection. Among Korean schoolchildren, control and strict discipline were seen as signs that parents cared about their children. For example, Korean mothers buy clothes for their children with no thought given to asking for their children's opinions. The children see this as a positive indication that their mothers are concerned that their sons and daughters look good when going to school or attending social gatherings. The American and Korean children have been exposed to different cultural values. Stricter control of children is valued in Korea, while parental permissiveness is far more common in the United States. Children internalize these values and then reflect on their parents' behavior with these values in mind. Some of the most rapid social changes involving important human behaviors can be seen in the behaviors of children. When Koreans immigrate to the United States, their children learn to value the more permissive norms in one generation. Korean-American children see their parents as rejecting if they are subjected to strict discipline. One place where the children are exposed to the new values is the school, and the various effects that stem from participation in a culture's educational system will be the focus of the next chapter.

5

FORMAL EDUCATIONAL EXPERIENCES

As discussed in the previous chapter, children are exposed to many opportunities to learn about their culture during the socialization process. For example, while observing adult relatives having an argument, they learn which issues people become upset about as well as methods for resolving interpersonal difficulties. When interacting with age peers, they can learn the benefits of compromise in contrast to the difficulties that arise when they insist that everyone follow their preferences. When answering their mother's questions about village gossip, they learn what issues are important to people outside their families. If they participate in organized group activities, they learn when the efforts of groups are more productive than the efforts of isolated individuals. These and many other opportunities to learn can be considered part of children's "informal education." The activities summarized by the term *formal education*, in contrast, are more organized, more predictable, and are marked by a number of features that can be found in cultures all over the world. The key features are that children leave their families for a certain number of hours each day, go to a designated place in the community called "the school," and interact with specialists known as teachers. There are certainly exceptions to this generalization, such as parents in highly industrialized nations who petition to keep their children home with the promise that they will provide formal education for their sons and daughters. But these exceptions should not keep people from examining one of the major institutions for socializing children: the special places called schools to which parents send their children (Cushner, 1990; Cushner, McClelland, & Safford, 1992).

There are few institutions within the countries of the world that have received more attention than the schools. Even when the topic might appear at first glance to be different, such as "intelligence," "learning," or "social change," a culture's schools quickly enter the discussion. A key aspect of intelligence, for instance, is how it is measured so that teachers and school administrators can best provide for the needs of children (Irvine & Berry, 1988). Teachers are constantly barraged by new advice from researchers concerning how children best learn, but the teachers must separate what is intellectually fascinating about the latest learning theory from what is truly helpful. When decisionmakers in government are contemplating major changes, such as the integration of a country's ethnic groups or greater attention to industrial competitiveness in the world economy, the school is very frequently the place where the changes are introduced (Anderson & Bowman, 1965; Tobin, Wu, & Davidson, 1989b). So many socialization experiences occur in schools, and societies expect so much of them, that efforts to understand human behavior around the world will be lacking if children's formal education is given too little attention.

This chapter reviews research in six important areas:

1. What changes in children's cognitive development occur because of participation in their culture's formal education? This is a difficult question to answer because research must separate the effects of formal schooling from (a) children's natural cognitive development as they increase in age and (b) the effects of other socializing experiences, such as the informal education children receive from working side by side with adults on tasks valued in their cultures.

2. Can classroooms be made more culturally appropriate to the backgrounds of children entering schools? Are there socializing experiences in which children participate *prior to their formal schooling* that prepare them to do well in school? Are there experiences children have that *interfere with* their schooling?

3. With some insights gained from the analysis of the questions posed in topic area number 2, are there interventions that educators can introduce so that more children can benefit from schooling? Are there benefits to be derived from involving the entire family, not just the children themselves?

4. Are there children from certain cultures who benefit from schooling more than children from other cultures? In North America, children of Asian descent seem to win more academic awards and go to college in higher numbers than children of European descent. Are these observations accurate and, if so, are there clear explanations of why Asian-Americans do well in school?

5. Do leaders in different societies identify problems that they feel can be addressed by changes in the school curricula? At what age are children targeted by leaders for major changes? Given that cultures have different goals and are changing in different ways,

at what age level (pre-school, elementary, secondary) can large differences in curricula be found?

6. There is a joke based on a series of questions: What is a person called who can speak two languages? Answer: A bilingual. What is a person called who can speak three languages? Answer: A trilingual. What is a person called who can speak one language? Answer: An American. In terms of languages that people can handle well in day-to-day interactions, Americans are in a *minority* (Hakuta, 1986). Most people in the world are fluent in more than one language, whereas the vast majority of Americans are fluent only in English. The important issue that arises is whether or not Americans are at an educational disadvantage given that competence in multiple languages is so rare. Is bilingual education, where children receive instruction in more than one language, a workable policy?

Before turning to these issues, it is useful to pinpoint aspects of formal schooling that can be found around the world. These are the etics (or culture-general factors: Chapter 3) to which emics specific to a culture can be added. Many of these characteristics of formal schooling, based on an analysis by Greenfield and Lave (1982), contrast sharply with descriptions of informal education as discussed in Chapter 4.

CHARACTERISTICS OF FORMAL EDUCATION

If people observe the institution called "the school" any place in the world, they are likely to observe a number of common characteristics. There will certainly be exceptions to this list, for instance when teachers and administrators make attempts to enrich the curriculum of their schools through innovative approaches. However, the characteristics are widespread enough to provide a good starting point for analyses of how schooling affects children. In addition, these characteristics are useful in describing the types of schools to which teachers are *reacting* in their attempts to be innovative.

(1) Schools are set apart from the context of everyday life. Children leave home and travel to a special place that is set aside for their formal education. In contrast to informal education, in which learning is embedded in everyday activities such as tending the garden and looking after siblings, formal schooling takes place during designated times. (2) Schooling involves specialists called teachers who are responsible for developing curricula and methodologies so that they impart their knowledge to students. This results in a system in which teachers decide what is to be learned. Only rarely are students able to designate topic areas that become part of the curricula. (3) Teachers are rarely members of students' families.

In many parts of the world, children are encouraged to become members of classrooms that are taught by someone from outside the family if their relatives happen to be members of the faculty. This contrasts sharply with settings where children learn informally by observing and working with various relatives. (4) Teachers are much more likely to be explicit about their goals and about ways these goals can be reached. This contrasts with informal education's implicit goals and tacit knowledge that were discussed in Chapter 4. For example, if students work together in groups, teachers are more likely to be explicit in their goals that children can learn certain content areas well through peer instruction *and* can learn how to work well with others on complex tasks (Johnson & Johnson, 1987; Kagan, 1990).

Another aspect of formal education involves the *emphasis* of a characteristic rather than its constant presence. When compared to informal education, (5) schools are more likely to be an institution where cultural change is introduced or reinforced. One reason is simply efficiency: It is far easier for a specialist in teaching to introduce new ideas to a class of 20 or more students than it is for far-flung and less organized sets of parents and relatives to introduce new material to children. It is certain, for instance, that schools in Eastern Europe and the republics formerly part of the U.S.S.R. will introduce new curriculum materials for the study of the political system known as democracy. (6) Schooling is far more likely to involve the practice of verbal interchange between teachers and students, with students able to ask questions about material that is not well understood. Informal education, on the other hand, is more likely to involve learning through observation of more expert people, whether those experts be older siblings, coaches, or other respected figures in the community. After a period of observation, learners try to imitate the more proficient people, probably engaging in more trial and error than a well-educated teacher would permit. Returning to point 4, above, concerned with the explicitness of instruction, a professional teacher is more likely to introduce tasks and goals that structure learning in a way distinct from pure trial and error. A teacher (7) is more likely to introduce general principles useful when solving a variety of problems rather than methods for solving one specific problem. If the topic was agriculture, a teacher would be more likely to discuss the contents of good fertilizer, crop rotation practices, and irrigation systems. This contrasts with the informal education method of learning how to plant a specific crop at a specific time in a specific place. The practice of teaching general principles in a classroom that might *later* be useful is known as "out-of-context" learning (introduced in Chapter 4). One danger is that some students benefit from this type of learning whereas others have difficulty seeing the relevance of general principles that seem to have no immediate application. This leads to the last characteristic of formal education suggested by Greenfield and Lave (1982). There is the danger that (8) some of the students will be less motivated in formal educational systems than in the informal settings provided by their culture. The grading system found around the world, for instance, leads to some students being labeled as "less capable," and this in turn affects their motivation. The efforts of policymakers to improve schools, as part of programs to deal with "culturally relevant curricula," "decreasing school dropouts" (called "school leavers" in some countries), and "basic life competencies" all reflect the fact that many students are not motivated to strive for success in schools.

CHANGES BROUGHT ABOUT BY PARTICIPATION IN A CULTURE'S FORMAL SCHOOLS

We will return to the problem of less-motivated students later in the chapter. The goal of working with such students, of course, is to increase the chances that they will experience success in school. But what is success? One way to answer this question is to examine the changes that occur in students who spend large amounts of time in school making adequate if not steller and prize-winning progress. A number of behavioral scientists deeply concerned about education have analyzed the changes that schooling brings (Rogoff, 1981; Scribner & Cole, 1981; Wagner, 1988; Cushner, 1990). The documentation of these changes is difficult since the contributions of formal schooling must be distinguished from maturation (children are able to do more as they grow older) and from the informal educational opportunities to which children are exposed.

One way to document the effects of schooling is to carry out research in cultures where children differ in the level of formal education that they receive. In some cultures, children who do not attend school (even though they may be very bright and able) can be compared with children who do. Keeping in mind the difficulties of making claims for schooling *above and beyond* other experiences in children's lives, a number of changes in students' abilities have been proposed.

THE USE OF MORE EFFICIENT LEARNING STRATEGIES. When faced with tasks that involve demands on people's memory, such as learning a list of words, children who have attended school are able to apply strategies that allow better performance (Cole, Gay, Glick, & Sharp, 1971; Cole & Scribner, 1974). Consider the following list of words:

red	cup	brother
knife	blue	sister
green	mother	spoon
plate	father	green

People are asked to study the words, the list is then taken away, and people are asked to recall the words that they remember. People are told that they can recall the words in any order that they wish. That is, people do not have to recall the words in the same order that they were presented.

Children who have attended school (hereafter called "schooled children") are more likely to use the very efficient learning strategy known as *clustering*. They are more likely to cluster the words into the categories "colors," "eating implements," and "family members." Very often, schooled children are explicit about this strategy, reporting that they put the words into various groups. They might not use the same labels for the word groups (for instance, they are more likely to use a phrase like "things on the kitchen table"), but the children clearly are organizing the information effectively in their minds. When people cluster information, they place *fewer* burdens on their memories. If they memorize the names of the clusters, these names then become cues for the contents within each cluster. Without the use of an efficient learning strategy such as clustering, the task becomes one in which people simply try to memorize 12 words, and this is both difficult and often rather boring. Based on research among the Kpelle in Liberia, Cole and his colleagues (1971) suggested the use of efficient learning strategies begins between the fifth and eighth grades. Students younger than this, and children of any age who had not attended school, did not impose any meaning (such as the names of clusters) on the words.

The exact reasons for the effects of schooling are not entirely clear. Rogoff suggested various types of reasons that might be called "test-wiseness" and "generalizable skills." Test-wiseness simply means that, given experience with such day-to-day activities as following the teacher's instructions, using paper and pencils, working along within time limits set for various classes in the school, and comfortableness with outsiders (here, the researchers) who come into classrooms with new tasks, schooled children are more prepared to do well in learning experiments. They simply know how to take tests well, and this is their only advantage over their unschooled peers. Test-wiseness is undoubtedly a factor, and good research takes this into account by allowing unschooled children extensive amounts of time to become familiar with the test materials, interactions with experimenters, sensitivity to any time contraints, and so forth (Dasen & Heron, 1981). Two of the more generalizable skills suggested by Rogoff (1981) are that, as part of their schooling, children learn familiarity with various ways of organizing knowledge, and they learn that many problems can be solved through the careful examination of information presented in the problem. Keep in mind that Cole and his colleagues found that children began to use ways of organizing information in the fifth grade. By that time, they would have been exposed to many lessons in which which information was clearly organized: history according to various significant events; science according to the steps involved in various experiments; mathematics according to recommended orderings of addition, subtraction, and multiplication when solving complex problems, and so forth. In mathematics especially, children learn that the information necessary to solve "word problems" is contained in the written or verbal information. In word problems, students are presented information ("John has two dollars and goes to a store where carrots cost fifty cents a dozen. How many carrots can John buy?") All the information is in the word problem, children learn, as long as they can find it. If students learn this fact, they are likely to apply it to the task of learning the list of words presented earlier. They might say to themselves (as children have told me after participating in research studies): "There is something in this problem that will make it easier to do as long as I can figure it out." If they bring this attitude, then they are likely to discover that the words cluster into clear groups.

GREATER FIELD INDEPENDENCE. If people are able to extract information from its surrounding context, they are said to be *field independent*. Consider Figure 3, a type used to test for field independence and called an embedded figure (Wilkin, 1967):

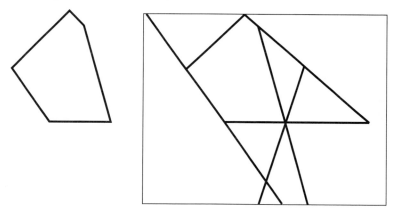

FIGURE 3. An "Embedded Figure"—a Type of Drawing Used
to Test for Field Independence.

If people can look at the small figure on the left, and quickly find it inside the more complex figure on the right, they are demonstrating the quality of field independence. They are able to extract or to find information in the complex figure, and are not distracted by the surrounding context or "field." They can find information "independent of the field." If people are *field dependent*, they are more likely to be attentive to the total context in which they find information. They are more comfortable making conclusions about the total package of information. If the total package of information (e.g., the figure on the right-hand side) demands that it be broken down into component parts, field-dependent people do not carry out such a task as quickly or as accurately.

Cross-cultural research (Witkin, 1967; Berry, 1979) has been concerned with the important question of whether socialization into different cultures has an impact on skills such as field dependence or field independence. Suggesting that there is indeed a relation between socialization and skills, Berry (1979) has done research on cultures in which the major subsistence activity is hunting. Berry argues that if subsistence activities demand certain skills, people will have to develop those skills or else their culture will not survive. Skills, then, can be viewed as an adaptation to the environment in which people find themselves. Further, adults will encourage the development of these skills among children. Hunting is a skill in which field independence is extremely useful. Consider hunting a brown deer living in a forest where the trees are similarly colored. Or consider hunting white seals in the Arctic where the snow-covered surroundings make the seals very difficult to spot. Field-independent hunters, who can extract information (the vague figure of a deer or seal) from the total context will have an important advantage in their quest for food.

Everyday words for the skills summarized by the terms "field independence" and "field dependence" are admittedly hard to identify. Possible approximations are "analytical" for field independence and "sensitive to context" for field dependence. Consider a meeting where 20 people are present. People express their various opinions about an important social issue. If asked what happened after the meeting, analytical people might focus on the views of individual persons. "Person A had one opinion, person B had another," and so forth. People sensitive to context may be more able to identify a sense of the group as a whole. They might be able to report, "I felt that the consensus of the group was that we should proceed in this specific way."

Although more studies would be desirable before firm conclusions can be put forward, Rogoff (1981) entertained the possibility that schooling leads to increases in field independence. One possible reason is that many tasks children are expected to master involve breaking a problem down into component parts. Complex mathematical problems have to be broken down into simpler steps. Information has to be extracted from complex pictures, figures, and graphs. The arguments that students want to make in their essays or in their public presentations have to be broken down and organized in an way to be understandable to listeners. These various tasks demand the sort of analytical skills captured by the concept, field independence. Ideally, increases in field independence will not come at the expense of the positive features field-dependent people possess. It is very useful if people can summarize the "sense of the group" after hearing many individual positions put forward. Another possible benefit of field dependence is that people are more sensitive to the needs of others (Witkin, et al., 1962)—they have more social skills in being able to deal with many different types of individuals. The "sensitivity of context" of field-dependent persons extends to sensitivity to others, who, it should be remembered, are part of the total *context* with which any one individual must deal. Given that many of today's social issues (drugs, housing,

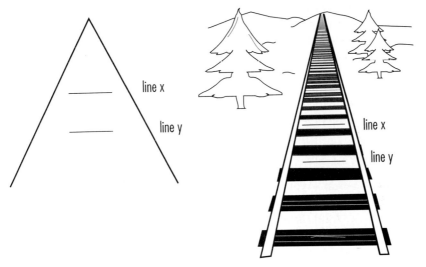

FIGURE 4. Drawings that Illustrate how
Three-Dimensional Information is Depicted in Two Dimensions.

poverty, diversity in the workplace) involve people and their special needs, social sensitivity should be encouraged whenever possible.

USING PICTORIAL INFORMATION. The interpretation of drawings and photographs is based on an understanding of how three-dimensional information is depicted in two dimensions. In Figure 4, consider the drawing on the right. The drawing is presented on a two-dimensional surface. The depiction of objects to the left and right of viewers, as well as up and down, correspond to the same two dimensions readily available on a flat surface. There are conventions (here, "perspective") that people learn to use when they need to depict or to interpret the third dimension involving the positioning of objects that are supposed to be seen away from the viewer, or "behind the flat surface of the page." In the right-hand drawing, the converging lines represent railroad tracks that are extending away from the viewer. The drawing of the railroad tracks indicates converging lines because that is what people see when looking at simliar objects in the real world. When looking in front of themselves in real-world situations, people see straight roads, long corridors, and railroad tracks converging as they extend into the distance away from viewers. There are other cues in two-dimensional drawings and pictures that indicate three dimensions. When objects are drawn so that they overlap, the proper interpretation is that one is in front of the other. In Figure 4, one tree is supposed to be seen as closer to the viewer than the other.

There are many places where children can become familiar with the interpretation of three-dimensional cues depicted on two-dimensional surfaces. Many children from middle-class homes in different countries have access to books with lots of pictures. Even before they begin school, they become quite skilled at identifying objects, indicating which are near and which are far away, and so forth. Schooling seems to impove this skill for children who have had experience with pictures, and it offers the opportunity to develop the skill for children who have had little exposure to two-dimensional drawings and pictures (Wagner, 1977; Rogoff, 1981; Segall, et al., 1990). The reasons for the effect of schooling in this case undoubtedly include exposure to many different types of drawings and pictures and practice in interpreting them.

An especially interesting finding is that schooled children can begin to make certain types of *errors* when interpreting pictures. These errors involve visual illusions (Segall, Campbell, & Herskovits, 1966). Both the left and the right sketches in Figure 4 are versions of the Ponzo illusion. If they demonstrate susceptibility to the illusion, viewers will report the top line (line x) as longer than the bottom line (line y), even when both are equal in length. Cross-cultural research has indicated that people in some cultures are more susceptible to the illusion than are people in other cultures (Leibowitz, Brislin, Perlmutter, & Hennessey, 1969; Brislin & Keating, 1976; Wagner, 1977). One explanation is based on the "ecological hypothesis." People learn to interpret cues in the physical environments in which they are raised. If there are many opportunities to see objects that seem to converge in the distance, then people will learn the cue that "converging lines tell me that certain objects are far away." People who are not raised in such environments are not as familiar with this cue to distance. For instance, people who live in rural communities with few buildings, few roads, and who see their flat farmlands extend into the horizon are not as familiar with the experience of clear lines converging in the distance. When asked to report which of the two lines is longer in different versions of the Ponzo illusion, they are more accurate. Since they are not as familiar with the cue that converging lines indicate distance, they do not use it when viewing the Ponzo illusion.

People familiar with converging lines (e.g., people in urban areas of the United States), are more susceptible to the illusion. They use the cue that converging lines indicate distance and make the unconscious interpretation that "since the top line is further away, it must be longer because objects in the distance look smaller." The interesting effect of formal education is that schooled children become more susceptible to the illusion than their unschooled peers (Wagner, 1977). This is especially true for the more complex versions of the Ponzo illusion (e.g., the version on the right-hand side, Figure 4). The more complex version has more cues to depth, schooled children learn how to use these cues, and consequently become more susceptible to the illusion. This illusion becomes an example of the use of cues, or habits of inference (Segall, et al., 1990, p. 75) that *most of the time* lead to correct decisions. After all, lines that converge in the distance *usually are* helpful in making decisions about the relative size of objects. In this case, however, a cue that is usually helpful leads to an error. Cross-cultural studies of other visual illusions (e.g., Deregowski, 1980) have attempted to identify the normal, everyday perceptual cues that people in different cultures learn to use. Much research has taken the view that visual illusions are not anomalies that are unrelated to anything else. Rather, illusions are helpful tools in the study of people's normal perceptual processes that happen to lead to mistakes in a few cases.

The feature of schooling that is common to these three skills is that children benefit from specific experiences commonly found in classrooms all over the world. They learn to organize information learned from their texts and from teacher presentations, and they apply organizational methods to new learning tasks. They learn to pick out key information in complex problems and to apply this to tasks meant to measure field independence. They learn to interpret cues in three-dimensional pictures and use these when asked to examine visual illusions. Some children come to school with a solid background that allows them to develop these skills readily. Others do not, but after several years some (not all, unfortunately) participate in so many classroom activities that they "catch up" to children with a better preschool background.

These observations lead to several more questions. What, exactly, is a good preschool background? If the background of children who are ready to benefit immediately from school attendance is known, will this be helpful to teachers concerned with the progress of children from other backgrounds? Are any aspects of the children's backgrounds related to cultural factors, as these have been discussed throughout this book? If so, can teachers *benefit from* knowledge of the cultural backgrounds of the various students who will be in their classes? These are some of the issues to which we now turn.

INTEGRATING CHILDREN'S CULTURAL BACKGROUNDS INTO THE SCHOOL

As was discussed extensively in Chapter 3, socialization into a culture involves behavior in social settings. Children become familiar with certain settings and are able to engage in appropriate behaviors so that they can achieve their goals. If they move to different settings, as in the example of families in India moving from rural to urban areas, they experience stress because they are unaware of the behaviors necessary to achieve their goals. Applying these concepts to the case of schooling, some children are well prepared to benefit from their formal education. Consider the three skills reviewed in the previous section: organizing information, the analytical ability to pick out key information in a complex problem, and interpreting information in pictures. Some children are socialized into settings where they are exposed to these skills by the time they are 3 or 4 years old. They are accustomed to organized play activities encouraged by adults. When playing with blocks, for instance, some parents sit down on the floor with their children and begin, "First we'll clear an area, then we'll get the blocks out, then we'll build a base, . . ." Many children have puzzles of various sorts where they have to analyze how to solve problems and then use a specific approach to reach a solution. Some puzzles children have bear a similarity to the embedded-figures task: In books of games their parents buy, children look at complex figures and are asked to find the three clowns, horses, or trees. Many of these same children have books with pictures and have conversations with their parents about the figures in the pictures, where things are in relation to each other, and so forth.

Many people take this for granted, but recall from Chapter 1 that this is an important insight about culture. People become so familiar with everyday aspects of their culture that they don't think about them, take them for granted, and are rather impatient with individuals who are not as familiar with those aspects. When aspects of culture related to schooling are taken for granted, however, the great danger is that children unfamiliar with these aspects will be shortchanged. One way of dealing with this issue is to ask: "What *are* children familiar with, given their socialization in their own culture, and can these skills and social settings be integrated into the school curricula? Important research on this question has been carried out (Laboratory of Comparative Human Cognition, 1986; Vogt, Jordan, & Tharp, 1987; Cushner, 1990), and some findings will be reviewed below. A good way of introducing this research, I believe, is to present findings about another aspect of middle-class American culture which (a) prepares children to benefit from school, (b) is a major part of classroom activities, and (c) which is extremely easy to take for granted.

CONVERSATIONAL PARTNERS. Children need to communicate with others to become competent native speakers of the language(s) employed by adults in their communities. Some of children's exposure to language takes place during give-and-take conversations with other native speakers. The important question related to preparation for school is: Who are these others with whom children interact? Heath (1983) argues that there are important cultural differences in answers to this question. In the American middle-class, mothers and fathers view their children as *conversational partners*. That is, adults engage in conversation with children, taking the point of view of children into account during the give and take of conversation. The diaries that Susan Braunwald and I kept of each of our daughters' language development were introduced in Chapter 4. Consider two other entries (Braunwald & Brislin, 1979, p. 30).

Laura is 17 months old. She is on the changing table and her mother is changing her diaper. Her mother senses that Laura wants to play.

MOTHER: I'll tickle you as soon as I put on your diapers.
LAURA: Now!

Cheryl is 14 months old. She is in the kitchen with her mother. A TV can be heard but not seen.

TV COMMERCIAL: Get rid of ring around the collar . . .

Immediately after she hears the words "ring around the collar . . . ," Cheryl begins to turn as she does when she plays "ring-around-the-rosie."

MOTHER: Yes, that's "ring-around-the-rosie." Good girl.

The point for discussion here is that both mothers are conversing with their children and are reacting to their attempts to communicate: Laura's desire to be tickled, and Cheryl's desire to play a game she knows. A number of researchers have pointed out that this adult willingness to communicate in this way with children is by no means universal (Ward, 1971; Heath, 1983; Rogoff, 1990). In many cultures, children are not considered appropriate conversational partners. Children hear their native language(s) spoken, but not during frequent conversations with adults.

In many, but not all, cultures, children are considered as appropriate conversational partners for adults.

Rather, children are much more likely to engage in conversations with age peers. Adults consider it strange to talk with children. When they do, they do *not* switch to a "baby talk" that is common in the middle-class United States when adults want to be sure that they are understood. For instance, the same diary study shows me saying "here's your wawa" when giving Cheryl the water she requested—I was using her word, not the adult word. Even though adults in the American middle class probably never think about such verbalizations, the fact that they interact with children in this manner is good preparation for formal schooling. If children learn to communicate with their adult parents, they will most likely be able to transfer this ability to communicate with their adult teachers. Children will also be prepared for their teacher's attempts to simplify language, a practice most American preschool and kindergarten teachers engage in frequently. The children will also be prepared to initiate behaviors, that is, to be the individuals who decide what will be done rather than just react to teachers' directions. Note in the two diary entries that it was Laura and Cheryl who began the tickling and dancing activities. This familiarity with the initiation of activities will be useful when the children are expected to make individual and original contributions during their formal schooling, such as bringing in objects from home and describing them during "show and tell" sessions.

INTEGRATING CHILDREN'S CULTURAL BACKGROUND: AN EXAMPLE. Without a great deal of conscious awareness, the parents of the American middle class prepare their children to benefit from formal schooling. Teachers learn to expect these well-prepared students and construct their lesson plans with the children's already-existing skills taken for granted. If the children begin their formal schooling without these skills, the risk is that they will not benefit from their attendance and will fall behind their better-prepared peers. Realizing these facts and also realizing that some of the reasons for friction in school are related to the children's cultural background, various researchers (reviews in Laboratory of Comparative Human Cognition, 1986; Cushner, 1990) have attempted to design school curricula that takes the children's culture into account. One of the most carefully documented efforts of this kind is the work with Hawaiian and part-Hawaiian children who attend schools in Honolulu and other parts of Hawaii as part of the Kamehameha Elementary Education Program (KEEP) (Jordan & Tharp, 1979; Vogt, Jordan, & Tharp, 1987).

As discussed above and as exemplified by child diary entries, one of the ways children are socialized is through conversation with others (Carbaugh, 1990). The KEEP researchers carried out careful research to determine who children talk to, and in what social settings they become comfortable (recall the discussion of social settings in Chapter 4), realizing that this information would be useful in understanding the children's formal schooling. Based on research carried out in the communities where the children resided, a number of important facts were documented. Given that both parents often have to work to cope with Hawaii's high cost of living, older children are frequently given responsibility for looking after their younger siblings. One way to look after siblings is to involve them in games and other group activities, and these efforts are often integrated with those of friends and *their* siblings. Consequently, Hawaiian children participate in group activities more frequently than do children from many other cultural groups (e.g., Caucasians originally from the mainland United States). Children become accustomed to integrating their own efforts with the goals of a group and are less insistent on the pursuit of their own personal goals. When instruction on the rules of the game or procedures needed for the group activity are needed, older children take responsibility. In turn, as the younger children become older, they pass their knowledge on to younger people. As a result, Hawaiian children become accustomed to the roles of teacher and learner within their peer group.

Another group activity in which children engage involves discussions of recent happenings in their lives or shared experiences within their communities. Called "talk-story," children sit around and tell what has happened to them in narrative form: who did what to whom, what happened as a result, who else became involved, and so forth. Adults also engage in talk-story, but it is more likely to be done with other adults so that story themes shared by adults (e.g., difficulties with members of the opposite sex, filling out tax forms) can be discussed. In other words, people in Hawaiian communities converse with each other in a format much like story telling. In addition to the fact that there is far more of this activity than is found in middle-class America, there is a procedural difference that is striking to outsiders. If the story is about a shared community happening, or if the story about one person's experiences bear similarities to recent events in the lives of others, people interrupt each other. Further, there is a great deal of overlap between the verbal contributions of one person and the additions to the story by others. People who were socialized to show good manners by *not* interrupting others, and by waiting for others to stop talking before making one's response, find it hard at first to participate in talk-story. If they use the conversation rules they learned during their socialization and wait a polite period of time before contributing, someone else will have already begun speaking!

Can these important cultural differences be integrated into the formal classroom? It is important to note that the *attitude* of teachers and school administrators is central in determining the answer to this question. Recall the discussion in Chapter 2 concerning the possibility of ethnocentric judgments when cultural differences are observed. School personnel *could* observe Hawaiian schoolchildren and could conclude that they have deficits that make it difficult for them to learn. They might point to overlapping conversations and conclude that the children are impatient and do not have an adequate attention span. They could point to the children's deference to group goals and conclude that the children are not independent enough to benefit from the many choices offered to them. On the other hand, school personnel could observe the children and could conclude that the children have been socialized in a different culture. This is neither good nor bad—it is simply a fact. The children bring a set of differences to school, and teachers and administrators have an opportunity to encourage the children to draw upon these aspects of their culture during their formal schooling.

The KEEP researchers made modifications to the elementary school curriculum based on cultural factors that they documented. Four have been reviewed: children play in groups, they defer to goals set by the group, they are accustomed both to teacher and learner roles within their groups, and they engage in talk-story conversations that involve interruptions and overlapping contributions. These factors were integrated into the methods through which teachers encouraged the development of various skills expected of schoolchildren. Methods for teaching reading provide a good example.

Teachers introduced cooperative group learning (Johnson & Johnson, 1987; Kagan, 1990). Students are divided into groups, and tasks are given to the group as a whole rather than to individuals. If one student doesn't understand an aspect of the task, someone in the group who does takes the teacher's role and offers an explanation or demonstration. Given their familiarity with this approach from their out-of-school playground activities, children find it easy to share information in the classroom. They also find it relatively easy to relate to the group goal that "everyone is expected to learn the skill," rather than the more individualistic, "some individuals will learn it very well and will receive a gold star." In learning to read, and in developing reading comprehension, the familiar talk-story method was adapted. Children would read sections of the book aloud, and then would *talk about* what happened in the stories. While doing so, children could also bring in personal experiences whose memories were triggered by some aspect of the reading assignment. Interruptions and overlapping verbal contributions were allowed. By hearing the reactions of other children, and by linking the content of the story to their own personal experiences, children developed their reading comprehension skills. They were able to show teachers and peers that they understood the content of the stories through their frequent contributions to group discussions. If their comments were not related to the story, the teacher and peers could ask questions or make suggestions that brought them back to the theme, characters, or plot of the story.

Evaluation studies of these classroom interventions showed very positive results. Compared to part-Hawaiian children taught in more traditional classrooms, KEEP children scored at grade-level on standardized reading tests. These are the same reading tests given to children on mainland United States (and which have probably been taken by a majority of this book's readers) to assess progress and to indicate areas (e.g., vocabulary, comprehension) that need improvement. Keeping in mind that the tests were designed to be compatible with the backgrounds of children in the American middle class, reaching grade level (e.g., third graders are indeed reading and understanding third-grade material) is a significant achievement.

LONG-TERM DIFFICULTIES. Is there a sad side to this good news? Unfortunately, the answer is "yes." After the children leave the KEEP program and enter traditional schools, they fall behind age peers from other cultural groups (e.g., Japanese-Americans, mainland Caucasians) and participate in a spiral called the "cumulative deficit phenomenon." That is, they might find themselves a little behind in the fifth grade. But since sixth-grade work demands the skills learned in the fifth grade, they get further behind as they proceed through junior high and later high school. These results from KEEP program research are consistent with studies that followed the progess of low-income, inner-city children from Milwaukee, Wisconsin. While initial results showed positive benefits of early educational intervention programs for 4- and 6-year-old students (Heber & Garber, 1975; Garber, 1988), these benefits were not maintained when students entered junior high and high school (Prasse & McBride, 1991).

With the impressive results of the KEEP program, why haven't programs been developed that assist children through their later school years? There are many answers. The research program that developed the classroom interventions was very expensive, and the competition for dollars is always difficult given that there are other demands on a school system (e.g., after-hours day care for the children of working parents; better teacher salaries; anti-drug education; organized team sports for females). The program also took many years to develop, and the original set of forward-looking administrators who first recommended that the program be funded had moved on to other jobs by the time the program had been successfully implemented. Another reason relates to the discussion of culture in Chapter 1 (p. 19). Recall that one aspect of culture involves the time necessary for change. If an important institution is part of a culture, as is formal schooling, it does not change quickly. The sorts of classroom activities adopted by KEEP involve many changes: The teacher is no longer the sole authority figure; groups work toward tasks; children interact with others in ways that are different from the well-managed classroom with which teachers are familiar. Many teachers are simply uncomfortable with these changes and, given the chance, will fall back on the familiar methods of the past that are not very different from those used during *their own* childhood.

Research on cultural differences in the classroom, then, faces a problem. Even if the benefits of programs are documented, there is absolutely no assurance that interventions sensitive to cultural differences will be adopted. Still, research must continue on this important topic. Researchers, and people who *are* willing to use the results of good cross-cultural research, must remain optimistic that their suggestions will receive careful consideration. Keeping this in mind, important research has been carried out that might shed light on the problem identified in the KEEP work: The benefits of the program introduced in the early elementary school years are not maintained as children become older and enter the later grades. This research has examined the role that the children's families play in the maintenance of skills that were developed during their formal schooling.

WORKING WITH THE ENTIRE FAMILY

Children in the KEEP program developed solid reading skills during their early elementary school years, but they did not maintain grade-level reading skills in the upper elementary and junior high school years. One reason may be that skills learned at school are not necessarily reinforced at home. If the children are reading well but have no opportunities to use their skills outside of school, they may feel that there is little link between the time they spend in school and the time they spend with their families. Further, if parents have little understanding of what goes on in their children's schools, they may be unable to reinforce newly developed skills even though they desire to do so. Recall the KEEP program involves a number of innovations. Even though the parents may be familiar with the underlying concepts used in developing the innovative methods (given their own socialization in Hawaii), they may be quite unfamiliar with how these concepts have been used in the school. It must be remembered that the parents most likely were exposed to very traditional classroom methods during their own schooling.

Kagitcibasi (1990) has advised researchers and educators to keep in mind that children will learn best if they see clear links between what they learn in school and what they experience at home. If different skills are called for, then confusion can result which interferes with the children's subsequent learning. Kagitcibasi argues that there are benefits to home-based schooling. Returning to the features of formal schooling discussed in the beginning of this chapter, bringing education into the home changes several of them. There is no longer a special place for schooling—it takes place in the familiar surroundings of a child's home. Ideally, children will be more motivated to take part in formal educational opportunities given the support of their parents and other family members. Other features of formal education remain. There are specialists called teachers, there is an explicit curriculum, there are sequences of questions and answers between teachers and children, and there are general principles introduced. There are also "in between" features in the sense that aspects of informal and formal education are involved. One such feature is that teaching responsibilities are shared between trained teachers and family members. Another is that the general principles can be applied to specific tasks around the home, such as gardening, cooking, child care, and other chores.

HOME-BASED SCHOOLING: SOME ADVANTAGES. The great danger with formal schooling is that if children develop skills in school, there is no guarantee that they can use and improve those skills any place else. If family members become involved in education, they are more likely to seek opportunities where the child's new skills can be used. One reason is familiarity: They simply know about and are not threatened by the new skills children possess. Another is that family members become more confident in *their own abilities.* Analyzing the role of mothers, for instance, Kagitcibasi (1990, p. 132) writes: "Specifically, helping the mother build self-esteem and competence, so that she can engage in cognitively oriented communication with her child, can help to foster the child's sustained cognitive development." Contributions to the education of parents are especially important in developing countries (such as Turkey, where Kagitcibasi lives and where she has carried out much of her research) since many adults have not had the opportunity to participate in formal educational programs of any kind.

Another advantage is that the benefits of home-based schooling are likely to generalize to other children who were not the specific targets of the original intervention. These include a child's younger siblings and the child's neighbors. Especially in rural areas, an outsider to someone's home is likely to receive a great deal of attention. When teachers arrive in a village and begin to introduce their educational program in someone's home, many neighbor children will gather around. If the teacher is able to integrate them and *their* parents into the program, the benefits will increase not only because more people are reached, but also because there are more people to provide reinforcement for skills developed during the program.

Home-based schooling also permits the introduction of various interventions meant to assist children and their families. If the goal is literacy, it is a relatively easy matter to use reading materials that deal with issues such as nutrition, family planning, and health education. If researchers use their imagination, they will be able to find opportunities to reach parents and their children if home-based schooling proves impractical because of travel distance and consequent expenses. Some communities have "feeding centers" where mothers come for nutritional supplements. Sometimes parents and their children have to wait until they can be helped by the nutritional specialists. During the waiting time, educators can involve the children in creative play activities that require the children to exercise various cognitive skills. Such efforts "can also get the mothers involved in such creative play in order to sensitize them to the importance of play for the cognitive development of their children and in order to encourage them to continue it at home" (Kagitcibasi, 1990, p. 133).

HOME-BASED SCHOOLING: AN EXAMPLE. Working in Turkey, Kagitcibasi, Sunar, and Bekman (1989) evaluated a four-year educational program carried out among low-income families in Istanbul. Components included the importance of frequent parent–child interactions, encouragement of feelings of competence as a parent, an introduction to various cognitive skills, and the importance of cognitive stimulation in the home.

Recall the important but disappointing finding from the KEEP research: Children did not maintain their grade-level reading skills as they moved into the upper elementary school years. In addition to the reasons already discussed, another may be quite subtle and difficult to identify. As children learn to read and find out information about important topics *on their own*, they become more autonomous and do not need to relate to their families and peer groups as often. This can be upsetting to parents who desire the quality of relatedness, which involves close ties and mutual interdependence among family members. If parents communicate their difficulty with their children's new-found autonomy, children may sense this and cease development of the skills that might be taking them away from the parents' desire for relatedness. Realizing this possibility in their own work in Turkey, Kagitcibasi and her colleagues (1989) dealt explicitly with the issue of relatedness verses autonomy. Prior to the introduction of their multiyear program, they asked mothers what they desired in their children. Over 80 percent of mothers expressed a desire for various types of relational behaviors, such as being good to family members. Autonomy actually angered mothers. Then a program (in this case, lasting 2 years) was implemented. In addition to introducing various cognitive skills mothers could pass on to their children, various relational skills, such as showing physical affection, helping, and supporting others were *reinforced*. The goal was not to interfere with existing cultural values. However, new concepts were introduced, such as the usefulness of autonomy when children go to formal schools, the importance of children being able to make some of their own decisions, and the value of children being able to set their own goals and working toward them.

Follow-up studies found that mothers who participated in the program learned to value their children's autonomous behaviors. This did not interfere with their continued desire for relational behavior: Mothers also wanted their children to remain close to the family. What happened, then, is that the program encouraged an important combination of behaviors that mothers learned to appreciate. The mothers continued to stress the importance of relational behaviors while learning about the usefulness of autonomous behaviors in certain social settings (e.g., formal schools, perhaps jobs later in the children's lives) in which the children will surely find themselves. An important point is that nothing is being taken away from children. The value of relatedness, including offering and receiving support, is retained while the benefits brought on by the new value of autonomy are added. Such syntheses of values and skills are not uncommon (Markus & Kitayama, 1991). In bilingualism, for instance, learning another language does not necessarily interfere with a language a person already knows well: Such interference is called subtractive bilingualism (Cummins, 1976; Hakuta, 1986). Instead, learning another language can be a positive aspect of people's education and can lead to increases in cognitive skills and greater numbers of opportunities in their lives (additive bilingualism). The possibility of adding to people's abilities, and not taking away strengths they already have, is an important goal in educational efforts that take cultural differences into account.

In the study carried out in Turkey, mothers learned to appreciate the importance that autonomy plays in formal schooling. After the full 4-year program, participating mothers had higher expectations of their children's school achievement and hoped that their children would stay in school longer. Children behaved in line with these expectations and demonstrated superior performance in school. A key concept here is *expectations*. Once mothers and children are exposed to a wide variety of cognitive skills, values, and supportive behaviors to reinforce school success, they learn to expect more out of their lives. They become more aware, for instance, of the role schooling plays in improving opportunities for people born into the less privileged, poorer classes within their societies. They can develop a positive view of their abilities (recall the elements of a positive self-concept and the benefits of autonomy that were included in the Turkish study) and can set their sights higher. An interesting question raised by this analysis is: Do people from some cultural groups set their sights higher than others, and if so, why? Recent research has addressed this question.

BENEFITING FROM FORMAL EDUCATION

Many journalists, as well as researchers, have made the observation that Asian-Americans are more successful in American schools than are members from other ethnic groups ("The new whiz kids" in *Time Magazine*, 1987; Hsia, 1988; Sue & Okazaki, 1990). More specific observations, documented in careful studies, include the fact that Asian-Americans are more likely than other Americans to graduate from high school, attend college, and graduate from college. They receive better high school grades and are frequently the winners in such competitions at the National Merit Scholarship Program, Presidential Scholars, and the Westinghouse Science Talent Search Program.

Calling Asian-American educational success "a phenomenon in search of an explanation," Sue and Okazaki (1990) analyzed a number of possible reasons. They could find no evidence for any genetic factor that would lead to the sorts of abilities that might give Asian-Americans an advantage in school. They could find no evidence that there might be an advantage given their social-class background (recall the discussion of social class in Chapter 4). In fact, Arbeiter (1984) provided evidence to show that the mean household income of Asian-Americans was lower than that of Whites. Setting these two factors aside, Sue and Okazaki (1990) focused on two other reasons: cultural differences in the socialization of children, and an innovative idea that they call "relative functionalism."

Cultural factors exist at a very high level of generalization, such as values that pervade a culture, and they exist at the level of very specific behaviors, such as typical and frequent parent–child interactions. When considering Asian-American success in school, appeals to values include the assertion that Asians are more likely to feel that success in school is important. Parents point to education as a way for children to better themselves, to make a contribution to society, and to find happiness. Parents are more likely to value the formal aspects of education, such as reading, test-taking, and grades, and will downplay other aspects such as a school's organized athletics program, extracurricular activities, and efforts to develop "the whole person." The value placed on education will be seen in more specific behaviors, such as parents monitoring the homework of their children, *expecting* more effort and achievement, making special efforts to provide a quiet place for children to study, hiring tutors when necessary, and encouraging children to put forth more effort on a day-to-day basis.

Insights into the behaviors and achievements of Asian-Americans can be stimulated by examining research carried out in Asia. Immigrants to the United States take many of their cultural values with them and try to find ways of maintaining them. Based on research carried out in Japan, Hess and his colleagues (1986) argued that the Japanese are likely to blame poor performance on a lack of effort. If they do not achieve, the way to improvement is through greater effort (Mizokawa & Ryckman, 1990). Work carried out in the United States indicated that American children were more likely than their Japanese counterparts to blame something other than their own effort if they did not perform well (Hess, Chang, & McDevitt, 1987). If they received a D-level grade, they were more likely to blame the test, or to claim that they studied the wrong material, than the Japanese. Compared to Japanese parents, American parents were more likely to blame the teacher, the school, or the curriculum for their children's poor grades. These differing interpretations of poor performance (or attributions about behavior: see Chapter 2) lead to different parent–child interactions. The Japanese parents are more likely to encourage the efforts of their children and to demand that their children work harder. Combined with the value placed on collectivism (Chapter 2; see also Kim, 1990), which encourages children to remain close to their parents and to show their love for their parents by pleasing them, children are likely to engage in more effort and eventually reap the benefits of higher grades.

Another cultural difference was documented by Ritter and Dornbusch (1989). Compared to members of other ethnic groups, Asian-Americans were more likely to believe that success in school had a relationship to success in life. That is, Asian-Americans believed that if they did well in school, this would increase their chances of achieving success in their later lives outside of school. Developing this concept, Sue and Okazaki (1990) suggested a set of ideas summarized by the term *relative functionalism*. This term is best explained by looking at the two component words. "Functional" means that people see a clear use to certain behaviors, or a clear link between one set of behaviors (e.g., studying hard) and others (e.g., good grades, praise from parents). "Relative" refers to one set of social settings in contrast to another. If one set of behaviors is seen as more effective *relative to others* (e.g., studying harder rather than blaming the teacher), then the first set of behaviors will be adopted. Sue and Okazaki argue that given prejudice and discrimination in the United States toward minority groups whose members have a different skin color and a different accent when using English, Asian-Americans cannot benefit from all areas in society. There are limits placed on them in areas such as politics, athletics, entertainment, leadership in various organizations, and so forth. Realizing this, they examine various aspects of society and try to identify those in which they will receive fair treatment. After such a search, Asian-Americans identify the area of formal education. Teachers are seen as appreciative of hard work and attentiveness, and will reward these qualities with good grades. Teachers are likely to give good students a "fair shake" regardless of their skin color. *Relative* to other parts of society, Asian-Americans expect that hard work in school will be functional to success in other arenas of life, such as the search for decent paying jobs and membership in various professions. Given that they internalize the link between success in school and success in other aspect of life, they work hard and demonstrate exceptional educational achievement.

This discussion of relative functionalism applied to an entire cultural group allows a review of a difficult concept first introduced in Chapter 1. This is the distinction between individual differences and cultural factors. There are *individual* White and Black Americans who view education as the road to success. I am certainly one of these. My parents made it very clear to me that financial burdens brought on by the Depression of the 1930s prevented them from going to college. If *their* children were to be more successful, then education was the avenue. This deeply held belief, however, is not widespread enough to be considered part of present-day American culture although it probably was earlier in the early twentieth century. Today, too many Americans do not see a link between education and success in life, spend as little time as possible on their schooling, and do not give sufficient attention to the education of their children. In contrast, the belief in the importance of education as leading to later success is more widespread among Asian-Americans. The argument is not that *all* Asian-Americans have this deep-seated belief. Rather, the argument is that the belief is widely enough shared to be considered part of Asian-American culture. Importantly, the issue of generational differences has to be integrated. A more precise statement of the findings is that the first few generations of Asian-Americans behave according to the relative functionalism hypothesis: Success in school leads to success in other aspects of society. Sue and Okazaki point out that among members of later generations, acculturation to American society shows its effects. Third and fourth generation Asian-Americans behave much like Americans in general: Some *do* behave according to the relative functionalism hypothesis and some do not. What *was* a cultural value, with its key component of being familiar and widespread among members of an ethnic group, has become "an individual differences" value. The key component of "individual differences" is that some people think and behave one way but other people think and behave in a manner quite different.

SCHOOLS AS SOCIALIZING AGENTS FOR THE NEEDS OF SOCIETY

The importance of success in school can be looked on as part of the cultural background of many Asian-Americans. Schooling is viewed as functional: It has uses for people in their quest for success and happiness in life. Are there other uses schools serve for people and for the societies that put tax dollars into formal education? The answer is clearly "yes." In many countries, the school is seen as a place where (a) desired changes in society can be introduced or reinforced and (b) where problems *not* addressed effectively in other parts of society can be treated. Consider some examples in the United States. During the first 50 years of this century, Black Americans made demands that they be integrated into society and that they be given the same rights as White Americans. After a number of Supreme Court decisions, action was finally taken. What was a major site of this action? The answer, of course, is the public schools. With the Supreme Court decision of 1954 known as *Brown vs. The Board of Education*, the concept of "separate but equal" schools was set aside and efforts were begun to integrate America's public educational system. Government officials felt they had more control over funds for schooling than for other programs in which massive integration efforts could have been undertaken. The schools became one of the major places where society tried to change itself in the area of race relations. As will be discussed in Chapter 7, lessons learned from the painful efforts to integrate schools were later applied to other parts of society, such as people's neighborhoods, workplaces, and *private* schools (Williams, 1987).

There are other examples of responsibilities that fall to the schools, especially when society's leaders feel that problems are not being effectively addressed elsewhere. People get into too many automobile accidents. Too many individuals drink alcohol to excess. Too few sexually active people, especially if they are young, know anything about birth control.

Many people get into trouble because of drug abuse, poor skills to manage their frustrations and aggressive tendencies, or a general disrespect for the country's legal system. The content matter of this book also is brought to the attention of schools: Not enough people know how to get along, or how to communicate effectively, with members of cultural groups other than their own. In all these cases, American schools are asked to add programs to their curricula so that society at large will function more smoothly. Consequently, programs in driver education, alcohol and drug abuse, police–community relations, intercultural interaction training, and so forth, are implemented.

The general concept, then, is that society identifies problems and schools are asked to deal with a number of them. Is this concept found in other parts of the world? Examining schools in Japan, China, as well as the United States, Tobin, Wu, and Davidson (1989b) answered "yes" and found that schools dealt with societal problems as early as the preschool level. One of their findings allows insights into a puzzling problem that has been faced by many American mothers who reside in Japan. Consider this example.

Margaret Blake was an executive in a fast food chain that was exploring the possibilities of introducing franchises in Japan. Accepting the assignment in Tokyo after a successful career in San Francisco, Margaret brought her 5-year-old son and placed him in a highly recommended Japanese preschool. Like many 5-year-olds, Margaret's son, named Mark, had already attended preschool in the United States. In fact, he had begun right after he was toilet trained at age 2. The preschool in San Francisco that Mark attended, in addition to offering good educational programs, also met Margaret's needs for day care. Margaret had long ago learned that Mark loved peanut butter sandwiches, and also usually ate his entire lunch consisting of a sandwich, fruit, cookies, and juice. So for his first day of Japanese preschool, Margaret prepared Mark's favorite type of lunch and took time off from work so that she could pick up Mark after his first day of school. She found that Mark was rather sullen, and on returning home he began to cry. Mark complained that the other children laughed at his sandwich, and even the teacher looked at Mark in a strange way during lunch. What is the source of the problem? (This incident is adapted from similar examples in both Brislin et al., 1986; and Tobin, Wu, & Davidson, 1989a.)

INTEGRATION INTO A GROUP. In Japan, one purpose of preschool education is to encourage the child to become part of a group. Especially in Tokyo and other large cities, children do not frequently have age peers with whom they can play until they start school. Land is so scarce and expensive in Japanese cities that people live in small apartments, and there is less land set aside for playgrounds than in other highly developed nations. So even if young children do meet age peers in their apartment buildings, there is little room for them to play together. The school becomes the place where children first learn to get along with others outside their immediate family. When asked, "What are the most important things for children to learn in preschool?" Tobin, Wu, and Davidson (1989b, p. 190) gave special attention to the three most important reasons each respondent gave. Eighty percent of Japanese respondents (both males and females were questioned) indicated that they expected children to develop sympathy, empathy, and a concern for others. In comparison, 20 percent of the Chinese and 39 percent of the American respondents listed sympathy, empathy, and concern for others among their most important expectations of preschool education.

What does this have to do with Mark's lunch? In Japan, children show their concern for others by becoming part of a very disciplined, well-behaved group. Visitors to Japanese preschools are amazed to see 5-year-old children clean up after lunch, without noise and without any need for disciplinary action, after the teacher simply indicates that lunchtime is over. The concern for others and the infrequency of disciplinary problems, however, come at the expense of individual expression. Children are expected to blend together into a classroom group and not to stand out as unique (Hamilton, Blumenfeld, Akoh, & Miura, 1991). This has implications for dress, for styles of interacting with others, for toys, and for the lunches children bring from home. A Japanese lunch consists of a predictable collection of foods placed in a box called a "bento." Anything other than a bento lunch is seen as overly individualistic, and 5-year-old Japanese children have had enough experience with the demands for uniformity that they find Mark's lunch unacceptable. In addition, bentos must be very carefully prepared, necessitating that mothers spend a great deal of time and effort on their children's lunches. As discussed in the previous section, Japanese culture places a great deal of emphasis on education. Mothers show their concern for their children's education in many ways, and just one is the preparation of lunches. Cultural differences lead to difficulties for Americans living in Japan. A mother living in Kyoto ran into the "nothing other than a Bento lunch" problem. So she learned how to make acceptable lunches. But her son came home crying. she said, "Now what's wrong? I made you a Japanese lunch." He said, in tears, "But you didn't cut the apple slices so they look like bunny rabbits like the other mothers do" (Tobin, Wu, & Davidson, 1989a, p. 38).

COMMUNICATION SKILLS. One way that Japanese children show a concern for, and empathy with, others is to behave in ways that are very similar to their age peers. This has important implications for communication skills. If people become empathetic with others in their group, there is no demand that members express their special needs with preciseness. If members have learned to be empathetic and concerned with each other, they will sense an individual's special needs without that person stating them clearly. In Japan, communication between people is successful when the *listener* understands what a speaker is trying to say (Lebra, 1976).

This emphasis on the listener's responsibilities for successful communication is quite different from the emphasis in both China and the United States. In these countries, *speakers* are expected to make their points clearly, and examinations of communication difficulties are more likely to focus on the speaker's errors. This cultural difference shows up in answers to the question about what children should learn in preschool. Adults in China and the United States felt that communication skills were important: 27 percent and 38 percent of the respondents, respectively, in the two countries. In Japan, only 4 percent of the adults felt that communication skills were among the most important things for children to learn.

One reason for emphasis on the speaker's skills is that in China and the United States, people must communicate with others who are very different from themselves. Readers will be familiar with the differences that must be transcended in the United States: Some are brought on by social class background, age, level of formal education, language of one's parents, accents within the English language, region of the United States where one was socialized, and so forth. While outsiders often view people in China as the same from one place to another, this stereotype is totally inaccurate. The differences among the Chinese are vast. In terms of population, the Chinese constitute almost 20 percent of the world's people. In terms of area, it is twice the size of Europe. The Chinese government recognizes over 50 official minority groups, most of whom have languages that are mutually unintelligible when members of these minority groups attempt to interact in face-to-face encounters. As Chang (1989, p. 36) states:

> Americans typically see China as a political, economic, and sociological monolith. Nothing could be further from the truth. Although under the mandate of a central government, the people and provinces of China are as different from each other as the countries of Europe. And it has always been this way in China, for thousands of years.

Given vast differences within a country, its citizens cannot develop the same empathy as expected in Japan with its one national language and long history of cultural traditions shared by all people who identify themselves as Japanese. If Chinese and Americans want to communicate with others, they cannot expect so much shared culture that listeners will understand what they want. Chinese and American *speakers* have the responsibility to communicate, and this is an emphasis in their education as early as the preschool level.

The Chinese make other requests of their preschools. One very important expectation has been brought on by a national policy to limit families to one child. Designed to curb population growth, the policy is at odds with a long cultural tradition of large families. Given the program's success, many adults worry about what they call the "4-2-1" syndrome

(Tobin et al., 1989a,b). The "1" refers to the child whose "2" parents and "4" grandparents are so attentive that the child may become spoiled and consequently not a hard-working citizen of China. When asked: Why should a society have preschools? 12 percent of Chinese adults answered: "To reduce spoiling and make up for deficiencies of parents" (Tobin et al., 1989b, p. 192). This figure is much larger than the 2 percent of adults in both Japan and the United States who were concerned about spoiling and other parental deficiencies. There was also more concern in China with preschools as "starting young children on the road toward being good citizens."

AMERICA'S EXPECTATIONS. Adults in the United States had expectations of preschools that were different than in China and Japan. Readers may want to guess what these expectations are, especially given the discussion in Chapter 2 on individualism and collectivism. In responding to the question concerning what is most important for children to learn, 73 percent of American adults expressed a desire for children's self-reliance and self-confidence. These figures were larger than the 29 percent of Chinese and 44 percent of the Japanese who had similar concerns. Self-reliance and self-confidence include the beliefs that people can set, work toward, and achieve their own goals, and can do so without total dependence on others. "I did it all by myself" is what American children say when solving a puzzle, and parents and teachers are happy when the children use this phrase when describing their efforts. Self-reliance is extremely useful in a highly individualistic society such as the United States where people must set and achieve goals *without* the constant presence of a supportive collective whose members can help out in times of trouble. Even with this emphasis on individualism, the importance of working cooperatively with others and developing a sense of identity that includes others *beyond oneself* is part of America's thinking about its schools. Tobin et al. (1989a, p. 45) observe:

> American folklore celebrates the loner and the self-made [person] and looks with scorn on the "ant-colony" mentality seen as characteristic of group-oriented cultures. But some Americans worry that in the celebration of individualism the threads that bind people to one another have been stretched too thin. They are looking to government, church, and community organizations—including preschools—for direction and for a sense of shared purpose and identity.

The balance between individualistic and group-oriented concerns will continue to be debated in the United States well into the twenty-first century. When applied to formal education, the question will be posed in the form: What aspects of American culture should be reinforced in the school and what aspects should be changed? One aspect of American society is the lack of appreciation given to people who are fluent in more than one language. In the conference that led to the publication of a volume on language learning, interpretation, and translation (Gerver & Sinaiko, 1978), both Europeans and Americans attended and shared ideas. The respect given to bilinguals was captured in this thought that attendees were asked to consider. Someone says, "We will be having a meeting where attendees speak different languages. Your interpreter has just arrived." In Europe, the concept "interpreter" has a positive image of a well-educated individual who possesses a valued skill. In the United States, the image is much more likely to be of an individual who speaks English with a noticeable accent, dresses in a slightly rumpled jacket with patches on the sleeves, is probably an immigrant to America, and in general does not command much respect. Can the schools do more to encourage respect for people who are fluent in several languages? This is one of the concerns of educators who have considered the introduction of bilingual education programs.

BILINGUAL EDUCATION

Few topics related to formal schooling have been the focus of more controversy than bilingual education (Paulston, 1980; Hakuta, 1986; Padila et al., 1991). There is little disagreement about one fact: If children participate in a bilingual education program, they receive instruction in different subject matters (e.g., reading, history, mathematics, science) in different languages. The key words are "subject matters." Bilingual education differs from foreign-language instruction because it goes beyond the typical class in French, Spanish, or German that students take under the label "foreign language requirement." Rather than being a separate class devoted solely to learning a new language, bilingual education involves various classes in which children learn the subject matter as dictated by the curricula established for the school as a whole. Beyond this fact, there is little agreement about the goals, purposes, problems, and advantages of bilingual education. One of the basic disagreements centers on the expectations adults in a community have for schoolchildren. Many adults feel that instruction in any language other than English places children at a disadvantage once they seek higher education or seek employment in the world outside school. They feel that instruction using another language involves time that should be spent using the language children need to succeed in the United States: English. Other adults feel that America has placed far too little emphasis on languages other than English and that this inattention has led to a decline in America's competitiveness within a global economy. Many of these same adults also feel that if some children already know a language before coming to school (e.g., immigrants from South America or Asia), then formal educational programs should be able to benefit from this blessing.

MAINTENANCE AND TRANSITION PROGRAMS. At least in terms of people who write letters to newspaper columnists and who contribute to the "letters to the editor" section of periodicals, there are four times as many people against bilingual education as there are in favor of it (Hakuta, 1986). Much sentiment against bilingual education will remain for decades given the deep-seated belief among many Americans that use of the English language is one of the demands of citizenship and is one of the unifying elements in a diverse society (a belief analyzed by Padila et al., 1991). Some of the negative sentiment, on the other hand, might diminish if a number of issues were better understood. One issue involves the goals of different bilingual education programs. There are two basic goals and consequently two different types of programs. In a *maintenance* program, children who already speak a language beside English are encouraged to maintain it. For example, a large number of children who *might* benefit from a maintenance program are native speakers of Spanish in the United States (Mackey & Beebe, 1977) and French in Canada (Lambert & Tucker, 1972). While maintaining their language skills that they brought to school, they also receive instruction in the English language and eventually use both languages in their subject matter instruction. The eventual goal of maintenance programs is to encourage the development of true bilinguals; that is, adults who are fluent in two languages.

In a *transition* program, children begin their schooling in their native language and are gradually exposed to more and more instruction in English. The transition, then, involves a move from the language they brought with them to the language introduced in school. Many transition programs have the goal of moving speakers of other languages into all-English instruction in two or three years. Contrary to popular belief, there are far more transition programs in the United States than there are maintenance programs. Educators who believe in the value of transition programs argue that certain general skills are transferable across languages (e.g., Mackey & Beebe, 1977). For instance, if children learn to read in one language, they have learned a general skill and as a result can read another language. The general skill called "reading" involves making sense of marks printed or written on a page, and it does not matter which language children use to develop this general skill as long as they *speak and understand* the language. Educators argue that it makes sense to teach these general skills to children using the tools (e.g., the Spanish or French languages) that the children already know. At the same time, instruction in the English language can be introduced, and children will later be able to use their general skills when asked to read materials written in English.

ARE CHILDREN NATURALLY PROFICIENT LANGUAGE LEARNERS?

In addition to discussing the maintenance–transition distinction as a source of disagreements, Hakuta (1986) analyzed other reasons why bilingual education has been the focus of such heated arguments. An additional reason is the belief held by many adults that children under about age 12 pick up languages naturally and easily. The argument goes that if speakers of other languages are put into an all-English curriculum, they will simply use their natural language-acquisition abilities and learn English. Hakuta (1986) argues that the "child as natural language learner" is a myth. *Some* children do learn other languages quickly, but others find it a struggle. It must be also kept in mind that many children who are non-native speakers of English will not have good support at home for other-language learning. Some children will downplay their English-language abilities for fear of distancing themselves from their parents and older siblings who may be far more fluent in Spanish, Chinese, Korean, or some other language. Just as in the research by Kagitcibasi (1990) reviewed earlier where mothers could become upset with the autonomy children show after school attendance, parents of children who are successful English-language learners may communicate subtle signs that they are uncomfortable with their children's progress.

Many adults who point to children's natural language-learning abilities are themselves immigrants who spoke another language on their first day of school, were placed in monolingual English classrooms, and were successful. "I learned English and did okay in school. Why all this fuss about special bilingual education programs that everybody admits costs a lot of money?" Again, the distinction is between *some* children and *all* children. Many adults did indeed thrive in America's classrooms without knowing a word of English on their first day of school. But others did not, dropped out, and had far less access to the benefits of American society. It was mentioned above that people who write letters to the editor are against bilingual education by a four to one margin. Many of these letter writers use the "I did it—why can't others?" argument. It must be kept in mind that these people have developed the literary skills and self-confidence necessary to write letters to the editor. School dropouts are far less visible when a "pro" and "con" count is made of these letters.

POLITICAL CONSIDERATIONS. Another important reason for the heated, sometimes unpleasantly hostile, debates about bilingual education is that political considerations are involved (Paulston, 1980). Whenever there are scarce resources that are desired by many different people, there has to be a system that allows decisions concerning the exact people who receive the resources (Brislin, 1991). In authoritarian societies, a limited number of privileged people make the decisions and the vast majority of citizens are not allowed to voice their preferences. In democratic societies, many people are allowed and are often encouraged to make recommendations concerning the distribution of resources. Although not always recognized as such (Crick, 1982), the system that allows people to participate in decisions concerning the distribution of scarce resources is called "politics." While often considered unpleasant words that polite people should avoid (Brislin, 1991), "politics" and "access to power" summarize the process through which people participate in decision making about important matters such as public education. As Crick (1982) points out, an absence of politics and a lack of power means that people have to accept decisions that affect them but that are made by others.

The role of politics in the distribution of resources becomes clearest when specific examples are examined. Bilingual education programs can be very costly. These programs often demand the hiring of new teachers who are themselves bilingual, or the hiring of bilingual aides who assist full-time teachers. The programs demand the acquisition of new textbooks and teaching materials. With some languages, such as Spanish and French, suitable materials might be readily available after examinations of schoolbooks used in Spain, Mexico, or France. With other languages, such as Laotian, Vietnamese, or any of the languages native to the Pacific islands, new materials might have to be prepared, and costs can mount quickly in any efforts to write new texts or to prepare new teaching materials. A major aspect of politics in a democratic society is that everyone who wants to contribute must have a chance to speak out. People who believe strongly in a certain position are happy to hear the speeches of supporters, but become frustrated when opponents (who have the same right to speak out) disagree. To increase the frustration, bilingual education is a topic about which many people feel compelled to speak without knowing much about it (Hakuta, 1986). At public forums, such as meetings of the board of education, people frequently begin by saying, "I don't know much about bilingual education, but I feel . . . "

Given its costs, people who favor other uses of public funds may feel that money invested in bilingual education will take attention away from other desirable programs. Consequently, opponents of bilingual education put forward arguments in favor of other programs, and in so doing participate in the competition for scarce resources. Examples of other programs that many people favor over bilingual education include special English-as-a-second-language classes (ESL), where well-trained teachers give instruction in English but with sensitivity to the background of students who are native speakers of other languages. Or, programs can involve very different aspects of the educational system such as a 3-year plan to raise teacher salaries, programs to encourage the best college students to enter the teaching profession, anti-drug workshops, or efforts to encourage schoolchildren to engage in volunteer work within their communities. All of these programs are worthy of consideration, and bilingual education has to compete against them in the political arena.

THE EFFECTIVENESS OF BILINGUAL EDUCATION PROGRAMS. If evaluations of bilingual education programs showed that native speakers of other languages were clearly benefiting from them, then this information would be very useful when proponents of bilingual education compete for funds in the political arena. Unfortunately, general or blanket statements that "bilingual education is effective" cannot be made. As Hakuta (1986, pp. 219–220) concludes:

> There is a sober truth that even the ardent advocate of bilingual education would not deny. Evaluation studies of the effectiveness of bilingual education in improving either English or math scores have not been overwhelmingly in favor of bilingual education. To be sure, there are programs that have been highly effective [discussed by Padila et al., 1991], but not very many. . . . An awkward tension blankets the lack of empirical demonstration of the success of bilingual education programs. Someone promised bacon, but it's not there.

This summary statement about the effectiveness of bilingual education programs brings up an important argument that will, in various forms, be found in several chapters of this book. The argument is that an understanding of complex programs is more likely to occur when very specific behaviors are investigated. Bilingual education programs are complex, but little is learned about them by asking the question: Does bilingual education help children? The key words in the quote from Hakuta (1986), above, is "there are programs that have been highly effective." More valuable insights into bilingual education would be forthcoming if research was done on exactly what happens in these successful programs. Is it the attitude of teachers? Is it a specific type of learning material that students use? Does it involve the sort of cooperative effort among students reviewed earlier in this chapter when the Kamehameha Elementary Education Program (KEEP) was discussed? We don't know the answers to these questions. The research on bilingual education, the results of which have been disappointing, has tried to answer the question: Does it work? Critics of this research feel that more useful information would be available if the questions had been: What types of bilingual education programs work with what age groups of children? From what social class backgrounds? With access to what other educational enrichments in their lives? Who are able to use what specific types of learning materials? Who interact with what kinds of teachers? and so forth. Paulston (1980) also recommended that research examine other outcomes of bilingual education programs *beside* classroom progress in subjects like English and mathematics. She recommends that researchers ask whether children stay in school until they graduate, whether they find employment after completing their education, whether they avoid drugs and alcohol abuse, and so forth. If bilingual education programs help speakers of other languages benefit from their schooling, its effects could well show up years later in their contributions to society.

The argument that complex human behavior is best understood by examining specific aspects can be applied in many areas. Returning to the analysis of the success of Asian-Americans in school, Sue and Okazaki (1990) argue that general appeals to "cultural differences" are not helpful. Much more specific behaviors have to be examined, such as the number of hours parents encourage their children to spend on their homework. The argument about understanding the specifics will also be found in the next chapter concerned with prejudice and discrimination. Many readers have probably heard the recommendation: Let's just bring people from different cultural groups together so that they can get to know each other—this will reduce prejudice! In actuality, such efforts can simply reinforce and even increase prejudice if people from the less-powerful groups feel that they are being ignored or exploited. Attention must be given to a very *specific* set of recommendations for programs to reduce prejudice, and this will be one of the topics covered in the next chapter.

CHAPTER SUMMARY

Many of the socialization experiences in which children participate take place within their culture's formal school system. Further, leaders in different societies frequently identify problems that are not being addressed effectively by other institutions, such as the family or the judicial system. These leaders often assign schools the task of finding solutions to these problems, and in so doing place expectations on schools that go beyond the teaching of traditional subject matters, such as reading, writing, and mathematics.

In contrast to informal education, formal schooling is set aside from everyday life, occurs in a designated place, and is organized by specialists in the teaching profession. Teachers are far more likely to be explicit about the goals of education and are more likely to introduce general principles that *may* have specific applications in other settings outside the school. The fact that formal schooling is removed from children's day-to-day activities with their families leads to the risk that some children will not see the relevance of schooling and will not be motivated to meet the teachers' expectations.

If children are successful in school, they are more likely to develop a number of cognitive skills than equally intelligent age peers who are not able to attend school (Rogoff, 1981). Three of these skills are the efficient organization of new knowledge; the analytical skill of extracting information from a complex figure or picture; and the more efficient analysis of pictures, especially the use of two-dimensional cues in depicting three dimensions. These skills undoubtedly develop from the typical school experiences of (a) learning to organize ideas presented by teachers in an efficient way rather than simply depending on rote memory, and (b) learning to pick out the *key* information necessary to solve particular problems from the *total* information presented in written or pictorial form.

Many educators feel that some children do better in school than others because some have socialization experiences prior to their first day of school that prepare them to benefit greatly from their formal education. Some come from families where there are many books in the home and where reading is an activity in which people frequently engage. Some children have experiences with puzzles, many of which are very similar to the sorts of tests used to analyze their analytical skills. An especially interesting cultural difference involves the concept, "conversational partners." Who are acceptable conversational partners for adults in various cultures? In some, the answer is "only other adults." In these cultures, adults rarely sit down with children and have a long conversation involving several rounds of verbal exchanges. In other cultures, such as the middle-class United States, it is considered quite acceptable for adults to have long conversations with children, and it is a recommended practice for children's language development. Children accustomed to adults as conversational partners will be far more prepared to benefit from interactions with their schoolteachers than children unfamiliar with such interactions with adults.

The fact that some children are familiar with adults as conversational partners is an example of socialization experiences that can lead to a smooth transition into their formal education. Various researchers have argued that there are various aspects of children's cultural background that, if recognized by school officials, can lead to greater success for the children (Laboratory of Comparative Human Cognition, 1986; Cushner, 1990). One of the most carefully evaluated examples is the Kamehameha Elementary Education Program (KEEP) in Hawaii (Vogt, Jordan, & Tharp, 1987). Research was carried out to determine what children are familiar with given their everyday socialization experiences. One finding was that Hawaiian children take part in group activities far more than children from other cultural groups. One group activity is called "talk-story" in which children have extensive verbal exchanges with others about familiar events, or stories, in their lives. Taking advantage of these socialization experiences, the KEEP researchers designed an educational program that involved a great deal of group learning. The program to teach reading integrated "talk-story." Children would read a story from a book and then discuss it with others in the manner with which they were familiar: many interruptions, many overlapping verbal contributions, and so forth. Evaluation studies showed that the program was very effective in teaching children in the early elementary school years to read at grade level. A disappointing finding was that children did not maintain their grade level reading skills as they moved into the upper elementary and junior high schools years.

One reason for the lack of skill maintenance may involve the children's families (Cushner, 1990; Kim, 1990). Skills learned in school may not be reinforced at home, not by any direct interference by family members but because they are unfamiliar and perhaps uncomfortable with the skills their children or siblings have developed. Realizing this strong possibility, Kagitcibasi (1990) introduced home-based schooling in her native country, Turkey. Teachers work with both children and mothers. Teachers suggest ways that mothers can interact with their children so that they can encourage their cognitive growth. Evaluation studies have shown that the mothers increase their own self-esteem and become more confident of their abilities to encourage their children's development. They become more comfortable with the autonomy their children develop in solving problems on their own *without* the need for as much dependence on the family. An especially interesting finding is that even though the home-based schooling is aimed at certain children and their parents, the skills developed are picked up by younger siblings. This generalization to younger children takes place during observations of the teachers' activities as well as from later interactions with their more knowledgeable peers and mothers.

In some countries, an emphasis on doing well in school, together with parental encouragement concerning homework, reading at home, and good grades, is so widespread that researchers have looked to cultural factors. Many observers, including journalists, researchers, and business-people concerned with education, have argued that Asian-Americans are highly successful in American schools. Attempting to identify cultural differences, Ritter and Dornbusch (1989) found that Asian-Americans, compared to other cultural groups in the United States, were more likely to believe that success in school had a strong relationship to success in other aspects of society, such as finding a good job and earning a good salary. Developing this idea, Sue and Okazaki (1990) argued that the hard work in school can be explained in terms of "relative functionalism." Asian-Americans examine various aspects of society and ask themselves, "Where will work be reinforced? Where will prejudice be least? Where will we receive fair treatment, regardless of our skin color or accent?" After their examination, they conclude that *relative* to other parts of society, hard work in school will bring rewards. Hard work will be useful, or *functional* in helping them to acquire the benefits that society has to offer.

Are there other uses that formal schooling serves for people? Research on this question has led to the important conclusion that schools are often treated as places to address some of society's problems. When other parts of society cannot deal with a problem effectively, it is sometimes turned over to the schools. In the United States, such problems include preparing people to drive automobiles, encouraging them to avoid drug and alcohol abuse, introducing racial integration, and practicing birth control. Society's leaders make demands of their formal educational system as early as the preschool years. In work carried out in Japan, China, and the United States, Tobin, Wu, and Davidson (1989a,b) found cultural differences in the expectations placed upon preschools. In Japan, schools are expected to encourage children to become part of a group and to become empathetic with and concerned about others. In China, schools are expected to deal with the "4-2-1" problem, that is, one child being spoiled by two parents and four grandparents who are overly attentive to the child's every wish. The schools are seen as the place where spoiling is to cease and where children will learn to be productive and hard-working members of Chinese society. In the United States, adults expect that preschools will encourage self-reliance and self-confidence among children. These skills are useful in an individualistic society in which people have to set goals and work toward them *without* the constant presence of a collective whose members are committed to helping each other. The future of education in the United States will undoubtedly include attention to the balance between individualistic strivings for personal goals and a concern for others, such as for the less fortunate who find themselves without homes, without skills for the job market, and without strong representation by influential political leaders.

Another aspect of formal education that may receive more attention is the value placed on fluency in more than one language. In a global economy, society should value bilingualism and multilingualism. One way this could be given attention is through bilingual education programs. Such programs, however, have been the topic of heated, often unpleasant debate. Many opponents of bilingual education feel that one of the unifying forces in a society is that all citizens should be fluent in one language (e.g., English in the United States). They feel that attention to other languages takes time and energy away from efforts to make children fluent in English. Educators argue that a mistake is often made when this position is put forward. Most bilingual education programs are *transitional* (Hakuta, 1986), meaning that children start school in the language of their parents (e.g., Spanish, Vietnamese), but move toward all-English instruction over a period of two or three years. Programs aimed at *maintenance*, where children are encouraged to keep and to develop their first language while simultaneously learning English, are less common.

Bilingual education programs must enter the political arena where many proposals for ways to improve children's schooling are considered. Many adults, just as concerned with the welfare of children as proponents of bilingual education, feel that other programs are more useful. These include instruction in English-as-a-second-language (ESL) by well-trained teachers; programs to bring society's brightest college graduates into the teaching profession; efforts to increase the status of teachers by increasing their salaries and giving them more decision-making power, and so forth. All these worthy programs have to compete for such scarce resources as funding, the attention of the school boards in various communities, and the support of concerned parent groups.

One factor that will influence the future of bilingual education programs is whether or not adults in America will value people's knowledge of more than one language, or whether adults will continue with the belief that "English only" language skills are sufficient. These attitudes toward language, in turn, will be influenced by how Americans view people who are different from themselves in terms of skin color, cultural values and practices, accent when using English, and so forth. To understand people's views of others who are different than themselves, we must understand issues such as stereotyping, prejudice, and discrimination. These are the topics addressed in the next chapter.

6

INTERGROUP RELATIONS:
CULTURES IN CONTACT

If there are three predictions we can make with certainty about the twenty-first century, they are that people will continue to experience death, continue to be taxed, and continue to experience extensive intercultural contact. As discussed in Chapter 1, an interdependent global economy, the worldwide movement toward democratic forms of government, the insistence of minority groups that their cultural heritages be recognized, and laws prohibiting overt discrimination all lead to the conclusion that people must be prepared to interact effectively with members of cultural groups other than their own. Various arguments about intercultural contact (also referred to frequently as intergroup relations: e.g., Stephan, 1985) have been made in the first five chapters of this book. In Chapter 1, the argument was made that one of the best ways to gain insights into cultural differences is to interact frequently with people from other cultures. When unchallenged by the presence of differences, culture becomes much like the air we breathe: We begin to take it for granted. We think about the air only when it is taken away, and we think about culture only when the familiar behaviors we learned during our own socialization *fail* to help us achieve our goals in different social settings. In Chapter 2, various theoretical concepts were discussed, one being the difference between individualism and collectivism in people's orientation toward others in their lives. Understanding this distinction allows advice to be offered for individualists about to interact extensively in collectivist cultures and for collectivists about to interact in individualist cultures.

In Chapter 3, some basic ideas about cross-cultural research methods were introduced. Suggestions were made concerning the understanding of complex concepts in different cultures. One approach is to identify aspects of the concepts that are common across cultures (e.g., intelligence as socially valued), and others that are specific to different cultures (e.g., intelligence as a quality involving "quick" versus "slow and careful" thought). When people from different cultures come into contact, the culture specific aspects must be given special attention. These are the aspects that will be most puzzling and most problematic for people encountering another culture for the first time.

In Chapter 4, the processes through which people are socialized into their own culture were discussed. One of the arguments made is that people are socialized to become familiar with a number of social settings in which important behaviors take place in their culture. One example is the family setting, involving many socializing agents in the traditional collective culture and fewer people in individualistic cultures. When there is culture change, such as the shift from a collective to an individualist lifestyle brought on by urbanization and the nucleation of families, stress can result when people are unfamiliar with the new social settings in which they are expected to interact. In Chapter 5, the differences between informal and formal education were discussed. Extremely impactful culture contact occurs in the institution called "the school." Children from some cultural backgrounds are far more prepared to benefit from schools than other children given that typical socialization practices (e.g., interacting as conversational partners with adults) are similar to practices encountered in the school. Other children have far more difficulty benefiting from school attendance given that the behaviors encountered there are so different from those with which they are familiar. Various interventions such as programs to prepare teachers to understand cultural differences, efforts to integrate behaviors with which children are already familiar into the school curriculum, and teaching in languages familiar to the children (e.g., through bilingual education programs) have been developed to ease the stress of culture contact.

Other examples of extensive intercultural contact will be examined in future chapters concerned with the workplace (Chapter 8), with general roles and gender differences (Chapter 9), and with the delivery of health-care services (Chapter 10). The pervasiveness of intercultural contact demands that its complexity be understood. Two chapters will be devoted to this topic. The present chapter draws from the work of behavioral and social scientists who have been concerned with the *difficulties* that intergroup contact brings to the people involved and to society at large. The starting point of this chapter is that we must understand the prejudicial attitudes and discriminatory behavior of people who would prefer to *avoid* intergroup interaction if they could. Much of this work has been done in the context of explaining long-standing stereotypes and intense negative feelings, for example, among Black and Whites in the United States. In addition to understanding the negative feelings, interventions have been studied that have attempted to improve intergroup relations, and the successes of such interventions have led to good advice that administrators of future intervention programs should consider. The next chapter (7), while not ignoring or even setting aside the difficulties involved in encouraging intercultural contact, begins with the assumption that many people recognize that intense prejudice and discrimination are no longer acceptable (Devine, Monteith, Zuwerink, & Elliot, 1991). In addition, the chapter assumes that many people are willing to communicate effectively with people from other cultures in the workplace, in schools, in their neighborhoods, and so forth. Given this willingness, the questions then become: What are the problems we will face given that intercultural contact will increase in the future? We are willing to be cooperative but realize that we need help. Are there insights from cross-cultural studies that will assist us?

This chapter on the difficulties of intergroup relations is organized into four sections:

1. understanding stereotypes, or generalizations that people make about others that ignore individual differences within the stereotyped group;
2. understanding the functions of prejudice, or the reasons why people have strong feelings about others who differ on dimensions such as skin color and cultural background;
3. understanding the *forms* that prejudice can take, especially those that involve discrimination such that members of certain groups are put at a disadvantage; and
4. understanding the types of interventions that have led to improvements in relations among people from different cultural groups.

STEREOTYPES

Stereotypes refer to beliefs about a group of people that give insufficient attention to individual differences among members of that group. Whenever statements are made that "Blacks are . . . ," "Native Americans do not . . . ," or "Japanese prefer . . . ," the content is stereotypical because there is no attention given to the differences among individual Blacks, Native Americans, and Japanese. Stereotypes refer to beliefs about any group of people, and so statements that describe "Republicans," "fraternity members," "career women," "full professors on this campus," or "graduating seniors" are stereotypical unless they clearly include recognition of differences within groups of people.

Much recent research on stereotypes has dealt with the ways in which people use their normal thinking skills on a day-to-day basis. Stereotypes should not be viewed as a sign of abnormality. Rather, they reflect people's need to organize, remember, and retrieve information that might be useful to them as they attempt to achieve their goals and to meet life's demands. This emphasis on normal thought processes has led researchers to borrow heavily from studies by psychologists and educators who investigate cognition and cognitive processes (Stephan, 1985; Messick & Mackie, 1989; Hilton & Von Hippel, 1990).

One important cognitive process, part of normal human thinking, is the development of categories. People cannot respond to each and every individual piece of information to which they are exposed. The vast majority of readers of this chapter will not know the brand name of the lightbulbs that are illuminating this page. The last time they road in a car, readers did not pay attention to the manufacturer of the various automobiles that they saw. Instead of this attention to detail, people form categories and then react to the categories as a unit. Regarding lightbulbs, people have at most three categories: sufficient illumination, burned out and in need of replacement, and insufficient illumination and in need of replacement by a brighter bulb. For automobiles, people probably have three categories: those that are going in the opposite direction, those going in the same direction as I am, and those changing direction that might come close to me. People then respond to the categories as if all members were the same. When driving, people don't respond individually to the interesting features of each car they see, such as whether it is a classic 1957 Chevrolet, whether it has had a recent paint job, or whether it has whitewall tires. If they did, they would pay insufficient attention to their driving and get into accidents! Rather, they use a category, such as "changing direction close to me," and then react accordingly.

Categories also exist for the people whom we know. As much as we might like, we cannot respond individually to all the people we see on an average day. If we did, we would never get from one place to another since we would have to stop and talk with so many people. Instead, we form categories. While walking 100 yards or more during daytime hours on a college campus, any one individual places other people into one of approximately four categories: (1) people not at all well known and who need no sign of recognition from the individual; (2) people known slightly for whom a nod of the head and a "hello" will do; (3) people who are better known, and for whom the individual needs to say a few more words, such as "How's it going?" or "Have you finished your term paper?"; and (4) people who are very well known and for whom the individual must stop and have a rather extensive chat. These four categories summarize information about the other people (in this case, how well known they are) and they also give guidance to the individual in making decisions about his or her own behavior.

Stereotypes are categories about people (Allport, 1954; Brislin, 1981). As such, they have all the features of categories, especially the organization of specific bits of information and subsequent reaction to the category as a whole. If there is a well-formed stereotype about some ethnic or cultural group, then people may use that stereotype when they interact with any one individual who is a member of that group. If people meet me, for instance, knowing only that I am Irish-American, they might use the information from the relevant stereotype: musical, hard-drinking, fun-loving, Catholic background, ancestors who came to America to escape famine, quick-tempered, and so forth. As with most stereotypes *applied to individuals*, much of this content is inaccurate.

Categories in general and stereotypes in particular are shortcuts to thinking. People have to make so many decisions about their behavior during a given day that they need guidance, hints, helpful rules, and so forth. Stereotypes serve this purpose. Assume that a White college student meets a tall, thin Black student for the first time. The White has to make a number of decisions: Should I assume a friendly demeanor or be more reserved? What should we talk about? Should I indicate that I want future interaction with this person? The White wants guidance, and the stereotype of Blacks can provide some. If the stereotype includes the belief that "Blacks are aloof and unfriendly toward Whites," then this gives guidance to the decision concerning a friendly versus reserved demeanor. If the stereotype includes the belief that tall Blacks are on campus to play basketball, this can guide the choice of a conversational topic. If the stereotype includes the belief that Blacks prefer to stick to their own group, this will influence the decision concerning future interactions. The key point is that attaching a stereotype to a person allows all the information in that stereotype to be brought to prominence in people's thinking. Stereotypes are found whenever people can use a label that they can attach to a certain group. When labels are used, they can place limits on the behavior of individuals who are assigned the label. In the business world, for instance (Morrison & Von Glinow, 1990), if the stereotype of women includes "inability to make tough decisions," they may not be given the types of job assignments that lead to promotion into the senior executive ranks. In a university or community counseling center, there could be a stereotype that Hispanic clients are less serious about working with a counselor since they drop out after a few sessions and do not return to the center (Atkinson, Morten, & Sue, 1989). This stereotype can affect decisions about funding priorities during the next budget hearings when administrators present their plans for the counseling center's future.

STEREOTYPES AS PART OF A CULTURE. If similar stereotypes exist about some labeled group generation after generation within a society, they become part of the culture (Biernat, 1991). They meet the criteria (Chapter 1) of culture-influenced behavior such as "widely shared," "transmitted from parents and other elders to children," and "the subject of memorable childhood experiences." Most readers will probably be able to think back on their childhood and remember an adult saying, "If you don't behave yourself, you'll end up just like the _____ !" The word that completes the sentence is the name of some downtrodden group in a community. My experience in working with Americans as well as citizens of Asian and Pacific Island nations is that virtually everyone remembers adults saying such things. The only difference is the *name* of the group that adults used to get children to behave themselves by eating their vegetables, completing their homework, or doing their chores.

A useful exercise for readers is to list the names of various groups in their communities. Then, write down various words that describe these groups. The words can refer to traits of people in the group, to their attitudes, or to behaviors that are expected of people in the group. Then, readers can compare their lists with those prepared by others. A number of features can then be examined. For a given group, is the content of the stereotype similar across various people who completed the exercise? What percentage of the stereotype is positive and what percentage is negative? Recall that stereotypes refer to descriptions of people that give insufficient attention to individual differences. Although the content of stereotypes could include terms that put the group in a favorable light, stereotypes more frequently include large amounts of very negative content. Another feature of the lists that can be examined is whether or not the stereotypes might influence various behaviors. For instance, might the stereotypes affect whether or not people will seek out future interaction with each other? Might the stereotypes affect the opportunities that people are offered? For example, Atkinson, Morten, and Sue (1989, p. 23) discussed how stereotypes can affect the advice given to people from different groups:

> If Black students are seen as possessing limited intellectual potential, they may be counseled into terminal vocational school trades. Likewise, if Asian Americans are perceived as being good only in the physical sciences but poor in verbal-people professions, counselors may direct them toward a predominance of science courses. . . . Many minorities may eventually come to believe these stereotypes about themselves. Thus, since the majority of stereotypes about minorities are negative, an inferior sense of self-esteem may develop.

AVOIDING THE NEGATIVE CONSEQUENCES OF STEREOTYPES.
Given that people cannot respond to the specific traits, needs, and goals of every individual whom they meet, they will have to group people together and then respond according to their knowledge of that group or category. In so doing, they run the risk of stereotyping the other individual and putting him or her at a disadvantage. What is the difference between making reasonable generalizations about other people and stereotyping? There is no easy answer to this question, and the area between "well-thought-out generalization" and "stereotype" is very gray. Over a period of 20 years, almost all meetings I have attended that dealt with intercultural interaction and cross-cultural research have generated charges that one or another speaker stereotyped members of some cultural group. It can be argued that I have done this in earlier chapters of this book. In Chapter 1, I discussed the case of women in the Philippines (and other parts of the world) who become upset when former romantic partners want to maintain cordial, friendly relations. In Chapter 4, I discussed the case of people in India who move from rural to urban areas, leave behind various support groups, and experience stress when adjusting to a new lifestyle. In Chapter 5, I discussed the development of reading programs that took

advantage of group activities with which schoolchildren in Hawaii are already familiar given their everyday behavior in their culture.

When looked at carefully, there are exceptions to all of these generalizations about people in the Philippines, India, and Hawaii. Some women in the Philippines are very gracious after the breakup of romances and are more than happy to maintain cordial friendships. Some Indians experience little or no stress after moving from rural to urban areas. Some children in Hawaii are not particularly familiar with the group activities that formed the basis of a new reading program. In fact, some children have to become familiar with the group activities (such as story telling, or "talk-story") *before* they can benefit from the reading program. In other words, there are exceptions to the generalizations. And this is one of the key differences between stereotypes and reasonable generalizations: When using stereotypes, people do not consciously consider individual differences. When thinking in terms of careful generalizations, people are constantly willing to entertain the possibility of individual differences (e.g., Toupin & Son, 1991). Nancy Adler (1991) has developed a checklist to help move people away from the negative consequences of stereotypes. Before discussing it, a case study in which I was involved may make some points about stereotyping clearer.

Virginia was a newly hired foreign student adviser at a large American university. She had received her own college degree in biology about 3 years ago, served overseas in the Peace Corps for 2 years, and then returned to the United States where she entered the job market. During her years in the Peace Corps, she observed large amounts of intercultural contact given that universities sponsored study tours through which students could receive college credit for overseas travel that combined "experiencing another culture" with reading and writing assignments. On a voluntary and informal basis, Virginia hosted a few of these groups, became interested in working with students, and began to search for jobs at colleges and universities after her return to the United States.

Although she hoped her job would involve developing various programs that would enrich the education of students at the university where she worked, Virginia found that much of her job involved a great deal of administrative detail. Were the visas of foreign students up to date? Were they taking the required courses that would allow them to graduate on time? Did they have adequate funds for housing, meals, and tuition? Could their spouses work in the community under the type of visa that they had? For Americans contemplating a year of study abroad, could they take courses whose credit would transfer back to the university, or would they have to attend school for another semester to graduate? Virginia dealt effectively with these administrative matters and occasionally found time to participate in enrichment activities, such as arranging for foreign students to serve as guest lecturers in various courses on campus and in nearby high schools. She had especially good working relations with a number of professors who called on her regularly to either give a lecture herself or to recommend one of the foreign students whom she knew. One of the professors was Charles Adams.

One day, Professor Adams phoned Virginia. He said, "I think I have one of the students you see frequently in one of my classes. Michael—he's from Nigeria. I've got a problem! Michael turned in a term paper in which he just wrote down words from a number of books—no citations, no indication that he was using the ideas of other people. It's a plagiarism case. I have to give him an 'F' grade, and I'm thinking of sending the information on to the Dean for possible disciplinary action. Do you have any advice?"

Fortunately, Virginia had studied some books on foreign-student advising where issues such as this were treated (e.g., Althen, 1984). Virginia explained that Michael came from a culture that had a different orientation toward knowledge. In Nigeria (and in many other cultures), knowledge is not attached to one person. Once somebody discovers something and writes about it, the knowledge is considered open and accessible to anyone who might use it. People feel free, then, to use passages from books (considered open knowledge) without the need to provide specific references concerning the exact source of this knowledge. There is not the demand, as there is in the United States and other parts of the world, to make links between the knowledge and the developer of the knowledge through conventions like references to books and articles, footnotes, and bibliographies. Virginia continued, "It's quite possible Michael was just behaving according to what is familiar in his culture and had no intention to cheat at all. I recommend that all this be carefully explained to him, but that it not be referred to the Dean." The professor accepted Virginia's recommendation. Both he and Virginia discussed what American professors consider to be "plagiarism." Michael understood and never had any more problems with his papers for other classes.

A few months after this incident, Virginia was asked to plan for the cross-cultural training program that would prepare *next year's* foreign students to benefit from the time they would be spending at the university. Remembering the stress Michael experienced when he heard that he might have to see the Dean concerning a disciplinary matter, Virginia decided to have a session on preparing term papers and theses. Realizing that the problem has arisen on North American and European campuses often enough to be called "the foreign student plagiarism issue" (Althen, 1984; Brislin, Cushner, Cherrie, & Yong, 1986), Virginia decided to behave according to the adage, "An ounce of prevention is worth a pound of cure." She reasoned that if foreign students learned about term paper preparation during the cross-cultural training program, they would be less likely to run into difficulties and experience debilitating stress.

Virginia proposed this to the advisory committee that was helping with plans for the orientation program. Several voiced objections. "You're stereotyping foreign students. Many know all about what Americans consider plagiarism, and they'll be insulted if you talk about it with them.

If you have such a session, it could be interpreted as saying that foreign students are ignorant, cheats, or both. You'll just be contributing to the stereotype that foreign students are not as good as American students." At this point, Virginia sought out the advice of others (including myself) who have engaged in cross-cultural research and have developed orientation programs to prepare people for extensive intercultural contact. She received conflicting views: Some said that the stress stemming from a major disciplinary action can be reduced if students are clear about what is expected of them in university classes. Consequently, a unit of plagiarism is appropriate. Others argued that such a session would label foreign students as "potential plagiarizers" and would contribute to negative stereotypes. What decision did Virginia make about the unit on plagiarism that would be covered during the orientation program?

Virginia decided to cover the plagiarism issue during the program, and she combined it with a treatment of the relationship between reasonable generalizations about people and stereotypes. She benefited from Adler's (1991, p. 72) checklist of concepts that people should constantly keep in mind whenever they *might* make a decision based on stereotypes. Alder argues that stereotypes should be:

1. Consciously held. People using stereotypes should be fully aware that they are thinking about an individual based on that person's membership in some labeled group. Further, people should be conscious that there will be exceptions to the stereotype and that they should even actively look for these exceptions. In so doing, people will be far less likely to put others at a disadvantage based solely on a label that can be attached to them. For example, people who work with foreign students can present information by saying, "There will be many exceptions and many students will have few problems in their coursework, but enough students have difficulties preparing term papers that we think that some key points should be discussed." The danger in unconsciously held stereotypes is that people make decisions that are based on little or no thought. For instance, if a professor believes that female students are so sensitive that they cannot accept firm feedback, he or she may give detailed suggestions about improving classroom performance only to males. Consequently, males receive far more opportunities to improve than do females. Or, if professors believe that minority group members are less capable, they may suggest that students tackle far easier topics for their term papers than other students. Consequently, minority group members have fewer opportunities to rise to challenges. These stereotypes are even more dangerous when they are so familiar to the professors that they are applied in an unconscious manner. The self-imposed intervention has to be self-generated thoughts such as, "I realize I might stereotype if I don't think about the different students in my classes. I must make sure that females receive the same sorts of feedback as males, and that minorities receive suggestions about their term paper topics that challenge them."

2. Descriptive. As much as possible, generalizations about people should describe behavior and should contain no evaluative commentary about the behavior. Further, there can be active searches for complexity to move people away from the oversimplified thinking that is so common in the use of stereotypes. For example, the statement can be made, "Some foreign students turn in term papers that do not meet the standards of professors in terms of how ideas are referenced and how bibliographies are prepared." This is a descriptive statement, and it allows the presentation of additional material, such as model term papers that received good grades. Complexity can be added if reasons are given for the different ways that students in various parts of the world prepare written work, as was discussed previously when the "openness of knowledge" was contrasted with the view that "ideas should be attached to the individuals who developed them."

3. Accurate. Whenever possible, careful searches should be made to determine whether the generalizations that people *might* put forward are supported by various types of evidence. Given that many people have very little contact with members of groups other than their own (Taylor, Dube, & Bellerose, 1986; Kealey, 1988, 1989), pure and simple ignorance can have a major impact on intercultural relations (Stephan & Stephan, 1984). One danger in using stereotypes is that people who hear them conclude that people in the labeled group behave in a manner different than people in other groups. For example, if people hear the statement that "foreign students have run into plagiarism problems," it is easy for them to conclude (perhaps erroneously) that "foreign students are accused of plagiarism more often than American students." If people who work with foreign students have access to the information, they might compare the number of American students who have had disciplinary hearings concerning plagiarism with the number of foreign students who have had similar hearings. If the numbers are similar (as they are on many campuses), they can add this information to the cross-cultural orientation program for foreign students. They can say, "We've checked, and foreign students have no more problems with plagiarism than American students, but it is so stressful to *anyone* who is called to a disciplinary hearing that we are covering it in this orientation program." Returning to the examples of constructive feedback to women and the suggestion of research topics to members of minority groups, the concern for accuracy can be added to the concern that generalizations be consciously held. After thinking about whether or not a stereotype is being applied, professors can ask themselves, "What hard evidence am I using when I deal with my female and minority group students differently than my Anglo male students?"

4. The first best guess. Any stereotype should be looked on as only providing guidance for a first guess about the way an individual might behave. Then, as people make a point of discovering more information about the individual, they move beyond the first guess with the conscious addition of new evidence and complexity (Toupin & Son, 1991), as already discussed. When people move beyond the first best guess, they often discover information that will be useful in their future interactions. Earlier, it was mentioned that Hispanic clients often do not keep their appointments at mental health clinics. If the counselors in the clinic quickly move beyond the first guess about "not serious about dealing with important issues," they can examine other information such as various demands on the client's time, transportation difficulties, the acceptability of what happens in a counseling session from the client's viewpoint, the cultural sensitivity of the counselor, and so forth (Atkinson, Morten, & Sue, 1989).

5. *Modifiable.* Once people show a willingness to move beyond a first best guess, they indicate a willingness to modify their generalization based on the additional information that they find. The modifications often take the form of adding great amounts of complexity to generalizations that recognize various exceptions based on differences in people's socialization experiences *within* a culture, their age, education, employment history, and so forth. One of the major "messages" of cross-cultural research, but at the same time one of the most difficult to communicate, is that there is often more difference *within* a culture than there is *between* two or more different cultures. For instance, there is likely to be more differences in the stress level within a group of Indian 20-year-olds who move from rural to urban areas than there is between these Indians and a group of 20-year-old Americans. This fact does not negate the necessity of studying stressful life experiences—it only reminds us that people are very complex and that simple statements are rarely very helpful. This fact can also direct people to sharpen their thinking with more complex questions such as why some Indians make the rural to urban move with little stress (e.g., presence of support groups in the urban area; Sinha, 1988), and why there is more stress among some 20-year-old Americans than others. In both cases, simple stereotypes are inadequate and people must modify them in the direction of more complexity.

PREJUDICE: ITS FUNCTIONS

The difficulty with stereotypes, of course, is that very few people put the amount of care into thinking about other groups to the degree contained in the five-point set of recommendations. Rather, people are much more likely to use oversimplified stereotypes that deny individuality and uniqueness to a person just because he or she can be conveniently labeled as a member of some group. In many cultures, stereotypes of certain groups are so negative, so pervasive, and have existed for so many generations that they can be considered part of the culture into which children are socialized. In these cases, the stereotypes become *part* of people's prejudicial feelings about other groups.

Prejudice refers to the emotional component of people's reactions to other groups. There is not only a set of beliefs about others, which are captured in stereotypes, there is also a deeply felt set of feelings about what is good and bad, right and wrong, moral and immoral, and so forth. Although prejudices can be positive, for example romantic feelings about Pacific Island nations as near-utopias that are unaffected by the ills of civilization (Daws, 1977), they more often refer to very negative feelings about others. Analyzing the components of the word, prejudices also involve a *pre-judging* of others based on limited knowledge and limited contact. There is a close relationship between negative stereotypes and prejudice since people have feelings (or prejudices) about various traits and beliefs (the content of the stereotypes) that others are seen to possess. Jordan (1989, p. 1119) also makes a link between the two when he argues that negative "stereotypes may be defined as the bundles of belief carried by the energy" of people's attitudes about other groups, or their prejudices.

Prejudices about other groups that differ in some way, such as skin color, accent, cultural practices, and social-class background, are a universal aspect of human behavior (LeVine & Campbell, 1972), found in all cultures and in all eras of recorded history. Despite vigorous attempts to change people in the direction of tolerance toward and acceptance of others (e.g., Miller & Brewer, 1984; Stephan, 1985; Adler, 1991), prejudices have been remarkably persistent and continue to be learned by children during their socialization. A good exercise for students is to think about their own socialization and to remember times when they were discouraged from developing close relations with people from certain groups and were *encouraged* to think negatively about them. Memories could include interventions by adults when the others were invited to a party, or when the others were found acceptable only in certain social settings (e.g., on athletic teams, but not study groups in school). If students compare their memories, they will undoubtedly find a striking amount of similarity. These memories frequently include the feelings that people from certain groups are in many ways inferior. They are less able to accept adult responsibilities, such as holding down good jobs. They are better suited for manual labor than managerial and professional white-collar jobs. The memories also include the advice that it is usually best to keep the others at a distance—people will benefit more from life's opportunities if they don't limit themselves by too much attachment to the other groups.

As they hear different adults giving such advice, children learn that there are clear "ingroups" and "outgroups" in their lives. A division of people into distinct ingroups and outgroups is another universal aspect of human behavior (LeVine & Campbell, 1972). Ingroups refer to those individuals about whom a person has positive feelings. Further, the person interacts with these others frequently and can depend upon them in times of need. These others are thought of as "similar to me," and their approval or disapproval of various behaviors are considered important. Outgroups refer to those individuals who are kept at a distance and about whom a person has far less positive feelings. Outgroup members are often viewed as "too different" to be considered as deserving of the person's time, effort, and concern. When people are asked to describe who they *are*, they often list the names of their ingroups, such as their family, group of friends, co-workers, and so forth. When asked to describe who they *are not*, they often list the names of their outgroups.

As the term is most frequently used, "prejudice" refers to negative feelings about outgroups. The most important reason why prejudicial attitudes are so resistant to change is because they serve clear functions for people. The concept of functions was discussed in Chapter 5 when possible reasons were suggested for Asian-Americans' success in schools. The concept of relative functionalism was introduced: Asian-Americans view success in schools as functional for achieving success in other aspects of society, such as respect in the work world and influence in their communities. Another word for functional is "useful." Hard work in school is seen as useful in the attainment of many goals in life. Prejudices also serve a number of functions—they are useful to people. Because they are so useful and because they have brought certain benefits to people (as described below), individuals who hold the prejudicial attitudes are resistant to change. The concept of attitudes as serving various functions was most fully developed by Daniel Katz (1960), and I have applied his framework to the case of prejudicial attitudes (Brislin, 1978, 1986). Prejudices serve one or more of four functions for people.

THE UTILITARIAN OR ADJUSTMENT FUNCTION. People hold certain prejudices because they lead to various rewards in their society and to the *avoidance* of punishment. These prejudices have a utility in helping people collect rewards. If people collect enough rewards valued in their society, they are very likely to experience a smooth adjustment into a comfortable lifestyle. Jordan (1989) argues that the White view of Blacks as inferior in abilities is long-standing and is an attitude that was brought to America by its earliest settlers rather than an attitude that developed after the importation of slaves. One reason was utilitarian: By viewing Blacks as inferior and not worthy of society's benefits, Whites could exploit Blacks as a cheap source of labor. Rather than work in the hot sun day after day, Whites could achieve a comfortable lifestyle by forcing Blacks to work long hours in the fields. If the Whites ever experienced a challenge to their consciences concerning this exploitation, they could justify their behavior by arguing that Blacks would be much worse off if they didn't have Whites to protect them and to offer them honest work. Even after slavery was eliminated, prejudicial views concerning Blacks continued to be useful. If Whites wanted jobs in the professions, such as law, medicine, or teaching at the college level, the widespread view that Blacks are less able meant that there was less competition for these well-paying, high-status jobs.

Understanding the utilitarian function means understanding access to rewards and the avoidance of punishment. In addition to insights into

American history, as in the example of slavery and institutionalized discrimination extending over centuries, the utilitarian function can be seen in people's everyday activities. In many parts of the world, people continue to be discouraged from interacting with individuals from certain outgroups. Assume that a husband and wife move into a neighborhood where prejudicial views prevail. They decide to work toward intergroup tolerance and harmony by seeking out interaction with many different people, including people whom the community leaders consider to be members of outgroups. A married couple may be able to withstand the pressure that community leaders put on them to "keep things the way they have always been." But what about the couple's children? Imagine the punishments that can be inflicted: taunting in the schools, lack of invitations to parties, being ignored on the playground during recess, having one's athletic talents ignored and not being given a chance for an honest tryout for the school team, and so forth. Few parents can maintain their stubborn insistence on intergroup tolerance in the face of such punishments inflicted on their children.

THE EGO-DEFENSIVE FUNCTION. People hold certain prejudices because they do not want to acknowledge various deficiencies. If they hold prejudices that blame outgroups for these deficiencies, people do not have to examine their own inadequacies. Certain prejudices, then, protect people's sense of self-worth. In everyday language, one person sometimes says of another, "He (or she) has a healthy ego." One way to protect, or to defend one's ego is to blame difficulties on other people. Prejudices against Jewish people have often had an ego-defensive component. Rather than examine one's own skills as they relate to potential success in the business world, it is easier to blame Jews for banding together and making it difficult for anyone else to start new companies (Allport, 1954). After the devastation brought on by World War I, German leaders blamed defeat on the Jews, thus protecting themselves from examining the mistakes that led to failure. Another ego-defensive prejudice stems from people's socialization into their culture (Chapter 4). People put large amounts of time and effort into learning acceptable behaviors in their culture. They come to believe that they behave in a "correct" and "proper manner." This is another cultural universal—people come to believe that their culture presents its members with the "best" set of guidelines for meeting life's goals. These beliefs become part of people's sense of personal identity— their ego. When members of other cultures behave in different ways, they are viewed negatively. These negative views allow the people holding them to protect their own sense of self-esteem. Additionally, if people automatically dismiss "different" behaviors as "unworthy of attention," they will not be motivated to examine their own culture to identify areas where changes in behavior (e.g., diet, conservation of resources, etc.) will yield benefits. For example, if Americans believe that their diet is the best in the world, they will not be motivated to examine diets common to other

cultures where there is less cancer, less heart disease, less obesity, and so
forth (Ilola, 1990, Chapter 10, this volume).

THE VALUE-EXPRESSIVE FUNCTION. People hold certain prejudices
because they want to express and to communicate values that they believe
to be correct, moral, and ethical. By viewing themselves as "right," they
put forward various prejudices that communicate their positive view of
themselves. The ego-defensive and value-defensive functions are related in
an important way. When people hold ego-defensive prejudices, they are
protecting themselves from admissions that aspects of themselves or their
culture may be inadequate. Ego-defensive prejudices allow people to *hide*
certain features about themselves from the rest of the world. When people
hold value-expressive prejudices, they are attempting to *communicate* what
they believe is correct. In sharp contrast to hiding their attitudes and
values, they attempt to make them as clear as possible. For example,
people who hold negative attitudes about members of a specific religious
group may view themselves as standing up for the "one true religion of
God." People who view people with a different skin color as inferior may

People who direct the behavior of others often become intoxicated with power.

view themselves as belonging to a superior race. When expressing these attitudes about religion and skin color, people are not hiding their beliefs about themselves—they are attempting to communicate that they are better than others.

As discussed above when the utilitarian function of attitudes was introduced, one reason for the centuries-long prejudice of Whites toward Blacks involved people's lifestyles. If Blacks were viewed as inferior, then Whites could exploit them as manual laborers and maintain a less arduous lifestyle themselves. Whites, then, became accustomed to dominating another race and exercising power over it. One of many evils that stems from dominance is that the people wielding power come to enjoy it, seek more of it, and come to view themselves as the only people who can use power responsibly (Kipnis, 1976; Brislin, 1991). Another reason for the long-standing domination of Whites over Blacks was that it reinforced White views of themselves as superior (Jordan, 1989). Power *is* intoxicating—it gives pleasure to people wielding it and eventually "goes to their heads." Lord Acton was correct: Power corrupts and absolute power corrupts absolutely. As Whites dominated Blacks decade after decade to obtain their cheap labor, they eventually came to believe that such an arrangement was natural, moral, and correct. White views that Blacks are fit only for manual labor came to serve their value-expressive needs. By keeping Blacks submissive, Whites could communicate clearly that they viewed themselves as worthy of their superior position in society.

THE KNOWLEDGE FUNCTION. People hold certain prejudices because such attitudes allow them to organize the various pieces of information to which they are exposed. There is a great deal of overlap between prejudices that serve a knowledge function and stereotypes. The major difference for the purposes of this presentation is that discussions of stereotypes usually do not include an analysis of the functions that they serve for people as they make various decisions in their daily lives. As discussed previously, stereotypes are bundles of information that are brought to mind when people think about a group label, whether that label is "Hispanic," "Black," "working woman," "Republican," or "fraternity/ sorority member." When the *content* of stereotypes supplies the "facts" that people use when making decisions, then the stereotypes are serving the knowledge function. For example, assume that parents are deciding on the school they want their children to attend, and that different schools are in neighborhoods that attract students from various racial and ethnic groups. If parents make their decision based on their beliefs about the abilities of children from different groups, then they are using stereotypes to serve the knowledge function. Or, assume that staff members in a counseling center can attend one of several conferences devoted to the special problems faced by members of different cultural groups. If they believe that people from some groups are more serious about working on their problems than others, they may make their decision based on stereotype-influenced "knowledge." If attitudes serve *only* the knowledge function, they can be changed as long as people can present more accurate knowledge. If educators, for instance, can demonstrate to concerned parents that there are no differences in the abilities and motivation of culturally diverse students within their community, the parents will cease to use this information in their decision.

The difficulty, however, is that attitudes rarely serve only one function. In the case of the parents making a decision about school, they undoubtedly possess views about other groups that they consider "knowledge." But they may also be insecure about their own abilities as parents and may hold prejudicial views about others so that they do not have to examine themselves (ego-defensive function). In addition, they may have developed the idea that they belong to a group that deserves special attention by the educational system given their superior status in society (value-expressive function). By maintaining such views, they make sure that more time, attention, and funding is devoted to the education of their children (utilitarian function). Given this complexity, attempts to change attitudes that deal only with the knowledge function are likely to fail given that the three other functions go unaddressed.

PREJUDICE: ITS FORMS

In addition to the necessity for understanding the functions that prejudices serve for people, it is also essential to understand the different forms that prejudices take when expressed (Brislin, 1986; Divine et al., 1991; Sears & Funk, 1991). Just as change programs will be successful only if they deal with the various functions that prejudices serve for particular people, the programs must also deal with the different ways those same people express their views about outgroup members.

INTENSE RACISM. Some people believe that virtually all members of certain outgroups are inferior in various ways and are not able to benefit fully from society's offerings such as education, good jobs, and participation in community affairs. Racism centers on the belief that, given the simple fact that individuals were born into a certain outgroup, those individuals are inferior on such dimensions as intelligence, morals, and an ability to interact in "decent" society. Other terms that end with "ism" also have the connotation that because of a fact surrounding their birth, certain individuals are less capable than others. For example, sex*ism* involves the belief that women are less capable than men in certain areas, such as leadership or decision making. Until very recently, many of the professions (e.g., law, medicine) discriminated against women out of the belief that men were more capable of making important contributions as professionals, executives, and powerholders. If individuals are denied opportunities because of their social-class background (the term "classism" is occasionally used), age, or ethnic group, these prejudices can be very similar to racism and sexism. The similarity is that people are denied opportunities because of a fact over which they have no control; for example, the class background of their parents, the year in which they were born, or the ethnicity of their ancestors (Brislin, 1988).

Currently, it is unfashionable in many parts of the world to express intense racist statements in public forums such as community meetings, offices, and classrooms. Such statements are more likely to be shared among people who know their listeners well and who feel that they will find an appreciative audience for their racist remarks. Discussing ways to measure various sorts of prejudicial attitudes, Ashmore (1970) presented items from different questionnaires that have been used in research studies. Many of these statements were designed to be worded in ways that capture the deep-seated feelings that intense racism involves. One such item is, "The many faults and the general inability to get along, of (*insert name of outgroup*), who have recently flooded our community, prove that we ought to send them back where they came from as soon as conditions permit." Another item is, "(*insert name of group*) can never adjust to the standard of living and civilization of our country due mainly to their innate dirtiness, laziness, and general backwardness."

The vast majority of people who read a book like this one that deals with understanding and appreciating cultural differences will undoubtedly cringe at feelings such as those expressed in these statements. Yet intense racism continues to exist, even though it may have gone "underground" in terms of its open expression. Still, readers may underestimate the current levels of intense racism given that they normally do not interact frequently with people who hold these views. Given that people are more hesitant to express intense views, the diagnosis of racism (and the other "isms") will not necessarily include people's frequent use of hate-filled statements. Rather, the diagnosis now centers on beliefs concerning inferiority. The belief in inferiority distinguishes racism from the other forms that prejudice takes, and the diagnosis of these other forms involve cues even more subtle than current expressions of racist attitudes.

SYMBOLIC RACISM AND REALISTIC GROUP CONFLICT. Certain people hold negative views about outgroups, not because they believe in their inferiority, but because they feel that the outgroup is interfering with important aspects of their culture. The people do not dislike members of the group as individuals, and their views are quite dissimilar from those that mark intense racism. Rather, people believe that the outgroups are interfering with the *symbols* of their culture, and these symbols can be abstract or concrete. Abstract symbols include (a) the belief in hard work as the backbone of society and (b) the importance of standing on one's own two feet and solving one's own problems. Concrete symbols include (c) the classroom as a place of learning the basics, not a place to deal with everyone's social problems, and (d) the job interview as a "level playing field" where some people should not have an advantage because they are from a minority group. Symbolic racism (McConahay & Hough, 1976; Kinder, 1986; Sears & Funk, 1991) centers on the attitude that minority groups are interfering with long-held values (that are captured by abstract and concrete symbols) in a culture. For example, people might dislike welfare programs because they believe too much money is being paid out to outgroup members unwilling to work (symbol "a," above) and who are unwilling to pull themselves up by the bootstraps and solve their own problems (symbol "b," above). Or, they may dislike the busing of students to achieve school integration because they feel it takes time, attention, and money away from the school's mission to teach reading, writing and arithmetic (symbol "c"). They may be against affirmative action programs in various organizations if they believe that outgroup members are being given unfair preferences in employment procedures that (they feel) should give equal treatment to all (symbol "d") and should focus on the ability to work hard for the employer (symbol "a," again).

Symbolic racism is expressed in terms of threats to people's basic values and to the status quo in people's culture with which they have become comfortable. When directly questioned, people assert that out-group members are "moving too fast" and are making illegitimate de-mands in their quest for a place in society. Symbolic racism is expressed by responses to questions such as these (from McConahay & Hough, 1976; the answer indicative of symbolic racism is noted in parentheses):

Over the past few years, (insert name of group) have gotten more economically than they deserve. (agree)

People in this country should support _____ in their struggle against discrimination and segregation. (disagree)

_____ are getting too demanding in their push for equal rights. (agree).

People who hold these views do not view themselves as racists, and so programs aimed at changing extreme racist views (such programs are presently the most common type) are doomed to failure. McConahay and Hough (1976, p. 44) are quite correct when they state that current change programs seem incomprehensible to holders of symbolic prejudices "and they do not understand what all the fuss is about. This enables racism to be considered 'somebody else's' problem while holders of symbolic views concentrate upon their own private lives."

In addition to the complexity of distinguishing intense racism from symbolic racism, a number of researchers have asked whether symbolic racism is different from what they call "realistic group conflict" (Bobo, 1983; Veilleux & Tougas, 1989). Recall the discussion of bilingual educa-tion in the last chapter. Bilingual education is expensive, and its support is dependent upon public funding. Many *groups* of people want to see public funding for other programs that members feel will improve education, such as increased teacher salaries, a "back to basics" emphasis on academics, repairs to buildings, and the attraction of the best and brightest college students to the teaching profession. These groups are engaging in competition for the same funds—they have a *realistic* conflict with other groups because there is almost never enough money for every group that wants its program funded. The competition for funds does not necessarily involve intense dislike of people from other groups, but it does mean that groups have realistic differences that they are trying to deal with as best they can. The people attempt to deal with their differences in the political arena, the place where various persons put proposals forward in the quest for scarce resources (Crick, 1982; Brislin, 1991).

When applied to relationships among people from different racial, ethnic, and cultural groups, arguments concerning realistic group conflict look at the competition for various scarce resources. Money is the most obvious scarce resource, as has been discussed in the example concerning funding for educational programs, but there are others. Other scarce resources include classroom space for one's children in good schools, honest interviews for good jobs, homes in crime-free neighborhoods, and access to the influence that elected politicians can wield. When different groups that happen to form around racial and ethnic criteria compete for these scarce resources, the result may be realistic group conflict. A given person might say, "I want my fair share of these resources, no more and no less. In my community, people seem to be forming political groups to compete for these resources based on their race and their ethnic group. To compete on an equal footing, I'll have to do the same and join members of *my* group." Disagreements exist concerning whether such action represents symbolic racism ("other groups are moving too fast, and so I'll have to work with my group to get our fair share") or whether they represent a realistic view that political action is more effective if individuals band together (Bobo, 1983). There is not enough evidence at present to make a choice between the two possibilities, and my guess is that the final synthesis of the relevant research will recognize aspects of both positions. A person can be quite irritated that minority group members seem pushy in their support of such policies as busing to achieve school integration (symbolic racism). That same person can then join a group of like-minded people who argue to both the school board and to the judicial system that money spent on a fleet of buses would be better invested in salary increases for teachers (realistic group conflict concerning the distribution of scarce resources).

Reconciliations and syntheses of the differing positions will undoubtedly involve complex analysis of *various* attitudes that people possess. Veilleux and Tougas (1989) developed a concept called "relative deprivation on behalf of others." If people from one group felt that members of another group have been deprived of certain rights, then the people were much more likely to reject views indicative of symbolic racism. For example, if men (who had good jobs) felt that women were disadvantaged in the workforce in terms of hirings, salaries, and promotions, then those men were more likely to endorse policies such as affirmative action. Using the terms suggested by Veilleux, if men spoke out on *behalf of others* and argued that women were *deprived relative* to the members of their own male gender, they were willing to endorse special efforts to provide opportunities for women. Other men who felt that women had not received negative treatment in the workplace were less enthusiastic about affirmative action. Regarding the men who felt that women had not experienced a lack of opportunities, different observers will have different conclusions that are influenced by *their* political positions. Some observers will view the men as "blind as bats," some will view them as symbolic racists, some will view them as uninformed, and some will view them as realistic.

TOKENISM. Consider this short case study. George is a staff member of an organization that sponsors overseas exchange programs for high school students. For example, 16- and 17-year-old Americans are sent to France where they reside with French families, and an equal number of French teenagers are sent to the United States where they reside with American families. These programs would be impossible without the willingness of families to sponsor the teenagers and to welcome them into their homes. The costs of the programs would be prohibitive if these students had to pay for their own housing.

George's job involved preparing the students for life in a culture other than their own, raising funds to pay for "extras" such as trips to historically important places within the countries, and finding families with a spare bedroom that they could offer to a visiting student. One week, he happened to be emphasizing the fund-raising and the "family finding" aspects of his job. George noted an interesting fact. The responses he received depended on the order in which requests were made. If asked to make a small donation to the program, adults were later far less willing to have a student live with them. On the other hand, if they had *not* recently been asked to donate money but were asked to welcome a student into their homes, they were more likely to say "Yes, a student can live with us." What might explain this relationshp between people giving money and their willingness to sponsor students in their homes?

The type of prejudice known as "tokenism" may be one reason for the pattern of behavior that George observed. Some people harbor negative feelings about an outgroup but do not want to admit this to themselves or to others. These people definitely neither view themselves as prejudiced nor perceive themselves as discriminatory in their behavior. One way they reinforce this view of themselves is to engage in behaviors that require little effort but which can be interpreted as supporting intergroup relations. By engaging in relatively effortless behaviors, people can persuade themselves and others that they are unprejudiced and can then later refuse to perform more difficult and important intergroup behaviors. For example, Dutton

Tokenism, such as contributing small amounts of money to charity,
can convince people that they are unprejudiced.

(1976) found that if people gave a small amount of money to members of an outgroup, they were later less willing to donate a large amount of their free time to a "Brotherhood Week" campaign that was to emphasize positive intergroup relations and goodwill. The small amount of money, then, was a token that allowed some people to persuade themselves they were unprejudiced and consequently did not have to prove themselves again by engaging in the more important, time-consuming behavior. The analysis of tokenism is similar for George's case. By donating money, people could demonstrate that they are in favor of overseas exchange programs, and consequently do not view themselves as unsupportive if they later refuse to accept the far greater responsibility of housing an exchange student. Knowledge of how tokenism works can be very helpful to administrators in charge of various programs that promote intercultural relationships. They should identify reasonable behaviors that can be expected of volunteers; for example, a reasonable number of hours to work, different types of hospitality, a reasonable amount of goods from retailers at wholesale cost, and so forth. Then, approach people with requests to engage in those behaviors. Do *not* approach people with requests for behaviors that are less demanding, such as contributing small amounts of money. If people agree to the less-demanding behaviors, they often will refuse the requests originally identified as reasonable and necessary for the program's success.

There are different types of tokens. If there are a few symphony musicians whose physical appearance marks them as minority group members, then administrators of the 100+ member orchestra can convince themselves that their hiring practices are nondiscriminatory. If a university has a small number of female or minority faculty members, administrators may place them on committees that are very visible in the community. By pointing to their representations on these committees, administrators can persuade themselves and others that they are making every attempt to involve females and minorities in university decision making. The danger to these faculty members is that the time spent being used as tokens on committees takes away from their teaching and research efforts. Teaching and research are far more important for job success and career development than are committee assignments.

ARMS-LENGTH PREJUDICE. Some people engage in friendly, positive behaviors toward outgroup members in some social settings but treat those same outgroup members with noticeably less warmth and friendliness in other settings. A colloquial term for treating people with little warmth is to say that they are "held at an arms length." The difference across social settings involves the perceived intimacy of the behaviors in which people are expected to engage (Triandis & Davis, 1965; Brislin, 1986; Triandis, Brislin, & Hui, 1988). Intimacy does not refer to sexual contact. It refers to how much personal information is shared among people. In some social settings, people are not expected to share large amounts of personal information. Examples are (a) relations with casual acquaintances within the organization where people work, (b) interactions between speaker and audience at a lecture, or (c) interactions at a catered dinner party. In such settings, people are not expected to provide personal information and instead can talk about such impersonal topics as the weather, recent policies in the organization that are affecting salaries, the speaker's topic during a question–answer session, and the menu at the dinner. In these settings, people can treat outgroup members in a very cordial, seemingly friendly manner. But for other settings where intimate behaviors are expected, such as (a) dating, (b) interactions during an informal dinner held at someone's home, or (3) relations between neighbors, people will interact in a tense, sometimes hostile manner. The people are uncomfortable treating outgroup members as equals in settings where they are expected to share some of their private thoughts.

I had read the early research concerning this form of prejudice (e.g., Allport, 1954; Triandis & Davis, 1965), but did not fully understand it until I saw it in action. My wife and I were entertaining a Caucasian social psychologist in our home. To make the story even more complex, this psychologist had written some very insightful, penetrating, and sensitive analyses of prejudicial attitudes. Our Chinese-American neighbor unexpectedly dropped by for a visit. The visiting psychologist became noncommunicative and ultimately rude when he left the room where we were sitting and trying to keep up a conversation in which everyone could participate. In my opinion, the psychologist was demonstrating arms-length prejudice. He could handle himself well in formal encounters with outgroup members, such as going to a public presentation where the speaker was Chinese or *writing about* the nature of prejudice toward outgroups. He was extremely uncomfortable in informal settings where he was expected to engage in relaxed, casual conversation, and where he was expected to discuss personal topics that go beyond such "formalities" as the weather. Arms-length prejudice is hard to detect since people who engage in it appear so tolerant and even respectful of outgroup members much of the time.

REAL LIKES AND DISLIKES. Certain people have negative feelings about a certain outgroup because members of the group engage in behaviors that the people dislike. People avoid interacting with the outgroup members, then, because the people want to avoid behaviors that they perceive as unpleasant, unhealthy, and even immoral. For example, I sometimes ask students this question: "How many of you use the smoking habit of others as a major reason for choosing how much interaction you have with these others?" As many as 50 percent of Americans in college classes have raised their hands to indicate that they use people's smoking habits as a reason to limit interaction with them. I then point out that this is an issue they will have to face if they decide to live in certain other countries. Smoking is much more common in certain countries (e.g., Japan, Turkey), and there are no policies to provide smoke-free places in restaurants and offices. If they live overseas, people who have a real dislike for the smoking habit may use their attitudes in deciding on how much interaction they will seek out with host nationals.

Treatments of real likes and dislikes have to include an understanding of people's everyday, normal behaviors. People *do* have strong aversions to certain behaviors and try to avoid them. No one person is so saintly as to be tolerant and forgiving toward all who engage in behaviors she or he dislikes. Many Americans who travel overseas bring back stories about the necessity of "bribing" public officials who engage in such duties as extending visas or providing government forms so that people can file various requests. These stories are especially frequent among Americans who travel to countries with extensive government bureaucracies but with a policy of low salaries for the bureaucrats (e.g., India). Americans complain that they have to wait incredible lengths of time to have the requests granted unless they slip some money to a government official. They view the money as a bribe, and providing bribes constitutes behavior that they dislike intensely. This then affects the amount of contact they have with host nationals. At times, the Americans can be assisted if a knowledgeable person tells them that the money should be viewed more like a "tip" in a restaurant that they are expected to leave if service has been adequate (Brislin, Cushner, Cherrie, & Yong, 1986). The salaries of waiters and waitresses are low, as it is for the government officials. "Tips" are viewed as part of their expected total take-home pay.

As another example, some people dislike others who complain and gripe all the time. If this is the case, they may find it difficult to interact with many Israelis. Katriel (1990) discusses the verbal ritual of "griping" in Israel. Griping is a common activity, so common that there is a term called "griping parties," in which people come together to share complaints about Israeli politics, economics, their jobs, and their everyday problems. Katriel (1990, p. 104) feels that

> Israelis' disposition toward griping seems to be nourished by a deep sense of frustration related to the perceived inability to partake in social action and communal life in a way that would satisfy the high level of commitment and involvement [that characterized the early, visionary settlers of Israel]. . . . The prevalence of griping suggests an overwhelming, culturally sanctioned concern with the public domain, on the one hand, coupled with a marked absence of widely satisfying participation channels, on the other.

Katriel also points out that not all subjects are proper conversational topics in griping sessions. Proper topics involve problems that might be addressed by the competent actions of somebody with responsibility and authority, and improper topics involve problems that are totally determined by fate. If visitors to Israel do not enjoy griping or listening to gripers, then that dislike will affect the amount of interaction they have with Israelis.

THE FAMILIAR AND THE UNFAMILIAR. Even if visitors were willing to participate in griping parties, they may be unfamiliar with the widely accepted norms that guide "proper" behavior during the parties. For example, visitors may be unfamiliar with the "action possible" versus "fate" distinction as marking proper topics for griping. Their unfamiliarity may lead to negative reactions, and the negative reactions may affect later intercultural contact. Even more complex—and admittedly very hard to deal with—is the concept that Israelis can gripe about an issue (e.g., extremely hard-line minority political parties), but visitors *cannot* comment negatively about the same issue. This reaction to outsider criticism is by no means limited to Israel. Many people are quite vociferous about certain problems in their country, for instance, Americans who complain about inadequate policies to assist the homeless in the United States. But Americans become upset when someone from another country comments on the same inadequate policies. The visitors may be avoided not because they disagreed with the Americans but because they were unfamiliar with the fact that "insiders" can say things openly that "outsiders" should keep to themselves.

In analyzing the familiar and the unfamiliar as it relates to intercultural contact, people should keep in mind some of the ideas addressed in Chapter 4. People who are socialized into one culture are likely to become familiar and thus uncomfortable with various aspects of their culture. When interacting in another culture, these people are likely to observe unfamiliar behaviors and to be challenged by new ideas. In turn, people's unfamiliarity leads to discomfort since they do not know how to engage in behaviors that are acceptable to others in the host culture. Consequently, people are likely to seek out interaction with members of their own cultural group that happen to be living nearby. Such "enclaves" of fellow countrypeople are very common, especially in large cities around the world (Kealey, 1989). In Chapter 2, advice was given to people socialized in individualistic cultures who were about to live in collective cultures (and vice versa: collectivists about to interact in individualistic cultures). Unless they receive very extensive preparation before living abroad (Bhawuk, 1990), they may have limited interaction with host nationals due to unfamiliarity. For instance, individualists may be offered membership in a collective, but may make mistakes due to unfamiliarity. Membership in a collective involves an extensive investment of one's time, and an extensive set of obligations as well as privileges, for which individualists are often unprepared. A collectivist may be offered extensive business opportunities in an individualist country but may be unfamiliar with the necessary behaviors for doing so, such as developing a network of "contacts" whose members help each other out on an ad-hoc rather than permanent and long-term basis. When people have difficulties and occasionally become frustrated with individuals from other cultures, the reason may not involve anything like intense racism as discussed previously. The frustration may be due to unfamiliarity with the behaviors expected by host culture members.

ARE SOME OF THESE BEHAVIORS BEST DESCRIBED AS PREJUDICES?
Many types of behavior have been described under the label "prejudice," ranging from intense racist beliefs involving perceived inferiority to unfamiliar behaviors for which people are poorly prepared. Does the term "prejudice" include too much? A strong case could be made that the answer is "yes." Prejudice involves negative feelings about other people. In three of the forms discussed here, a case can be made that people have views about outgroups that do not necessarily involve these negative feelings. In (1) realistic group conflict, people may simply join forces with ingroup members to compete for scarce resources, such as funding for a community mental health center. Outgroup members may compete for the same public funds, but may prefer that money go to preschool education programs. Conflict exists since there may not be enough money

to fund both worthwhile projects. The two groups, however, may not harbor negative feelings about each other—they may simply recognize that they prefer different allocations of funds. In (2) real likes and dislikes, individuals may make a distinction between the behavior of people and the people themselves. For example, Americans may dislike smoking, but may realize that there have been no extensive and well-funded public health campaigns against smoking in other countries. They may be able to set aside their attitude toward smoking and seek out the stimulation that interaction with people from other cultural backgrounds can bring. In considering (3) the familiar and the unfamiliar, the argument is similar. Individuals may be able to distinguish unfamiliar behaviors from the persons who engage in those behaviors. If they, too, desire the stimulation that intercultural interactions can bring, they may be able to find opportunities to practice the unfamiliar behaviors such that they can later interact effectively across cultural boundaries.

I believe that there are indeed cases like these three in which relations among ingroups and outgroups that involve conflict, disliked behaviors, and unfamiliar behaviors are not necessarily prejudicial. Just as often, however, *attitudes* turn negative and prejudices about outgroups develop. If people lose in the competition for scarce resources, they often develop negative views about their successful opponents. If people dislike certain behaviors, they often generalize their attitudes about the behaviors to the persons who practice them. If people are unfamiliar and uncomfortable with certain behaviors, they often *do not* take the time and trouble to practice them so that they can interact smoothly with others. Given the continuing unfamiliarity, ingroup and outgroup members continue to keep their distance. Over a number of years, this "distance" becomes the norm: "the way things are done around here." This absence of interaction across ingroup–outgroup boundaries is the major reason I have discussed the three forms of behavior in a discussion of prejudice. Even though there may be no negative attitudes about outgroups involved, the *result* of realistic conflict, dislikes, and unfamiliarity is the same as for prejudice: People are not interacting effectively across ingroup–outgroup boundaries. Rather, people are keeping their distance and interacting far more within their ingroup than with outgroup members. Given this pattern of behavior, stereotypes develop since people do not have the extensive interaction with *individual* outgroup members necessary to break down conclusions about a category of people. For example, White college students may not have the necessary interaction with Blacks on their way to law, medical, and business schools to break down the stereotype of "Blacks are here to play basketball." Eventually, unchallenged stereotypes can have an effect on attitudes, for example, that Blacks may be great in athletics but inadequate in the classroom.

The most effective way to break down negative stereotypes and to challenge negative attitudes is to encourage *carefully thought out* contact among ingroup and outgroup members. The emphasis is on "carefully thought out" because contact itself is no guarantee of positive intergroup relations. If readers have heard somebody say, "let's just bring people together so that they'll get to know each other and this will reduce prejudice," then readers have heard an oversimplification. A great deal of research has been undertaken to identify the *type* of contact that is effective, and people who study the research will find some very helpful guidelines for interventions designed to improve intergroup relations.

INTERVENTIONS FOR EFFECTIVE INTERCULTURAL INTERACTION

An extensive body of research has focused on the question: What types of contact best encourage the development of positive intergroup relations? The shorthand term for the research has been called, "studies of the contact hypothesis" (Allport, 1954; Amir, 1969; Cook, 1969; Brislin, 1981; Stephan, 1985; Miller & Brewer, 1986; Cushner, 1990; Leong & Kim, 1991). Since Gordon Allport's highly influential book on prejudice published in 1954, researchers and practitioners have known that contact itself does not necessarily bring about positive benefits. In many cases, contact simply reinforces existing prejudices. For example, there may be extensive contact in a factory where people appear to work cooperatively on the products that their employer manufactures. However, if the managers are from one ethnic group and the laborers from another, the contact may simply reinforce the existing stereotype that members of one group are fit for leadership and members of another group are happier in subservient roles.

Intervention programs that have the goal of improving intergroup relations are based on the assumption that administrators of the programs have *some* control over what happens when people come into contact. That is, the program administrators must have the ability to intervene in ways that should improve intergroup relations according to guidelines developed by researchers and experienced practitioners. Several of the guidelines are especially important (longer treatments in Brislin, 1981; Stephan, 1985).

EQUAL-STATUS CONTACT. The guideline most frequently suggested is that people participating in intergroup contact should have equal status. Members of the various groups should have equal power, should be treated equally by program administrators, and should have equal access to rewards. In efforts to desegregate schools, for example, students from various ethnic groups should receive equal amounts of attention from teachers and should have equal access to rewards, such as good grades and active participation in school activities. In public housing projects, people from different groups should have equal access to the homes considered "the best," such as those with the best views or with the easiest access to shared facilities such as playgrounds. In the workplace, equal-status contact means that people should have equal access to benefits, such as advanced training opportunities, salary increases for meritorious work, and promotions.

In Chapter 5, reasons for Asian-Americans' success in schools was reviewed. One reason suggested was based on the concept "relative functionalism." I believe that equal-status contact contributes to the explanation of exactly what relative functionalism means. Compared to other parts of society, and even other aspects of school, such as athletic activities and elected student government positions, Asian-Americans perceive that they will experience equal-status contact in the classroom. If they perform well in their studies, they have equal access (along with hardworking students from any ethnic group) to rewards, such as teacher approval, good grades, and listings on the honor roll. Work in the classroom is perceived as functional in leading to success, and one reason for this perception is that Asian-Americans feel that they will be treated equally by teachers.

In some cases, equal status in the contact situation may not go far enough. Considering the case of Blacks in the United States, Riordan (1978) feels there has been such a long history of discrimination that special steps are needed. Riordan fears that an equal-status contact experience between Whites and Blacks may not have enough impact to counter years of experience with unequal status. One suggestion for program administrators is to arrange experiences in which Whites have contact with *higher status* Blacks. Within the contact setting, Whites have to interact with Blacks who are better educated, more articulate, and have more abilities to contribute if people are to work cooperatively on various projects. Riordan feels that interactions with higher status Blacks will be more likely to offset the familiar "status quo" in which Whites are both more numerous and in superior positions.

I feel that these concepts of equal status and higher status contact help explain White reactions to life in my home, Hawaii. Many Caucasians from mainland United States settle in Hawaii given its climate, outdoor lifestyle, clean air, and so forth. However, some stay only a few years and move back to the mainland. There are many reasons: Hawaii has a very high cost of living; given the number of people desirous of jobs, salaries are not very high; people find that they genuinely miss their families and old friends, and so forth. But another reason is that many Caucasians come from parts of the country in which they are clearly the majority and clearly hold down the most powerful and influential jobs. They may interact adequately with members of minority groups, but more often in the sort of "arms-length" manner discussed earlier. Many Caucasians can be polite in formal settings, but do not seek out interactions with minority group members during their voluntary free time. In Hawaii, however, they will inevitably experience people from culturally diverse groups who hold down powerful positions. Japanese-Americans,

Chinese-Americans, Filipino-Americans, and others hold down high-level positions, such as elected congresspeople, judges, chief executive officers, school principals, college professors, and so forth. Many of these positions represent much higher status than those held by Caucasians who decide to settle in Hawaii. Some Caucasians benefit from interactions with high-status people from culturally diverse groups and become much more tolerant and appreciative of cultural differences. Other Caucasians become uncomfortable and move back to mainland United States.

SUPERORDINATE GOALS. Administrators can also give attention to the tasks on which people work during their intergroup contact. The most effective tasks are directed toward "superordinate goals" (Sherif, 1966), or goals that are desired by everyone *and* that demand the efforts of everyone involved. When people work together to achieve goals valued by all, prejudicial attitudes have to be set aside or else people will not accomplish anything. Instead of sniping at each other, people will put their efforts into hard work if the goals for which they are striving are important to them. For example, superordinate goals have been integrated into classroom activities designed to improve the learning of new material. In one type of cooperative group-learning activity (Aronson & Osherow, 1980), students become members of four-person groups. In desegregated classrooms, teachers make a point of maximizing the cultural diversity of each group. If Blacks, Anglos, Hispanics, and Asian-Americans are represented in the classroom, they become members of culturally diverse learning groups. The teacher gives part of the lesson to each student, who has to share his or her part with the others. To achieve the superordinate goal of learning the entire lesson and achieving teacher praise as well as good grades, the students have to work cooperatively and make sure that all group members have mastered the entire lesson. Research has shown that students learn as much from this approach as from traditional "teacher-centered" activities such as lecturing, *and* the students become more tolerant of classmates from different cultural backgrounds.

Of course there are various types of superordinate goals. In athletics, the goal is to have a winning team, and the time and energy that might be spent on prejudicial attitudes toward teammates from minority groups has to be invested in developing the skills necessary to compete successfully in the league. In international business activities, goals include profits and the successful acquisition of a niche in the marketplace. Great amounts of money and energy have been invested in cooperative efforts among businesspeople from such countries as Japan, the United States, and Germany. When business goals are very clear, people become motivated to find ways to harness cultural differences in the pursuit of success (Adler, 1991). This motivation replaces the useless complaints about businesspeople in different countries who "don't do things the way we do."

INTIMATE CONTACT. When researchers and practitioners make recommendations that contact be intimate, they are not referring to sexual relations. Rather, they are referring to the sharing of personal information. Most people share much more personal information about themselves with ingroup than with outgroup members. Further, most people have a rather well-rehearsed set of statements about themselves that they use when meeting strangers and/or outgroup members. Typical examples of well-rehearsed, *nonintimate* statements are one's name, schools attended, name of one's hometown, and perhaps a few words about hobbies. These statements reveal little about the person.

In contrast, intimate statements are shared with ingroup members. These usually contain much more emotional content and include thoughts about people's personal ambitions, worries, troubles they are having, successes and failures in their interpersonal relationships, and so forth. The advantage of intimate contact is that it is far more likely to break down the barriers between "us" and "them." When people reveal personal information about themselves, they are more likely to be seen as individuals rather than as members of a category. Further, the sharing of personal information often leads to the discovery that others previously considered as "them" have some of the same feelings, concerns, and ambitions. Again, this leads to a breakdown of ingroup–outgroup barriers.

In one of the first studies of extensive intergroup contact, Deutsch and Collins (1951) studied the reactions of Black and White residents in an integrated housing project. The project included small apartments for families along with shared facilities, such as laundry rooms and playgrounds for children. Even though they may have preferred to stick with their own ethnic group, there were a number of opportunities for intergroup contact. One set of opportunities took place in laundry rooms. It was more interesting for Whites to chat with Blacks than to stare blankly at their clothes tumbling in the dryer. Another set of opportunities took place on the playgrounds. Four- and 5-year-olds, too young to be attached to the prejudices of their parents, would play together regardless of skin color. Children would follow each other as they reported back to their parents at the end of playtime. Children would meet each other's parents, and eventually the parents learned to recognize each other, having been introduced (in effect) by their children. Parents would eventually chat while watching their children on the playground. Over time, the chats would move from topics such as the weather and the quality of the washing machines to the sharing of personal information. Blacks and Whites learned that they shared many of the same concerns: the job market in their community, the quality of schools for their children, problems in balancing the family budget, taxes, problems in the romantic liaisons of friends and relatives, and so forth. The discovery that people shared these concerns and experienced similar problems helped to break down ingroup–outgroup boundaries based on skin color. Ashmore (1970, p. 320) argues in a similar manner: "Intergroup friendship causes a redeployment of motivation with respect to the intergroup attitude. The prejudiced person wants to hang onto his [or her] prejudice; but becoming friendly with a member of an outgroup makes [the person] more amenable to information that favors tolerance."

THE CANDID TREATMENT OF DIFFICULTIES. Enough is known about intergroup relations that program administrators can identify problems that will almost inevitably arise. My recommendaton is that these be given explicit attention during the program. It is far better to deal with difficulties when suggestions for their alleviation can be presented than it is for people to face the difficulties *after the program* without guidance for dealing with unforeseen problems.

For example, people can become quite tolerant of outgroup members in the contact program arranged by knowledgeable administrators, but this tolerance might not transfer *to others* outside the program. If the contact is between Blacks and Whites in the integrated housing project discussed above, for example, people may become quite tolerant of outgroup members who live in the housing project. There is no assurance, however, that these positive feelings will transfer to other outgroup members in the community at large. Challenges have been made to people's previously existing categories (left-hand side, Figure 5). The difficulty is that people may simply develop a new and smaller category that splits off from the previous, all-encompassing category (Brewer & Miller, 1984). This can be seen in the right-hand side in Figure 5. People then have two categories: almost all outgroup members, and those few in my housing project. The larger category remains almost untouched, and so people are likely to treat outgroup members outside the housing project in a prejudicial manner. I recommend that this problem, called "splitting," be treated as part of the material presented to participants during the contact program. I also recommend that administrators point out that "participants in programs such as this one often report that they grow to like each other. This does not mean that they will show the same affection toward outgroup members outside the program. We must keep in mind the possibility of splitting, or the development of a new category that contains only the outgroup members met in the contact situation."

When writing about Black–White relations some years ago, I referred to the splitting problem as the "Lena Horne–Harry Belafonte effect"

FIGURE 5. A Representation of "Splitting" in Intergroup Relations.

(Brislin & Pedersen, 1976). It is easy for Whites to like these handsome entertainers—it is easy to split them off in a separate, small category. It is harder to be tolerant of all outgroup members, not all of whom can possibly be as attractive as these two singers. The name of the effect might have to be changed so that it is understandable to younger audiences. Suggestions are welcome. Would the "Whitney Houston–Michael Jackson effect" capture the same concept?

Knowing about difficulties such as splitting helps administrators plan the content of their programs. One way they can continue to challenge the large preexisting category of "all outgroup members" is to make sure that people have contact with many outgroup members who have different abilities and characteristics. If people learn to interact with diverse outgroup members, they may have their preexisting category challenged so many times and *in so many different ways* that they no longer find the large category useful in thinking about others they might later meet.

There are many other issues that can be covered as part of the recommendation to prepare people for the difficulties they will face during extensive intercultural interactions. Many of these are based on the realization that many people are (a) *willing* to be tolerant and to seek out opportunities for intercultural contact but (b) do not know enough about other cultures and ethnic groups to be *comfortable* during the contact. Further, they may find that (c) intercultural interactions involve behaviors that are both frustrating and irritating because they are so poorly understood. Such problems will be the focus of the next chapter.

CHAPTER SUMMARY

One prediction about the future that can be made with absolute certainty is that there will be far more contact across cultural boundaries than there has been in the past. Such contact will challenge people's preexisting beliefs about others, their attitudes, and their behaviors, and it will also challenge administrators (e.g., school principals, employers) who must guarantee the equal treatment of individuals regardless of skin color or cultural background.

Challenges to preexisting beliefs immediately bring up the problem of stereotypes. Whenever there are individuals who can be grouped together or categorized in some way, then stereotypes become part of people's thinking. When people use stereotypes, they ignore individual differences among the members of the group or category. Many stereotypes are used without much thought, as when people talk about "the Republican position on taxes" or "women's ways of making decisions." In actuality, there can be large differences in the positions taken by different Republicans and in the ways that different women make decisions. Stereotypes can involve any group of people, or any category whose members are people, but the term is most often used when it refers to people's beliefs about outgroup members who have a different skin color and are from a different ethnic or cultural background. Stereotypes provide shortcuts to thinking and allow people to make decisions without a great deal of mental effort. Assume a White student has the opportunity to approach and to chat with a Black student at a campus reception. If the stereotype of Blacks include the belief that "Blacks don't particularly want to interact with Whites and prefer to stick with other Blacks," then the White student has assistance in making his or her decision. The decision will be to avoid contact with the Black and to seek out someone friendlier at the reception. One of the difficulties in such decision making is that once a person is put into a category, all the information from that category becomes available. In the business world, a stereotype of "women executives" may be that they cannot make tough decisions. If a young woman with an advanced degree in business seeks a serious interview for an executive-level position, her individuality may be denied if she is simply put into the convenient category of "female in the business world." All of the information from the category becomes available to decisionmakers, and she may be denied the interview because she is seen as unable to make difficult decisions.

In this busy, stress-filled world, people seek shortcuts when thinking about the many others whom they might meet on a day-to-day basis. They *must* form generalizations about others, since they do not have sufficient time to examine the individuality of every person they see. The goal should be to *improve* the generalizations, and Adler (1991) recommends using a 5-point checklist. If people use stereotypes, they should be (1) quite conscious of this fact. People should also consciously look for exceptions and ask themselves if they are making decisions based on stereotypes. Generalization about people should be (2) descriptive and have as little evaluative content as possible. The danger of evaluative content is that people will judge "goodness or badness" based on their own standards and will be insensitive to cultural differences concerning these standards. Careful searches of available evidence should be made to determine if the stereotypes are (3) accurate. What evidence exists, for instance, that Blacks do not want intergroup contact or that women cannot make tough decisions? Stereotypes should also be considered only as a (4) first best-guess about outgroup members that will be sharpened through firsthand experiences with many different others. Consequently, stereotypes will be (5) modifiable rather than rigid and will include an important fact: There are often more differences *within* the members of a category than there are *between* the members of two categories.

A major difficulty, of course, is that most people are not willing to put this much effort into their stereotype-influenced thinking. One reason is that many stereotypes are the result of deep-seated attitudes toward outgroups, and any discussion of attitudes and feelings about outgroup members immediately brings us to the topic of prejudice. As Jordan (1989, p. 1119) pointed out, "stereotypes may be defined as the bundles of beliefs carried by the energy" of people's prejudicial attitudes. Prejudices refer to the emotional content of people's reactions to outgroups, and the root words help explain its meaning. There is a *pre-judging* of outgroups based on limited information, and the judgments are based on emotion rather than careful thought. There is a far greater likelihood of negative than positive feelings in people's judgments.

Prejudices remain—sometimes generation after generation—within a culture because they serve various functions or uses for people. Four functions have been suggested. If a prejudice serves an (1) adjustment function, it helps people to obtain rewards and to avoid punishment in their culture. If people view certain outgroup members as lazy and as unable to hold down good jobs, this is functional for those people. It means that they will have less competition for good jobs given that the outgroup members are never even considered for interviews. If a prejudice serves an (2) ego-defensive function, it means that people can hide negative aspects of themselves they don't want to admit publicly. Rather than admit that they do not have the necessary skills for success in the business world, for example, they might charge that certain outgroup members conspire to keep all the good business opportunities to themselves. This conspiracy charge has long been part of anti–Semitic prejudices. Ego-defensive prejudices *hide* certain traits. If people want to *communicate clearly* certain information about themselves, they may hold prejudices that serve the (3) value-expressive function. For example, they may want to communicate clearly that they belong to the "one true religion of God." They may communicate this by viewing other religions as wrong-headed or even evil. Other prejudices serve the (4) knowledge function. Attitudes serving this function help people organize what is "correct" and what is "incorrect" in their culture. For instance, assume parents are deciding which school their children will attend next year, and that they have four or five possibilities. If part of their "knowledge" is that one of the schools attracts members of a certain ethnic group and that people from this group are not terribly serious about the importance of good schools, then the parents may eliminate that school as one of the possibilities. Their "knowledge" helps in their decision making.

Many attitudes serve several functions. Children may adopt a certain prejudice (e.g., "those outgroup members are not as good as us, so don't interact with them") to avoid being punished by their parents (adjustment function). They may maintain this attitude as adults so that they can use the outgroup as an excuse for their own shortcomings (ego defensive) or to clearly demonstrate that they belong to a superior group (value expressive). They may use "information" about the outgroup in making decisions (knowledge function). Programs aimed at changing prejudices often address only the knowledge function. For instance, information is presented about successful people from the outgroup, the concern parents express toward their children, how admitted difficulties such as the outgroup's living standard can be explained by the denial of opportunities for betterment, and so forth. While possibly successful in challenging the knowledge function, the prejudices often remain given that the other three functions are not addressed.

In addition to understanding its functions, an understanding of prejudice demands that the various forms it takes be recognized. The most virulent form is (1) intense racism. When people believe that certain individuals are inferior simply given the fact that they were born to parents from an outgroup, then they are guilty of racism. Examples of racist feelings are that certain outgroup members are naturally ignorant and cannot advance to a decent standard of living. The public expression of racist sentiments has become unfashionable, and consequently the prevalence of intense racism is difficult to establish. When people believe that outgroup members are interfering with valued aspects of a culture, such as the importance of hard work and raising oneself by the bootstraps when faced with difficulties, they may be expressing either (2) symbolic racism or may be recognizing realistic group conflict. Symbolic racism involves the beliefs that outgroup members are getting more than they deserve and are receiving *too much* support in their struggle against discrimination. If people recognize realistic group conflict, it means that they are competing for society's scarce resources, such as public funding for their favored programs. Some groups compete for such resources by organizing around racial and ethnic affiliations. This type of behavior may not involve prejudice—it may simply involve the realization that political action is more effective when people join together.

In (3) tokenism, people engage in unimportant behaviors on behalf of outgroups so that they can convince themselves that they are unprejudiced. Given this self-definition, they do not have to engage in more important, challenging, and time-consuming behaviors. (4) Arms-length prejudice involves apparent tolerance in formal situations such as meetings in the workplace, but rejection in more intimate settings such as informal interactions in one's home. The difference seems to involve the necessity of communicating personal information. "Safe" topics, such as the weather and business conditions, can be discussed in formal settings. Informal settings call for the sharing of information usually reserved for ingroup members. While not always involving prejudicial feelings, (5) real likes and dislikes and (6) familiar and unfamiliar behaviors can lead to preferences for interaction with ingroup members and the avoidance of outgroup members. No person is so saintly as to be tolerant of all behaviors. For example, if Americans dislike the smoking habit, they will have a difficult time interacting cordially in cultures where far more people smoke than in their own country. If people are unfamiliar with certain behaviors common in a culture, such as communication rituals involving subtle rules for what are proper and improper topics in gripe sessions, they may feel unwelcome even if invited to interact with individuals from that culture.

Encouraging people to practice unfamiliar behaviors is one goal of formal programs that encourage intergroup contact. Another is greater openness toward, and tolerance of, individuals previously rejected as outgroup members. A number of guidelines are available to administrators of such programs, whether those programs take place in schools, the workplace, neighborhoods, the military, or elsewhere (longer treatments of various guidelines can be found in Brislin, 1981; and Stephan, 1985). Administrators should make efforts to ensure that all people involved in the intergroup have equal status, or equal access to the rewards and benefits of the school, workplace, or neighborhood. At times, the status of certain groups *outside* the contact setting will be so much lower (e.g., Blacks in the United States) that efforts should be made to expose people to individual outgroup members who possess very high status. Administrators should also encourage people to work toward superordinate goals, or goals that are desired by all and that need the efforts of all. When they work toward goals they deem important, people often set aside the energy they need to maintain prejudices and instead invest it in goal attainment. Intimate contact should be encouraged in which people have opportunities to share personal information. When people discover that many of their concerns about life are shared by outgroup members, it becomes harder to maintain rigid distinctions between "us" and "them." Still, it must be recognized that increasing intergroup tolerance will always be a difficult undertaking. Some of the difficulties should be treated candidly by administrators. For example, people often become tolerant of outgroup members they meet in the contact setting, but this does not transfer to individuals whom they meet elsewhere. One reason is that people form a category of "outgroup members I had contact with" that is distinct from "outgroup members in general." Administrators can address this issue by encouraging people to meet as many different outgroup members as possible so that their unique traits constantly provide a challenge to the all-encompassing category.

The tendency to form a separate category of favored outgroup members and to distinguish this from a more general category is just one example of the difficulties involved in encouraging more intercultural interaction. Even if people seek out increased intercultural contact and are generally tolerant of individuals from other racial and ethnic groups, they may find that actual interactions with outgroup members are often puzzling and unsuccessful. Further, they are unable to discern the reasons for the difficulties. This theme of "difficulties despite good intentions" will be examined in the next chapter.

7

INTERACTING SUCCESSFULLY WITH PEOPLE FROM OTHER CULTURES

If people learn to understand some of the major difficulties that stem from extensive intercultural interactions, such as the forms and functions of prejudice discussed in Chapter 6, they may feel ready to seek out relationships with individuals from other cultural backgrounds. They may, however, experience difficulties because they fail to understand cultural differences that have an impact on the formation and maintenance of interpersonal relationships. Further, because the people are very well-intentioned in their pursuit of positive relationships, they may become very frustrated if their intentions cannot be translated into behaviors. They may conclude, "I tried my best and I don't think my failures are due to my prejudices. But I just can't seem to communicate with those other people, and I'm not going to continue trying!"

These frustrations—and suggestions to alleviate them—are the focus of this chapter. Even though frustrations will be common in the development of relationships across cultural boundaries, I feel that the tone of this chapter is "positive" in contrast to the tone demanded in the previous chapter's discussion of stereotypes, racism, prejudice, and discrimination. I assume that many people either accept the fact that effective and respectful intercultural relationships are necessary or they actively look forward to developing these relationships. I realize that I will not be addressing the needs of everyone, since many people will prefer to retain their prejudicial outlook and will interact only with individuals much like themselves. However, there are large numbers of people who will be able to overcome the problems that stem from prejudices and stereotypes (the previous chapter) and who will seek out intercultural relationships. The content of this chapter will hopefully be of assistance to these people.

Another way to view the relationship between the previous and the present chapters is to ask: After dealing with prejudice, are there still problems that remain? The answer is "yes." Many of the remaining problems stem from unexamined aspects of one's own culture. Recall the presentation in Chapter 1 on "well-meaning clashes." People from different backgrounds come together and have every good intention to interact effectively, but there is a clash. The clash is usually based on a violation (from one and/or the other person's viewpoint) of what should happen in an interaction that is *meant* to proceed smoothly. In Chapter 1 the example was given of a Japanese student pursuing a graduate degree at an American university. He expected an invitation to a late-Friday afternoon social gathering. The American students were behaving according to their expectation that "the word will get out and everyone who wants to come will just show up!" No one is prejudiced—no one is trying to be unpleasant—but there is a clash. The result is that the Japanese student is frustrated in his desire to develop effective intercultural relationships. Various reasons for such well-meaning clashes will be discussed in this chapter.

When people are willing to move beyond the problems brought on by prejudicial thinking, they want to experience success in their efforts to develop intercultural relationships. What does success mean?

SUCCESS IN INTERCULTURAL INTERACTION

A four-part definition has been developed to analyze exactly what it means to be "successful" when engaging in extensive intercultural interactions (Hammer, Gudykunst, & Wiseman, 1978; Brislin, 1981; Hammer, 1989; Kealy, 1989; Bhawuk, 1990). A person must satisfy all four parts—two or three parts out of the four is not sufficient.

People must feel (1) that they are having successful relationships with people from other cultures. They must show respect, seek out activities of mutual interest, work cooperatively on projects, spend part of their voluntary free time with others, and so forth. In short, relationships should be warm and cordial and people should look forward to their intercultural interactions. In actual research projects, this aspect of success is based on people's self-reports concerning their interactions with others. People simply tell about their interactions and label them as successful and unsuccessful. While it would be desirable to follow people around and keep careful records of their interactions, practical considerations and ethical principles (especially the invasion of people's privacy) make such research almost impossible. Given the dependence on people's self-reports, it is important to add a second part to the criteria of success. (2) Individuals in the other culture (sometimes called "hosts") must feel that the interactions are warm and cordial, reflect respect, involve cooperation, and so forth. This insistence on the two parts reflects awareness of a type of person that many readers have probably encountered. Some people *report* that they have many friends and that they are gracious and cordial, but *others report* that those people are abrasive, unfriendly, and should be avoided!

Most extensive intercultural interactions involve tasks of some kind. Foreign students want to obtain college degrees within a reasonable amount of time; businesspeople want to start or to maintain joint ventures in other countries; diplomats want to develop treaties; technical assistance advisers want to develop projects of use to the host country, and so forth. Even if an intercultural relationship develops outside a workplace, there are often tasks on which people cooperate: visa extensions; help in the dreadful task of filling out unfamiliar tax forms; help in guiding people through bureaucracies if legal, government, or medical interventions are needed; and so forth. Another part of the definition of success, then, is that (3) tasks be accomplished in an efficient manner. As will be discussed later in this chapter (and in Chapter 8 concerned with the workplace), task accomplishment often involves dealing with cultural differences. The final part of the definition (4) is that people should experience minimal stress due to the fact that they are dealing with individuals from other cultures rather than from their own culture. Life is stressful, and so the definition cannot include the assertion that there should be *no* stress. If people are in an organization working to meet an upcoming deadline, or if they are competing with other companies for lucrative contracts, or if they have an abrasive boss, they will experience stress. The definition of success in intercultural relations suggests that there should be no *additional* stress brought on by the fact that the others with whom people work (e.g., co-workers and boss in the examples) and/or interact frequently are from a different cultural background.

When stress becomes overwhelming people often experience the intense emotional reaction known as "culture shock" (Oberg, 1958; Bock, 1970; Furnham & Bochner, 1986). Stress arises when people cannot meet their everyday needs as they would in their own culture. They cannot communicate, they cannot make themselves understood, they cannot figure out why hosts behave the way they do. The familiar ways of behaving, learned during their socialization, do not work in the other culture. As a result, they experience a sense of loss and a sense of *shock* that others behave so differently and seem to have such a different worldview (Solomon, Greenberg, & Pyszczynski, 1991). It is important to note that culture shock is not an indication of failure to adjust to another culture. Often, it is a "signal" that people are interacting with host nationals in a way such that they will surely experience differences and will encounter challenges to their worldviews. People who do *not* experience culture shock may be so rigid as to not see cultural differences where they clearly exist; or, they may be interacting only with fellow nationals who happen to be living in the other country.

Assuming that people are positively inclined toward developing intercultural relationships and want to achieve success according to the four-part definition, what should they do? Is there good advice they should keep in mind? Are there specific steps they can take to increase their chances of success? To provide answers to these questions, the remainder of this chapter deals with three approaches to helping people achieve success.

1. The qualities of the individual. One approach involves studying the qualities of individuals who achieve success in extensive intercultural interactions in contrast to people who do not. "Qualities of people" refers to various traits within their personalities, to their abilities, and to their attitudes.

2. Difficulties in face-to-face conversations. To develop relationships with others, people have to engage in conversations about various tasks, about potential social activities, about outlooks on life, and so forth. There are cultural differences in the ways that people converse with each other that can lead to irritations and to decreases in people's willingness to seek out future conversations. If these difficulties can be identified, irritations may be less intense because people know what to expect. At times, however, these difficulties are almost invisible. Just as people usually have few opportunities to examine their culture and to identify how culture affects their behavior (Chapter 1), people rarely have opportunities to examine how the *ways* that persons communicate affect success and failure in their interactions.

3. Formal training programs. People may decide they are unprepared for the difficulties they might face. They may want to take advantage of intercultural training programs, or formal efforts to prepare people to live and work in cultures other than their own. Various types of programs exist that are aimed at providing people with information, encouraging greater sophistication in their thinking, and preparing them for the emotional confrontations that extensive intercultural interactions can bring.

QUALITIES OF THE INDIVIDUAL

Many researchers, working in different parts of the world, have identified a core set of traits that seem to distinguish people who are more and less successful in their intercultural interactions. For example, work has been carried out with Canadian technical assistance advisers working in Africa and Asia (Hawes & Kealey, 1981; Kealey, 1989), American Peace Corps workers in various parts of the world (Harris, 1973), Japanese businesspeople working in the United States (Black, 1990), immigrants from Asia settling in North America (Berry, 1990), students from various parts of the world pursuing college degrees in countries other than their own (Klineberg & Hull, 1979), and German businesspeople contemplating expansion into marketing efforts in other countries (Dichtl, Koeglmayr, & Mueller, 1990). Further, reviews exist that attempt to integrate these studies and others (Brislin, 1981; Kealey & Ruben, 1983; Spitzberg, 1989). While all these studies and reviews do not use the same terms, and while there is certainly no total agreement, I believe there is good evidence that a number of identifiable traits increase the chances of success in intercultural interactions.

CULTURAL FLEXIBILITY. As discussed in Chapter 1, the culture in which people are socialized provides a great deal of guidance for choices about everyday behaviors: what and when to eat, what activities to pursue, how to talk with higher-status people, and so forth. Cultural flexibility involves changes in one's behavior to meet the demands of situations found in other cultures. Many businesspeople working in Japan, for example, have commented on a difference between Americans and Japanese (e.g., Chesanow, 1985). When negotiating with the Japanese, Americans like to get right down to business. They were socialized to believe that "time is money!" They can accept about 15 minutes of "small talk" about the weather, their trip, and baseball, but more than that becomes unreasonable. The Japanese, on the other hand, want to get to know their business counterparts. They feel that the best way to do this is to have long conversations with Americans about a wide variety of topics. The Japanese are comfortable with hours and hours, and even days and days, of conversations concerning "small talk" issues. One reason is very pragmatic. The Japanese want to determine if they can trust their potential American counterparts. *If* business dealings are agreed upon, they want to know that any eventual problems can be settled by appealing to their feelings of trust for their American counterparts. The Japanese *do not* want to settle difficulties by bringing in lawyers who will hash out or litigate a settlement. Rather, the Japanese want to place a phone call and say to their American *friends*, "We have a problem. Can you take care of it?" The Japanese feel that the best way to develop this trusting, friendly relationship is to have long conversations during which people get to know each other and can constantly demonstrate their goodwill.

People working in Japan will have a greater chance of success if they possess the trait known as "cultural flexibility." The opposite of flexibility is rigidity: Rigid people behave in a very limited set of ways and believe that other ways are incorrect or even silly. Flexible people can modify their behavior to meet the demands of the culture in which they find themselves. Following the points made in the above example, overseas businesspeople in Japan will demonstrate flexibility if they are willing to engage in long discussions of "small talk" issues, show that they are trustworthy people who will be good friends, and communicate clearly that they will later solve problems the way that friends do. Friends do not bring in lawyers—rather, they come to each other's aid in times of need.

Analyzing the experiences of Japanese businesspeople working in the United States, Black (1990) provided another example of cultural flexibility. One way that people reduce stress is to have hobbies. It is difficult to pursue some hobbies when working in another country given that no one else is interested, materials are not available, and so forth.

Culturally flexible people can find activities that interest them. They can replace valued activities from their own culture (e.g., cricket in Great Britain) with those available in other countries (e.g., baseball in the United States). Rigid people will be less able to modify and to replace valued activities, and consequently will not reap the benefits that enjoyable hobbies can bring.

ENTHUSIASM ABOUT FORMING INTERCULTURAL RELATIONSHIPS.
Some people actively want to establish close relationships with people from other cultural backgrounds. Rather than simply tolerating such relationships as a necessity for task accomplishment, they look forward to the stimulation that intercultural relationships can bring. Some people even look forward to having aspects of their *own culture* challenged during intercultural interactions. They realize that understanding the underlying reasons for these challenges is an excellent way to increase one's learning about one's own *and* other cultures.

There are also practical results that people will achieve if they carry out their goals of forming intercultural relationships. Adjustment to other cultures is hastened if people have "cultural informants." When people have difficulties, cultural informants can provide information that can help alleviate problems. They can answer variants of this question: "Is there something about culture and cultural differences that is causing this problem I am having." For example, assume that an American business-person in Japan is impatient with the length of time it takes the Japanese to make decisions. If the American has developed good intercultural relationships, one or more Japanese friends may be able to take on the role of cultural informant. When questioned about decision making, the informant could point out that Japan is a more collective culture than the United States (see Chapter 2). In Japan, the feelings of all group members are very important. Each person in the workplace who might be affected by the decision has to examine all the proposals that the American puts forth (Hijirida & Yoshikawa, 1987). Each Japanese individual makes a mark or "signs off" on the proposal after he or she approves it. Because so many people have to read and sign off, a great deal of time is needed. Interestingly, even though it may take a great deal of time to reach a decision, *implementation* might be rather fast. Since all the Japanese business-people involved know the content of the proposal, have expressed their approval, and feel involved in the decision making process, they will be able to implement plans quickly. In the United States, on the other hand, decision making may proceed quickly because so few people are involved in the process. A few high-level executives may make the decision and pass "orders" on to subordinates. Implementation may take a long time because subordinates either resent not being consulted, do not know how to go about implementing the part of the proposal that deals with their department, have not developed good communication links with others in the organization, and so forth.

The best cultural informants have themselves had experiences in other cultures. As discussed in Chapter 1, "culture" and "cultural differences" are difficult concepts to grasp unless people have firsthand experiences. Given such experiences, during which they had to make adjustments, people learn that culture is much more than an abstraction. With this knowledge, they can then assist others in the role of cultural informants and answer questions about adjustment to other cultures. In the example of businesspeople in Japan, for example, the best cultural informants will be Japanese who have been overseas for one reason or another. Perhaps they had an overseas assignment for their company; perhaps they went to college in another country; or perhaps (years ago) they participated in an overseas exchange program for adolescents sponsored by AFS International or Youth for Understanding. Whatever the exact experience, they had to adjust to another culture, encountered confrontations with their expectations, were frustrated in their desire to be understood, and so forth. Given their firsthand knowledge of what is involved when people adjust to another culture, combined with their knowledge of Japanese culture learned since they were children, they make good cultural informants.

EFFECTIVE CONFLICT RESOLUTION. No matter how well prepared people are, and no matter how much help cultural informants can offer, people will encounter misunderstandings and conflicts when interacting in other cultures. One key to success in intercultural interactions is the ability to deal with the conflict such that long-term relationships are not threatened. Consider the following short case study (based on research by Saraswathi & Dutta, 1988).

Vasanthi was a foreign student from India studying at a university in the United States. She came from a family that would be considered "conservative" in India regarding the importance placed on traditional values. Consequently, even though she was 23 years old, she had little experience socializing with men outside her family. Paul, from Boston, Massachusetts, was one of her fellow students in a statistics class. Vasanthi was a very good statistics student, so good that she could offer help to others. Paul was quite grateful for all the help that Vasanthi offered to him, and presented her with a box of candy and a bouquet of flowers at the end of the semester. "I bought these for you," Paul told Vasanthi. "I was afraid that I was going to flunk, but your help allowed me to pull a 'B'." Obviously uncomfortable, Vasanthi accepted Paul's gifts but did not show any signs of appreciation and did not say "thank you." Paul concluded that Vasanthi was ungrateful and didn't seek out further interaction with her.

What mistakes were made? Studying the experiences of Japanese businesspeople in the United States, Black (1990) found that one predictor of success was the ability to solve conflicts in a manner that was collaborative, issue-oriented, and allowed for the development of mutual understanding. Rather than conclude that Vasanthi was an ungrateful person, Paul might have asked himself, "Are there cultural differences that may be causing difficulties?" By asking this question, Paul moves *away from* Vasanthi's personality as a cause of problems to an issue based on people's cultural background. Focusing on a cultural difference is far less threatening, and is far less likely to cause hurt feelings, than focusing on personalities. A focus on cultural differences also allows a collaborative effort toward dealing with the problem, since the misunderstanding is caused by the clash of two cultures, both of which must be understood. With a collaborative focus on culture and cultural differences, people also have the opportunity to develop a mutual understanding of why they behaved as they did.

In this case, there are many differences. Vasanthi has not had much practice receiving gifts from men, while Paul may have participated in many exchanges of gifts. Vasanthi does not know how to interpret Paul's gifts—is it a romantic gesture, a sexual advance, a symbol of thanks for help received, or something else? Vasanthi may be especially confused by the attention of American males if she is quite content to have her husband chosen by her parents. Other possibilities are even more complex. If Paul and Vasanthi had been spending a great deal of time together studying statistics, Vasanthi may have developed warm (nonsexual) feelings toward him and may look at him as a member of her collective. She may feel that Paul will always be close to her and will be one of the people she can call on in times of difficulty. People in the same collective don't have to say "thank you" when one member helps another. People in the same collective know their efforts are appreciated and that there will be many opportunities to reciprocate in the future. What Paul interprets as a rejection, then, may be the exact opposite: The absence of a clear "thank you!" can be interpreted as a sign of acceptance.

When conflicts occur, the best way of resolving them is to avoid conclusions about people's personal quirks and to search for underlying issues that will not threaten people if raised and discussed openly. A few days after the incident, for instance, Paul might engage Vasanthi in a discussion of gift giving in the United States and India. During discussion of this nonthreatening topic, information can be exchanged that can increase the chances of mutual understanding.

WILLINGNESS TO USE VARIOUS WAYS TO COMMUNICATE. To develop intercultural relationships and to intervene effectively when conflicts arise, people must be able to communicate effectively with others. The more ways in which people can communicate, the better. Two ways will be discussed here: use of the host culture's language, and nonverbal communication.

When people find themselves in settings where a different language is spoken, for example on international assignments, various aspects of oral communication must be understood. One is the distinction between knowledge of another language and the willingness to use it. In many cases, people's knowledge of another language is good enough so that they can enter various social settings and make their ideas known. However, they do not take advantage of these opportunities because they are afraid of making blunders. Given that they do not practice their language skills, they do not improve. Further, they do not benefit from the feedback that native speakers offer when mistakes are made. The fear of making mistakes is probably one reason why children *seem to be* more effective language learners (Hakuta, 1986). Adults, who pride themselves on their hard work, success in life, and status within their societies, do not like to think of themselves as people who make a lot of blunders. They may be very reluctant to enter social settings in which they might make mistakes, and mistakes are inevitable when using an unfamiliar language. Children, on the other hand, are not as concerned with protecting the self-image of "a competent and successful person." Children use their language skills in the school, on playgrounds, and in their neighborhoods. They can practice their skills, accept and benefit from the feedback they receive, listen to native speakers, and so forth. Consequently, they improve.

Returning to the problems faced by adults, there is an interesting link among the qualities of individuals under discussion here. If people are flexible and obviously enthusiastic about developing positive intercultural relationships, they are forgiven a certain number of mistakes. That is, hosts will forgive people from other cultures who sometimes use the host language incorrectly and even make social errors, such as speaking out of turn, bringing up a topic for discussion before others are ready, and so forth. The sense of people's overall goodwill and positive attitude toward intercultural relationships will outweigh a collection of mistakes. This aspect of intercultural contact is very similar to Hollander's (1985) concept of "idiosyncrasy credit" when analyzing the behavior of leaders in various organizations. If leaders work effectively on behalf of their groups *most of the time*, they are allowed to deviate once in a while from the group's preferences. Through their good works, they earn idiosyncrasy credit they can "cash in" when they find themselves unable to pursue a certain goal that their groups want to see accomplished. Given sufficient idiosyncrasy credit, they can refuse to pursue a certain goal and still retain their positions as leaders. In intercultural encounters, overall goodwill, respect, and enthusiasm allow people to generate "credit," and their credit allows mistakes to be ignored or forgiven.

People also communicate through nonverbal means (Hall, 1959, 1966). The study of nonverbal communication has become a speciality that has generated a great deal of research, and only a few highlights can be described here. In general, nonverbal communication refers to information exchange (or difficulties in such exchange) that do not involve oral or written forms of language. Examples are gestures, positionings of the body, tenseness of the body, facial expressions, and so forth (Damen, 1987). There are few cultural universals except the general advice that all cultures communicate through both verbal and nonverbal means, and that people should not draw conclusions concerning nonverbal behaviors without a great deal of knowledge. Understanding nonverbal interactions involves developing knowledge of many specific gestures, expressions, uses of the body, and so forth. For example, during face-to-face encounters, many Pacific Islanders flash their eyebrows in an up-and-down movement when listening to another person. If the person receiving eyebrow flashes is an American woman, she may be very disconcerted if she perceives the flashes as a sign of romantic and/or sexual gesture. In actuality, the eyebrow flash is merely a sign that the listener uses to communicate the message, "I am following what you are saying," and it has no meaning beyond this message. The equivalent in American English is the *verbal* "uh-huh" or the nonverbal slight head nod, both of which indicate that the listener is following (not necessarily agreeing with) what the speaker is saying. The distance people keep from each other is also a means of nonverbal communication. In the United States, if a man and woman meet each other for the first time, a typical distance they keep from each other is two-and-a-half to three feet. If they stand closer than that, it can be interpreted as a sign of more than casual interest in each other. In Latin America (Hall, 1966), on the other hand, the typical distance people stand from each other while conversing is about two feet. There is no special message of "desire for more interaction in the future" when people maintain this distance. Difficulties arise when Americans impose their interpretation of what a two-foot distance means during interactions with Latin Americans.

A willingness to communicate, then, refers not only to spoken and written languages but also to nonverbal behaviors. People who want to establish close intercultural relationships are well-advised to learn about nonverbal behaviors and to engage in as many as possible. Such behaviors can include much more touching than they are accustomed to, more bowing, longer periods of silence, different sets of gestures, greater use of the hands when speaking, greater sensitivity to the way time is used, and so forth (Damen, 1987). As with uses of the spoken and written language, people are forgiven a certain number of mistakes in nonverbal behaviors if their overall enthusiasm and goodwill concerning intercultural relationships is high.

DIFFICULTIES IN FACE-TO-FACE CONVERSATIONS

There is admittedly an ambiguous term in the last sentence. People may be forgiven "a certain number of mistakes," but when is this number too large for effective intercultural interaction to continue? No firm answer can be suggested because an answer is dependent on so many factors. For instance, the answer will be dependent on how many favors one person has done for others, how long the intercultural relationship has existed, the personalities of the people involved, the current political climate in a country concerning how much intercultural interaction is desirable, and so forth. Another factor is how much people know about the *style* in which people from different cultures communicate. Consider the behavior of two people who want to communicate with each other. "Style" refers to factors such as the manner in which people make their contributions to the conversation, the actual amount of talk (versus silence) that they prefer, and the degree of comfort and familiarity people communicate when introducing various topics. Analyzed by researchers such as Philipsen (1975; 1990a,b), Kochman (1981), and Carbaugh (1990a,b), communication style is one of the more difficult aspects of intercultural encounters to discuss. People are unaccustomed to examining stylistic differences as a reason for intercultural misunderstandings. Assume that two people meet, have a one-half hour conversation, and then go their separate ways with the conclusion that they don't particularly want to have any more interaction with each other. What could be the reasons? People *can* focus on such reasons as the lack of any common interests that could be discussed, such total disagreements on certain issues that there would be little gained through further conversations, and personality factors such as dominance ("never letting anyone else speak") or abrasiveness. People are less able to focus on stylistic factors, such as expressiveness or the use of silence, as reasons for the decision to limit further contact. Further, people may make mistakes if they fail to make distinctions between stylistic factors and personality factors. If they encounter a person who is very expressive in putting forth his or her contributions to the conversation, they may mistake expressiveness for "pushiness" or even "rudeness" (Sakamoto & Naotsuka, 1982). If they experience large amounts of silence during a conversation, they may focus on this stylistic feature but mistake it for "boredom" or "lack of interest in pursuing a relationship."

One reason for the difficulty of analyzing stylistic features is that there is no widely accepted language for talking about them, or no convenient set of terms that people can easily use. People *can* talk about personality factors (e.g., rudeness) and about the results of conversations ("I don't want any more interaction with that person!"), but they are less able to talk about the manner in which people interact as a reason for difficulties. One reason is that a person's cultural background provides guidance for conversing with others. In American culture, for example, guidance includes not interrupting, not dominating conversations, filling in periods of silence with small talk, and so forth. Keeping in mind the discussion in Chapter 1 that people take such cultural guidance for granted, they find it difficult to analyze cultural differences in communication style. For example, they find it difficult to consider that there may be cultural differences in the desirability of interrupting others (discussed in Chapter 5), putting one's ideas forward in a very vigorous and seemingly dominant way, or the acceptability of long periods of silence. However, if persons learn to analyze stylistic features and to recognize their importance, they are likely to have far more success in developing and maintaining intercultural relationships. They will learn to accept stylistic features as the products of cultural guidance and will not automatically interpret use of the features as signs of intercultural difficulties. Three examples will be considered here: the use of silence, the importance placed on a very expressive style, and the use of a warm and open style that appears to signal an interest in future interactions.

As part of these examples, the behaviors of people in three cultural groups will be examined: Native Americans, Black Americans, and middle-class Anglo Americans. As with all discussions of cultural influences upon behavior, the possibility of unreasonable stereotypes must be kept in mind. As discussed in Chapter 6, statements about cultural differences and culturally influenced behaviors must be carefully made. The three examples provided below will describe cultural norms—specifically, behaviors frequently found in three cultures. There *will be* exceptions. There will be individual Native Americans, Blacks, and middle-class Anglo Americans whose behavior is not well captured by these descriptions. Any generalization about culture and behavior provides a "first best guess" (Adler, 1991) about the differences persons who engage in intercultural encounters can expect. These first guesses should always be open to modification based on specific encounters with specific persons in the other culture.

SILENCE. The importance of stylistic features in communication can most readily be seen in actual examples of their use. Consider the following example.

John is a Native American who was raised on reservation lands in a rural area of Arizona. Having done well in his studies in a nearby high school, he won a scholarship to study at a university about 500 miles from his home. The scholarship was adequate to cover his basic support, such as tuition payments, board and room in the university dormitory, and books, but it did not allow "extras," such as frequent trips home. After his freshman year, he returned to his community for the first time in nine months. His parents met him at the bus station. They said nothing when they saw him. All silently got into the family car and drove home, again with no verbal communication. Stopping for groceries on the way home, John noticed a very attractive young lady who was stocking shelves. He later learned that she was a Native American named Irene and that her family had recently moved into the community. John looked at Irene, and Irene returned John's gaze while quickly looking up from her work, but no words were exchanged. John and his family paid for their groceries, got into their car, and continued home. With few exceptions (such as announcements about dinnertimes on various days), John and his family spoke very little to each other for the next few weeks. Are there any signs that John is having difficulties either with his family or with members of his community?

The answer is "no." John is encountering behaviors that are very common among Native Americans (the specific case studies from which this discussion draws are based on interviews with Western Apaches: Basso [1970]; see also Braithwaite [1990]). In many Native American cultures, silence is used as a response to ambiguity, especially when the ambiguity involves people's role relationships and relative status. *Role* is a term that refers to expected behaviors given some sort of label that people use when describing each other's positions within a society. Within a culture, there are behaviors that are expected of such role labels as "professor," "boss," "son," "secretary," "mother," and so forth. When entering a new community, people may be uncertain about the role expectations that *others* have. Silence as a response to ambiguity is one of several possibilities guided by one's culture. In other cultures (e.g., middle-class America), a frequent response when encountering ambiguity is to engage in small talk. If John and his parents were Anglo Americans, for instance, they would be likely to engage in small talk about the weather, the names of courses John has completed in college, recent events in the community, and so forth. On seeing Irene and deciding that he found her attractive, John might engage in such conversational openings as: "Where is the cheddar cheese?" or "How long have you been working here?" For many traditional Native Americans, silence is preferred.

What are the sources of ambiguity? There are at least two very clear sources in this story as analyzed by Basso (1970) and expanded upon by Braithwaite (1990). John's parents may fear that he has changed as a result of his study at the university, given that the predominant influences there are dictated by Anglo culture. "Uppermost is the fear that, as a result of protracted exposure to Anglo attitudes and values, the children have come to view the parents as ignorant, old-fashioned, and no longer deserving of respect" (Basso, 1970, p. 220). Parents are unlikely to question John directly about his experiences. This would place John in the uncomfortable experience of being directly interrogated, and this sort of behavior is frowned upon in Native American culture. Instead, the parents just wait silently. Eventually, John is expected to talk. Based on the sorts of topics he chooses to discuss, and the respect he shows to people based on his verbal and nonverbal behavior, the parents (and others in the community) can decide whether or not he still values his Indian identity or whether or not he has assimilated himself into Anglo culture. There is no pressure placed on John to begin speaking. This would interfere with John's choices about his own behavior, and this *avoidance of interference* is valued in his culture.

In his decision concerning how to communicate with Irene, there are several sources of ambiguity. John does not know Irene's family, since Irene (perhaps along with family members, perhaps not) has only recently moved into the community. Irene's family may have a higher status than John's, and this will influence how John behaves. Note how this is different from Anglo norms. During his stay at the university, even though John may be the son of a mechanic, he can approach and chat with a female classmate who is the daughter of a millionaire company president. Another source of ambiguity is that John and Irene do not know enough about each other, and have not known each other long enough, to have extended conversations according to cultural norms. "The Western Apache draw an equation between the ease and frequency with which a young couple talks and how well they know each other. Thus, it is expected that after several months of steady companionship sweethearts will start to have lengthy conversations" (Basso, 1970, p. 219). The desirability of silence is especially encouraged in young women because Native Americans equate silence with modesty. Further, if young women are overly fluent in conversations with men, this can be taken as a sign of too much experience with many men. In extreme cases, talkativeness may be interpreted as a willingness to engage in premarital sexual relationships, a practice frowned upon by elders.

There are other social settings that call for silence. These include meeting strangers for the first time, encountering and interacting with someone who is extremely angry, or consoling someone during times of grief, for instance, following the death of a spouse. As with the other two social settings of coming home to one's family and communicating with members of the opposite sex, ambiguity is involved. People don't know what to expect of others they meet for the first time. Are they individuals who bring goodwill with them, or are they out to cheat people and then leave the community? When encountering someone who is angry, people are unsure of how the other person will behave. The other may become so upset that he or she will harm others. Talk might increase the intensity of the person's behavior. It is considered best to wait silently until the person's anger is discharged, or until the person walks away. While consoling a person who is experiencing grief, there is often no need for talk since the people involved know that they care deeply about one another. In addition, people who are grieving over a loved one sometimes lose control of their emotions (Basso, 1970). Rather than encourage loss of control through talk about good times remembered from the past, it is considered best to remain silent.

The value placed on silence can have an impact on intercultural communication. I have spoken to several Anglo Americans who have taken jobs on American Indian reservations, often in the role of teacher. On arrival at the schools where they would be teaching, these people naturally expected a few words of welcome. Instead, they encountered silence. "Practically nobody spoke to me for six months!" one person remembered. The Native American use of silence in these cases is again a response to ambiguity. Indians will be concerned about how well-intentioned these Anglo newcomers are, whether they will be "fizzlers" who leave in a few months, whether they are bleeding-heart liberals who want to bring their "better" way of life to the Indians, and so forth. By observing the newcomers and waiting quietly for them to display their attitudes and intentions, long-time community residents can draw conclusions concerning whether or not extensive communication is advisable. Once a judgment is made that the newcomers are good people, verbal communication will begin.

EXPRESSIVENESS IN COMMUNICATION STYLE. Another feature of face-to-face communication is the degree of expressiveness that people use when conveying messages. *Expressiveness* can include the amount of emotion that people communicate in their choices of words and voice tones, the amount of body movements, the intensity with which they communicate disagreements with others, and the amount of boasting or bragging used when describing themselves (Kochman, 1981). Consider this example.

Harry is an Anglo American student taking a class in social psychology. The class instructor encourages a great deal of student participation, and so she approves Harry's plan to invite two Black students to come to class when the unit on "stereotypes and prejudices" is treated. Harry invites two Black students, Darrell and Jennifer, whom he met in the dormitory where he lives. As far as Harry can determine, Darrell and Jennifer are not particularly well acquainted.

Prior to class, Harry asked the two students to prepare a few remarks concerning their personal experiences with stereotypes and prejudice. Harry told the students he would simply introduce them, moderate any discussion, and help with the question–answer part of the class session. After introducing the two students, the discussion proceeded as follows:

DARRELL: America is a racist society! Blacks are not allowed the same opportunities as Whites in education and in organizations where they seek good jobs. As a result, many live in poverty.

JENNIFER: I personally have not experienced much prejudice. Sure, some people don't like Blacks and discriminate, but this is true of any group, including ethnic groups like the Polish or the Irish, even though they are all Caucasians.

DARRELL (with a great deal of emotion in his voice, and with a great deal of obvious tension in his body): How can you say that? If you have two applicants for a job with equal qualifications, one Black and one White, you know damn well that the White will get the job.

HARRY (trying to keep tensions from increasing): Since this is a college classroom, I think we should try to be less emotional in our contributions to the discussion.

JENNIFER (with just as much emotion in her voice as Darrell): No, let him have his say! I just think that Blacks have to stop whining and complaining about Whites and instead focus on their own behavior. I don't know any Whites forcing Black

14-year-old unmarried girls to get pregnant and have babies. Even Jesse Jackson talks about the problem of "Black babies having babies."

DARRELL (still visibly upset): That's easy for a member of the Black middle-class to say. These 14-year-olds you talk about were born into a poverty-stricken segment of society created by Whites!

Concerned that people's emotions had gotten out of hand, Harry called an end to the discussion. What was the problem?

From the Black viewpoint, there was no problem. The only problem is that the Black and White styles of discussion have clashed. As analyzed by Kochman (1981, 1990), Blacks value a very expressive style when they communicate. Perhaps as a result of years and years of being forced to hide their feelings and to defer to Whites (slavery, Jim Crow laws, segregated schools, neighborhoods, and churches), Blacks developed a very expressive communication style when in the company of other Blacks. The desire to express emotional intensity is part of being human. People did not want to suppress it, and so they used what opportunities they could to express themselves freely. For Blacks, these opportunities existed only when Whites were not present: in churches, Black-only dance halls, street-corner rap sessions, and so forth. After the Civil Rights movement of the 1950s and 1960s, and resulting legislation that allowed Blacks greater movement in society, Blacks did not have to limit their style according to the type of people they found in any given social setting. If they wanted to express themselves, they could do so, no matter who else was present!

Expressiveness includes the amount of emotion people put into their discussions about controversial matters. In the example, Darrell feels that he should put his position forward vigorously and with clear emotional intensity. In fact, part of the norms surrounding the style is that by putting forward his ideas in an intense manner, he is complimenting the others in the classroom. In effect, he is saying, "I respect you enough to put my position forward vigorously. I don't feel that you want me to beat around the bush. If you disagree, that's fine, just pay me respect by putting *your* position forward so that I can understand it clearly." Jennifer follows the expectations Blacks have by communicating her position in a manner just as intense as Darrell's. It is important to understand that Jennifer and Darrell do not necessarily view their contributions as attacks on each other. They are showing each other respect by allowing each other to put their positions forward (note Jennifer's comment to John, "let him have his say"). There is no evidence in this example that Jennifer and Darrell are upset with each other. They both have opinions; they disagree; they raise their voices. So what? They have expressed themselves and shown respect for each other. This is what is important according to Black norms concerning communication. As Kochman (1990, p. 204) points out:

Blacks' capacity to deal with intense emotional outputs is relatively greater than that of Whites because Blacks have greater experience of being confronted with them. Reciprocally, this capacity also gives Blacks acting in response to their own feelings greater freedom to express them intensely, knowing that others have developed the capacity to receive them without becoming overwhelmed.

When interacting with Blacks who feel that they should express themselves openly, Whites often become upset. The norms for conversation, according to the Whites' cultural background, is that people should not say things that might upset someone else. Since disagreements about important issues can upset people, it is better to find topics for conversation on which everyone can agree. Or if a controversial topic must be discussed, as they must in college classrooms, then people should do so in a calm, level tone of voice (recall Harry's request, "I think we should try to be less emotional"). So it is Harry who eventually becomes so uncomfortable that he tries to bring the conversation to a close. One difficulty people have in analyzing encounters, such as presented in this example, is that they are not prepared to talk about the fact that communication style, not just content, can cause difficulties. Given the inability to talk about style, they are likely to leave intercultural encounters with the vague conclusion that the conversations did not go well, but that they do not understand exactly why. Not knowing the reasons for difficulties causes stress, and the easiest way to avoid further stress is to avoid future intercultural encounters. If people understood that communication style can cause difficulties, and if they have some concepts to use in the analysis of problematic intercultural encounters (e.g., differing views of silence, the importance of expressiveness), they would not become as upset.

A WARM AND OPEN STYLE. The two examples discussed previously have dealt with Native American and Black American cultures. The approach taken was to analyze difficulties that an outsider might have in communicating with members of these two cultural groups. It must be kept in mind that all cultures have norms that can be misunderstood, or can be considered irritating, by outsiders. Consider the following example (from the research of Klineberg & Hull, 1979; and Triandis, Brislin, & Hui, 1988) of behavior that draws on communication norms commonly held in middle-class Anglo culture in the United States. The discussion of individualism and collectivism in Chapter 2 introduced concepts that are helpful in analyzing this example.

Simalee is a student from Thailand studying at a large university in the Midwestern United States. The university has an active program that encourages interaction among American and foreign students. In securing funding for this program, supporters argued (to the state legislature) that

Americans must learn about interaction across national boundaries given developments in the world's economy and political systems. Americans can prepare themselves for international experiences in their later lives through cooperative activities with foreign students.

Shortly after her arrival on campus, Simalee was invited to a reception for new students at the university. The international programs office had organized this reception, and its staff also invited some American students. At the reception, Simalee met an American student named Lisa. Lisa was very warm and open, asked about Simalee's interests, and even was able to suggest a few ways that these interests could be pursued in the United States. Simalee and Lisa talked for about 15 minutes before Lisa left the conversation and began to talk with someone else at the reception. Just before leaving, Lisa said, "I hope we get a chance to talk again soon."

About two weeks later, Simalee was walking across campus. She spotted Lisa about 100 feet away. As Lisa approached her, Simalee smiled and said "Hello." Lisa looked at Simalee with a rather vague expression on her face, then suddenly remembered the interaction at the reception two weeks ago. Lisa also said "Hello," but hurried on since she was late for her next class. Simalee walked back to her apartment, puzzled at the rather cool way that Lisa treated her. In contrast, Lisa arrived at her class and did not give the interaction with Simalee much thought. What are possible reasons for these differing reactions?

Lisa was socialized to behave in a way that is quite puzzling and disconcerting to people from many other parts of the world. She learned a communication style that allows a person to meet others quickly, put them at ease, find topics of conversation that both can talk about, and then leave the conversation in a way that is not considered abrupt. Part of the style involves a warm demeanor, a great deal of smiling, a relaxed body posture, and sense of enthusiasm and excitement about being present in the conversation. This style is useful for individualists like Lisa (Chapter 2). Since she does not have a collective or a support group constantly with her, it has been necessary for her to solve her own problems. The category "problems" is meant to be broad, and includes items such as the need to make friends, finding someone to fix a car, discovering how to drop a course, arranging for a ride home before holidays, and so forth. A communication style that allows an individual to meet others quickly, and to discover whether or not others can help, is very useful. Others in Lisa's culture know about this style and can interpret her seeming warmth and enthusiasm as simply the way people behave when they meet others for the first time.

Simalee, on the other hand, is from a collective culture. Since she has a constant support group on which she can call, she does not need to develop a communication style that allows her (as an individual) to meet others quickly. When she does have to go outside her collective, as she must if she studies overseas, she is much more likely than Lisa to be quiet, tentative, and careful during her conversations. So she is likely to be quite puzzled when she meets someone like Lisa at a party or at a reception. Her attribution (Chapter 2) of Lisa's warm behavior is likely to be, "This woman is showing interest in me, personally." Since she has *not* met hundreds of people with a similar style, Samalee has not learned to view the style as very typical among people in middle-class American culture. When she meets Lisa two weeks later on campus, then, she is very puzzled that Lisa does not continue her warm style. She is likely to view Lisa's behavior as a personal rejection. Further, she is apt to make negative attributions about Lisa. Readers might want to guess what these attributions will be. A hint is that the attributions consist of words that will be familiar to native speakers of English, but which those same native speakers do *not* necessarily use in the course of an entire month. Given this relative infrequency of use, native speakers are surprised to hear the words used by foreign students who are expressing themselves in a second or third language. The words are "superficial" and "insincere." Simalee is likely to conclude that since Lisa is so inconsistent in her behavior, warm one time and cold the next, that no further interaction is possible.

What are Lisa's attributions about the same behaviors? Lisa would argue that she was simply using the social skills and the communication style that her parents taught her: "be polite," "talk about things the other person is interested in," "keep the conversation flowing," and so forth. She would further argue that she was simply being nice to the foreign students she met at the party. When asked to interpret the second interaction on campus, she would argue that she talked to a lot of people at the reception and could not possibly remember the names of everyone. She had also talked to a large number of people over the two-week period between the reception and meeting on campus, again interfering with her memory of any one encounter. She was also in a hurry to class—surely people understand that reason for not being able to stop and chat!

The contrast between the warm and open communication style familiar to many Americans, and the more reserved style of people from other parts of the world, can have more intense consequences than those in this example. D.P.S. Bhawuk, from Nepal, worked with me for two years and prepared a summary of his thinking about the movement of people across cultures (Bhawuk, 1990). One of his observations was that males and females from different cultures can draw very different conclusions about romantic intentions. The danger is that if a young man from an Asian culture interacts with an American woman who employs the warm and exuberant style under discussion here, the man may attribute the style to a romantic interest in him, personally. For example, assume that an American woman helps an Asian male on a class assignment. The Asian (following norms in his culture) offers a small gift to show his appreciation. The American woman responds, "I just love it!! It's so great!! How thoughtful of you!!" The Asian may conclude that the comment about "loving it" extends to him, personally. Training programs to prepare American women to live in Asia often include treatments of this issue.

*A highly expressive style of communication can be misinterpreted
by people unfamiliar with it.*

The advice is that when interacting with males, tone down any natural exuberance in one's communication style. If this is not done, males will interpret the exuberance as a sign of romantic or sexual interest. This is difficult for many women to do because the style is so natural for them. Another reason for the difficulty of changing one's style, as previously mentioned, is that people are unaccustomed to talking about it. People have terms for disagreements about the content of their conversations, but not as frequently the style in which the conversation takes place. One of the ways to find out about subtle and underdiscussed issues of this kind is to seek out training programs that prepare people for successful inter-ultural experiences.

TRAINING PROGRAMS FOR MORE EFFECTIVE INTERCULTURAL INTERACTION

When they know that they will be engaging in extensive inter-cultural interactions, some people have the self-insight to know that they are not well prepared. If they know what culture is, and know how cultural differences affect interpersonal encounters, they may be able to say to themselves that they need more information. Many researchers and educators have been involved in the development of cross-cultural training programs, or formal efforts to prepare people to live and work in cultures other than their own (Landis & Brislin, 1983; Martin, 1986; Paige, 1986; Brislin, 1981, 1989; Bhawuk, 1990). The intercultural experiences for which people can be prepared include assignments in another country (e.g., Americans about to work in Japan), or extensive interaction among members of culturally diverse groups within a large country (e.g., His-panic Americans about to interact with Native Americans).

The goals of cross-cultural training are to prepare people for inter-cultural interactions so that they have a greater likelihood of meeting the four-part criteria of success discussed in the first part of this chapter. Success involves (1) positive feelings about the development of intercultural rela-tionships, (2) the reciprocation of these feelings from members of other cultural groups, (3) task accomplishment, and (4) minimal stress stemming from intercultural misunderstandings and difficulties. The content of train-ing programs often includes attention to people's thinking and cognitions, to their attitudes and feelings, and to their actual behaviors. In encouraging people to consider their thoughts, feelings, and behaviors, the adminis-trators of programs (most frequently called "trainers") often use critical incidents and case studies that capture commonly encountered intercultural difficulties (Brislin, Cushner, Cherrie, & Yong, 1986). Ideally, the inci-dents and case studies include experiences with which all program partici-pants (called "trainees") can identify. Given that they identify with *aspects* of the incidents (e.g., disagreements, the breakup of romances, failure to perform well in a job interview, a poor grade on a test), trainers can then point out how cultural differences affect the outcomes described in the incident. There is a two-part structure, then, to good critical incidents: elements with which everyone can identify, and additional information concerning cultural differences. Most often, the cultural information will be new and unfamiliar to trainees. But given that they understand *some* of the incident (the elements with which they can identify), they are likely to become interested in the cultural information so that they can diagnose the reasons for the difficulties presented in the incident.

An example should make the use of critical incidents clear, and it also allows a discussion of how the three-part analysis of thoughts, feelings, and actual behavior can be treated in training programs. Many training programs cover a critical incident similar to the one following (Foa &

Chemers, 1967; Brislin et al., 1986) because the difficulty treated is so commonly experienced.

Yoshiko is a student from Japan studying for a graduate degree in the United States. At her university, she enrolled in several graduate seminars that had only 10 or 12 other students. The professors in these seminars expected that the graduate students would contribute a great deal to discussions of current research issues, and that long lectures would be an uncommon event. The professors assigned students to prepare short presentations on various topics. The students would then present their ideas to class, and the other seminar participants would then contribute to the discussion of the issues raised in the presentation. Yoshiko was not familiar with this style of participation, given that she was far more accustomed to sitting quietly and taking careful notes while hearing lectures prepared by her professors. She was also unaccustomed to asking questions of her professors, as this was not a common practice during her undergraduate education in Japan. Her American colleagues were also accustomed to taking notes, but they were more familiar with the professors' expectations that they contribute given their participation in small classes (e.g., senior seminars) during the last two years of their undergraduate studies.

Yoshiko was friendly with Barbara, one of the other students in her department, and the two were participants in the same graduate seminar that dealt with the most recent research in personality testing. The professor asked Yoshiko to give a short presentation on projective tests. Yoshiko worked hard, prepared a clear handout for the rest of the class, and spoke for about 30 minutes. After her presentation, Barbara brought up several recent studies that Yoshiko had not discussed, and mentioned that these were on the "cutting edge" of current thinking about personality and its measurement. Other students also made contributions based on their thinking about the present and future status of projective tests. Barbara thought that the session went very well. After the session, however, Yoshiko told Barbara that she could not go to lunch with her, as they had previously planned. Since Yoshiko seemed a little upset after the session, Barbara wondered if something was wrong. She couldn't think of anything. "Yoshiko presented some interesting material and it stimulated a lot of discussion. I should think she would be pleased," Barbara thought. Is there a cultural difference that could be affecting the outcome (the broken luncheon engagement) of this incident?

The answer is "yes," and the reason involves a concept known as *differentiation*, and specifically differences among the expectations concerning how friends will behave. What behaviors are expected of friends? Most people will list answers, such as spending free time together, sharing emotional experiences, helping each other out in times of need, and so forth. In the language of Chapter 3, these are undoubtedly the etic or universal expectations of friendship. But there are other, emic, elements that differ from culture to culture. In the United States, a friend can be a constructive critic who makes helpful suggestions in a public forum (let's shorten this to "helpful public critic"). In the incident, Barbara feels that she is being a good friend. She listened attentively to Yoshiko's presentation during the seminar, and then made some helpful suggestions. The cultural difference here is that Yoshiko's does not expect friends to make critical remarks in public, no matter how positive the motivations are behind the suggestions. Yoshiko's expectations are that friends engage in supportive behaviors, not public criticism. Returning to the concept introduced in the first sentence, Yoshiko has more differentiated categories than Barbara as they apply to the behaviors experienced in this incident. Yoshiko has the same etic expectations for the behavior of friends (free time, sharing of emotions, etc.), but does not expect helpful public criticism. There may be helpful critics in her life, but these are not her friends. Helpful criticism is a behavior expected of people in another category. Consequently, Yoshiko feels betrayed. She was planning to engage in a friendly behavior, such as lunch with Barbara, but she felt that this was totally inconsistent with Barbara's public criticism.

Barbara, on the other hand, does not differentiate the behaviors described in the incident. Her expectations of what friends do include the same etic elements as Yoshiko's, but they also include the behaviors associated with being a helpful public critic. Consequently, Barbara does not see any difficulties with criticizing Yoshiko and then having lunch with her. The two behaviors are part of the same category.

The advice for people participating in cross-cultural training programs, then, is to examine incidents such as this one and to identify cultural differences that can be causing difficulties. A good starting point is to assume that people are trying to get along with others and trying to communicate effectively, but they have difficulties because they cannot recognize cultural differences. At times, insights into cultural differences can be gained by asking: Are people from one culture making differentiations within a category that people from another culture are *not* making? If so, can this be causing difficulties? Learning to understand difficulties based on differentiations can be useful in analyzing misunderstandings within one's own culture. Readers might try to identify a recent misunderstanding or set of irritations that had differentiation as a basis. For example, Protestants who call themselves "Baptists" recognize *many* distinctions within this category, and they are irritated when outsiders lump all Baptists together and make the same predictions about their religious beliefs. Faculty members have misunderstandings with secretaries when discussing instructions for the preparation of documents. The faculty members may have one word-processing program in mind that allows certain tasks to be done easily, while the secretaries may have switched to another. While not using the term, secretaries may complain that the impatient professors are not making proper differentiations between what various word-processing programs can do. Automobile mechanics find it difficult to help customers who complain of a rattle under the hood of their cars. The mechanics can differentiate the various parts of a car found under the hood. If all of these parts look and sound about the same to customers, communication is made difficult.

Looking for misunderstandings based on differentiations can often lead to very specific behaviors that allow effective communication to take place. Yoshiko did not have "helpful public critic" as part of her expectations of what friends do. However, a friend can be a "helpful *private* critic." If Barbara decided to behave according to Yoshiko's expectations, she could schedule an informal private meeting. There, Barbara could calmly make suggestions that could lead to improvements in Yoshiko's work. Even within the activities of this meeting, Barbara would want to work within Yoshiko's expectations. Barbara should keep the tone of the meeting as pleasant as possible. She should tell some jokes, and make sure that she says a number of good things about Yoshiko's presentations. Suggestions for improvements should be made only after these more positive preliminaries, and they probably should not take up more than 25–30 percent of the time that Barbara and Yoshiko spend together.

Note how the elements of this critical incident meet the suggestions for good cross-cultural training materials. Virtually everyone has been in a social encounter where they received more criticism than they thought they would. Everyone has also been disappointed when friends behaved in a manner other than the way that was expected. Given these common-alities to which everyone can relate, cultural differences can then be added to explain what can happen when the people involved are from different cultural backgrounds. In this case, people can also relate to one of the underlying bases for the difficulties, the differentiation of categories, given that this has undoubtedly caused some misunderstandings or irritations in their own lives.

The best cross-cultural training programs give guidance to people's thinking, feelings, and actual behavior. In fact, recommendations concerning the content of training programs is sometimes organized according to these three aspects of people's reactions to intercultural encounters (Brislin, 1989). It's useful to examine this same critical incident and to make recommendations concerning the thinking, feelings, and behaviors of trainees who might find themselves in similar encounters.

ATTENTION TO PEOPLE'S THINKING. Good cross-cultural training makes people's thinking more sophisticated. For example, it can assist people in developing new categories so that they can understand specific examples of those categories during their cross-cultural encounters. With-out categories that allow an understanding and interpreting of events, intercultural encounters become strange, puzzling, and upsetting. But with knowledge of appropriate categories, people can examine encounters and put them in proper perspective (Gardner, 1985). This assists greatly in the development of tolerance for behaviors that would *previously* have been labeled as strange, backward, or inferior.

In the incident, Barbara and Yoshiko have difficulties because their categories of "what friends do" have different elements. "Helpful public critic" is part of Barbara's category but not Yoshiko's. Further, Yoshiko differentiates behaviors into two categories: friend and public critic. The assumption behind cross-cultural training is that if people understand what categories are, and what it means when people in a certain culture differentiate categories, they will be better prepared for intercultural encounters. When faced with a difficulty similar to that depicted in the incident, they can say, "I shouldn't become upset. The other person is simply using a category, 'friend,' that has different content than mine." With this understanding, people can continue in their intercultural relationships without the emotional reaction that they have been betrayed or that they have been treated in a manner totally inconsistent with previous behaviors.

Another way training can encourage more tolerance and sophistication is to help people understand the nature of thinking itself. For example, people are much more influenced when an event happens to them, personally, than when they read about an event (Kahneman & Tversky, 1972; Brewer, 1979). If people read about a 3-year-old child who needs a kidney transplant, for instance, they may sympathize with the child's parents but will probably quickly forget about it given the many events that compete for their attention during the typical day. If it is *their* 3-year-old child who needs the transplant, the parents obviously become intensely involved and the search for a new kidney becomes the most important goal in their lives.

The difference in emotional intensity between reading about an incident and experiencing it personally will not always be as great as in this example of a child's health, but it is always present to some degree. When behaviors are personally targeted at people, those individuals will interpret them as more important, as more impactful, and as demanding more attention. It is exactly this aspect of people's thinking that can be introduced in good cross-cultural training. In the example involving Barbara and Yoshiko, the two women are certainly involved in a personal way, and are likely to interpret the behaviors as being personally directed at them. This will cause more intense reactions than if they had read about the incident, or if they had simply observed the same interaction between two other people in the seminar. If Barbara and Yoshiko react with intensity, however, it may be more difficult to "patch up" the misunderstandings at a later date. On the other hand, they may be able to maintain cordial communications if they understand the impact of events that *seem* personally directed. In effect, they can say to themselves, "I am tempted to interpret these behaviors as personally directed at me, and this can cause intense reactions. Since we are from different cultures, however, there are lots of reasons for misunderstandings. There may be *nothing* going on here directed at me, personally. I'm going to wait until I find out more!"

ATTENTION TO PEOPLE'S FEELINGS. There is a strong relationship between people's thinking and their feelings or emotions (Markus & Zajonc, 1985). People observe or experience behaviors and then interpret them in various ways. If they are disagreeing with someone and interpret a certain statement as an insult, they will become upset. If they interpret *that same statement* as simply the other person's way of advancing the discussion, they will continue the discussion with an absence of negative feelings. In addition to helping people think about and interpret events so that their emotional reactions cause as few difficulties as possible, good cross-cultural training recognizes that people are not always able to simply "interpret away" all events that can cause intense reactions. Certain behaviors people experience are so contrary to their expectations, based on their socialization in *their own* culture, that they cause emotional reactions when encountered in *other* cultures. Good cross-cultural training can prepare people for these types of emotional challenges.

In the incident involving Barbara and Yoshiko, both individuals will have emotional reactions. Yoshiko will be upset because she thinks that Barbara is withdrawing her friendship, and Barbara will be frustrated when she learns that the time and effort she put into being friendly was misunderstood. Even if the two individuals understand some of the underlying concepts, such as categorization, differentiation, and the expectations of what friends do in different cultures, they will still likely have emotional reactions. Sometimes, understanding the underlying concepts behind people's behaviors is enough to inhibit the emotions that stem from a reaction such as "strange" or "unfamiliar." If Americans doing business in Asia, for instance, realize that business cards are exchanged far more frequently than in the United States, they will simply pay $50 and have some cards made. As a result, they will be prepared to exchange cards and will experience no emotional problems when meeting Asian business-people. At other times, an understanding of underlying concepts is not sufficient. People can *know about* the uses of silence, discussed earlier in this chapter. They may have participated in a good cross-cultural training program where information on "silence as communication" was shared. But when experiencing interactions that involve long periods of silence, they still become upset! I have been in such interactions and still find them bothersome. I am tempted to fill the empty time with small talk, and I have to constantly tell myself, "Filling time is not required in all cultures like it is in the one in which I was socialized!" But if measuring instruments were strapped on to my body, I am sure that they would show increased blood pressure, increased heart rate, and increased respiratory rate during these periods of silence.

One way to prepare people for emotional reactions is to encourage them to actually participate in impactful experiences during cross-cultural training programs. For example, Yoshiko would be confronted with criticism in a public setting, and Barbara would interact with a person who misunderstood her friendly manner. The specific technique is called "role playing," and it is quite an effective training approach (Elms, 1972; Gudy-kunst & Hammer, 1983; McCafferey, 1991). Trainers identify a set of potentially problematic intercultural experiences, and trainees then take various "roles" or parts in the mini-drama. For example, assume that there is a training program to prepare Asian students for their graduate-level degree programs in the United States. The trainers decide that "participating in a small seminar" involves a good set of experiences to cover because Asian students are often unfamiliar with the expectations that they participate vigorously in interactions with professors and fellow graduate students. One Asian student would role-play Yoshiko, an Ameri-can would play Barbara, and others would role-play the professor and graduate students who contribute to the discussion. The assumption behind role playing is that by actually experiencing what frequently happens in real intercultural encounters, people become prepared for the emotional reactions that follow from such encounters. If the Asian role-playing Yoshiko faces disagreement from others, there *is* an emotional reaction even in the somewhat artificial setting provided by the trainers. Other emotional reactions will result from the expectation to "speak up" in the seminar, since this is what good graduate students are supposed to do. The student assigned the role of Barbara will also have an emotional reaction when she has to "play out" the experience of having her friendly behavior misunderstood. Other behaviors she might experience are en-couraging international students to both speak out and to accept criticism and constructive comments graciously.

There are a number of benefits to role playing. In actually playing out the behaviors, such as those involved in a seminar, people do not work from a completely prepared script. Rather, the trainer suggests general guidelines and people then make up the script as they go along. When people play their roles in this manner, they frequently find themselves saying things that they have never thought through completely prior to the training program. Later, they think through their statements and say to themselves, "Why did I say that? Did I really mean it?" This very private set of thoughts contributes to a unique learning experience that is especially impactful since the individuals involved designed it themselves as they role played the scene. For example, a student playing one of the graduate students in the seminar might find himself or herself asking, "Yoshiko, what do you think about this issue, based on your experience in Japan?" Later, that student might think, "I wonder if I said that because I was really interested in the point of view of people from other cultures." This is an important self-generated thought that the person should care-fully examine. The appreciation of other people's viewpoints, of course, is central to effective intercultural interactions.

Decisions concerning whether or not to use role playing should not proceed without considering its potential disadvantages. In a chapter with the especially intriguing title "Role Plays: A Powerful But Difficult Training Tool," McCafferey (1991) discusses a number of disadvantages.

One is that the content of the role plays can become so emotionally arousing that the trainees become extremely upset, so much so that they are unable to continue in the training program. Human behavior is very complex, and a role play that seems totally innocent and unthreatening can trigger intense reactions in just one trainee. When one trainee is obviously debilitated, of course, the training must come to an end until that person's needs are thoroughly addressed. For example, a trainer might feel that some basic ideas about male–female dating relationships should be covered so that international students are introduced to some aspects of campus social life. The person role-playing a male who wants a date may *just happen* to have a set of mannerisms similar to the person who tried to rape one of the trainees a few years ago. The trainee becomes very upset due to a specific set of circumstances that no trainer could possibly foresee. Reactions such as this happen frequently enough for Jim McCafferey to have chosen the title that he did. The recommendation for role playing as a training technique is that it should only be used by very experienced people who have guided its use many times. Inexperienced people should apprentice themselves to others who have used role playing frequently, in many places, and with many different types of trainees. In the training programs I have organized, I add a number of "rules" that all trainees agree to prior to their actual role plays. These include (1) working together in small groups for about 30 minutes going over what will later actually happen in the role play; (2) working from one or more of a collection of 100 critical incidents (Brislin, et al., 1986) that everyone can read prior to the role plays; and (3) accepting the rule that once the basic events that will occur in the role play have been formulated, there will be "no surprises." No one will say anything (e.g., a criticism Barbara makes about Yoshiko) that is different from the sorts of statements to which people agreed during the 30-minute planning session. It is the suprises that cause intense reactions since people are totally unprepared. This point is covered as part of the introduction to the role playing exercises. In my experience, if people accept the rules, then the time devoted to role playing is well spent. Even with the possibility of intense emotional reactions being carefully avoided, there are still many behaviors that occur during role playing that provoke discussion and that provide specific examples of newly introduced concepts.

ATTENTION TO PEOPLE'S BEHAVIORS. In addition to people's thinking and to their emotional responses, cross-cultural training can also deal with actual behaviors. For the purposes of this discussion, *behaviors* refers to the actions of people that can be observed by others as well as by themselves. The first part of this informal definition is important, of course, since people's behaviors that are observed by others are often the only basis the others have to make decisions about matters such as the desire for future interactions. The latter aspect is also important because people monitor *their own* behaviors and draw conclusions about it. For example, when deciding what courses to take next semester, a student might say to himself or herself: "There is a course in international diplomacy. Am I interested? I attend a lot of meetings organized by the international student group here on campus. I guess I can do okay in the course."

In good cross-cultural training programs, people can be asked to focus on the actual behaviors they perform in a wide variety of social settings (Cushner, 1989). Then, they can examine those behaviors and decide if some should be abandoned or modified so that the chances of success are increased when residing in other cultures. For example, recall that one of the four criteria of success discussed in the first part of this chapter is that people from other cultures must develop positive relationships with hosts. So how, exactly, can this be done? Trainees might be asked to write down exactly how they would develop positive relations with others in their own culture. Then, trainers can guide examinations of whether or not these same behaviors will be helpful in developing relationships in the host culture. If the trainees are from collective cultures, for example, they might write down that the development of new relationships often stems from introductions arranged by relatives or long-term friends. Help with meeting new people, then, is one of the expectations people have, given their loyalty to a collective. If they are living in an individualistic culture like the United States, however, the trainees will probably not have a supportive collective that accompanies them. They will have to develop positive relationships through another set of behaviors. Trainers can then guide these persons into listing a set of behaviors that are more appropriate in the host culture, and they can help trainees rule out behaviors that are possible but extremely difficult. For example, trainees *might* list that they can walk up to people (e.g., in the student union or library) and simply introduce themselves. While a possibility, trainers would have to point out that this is difficult even for socially skilled people who have lived their entire lives in the United States. A better possibility is to attend gatherings where it is expected that people introduce themselves, such as at receptions sponsored by various groups on campus. Another possibility is to encourage trainees to list their interests and hobbies (e.g., dance, drama, politics, computers) and to guide them toward various on-campus clubs where they can meet like-minded people.

In the incident involving Barbara and Yoshiko, both individuals could list behaviors that they could then modify, abandon, or develop. Yoshiko could list that she needs to speak up and to accept criticism graciously, and she could practice these as part of role playing exercises. Yoshiko could also perform these as part of "homework" exercises outside of the cross-cultural training session. Later, she could report back to the trainer and could discuss the results of her efforts. Barbara could practice ways of keeping her comments to herself during the seminar session, especially when she finds herself in social settings with Asian students who have probably *not* been exposed to a good cross-cultural training program.

She could *later* take her fellow student aside and offer her feedback in the manner more acceptable to Asians. She could also practice explaining how constructive criticism is offered in American seminars, thus preparing the Asian student for future encounters in other seminars whose participants are not as knowledgeable about cultural differences as Barbara.

I have had arguments with many people about this segment of a cross-cultural training program. Others argue that people shouldn't be asked to modify their behaviors because they would then be false to themselves. If they follow the advice to list and to modify behaviors, they will be inconsistent with their own natural preferences to behave in the manner that they always have. Further, they argue, people would be treating individuals from another culture in a dishonest and even dis-respectful manner. In the case of criticism in public, for example, some individuals argue that foreign students should learn to "take it" and that Americans are saying that the students don't have the maturity to do so if Americans wait and give their comments in private. People from other cultures deserve our honest reactions to their behaviors, they argue. Neither one will understand the other if each modifies their preferred behaviors. I respond that there are always modifications in preferred behaviors to meet the demands of various social settings. If people have a proposal to make, they surely behave in a different manner if they are sharing it with friends versus discussing it with the powerholders who have the authority to grant or withhold support. If people receive a perfectly dreadful gift from an 8-year-old child who made the present with his or her own hands, they do not give their "honest" reactions to the child. Rather, they modify this behavior and respond in a gracious manner, telling the child how wonderful the gift is. Modifying one's behaviors to meet various demands in life is part of social skills (Brislin, 1991). When interacting with people from different countries, the rec-ommendation for this type of behavior modification is to take into account the cultural background of the other people. With respect to the objection that people won't learn to understand each other if behaviors are con-stantly being modified, my response is that good cross-cultural training programs recommend that trainees become involved in many activities within the host culture. In so doing, they will meet all kinds of people, many of whom will not know how to modify their behaviors even if they wanted to do so. In the United States, for example, they will meet many Americans who engage in typically American behaviors! To maintain the enthusiasm of trainees for continuing the recommended involvement, it is essential that they have *some* successes. These successes, especially during people's first few months in a new culture, are more likely to happen if hosts are sensitive enough to take people's cultural background into account when making decisions about their behaviors.

IMMERSION INTO ANOTHER CULTURE. In addition to increasing the chances of successful intercultural encounters, another reason to modify actual behaviors is that change is sometimes necessary for survival in another culture. If such behaviors can be identified, they can be practiced during training programs. Gregory Trifonovitch (1977) has been involved in training Peace Corps volunteers and American schoolteachers who accepted two-year assignments in rural villages on various small Pacific Islands. Having lived on such an island himself, Trifonovitch knew the changes in everyday behaviors that would be necessary for survival and for a chance (at the end of two years) that the volunteers and teachers would consider their sojourn successful. Consequently, he designed a training program that immersed people into another culture. All trainees flew into the airport in Honolulu, Hawaii. From there, they were taken to rural parts of Molokai or Oahu, two islands in the Hawaiian chain. There they found the village in which they would live during their two-week training program. Built to be as close as possible to the sorts of villages in which they would be living for two years, trainees had to learn to meet their everyday needs in ways new to them. There were no grocery stores, so they had to gather their own food, such as coconuts and fish. There was no radio or television, so they had to entertain themselves. There was no plumbing, so they had to find fresh water and make provision for the disposal of human wastes. There was no public transportation, so they had to walk or learn to travel by boat, necessitating awareness of ocean currents and tides. They also had to learn to tell time by the position of the sun and stars in the eventuality that their clocks might stop—there was to be no access to repair shops. The staff for the training program included Pacific Islanders who could teach the behaviors necessary for success, and who could also answer questions and make presentations concerning life in rural island villages.

This immersion program represents one of the most intense experiences ever developed for the preparation of people about to enter another culture. Some trainees learned what was necessary for success in a Pacific Island community and left the training program well prepared for their two-year assignments. Others did not survive the training and went back to their homes, canceling their agreements to serve in the Peace Corps or to become schoolteachers. There are many possible reactions to the finding that some trainees dropped out. One is that the training program was too intense and "burned the trainees out." Consequently, the trainers should lessen the intensity of training to encourage more graduates to see it through to completion. Another reaction is that the training program should retain its intensity and realism. After all, people will be living in remote island villages. They *should* be exposed to the demands that such intercultural assignments will bring. Further, it is far less expensive and less stressful to leave a training program and return home than it is to leave the actual assignment sometime during the two-year period.

Recognizing the complaints and the admitted stresses of organizing and administering immersion training programs, Trifonovitch (1977) argued along the lines of the second reaction. People should be exposed to the behaviors necessary for success during training, and should then make their own decisions about the future. When people decided to leave the training program and cancel their two-year agreements, Trifonovitch responded in an interesting and intriguing manner. He threw a party for them! He announced that the party was to celebrate the people's self-discovery. Living on a Pacific Island is not for everyone, he would say. There is nothing wrong with this fact—lots of very decent people simply would not be happy on such an assignment. They would be far happier spending the two years somewhere else. Other people learned a lot during training and were prepared for life in the Pacific. That's fine too! But there is nothing inherently better about one set of people compared to the other. By focusing on self-discovery, Trifonovitch encouraged the dropouts to look upon training as a success rather than as a failure. Everybody involved learned a great deal about themselves, and this is what is most important in the search for happiness in life.

Trifonovitch's decision concerning how to respond to trainee drop-outs is a good example of tolerant behavior and of good managerial skills. Intolerance stems from insistence on one type of behavior and the demonstration of obvious disapproval when there are deviations from the preferred behaviors. In the example of this intense training program, an intolerant response would be that everybody should keep a stiff upper lip and "stick with" the training until its completion. Such intolerance, however, can lead to poor adjustments of people to their work. Extremely unhappy people will not be good schoolteachers, and young islander students will suffer. Tolerating different behaviors, and developing a sensitivity to the fact that not all people will find satisfaction in the same types of work, are necessary if individuals are to become good leaders and managers in the workplace. The importance of understanding cultural differences as they apply to the world of work is the topic of the next chapter.

CHAPTER SUMMARY

Even when people are unprejudiced and have no intention to discriminate against people from other ethnic groups, there still can be problems in their intercultural interactions. Some of the reasons, including the style people use when interacting with others, are very subtle and hard to understand. Further, there is no convenient language widely available that allows people to discuss the intercultural difficulties that might be called, "beyond prejudice and discrimination." Consequently, special training programs often have to be established during which the difficulties can be discussed openly.

If people are to overcome misunderstandings and be more successful in their intercultural interactions, an understanding of "success" is necessary. A four-part definition has been suggested: (1) people enjoy interacting with individuals from various cultural backgrounds; (2) these feelings are reciprocated by those culturally diverse individuals; (3) the tasks that people want to accomplish (e.g., obtaining a degree, negotiating a contract) are completed within a reasonable amount of time; and (4) there is no additional stress brought on because the people working together are from different cultural backgrounds. All four parts are necessary to be successful: three out of four are not sufficient! For example, interactions can be imagined in which people (1) enjoy their interactions, (3) get their work done, and (4) feel little stress. However, individuals from other cultural groups (in reference to number 2 of the success definition) may dislike these people, feel they are insensitive, and argue that they are not bringing in diverse viewpoints to the task at hand.

People with a certain set of traits and skills have a greater chance than others for achieving success in their intercultural interactions. If people are *culturally flexible*, they are able to make changes in their behaviors that meet the demands of various social settings. If flexible American businesspeople find themselves in Japan, for example, they are willing to engage in much more "small talk" than if they were doing business in their own country. The Japanese want to know their business counterparts *as people*. Chats about people's backgrounds and interests allows them to get to know one another. One reason is very pragmatic. If problems arise in business dealings, the Japanese strongly prefer that the involved people work cooperatively, with mutual trust and goodwill, toward a solution. The Japanese do *not* want to bring in a team of lawyers. The long hours spent on small talk is their way of determining whether or not potential counterparts can be trusted to bring goodwill to the negotiations. Some people are actively *enthusiastic* about developing intercultural relationships. Rather than just tolerating such interactions as necessary for task completion, they actively look forward to the stimulation that intercultural relations can bring (Fontaine, 1990). Enthusiasm also encourages people to use *various ways of communicating effectively* with others. For example, they become willing to put in the hard work necessary to learn another language, and to learn the nonverbal behaviors necessary for good communication. One of many reasons that children seem to be better language learners than adults is that they are more willing to engage in conversations during which they make mistakes. They are not as embarrassed, learn from their mistakes, and continue conversing. Many adults, on the other hand, do not like making mistakes in public and consequently do not give sufficient time and attention to practicing their language skills. An enthusiasm about developing intercultural relations can help to overcome the discomfort that results from making mistakes.

Successful people also have methods to resolve conflicts effectively. Just as mistakes will inevitably be made when people struggle in another language, so will mistakes be made when developing close intercultural relationships. No person can be prepared for every eventuality that will occur in their futures. Interestingly, the *more* people develop intercultural relations, the more difficulties they are likely to have. Culturally influenced norms will be violated, conversational topics will be raised at the wrong time, polite comments to pass time will be taken seriously, and so forth. It is relatively easy to avoid such intercultural mistakes—just avoid any interaction with people from other cultural backgrounds! The alternative to this decision is to possess the skills that allow *effective conflict resolution*. Black (1990) identified such skills. If people could address difficulties in a collaborative manner, focus on issues instead of personalities, and work toward mutual understanding, conflicts would not necessarily interfere with the long-term development of intercultural relationships. Focusing on cultural differences can frequently be part of this conflict-resolution approach. One person might say to another, "We disagreed the other day on an issue. I wonder if the fact that we are from different cultures, and have different ways of doing things, could have been a part of the disagreement." Focusing on cultural differences takes away the more threatening focus on personalities. If people have developed "cultural informants," they will be better able to use this conflict-resolution approach. A cultural informant is a knowledgeable individual who can answer queries when difficulties arise. If a businessperson can't understand the reason for all the small talk in Japan, a Japanese cultural informant can point out, "It's a way of developing trust, and a lot cheaper than a team of lawyers!" Cultural informants are often individuals who have lived in another country. For instance, the Japanese cultural informant may have attended college in Europe. As a result of his or her own cultural experiences, the informant knows what adjustment to another culture is, how people can misunderstand everyday encounters, how people's cultural background can affect their everyday behavior, and so forth.

Cultural informants may also be able to give advice and offer very subtle reasons for misunderstandings that might be missed by well-meaning people who have not previously engaged in extensive intercultural interactions. One set of subtle reasons can be summarized by the term "communication style." People have vocabulary terms that allow them to talk about disagreements and misunderstandings that stem from the content of their communications with others. They are not as likely to have terms that allow them to discuss differences in the style people use when they communicate. Three examples of stylistic differences are the use of silence, expressiveness, and warmth and openness that seems to signal a desire for further communication. As with many examples of cultural differences, concepts become especially clear when the styles of people from different cultures are contrasted. In any discussion of style, it is important to remember the danger of stereotypes (Chapter 6). Stylistic features will be discussed that are commonly found among members from identifiable cultural groups. This does not mean that all members of those cultures behave in the same manner. The possibility of individual differences must be constantly kept in mind.

Silence is commonly found as part of communication style among Native Americans. When Anglo Americans interact with Native Americans, they often want to fill periods of silence, feeling that too much silence is a sign that interpersonal interactions are not proceeding well. As a consequence, Native Americans may conclude that the Anglos are frivolous people who talk even when they do not have anything to say. Native Americans use silence in social settings involving ambiguity. When meeting a stranger, for example, it is ambiguous whether or not the person brings goodwill or intentions to take advantage of people. Native Americans prefer to wait until the stranger demonstrates his or her intentions before they engage in conversations. When a young man or woman comes home from a year at an urban university, the family does not know whether or not the student has adopted "white man's ways." The family members feel that it is best to remain silent until the student demonstrates whether or not Native American ways are still respected.

Many Black Americans commonly employ a very expressive style in which they put their emotions "up front" (Kochman, 1981, 1990). In contrast to the socialization of many Anglo Americans who are told to keep controversial opinions to themselves for fear of offending people, Blacks feel that they are showing respect to others when they communicate their feelings in an expressive manner. They then expect others to do the same. If there is disagreement, that is acceptable since the most important goal is to express oneself openly. Anglo Americans can leave intercultural interactions with the feeling that Blacks were too intense and not willing to listen to anyone else. Blacks may leave the same conversation feeling that the Whites never have anything to say and are uncooperative when dealing with controversial issues because they keep their opinions to themselves.

Anglo Americans commonly employ a very warm and open style when meeting people for the first time. One reason is that many were socialized into an individualistic culture. Since they do not have a supportive collective to call on when they need assistance on everyday matters, such as obtaining help with job searches and repairing cars, they develop a warm and open style that allows them to meet others quickly. Then, help can be sought from these newly met others. This style can be very confusing to people not familiar with it. If people were raised in a collective culture, they did not have to develop a style that allowed them to meet others quickly. This was a task for which help could be sought from members of one's supportive collective. When they *do meet* warm and open individuals, they feel that those individuals are treating them in a manner that shows special interest. The attributions (Chapter 2) are quite different. The individualists conclude that they are simply using the social skills their mothers taught them. The collectivists conclude that the people they recently met are superficial and insincere.

Examples of intercultural difficulties such as this can be effectively addressed in cross-cultural training, or formal efforts to prepare people to reside and work effectively in cultures other than their own. Good training programs address people's thinking, feelings, and actual behaviors. Assume that trainers want to cover the (commonly experienced) problem of how people can disagree with their friends. In some cultures, such as middle-class United States, people can read a friend's proposals, and then make public suggestions concerning how some points can be changed and thus improved. In other cultures this is not possible—friends *do not* disagree in public. In addressing people's *thinking*, trainers would point out that roles are being differentiated. In some cultures, the category "friend" can include a person with whom one spends a lot of free time and with whom one disagrees in public. In other cultures, these roles are differentiated: The same people cannot engage in both behaviors. The people who are one's friends are different from people who can disagree in public. A person who differentiates the roles, then, would feel that an individual is withdrawing his or her friendship when engaging in the role of "public critic".

In addressing people's feelings, trainers would encourage individuals to actually encounter challenges to their cultural background during the training program. The assumption is that people will inevitably encounter challenges after training, and so it is best to prepare people during formal programs when there are helpful and knowledgeable individuals who can assist in the process of adjusting to another culture. It *is* emotionally arousing to have one's expectations disconfirmed. If people expect friendship, they are upset to find a critic! During training, people can role-play such encounters, with one trainee acting out a person who makes a short presentation, another who disagrees, another who acts as a cultural informant who has experienced such encounters in his or her own life, and so forth. If people learn about potential emotional challenges during training, they are better prepared to deal with these during their actual intercultural encounters after the training program ends (Cushner, 1989).

In addressing people's behaviors, trainers would encourage people to think about changes in their day-to-day actions that could increase the chances of success. Some examples have already been covered: Americans should be more willing to engage in extensive small talk in Japan; Anglo Americans should not rush to fill periods of silence when interacting with Native Americans; Black Americans might make sure that they are encouraging Anglos to communicate their feelings openly and to hold nothing back. In the example involving friendship and disagreement, people might practice responding to disagreements in a gracious manner and using the suggestions of others to improve one's work. Or, people who *might* express their disagreement in a public meeting might wait and share their reactions in a private conversation with their friends.

When people are willing to modify their behaviors to meet the expectations of people in other cultures, they are demonstrating that they are tolerant individuals. They are communicating the point that there are many ways to behave and that the ones with which they are most familiar, from their own socialization, are not necessarily the best for all people in all parts of the world. People who happen to be socialized so that they are familiar with a different set of behaviors should be respected. Tolerance for the differences brought on by one's ethnic heritage, cultural background, religion, gender, sexual orientation, and medical history is becoming an increasingly important issue in various parts of world. Just one reason is that tolerance, and ideally enthusiasm, concerning differences will be necessary in the world of work because leaders need to integrate the various contributions people can offer. Leaders will be able to encourage more contributions if they appreciate differences and avoid forcing everyone to behave in exactly the same manner. This is one of the topics addressed in the next chapter that deals with cultural differences in the workplace.

CULTURE'S EFFECTS ON
THE WORLD OF WORK

The prediction has been made several times in this book that the future will bring the necessity for people to make more decisions about intercultural interactions in which they might participate. This fact about the future led to its treatment in two chapters, one on the difficulties to be overcome (such as prejudice: Chapter 6) and the other on more subtle issues once people have made the decision to seek out intercultural interactions (e.g., communication style: Chapter 7). One of the important aspects of decision making concerns the range of settings in which people find themselves. In some settings, there is more freedom of choice concerning intercultural interactions than in others. Many people, for example, choose to live in neighborhoods where most of the other residents are from a background similar to themselves. Or, they choose to spend most of their voluntary free time with people who are culturally similar. In other settings, there is less choice. In many countries, if parents want their children to attend public schools, the child will inevitably encounter classmates from a variety of cultural backgrounds. Laws in these countries dictate that schools are to be integrated and that there can be no discrimination on the basis of skin color, ethnicity, and a number of other factors. If parents want to circumvent these laws, they have to seek out or establish private schools and must pay sizable tuitions. Even with private schools, governments can demand integration if the schools seek out public funds (e.g., for school lunches, tax dollars that support military dependents, and so forth).

Another setting where there is less choice than in one's voluntary free time is the workplace. There have been massive changes in the composition of the workforce in countries such as the United States over the past 50 years. Years ago, a White male could accept a job in a large organization and find himself in the company of people who were much like himself. Today, a host of laws demand that organizations recruit and hire females, Blacks, Hispanics, the handicapped (Gaylord-Ross, 1987) and so forth. In addition to intercultural interactions with co-workers, many American workers will find themselves in jobs involving international contact. Either they will accept overseas assignments (Adler, 1991) or will find themselves working in organizations located in the United States but owned by foreign nationals (Rigby, 1987; Nath, 1988). Those foreign nationals may hire executives from their own and other countries, forcing Americans to work for a boss born and socialized in another culture. The Americans, then, have a choice between (a) quitting their jobs or (b) learning to work effectively with people from other cultures. This chapter is meant to provide helpful concepts for people who choose the second alternative (b).

Just as in the contrast between Chapter 6 concerned with prejudice and Chapter 7 concerned with successful communication, people can bring a negative, neutral, or positive attitude toward intercultural relations to the workplace. With a negative attitude, people may act in a discriminatory way toward outgroup members, denying them opportunities such as difficult assignments that allow them to prove their worth to the organization. With a neutral attitude, they may merely tolerate cultural differences and try to minimize their influence in the workplace. With a positive attitude, on the other hand, people will actually look forward to the stimulation that cultural differences can bring (Cushner, 1989; Martin, 1989). They will benefit from the differences that workers will bring to their jobs. Employers, for instance, will value the diverse experiences that members of their workforce have had and will attempt to benefit from their varied backgrounds, language skills, types of education, travel, "contacts" with influential people in various communities, and so forth. With this positive attitude, cultural differences will be looked on as a potentially rich fruit orchard that should be treated with care and enthusiasm.

Four general topic areas will be covered in this chapter involving the relation between culture and work.

1. Since much relevant cross-cultural research on worker values is based on a method of statistical analysis involving ecological correlations, an understanding of the difference between this and the more familiar analysis based on individual-level correlations is necessary. Understanding the two types of correlations also allows further treatment of a theme introduced several times in previous chapters (e.g., 1 and 5): the distinction between individual and cultural differences. When interpreting individual-level correlations, researchers can focus on aspects of people. When ecological correlations are based on data collected in various countries, researchers can suggest interpretations based on cultural differences.

2. When moving between cultures, people are likely to confront differences in work values that involve individualism versus

collectivism, power distance, uncertainty avoidance, masculinity versus femininity, and (in Asia) Confucian dynamism.

3. Leadership has been a focus of active research, and investigations have moved beyond descriptions of the traits of leaders to a greater sensitivity to the social context in which leadership takes place.

4. In many parts of Asia, subordinates prefer a leadership style known as "paternal authoritativeness." This is a very puzzling style for many Americans, and is a source of difficulties for Americans who accept leadership positions in Asia.

UNDERSTANDING ECOLOGICAL CORRELATIONS

When people work in a country other than their own, or work in an organization owned and operated by foreign nationals, they will inevitably encounter a number of challenges to their expectations. The challenges will be especially impactful if they have held other jobs in their own country and have interacted with few co-workers from culturally different backgrounds. Many resulting frustrations will stem from the realization that the behaviors *they* thought appropriate in the workplace are considered unacceptable by members of the other culture.

A number of helpful guides have been developed that can assist people adjust to the workplace in other cultures (Brislin, et al., 1986; Miller & Kilpatrick, 1987; Adler, 1991). An especially helpful set of five concepts has been developed by Geert Hofstede and his colleagues (e.g., Hofstede, 1980; Hofstede & Bond, 1988; Chinese Culture Connection, 1987), and these have generated a great deal of research by other scholars (e.g., Earley, 1989; Kim, Park, & Suzuki, 1990). To use these concepts in analyzing intercultural behavior in the workplace, it is first necessary to understand the meaning of *ecological correlations*.

Let's begin the discussion with an explanation of "correlation," a topic that students may have covered in other classes. A correlation is a mathematical statement that communicates the association between two variables. For example, most readers have taken a set of tests during their high school years in anticipation of attending college. These test scores were part of the application materials that people presented to various colleges. The test scores (the most common is the Scholastic Aptitude Test, or SAT) is considered valuable since performance on it is *associated* with success in college. The mathematical relationship, or correlation, between test scores and college grades is positive ($r = .30$ to $.45$, depending upon the college). This is not a perfect relationship, but it does provide useful information to college administrators and counselors who work with students. The interpretation of correlations must always be made carefully. In this example, test scores do not cause good grades, of course. Rather, there are most likely aspects of human behavior (such as verbal and mathematical skills) that are both tapped by the test *and* that are useful in the college classroom.

The association between test scores and college grades is summarized by an individual-level correlation. The word *individual* indicates that each piece of information was gathered from distinct people: Person A provided both test scores and his or her college grades, as did persons B, C, D, and so forth. A mathematical formula was applied to the two sets of information, and the results were summarized in the form of a correlation coefficient (indicated by the letter r as mentioned above). Individual-level correlations allow researchers to suggest reasons for the association between test scores and college grades, and the reasons almost always focus on the traits, abilities, and other aspects of *people*. Correlations usually entertain a number of reasons for their existence. Some researchers suggest that the tests measure important abilities, such as reading comprehension, and such abilities lead to good grades. More skeptical researchers say that the tests simply measure test-taking skills, and these same skills are later used when taking mid-terms and finals in the college classroom. In both suggested reasons, note that the explanations involve aspects of people.

In individual-level correlations, aspects of people are the units of analysis. Some important cross-cultural research (Hofstede, 1980; Chinese Culture Connection, 1987) has involved the use of ecological correlations. In *ecological correlations*, aspects of a society or countries as a whole are studied. The use of different countries probably provides the clearest example. First, the gross national product (GNP) of each country might be listed; second, the amount spent on public education for children 5 to 18 years of age is listed for these same countries. There will thus be two entries for countries, such as Japan, Canada, Great Britain, Australia, the United States, and so forth. A correlation coefficient can be computed, and an association established: The greater the GNP, the greater the amount spent on public education. Interpretations of ecological correlations must focus on aspects of the units of analysis, in this case the countries. One interpretation is that countries with a high GNP have citizens who earn good salaries, and thus provide a tax base out of which public education is funded. Just as with individual-level correlations, ecological correlations encourage more than one explanation. Another interpretation is that countries with a high GNP can afford to support an efficient tax collection system, and it is this efficient collection of "taxes due" that is more important for the funding of public education.

Ecological correlations can also involve widespread norms in a society. *Norms* refer to guidelines about behavior that are widely accepted. It is the norm in America that children are taught to read—large sums of money are put into public schools. This is a fact about society. Given this fact, there are (of course) individual differences—some children read better than others. As another example, a norm in society (that could be used in the analysis of an ecological correlation) is that people are expected to work well with others on group-defined tasks. As will be discussed below, this *is* a norm in societies called *collective* (e.g., Japan), where people are more likely to pursue their goals in cooperation with others. Within a society, there will be individual differences—a given person may be able to work cooperatively with others better than another individual. That second person, however, may have to develop his or her cooperative skills to accomplish goals given the *societal norm* that people are expected to work well with others.

It is very important that ecological correlations not be interpreted as individual-level correlations (and vice versa) since mistakes can be easily made. In a classic treatment of ecological correlations, Robinson (1950; see also review by Nachmias & Nachmias, 1987) analyzed the relation between birth outside the United States and literacy. When analyzed as an ecological correlation, the association was positive. Specifically, when major regions (e.g., Northeast, Deep South, Midwest, Far West, etc.) were analyzed, the more people who were foreign born, the higher the literacy rates. When an individual-level correlation was computed, the association was in the opposite direction! That is, if an individual was foreign born, he or she was less likely to be literate than a native-born individual. What could cause this striking difference? The key to analyzing the difference is to return to the basic piece of advice presented previously. In interpreting individual-level correlations, look at aspects of people. In interpreting ecological correlations, look at aspects of the unit of analysis, in this case regions of the United States. One interpretation of the ecological correlation is that different regions of the United States have public education systems that differ greatly in quality. Ambitious, hard-working, or already-literate foreign-born immigrants settle in those regions with good educational systems. Thus certain regions attract many immigrants who already are or who quickly become literate. One interpretation of the individual-level correlation is that native-born people have had longer exposure to the language in which literacy tests are given (English), and so can be expected to perform better. Note that one explanation does not contradict the other. They can both be correct. One explanation deals with an association between information at the "ecological" level, and the other deals with information at the individual level. When people interpret ecological correlations as if they were individual-level correlations (a very easy temptation!), they are said to be guilty of the ecological fallacy.

In the subsequent treatment of ecological relationships in this chapter, the unit of analysis will be the country in which people work. In an influential research project, Hofstede (1980; 1991; Hofstede & Bond, 1988) assessed the values of workers in over 50 countries. These people worked for branches of the same multinational organization, International

Business Machines (IBM). The results from individual workers were analyzed by examining the average scores of people in various countries: Japan, USA, Germany, the Philippines, and so forth. Statistical analysis then dealt with the average scores of workers in different countries. For instance, the average scores (on the values assessment instrument) of workers in Japan, the USA, Germany, and so forth, could be related to the gross national product of those same countries. The unit of analysis is at the level of countries. Consequently, to interpret the project's results, we must understand the nature of ecological correlations. We must focus on the unit of analysis, the countries in Hofstede's research, and examine aspects of those countries in interpreting results. Hofstede and his colleagues have identified five factors that they argue are helpful in understanding work differences in various countries.

VALUES THAT INFLUENCE BEHAVIOR IN THE WORKPLACE

In this section, five values that affect behavior in the workplace will be discussed. The values were identified through research based on ecological correlations, and to interpret these correlations we must look at aspects of the countries in which the research took place. Ecological correlations are sometimes more difficult to interpret than individual correlations. We know lots of people with different traits and abilities, and so we can suggest reasons why two traits are correlated when information is gathered from these individuals (recall the example of test scores and college grades). It is often harder to identify aspects of societies or countries that assist in the interpretation of ecological correlations since most people are not intimately familiar with very many societies other than the one in which they were socialized. Yet knowing about aspects of various societies (or major segments within a society) is important in making decisions about behavior. Recall the ecological correlation between number of foreign-born people in a region and literacy rates. One suggested reason for this ecological correlation is that certain regions have good educational systems that attract immigrants eager to learn English. This fact could be very useful, for instance, to a teacher who has job offers from school systems in several American cities located in different regions. If the teacher feels that he or she can make a contribution to the education of immigrants, the level of funding for educational programs in the different cities can be a factor in the decision concerning which job to accept.

One technique for interpreting ecological correlations, then, is to imagine that one is living and working in different parts of the world. This chapter covers that part of people's lives that involves their work. By imagining typical workplace behaviors in their own (familiar) country with behaviors expected in other countries, research based on ecological correlations can become clearer. The following incident (adapted from a case study presented by Chernin [1990]) involving an American working in Japan should make the subsequent discussion of value differences clearer. In this incident, the American encounters differences in the five values identified in research by Hofstede and his colleagues (Hofstede, 1980; Hofstede & Bond, 1988).

Peter Reed, a computer software specialist, had developed a good reputation as a programmer in the United States. Seeking new challenges, he accepted an appointment as a software specialist in his company's branch office in Tokyo. In his own country, Peter had a reputation as a very creative programmer, and part of his preferred workstyle involved working on a number of different projects at the same time. If there was a stumbling block in one project, Peter often found that he could clear his mind by working on one or even two other projects. His mind refreshed, he could then return to the original project with a fresh outlook and a range of potential solutions to problems. Managers in the American branch encouraged this workstyle because they saw that Peter was very productive when allowed to work in his own preferred manner. The managers were also very tolerant when Peter (and other productive workers) deviated from written policy in such activities as lateness to work, lunch hours that extended beyond 60 minutes, number of workbreaks during the day, and so forth. As long as the employees were productive, rules were loosely enforced.

Peter arrived in Tokyo and met his immediate superior, Mr. Hirumi Watanabe. The relationship between the two started out well since Mr. Watanabe recognized Peter's abilities and the quality of his work. After about three months, however, tensions began to arise. Peter enjoyed going off by himself when faced with a difficult problem, sometimes sequestering himself in the company library and foregoing lunch with his co-workers. When he did have lunch with co-workers, he was surprised that males usually ate with males, and the females in the company ate with other females. Accustomed to more integration of males and females in his own country, he would sometimes ask females to join his lunchgroup, but his invitations were received with obvious discomfort. When he was late coming back from lunch or late coming to work, Mr. Watanabe reacted negatively. At first, the negative reactions consisted of frowns. Finally, Mr. Watanabe had to ask Peter to be more careful about observing company policy. Mr. Watanabe was also frustrated at Peter's habit of working on different projects at the same time and not giving enough attention to the one that he (Watanabe) considered the most important. Mr. Watanabe did not seem to appreciate Peter's preferred style in which working on a second and third project would eventually help solve difficulties encountered in the first and highest-priority project. It was clear to everyone who knew of Peter's work that he was one of the most productive workers in the company. He was clearly not abrasive, or unpleasant, and he clearly enjoyed interacting with his Japanese co-workers. Yet he was unhappy in his assignment, and Mr. Watanabe was not pleased with Peter's contributions. Peter recognized that he was unhappy, and that he was not getting along very well with Mr. Watanabe, but he was unable to "put his finger on" the reasons for the difficulties. Eventually, Peter was forced to consider changing companies.

What are the reasons, all involving cultural differences, for Peter's difficulties? Five reasons will be discussed here, all involving generalizations about culture and cultural differences. The five are (1) individualism contrasted with collectivism, (2) power distance between bosses and subordinates, (3) uncertainty avoidance, (4) masculine and feminine goals in the workplace, and (5) the influence of Confucian thought on people's values. As discussed at length in Chapter 6, the possibility of exceptions must always be kept in mind whenever generalizations are applied to specific cases. I believe that these generalizations provide a good starting point for the analysis of intercultural difficulties, but people should always be willing to move beyond the generalizations as they acquire more and more information from their own firsthand experiences.

INDIVIDUALISM AND COLLECTIVISM. One of the strongest distinctions that people adjusting to other societies must face is the relative emphasis on individualism and collectivism. These concepts were introduced in Chapter 2 as they apply to the behaviors of individual persons in various cultures. Hofstede (1980, 1986) found that the concepts also were important at the ecological level. In collectivist societies, goals are much more likely to be attained through group effort, and the organization of various institutions within a society are more likely to be based on groups. Consequently, there is a great deal of value placed on people being part of groups, and working toward their goals as group members. In individualist societies, there are more institutions in society that allow people to work toward their own personal goals. If they *choose*, they can pursue some of these goals as part of groups. For instance, they can join a political action committee to work toward the election of a particular candidate for governor. There are at least two differences in the formation of these groups in individualistic versus collectivist societies. In individualistic societies, there is a choice. A person can join a group to pursue a goal, or she or he can work toward the goal without much interaction with others. In collectivist societies, it is far less likely that a person would consider working alone since the *expectation* is that people will integrate their wishes with those of others. The second difference involves the time frame of group membership. In individualist societies, the group is likely to exist only as long as it serves the needs of the individual members. In the example of the political action committee, the group will exist until the results of the election for governor are counted. After the group's goal has been accomplished (or after there has been a clear failure), the group's members are likely to go their separate ways. In collectivist societies, the groups with which people are involved are likely to be a permanent part of their lives (Hui, 1990). People are far more likely in collectivist societies to have very lengthy (if not lifelong) ties to their extended family, to their organization, to their school alumni group, and so forth.

Understanding individualist and collectivist societies has many important and interesting implications. When interacting in collectivist societies, a person is not seen as just an individual with his or her own qualities. The person is also seen as a member of some group. Before my first lecture tour in Japan, a knowledgeable colleague advised me, "Be sure to have business cards made. On the business card, be sure to include your title within your organization. The higher-sounding your title can be and still represent an honest indicator of your position, the better. You have to keep in mind that part of your identity as a person in Japan is your position in your organization. If people don't know where you stand in a group, you will not have an existence for them!" Socialization (Chapter 4) in a collective society involves sensitivity to people's lifelong participation in groups. The work of Tobin, Wu, and Davidson (1989) in China, Japan, and the United States was discussed in Chapter 5. As part of their work in Japan, they observed one preschool classroom in which there was a very ill-mannered, unruly boy who was clearly interfering with the schoolwork of the other students. A few well-behaved students complained to the teacher. While it might be expected that the teacher would intervene, she took a different approach. She told the well-behaved students that it was *their* job to deal with the unruly youngster. She told them that the ill-behaved student must learn to work cooperatively with others, and part of the class's responsibility is to make efforts so that the isolated individual becomes integrated into the group. She also said that there will always be a few unruly people with whom the cooperative students will later have to deal. It is best to learn during preschool how to get along with difficult people and to avoid becoming visibly upset at these individuals.

Returning to the case study of Peter Reed's adjustment to the Japanese branch of a multinational corporation, Mr. Watanabe felt that Peter was not being cooperative enough. He worked too frequently by himself, and he did not participate in the smooth-functioning lunch groups that his co-workers enjoyed and looked forward to as a major part of their workday. Many lunch-hour conversations in Japan are job-oriented. Mr. Watanabe felt that if Peter had a problem with one of his projects, he could obtain assistance from others if he would simply share his difficulties and ask for suggestions. Mr. Watanabe, recognizing Peter's talents, also felt that he could be of assistance to other co-workers when they needed suggestions. Peter, of course, was not as accustomed to making contributions through a group. In the United States, his supervisors were tolerant of his preference to work alone, realizing that this was the style that allowed him to be highly productive.

The value placed on working in groups has many implications. One has been documented by Gabrenya, Wang, and Latane (1985), who reasoned that there will be less "social loafing" in collectivist societies. Social loafing occurs when people make fewer contributions while working with others than they would if they were working alone (Latane, Williams, & Harkins, 1979). If five individuals working alone each generate five solutions to a complex problem, then these individuals are responsible for 25 solutions. Assume that all 25 of the solutions are quite different. If people are put into a five-person working group, and if the group generates only 15 or 18 solutions, then people may be guilty of social loafing. Certain group members may relax, letting others do most of the work. Another reason that individuals may not work as hard in groups is that their personal efforts are less visible. If a group generates 28 or 30 solutions, the contributions of the individual members are hard to recognize. Realizing the relative invisibility of their efforts, individual group members may "slack off."

Gabreyna and his colleagues (1985) found that social loafing was more common in an individualist culture (United States) compared to a collectivist culture (Taiwan). The Americans in the study were more productive when working alone than when working with others. The Chinese not only avoided social loafing; they also were more productive when working with others than when working alone. Gabrenya and his colleagues referred to this finding as indicating the possibility of "social striving." The value placed on being part of a group is so strong in collective societies that people actually benefit from working with others. Working with others helps people raise their productivity beyond the level they would achieve when working alone. The realization that groups can generate social striving is another reason for Mr. Watanabe's disappointment with Peter's behavior. Mr. Watanabe, based on his own socialization and experiences in his culture, feels that Peter would be even more productive if he could integrate himself into the workgroup. Peter may feel that the time and energy spent on working with others will interfere with his productivity and will reduce the originality and creativity of his own unique contributions.

POWER DISTANCE. A second dimension that is important in understanding cultural differences in the workplace is called "power distance." This dimension refers to the *amount of distinctiveness* among various groups in their access to power and in their relative status levels. The word *amount* is important. All societies have different status levels, and people with high status have more access to power and to various comforts that society has to offer. People who are wealthy, who are well educated, who come from families that have wielded power for many generations, and who have many "contacts" in government and professional circles are likely to have more status than the less educated and the poorer individuals in a society. In the workplace, executives have more power than factory workers, and office managers have more power than secretaries.

The difference across various societies involves the amount of power that high-status groups have relative to lower-status groups, the degree to which the distinctions are built into societal intitutions, and people's acceptance of power differences as normal. Cultures referred to as "low power distance" are guided by laws, norms, and everyday behaviors that make power distinctions as minimal as possible. The United States is considered a "low power distance" country. Yes, members of the United States Senate have a great deal of power, but the less-powerful citizens can remove a senator when he or she is up for reelection. Yes, executives have more power than factory workers, but workers can join together in unions and challenge the policies that executives establish. There can also be friendly contact across the executive–worker distinction when the individuals involved share similar interests in golf, bridge, or other activities. Yes, office managers have more power than secretaries. But office managers are very unwise if they do not treat secretaries well and if they fail to listen carefully to the secretaries' suggestions concerning improvements in the workplace. Further, there are explicit limits to the power that managers possess, as can be seen in laws and company policies that attempt to prevent sexual harassment. In general, workers in low power distance countries feel more freedom to disagree with their bosses than workers in high power distance countries. Yes, it is never easy to meet with one's boss and to express disagreement. But again, the distinction refers to the *amount* of comfort people feel when disagreeing. In low power distance countries, people feel more comfortable disagreeing. In high power distance countries, people feel very uncomfortable, so uncomfortable that they often don't do it.

In some high power distance countries, people accept status distinctions as normal and are not upset when high-status people exert their power. For example, Bond, Wan, Leong, and Giacalone (1985) compared people's reactions to insults in a high power distance country (Hong Kong) and in a low power distance country (United States). People in Hong Kong were less upset when they were insulted, as long as the insulter was of high status. When people accept status distinctions as normal, they accept the fact that the powerful are different than the less powerful. The powerful can engage in behaviors that the less powerful cannot, in this case insult people and have the insult accepted as part of their rights. Colleagues and I (Triandis, Brislin, and Hui, 1988) suggested that people from low power distance countries who were socialized *not* to accept such status distinctions will find this one of the most difficult cultural differences with which they will have to cope.

In a number of countries, people *accept* the fact that there are sharp status distinctions but do not necessarily like this fact. Early and Stubblewine (1989) studied the ways British workers used feedback provided by their supervisors. Great Britain is not one of the countries highest in power distance, but there is enough to be noticed by people from a country very low on this dimension (e.g., Israel or New Zealand). Whereas studies in other countries (e.g., Japan: Reitsberger & Daniel, [1990]) have shown that workers benefited from feedback, the British workers actually resented the information that was offered to them by supervisors. Earley and Stubblebine (1989, p. 177) offered this explanation.

> ... English society is characterized by an entrenched class structure such that shop-floor workers perceive themselves as quite different from managers. ... English workers have structured their unions so as to retain control over their environment. The trade union system can be interpreted as a formalized structure that reduces the capacity of managers to influence shop-floor workers. The high power distance found in England reflects a hands-off approach that workers expect from their superiors.

When managers in England give feedback, then, workers consider it inappropriate and are unlikely to use it.

Power distance is involved in the case study involving Peter Reed and his Japanese boss. Japan is higher on the power distance dimension than is the United States. Mr. Watanabe believes that the boss has a right to direct the behavior of his employees. He is accustomed to his workers saying the equivalent of "yes, sir!" when he makes a suggestion. Peter certainly knows that Mr. Watanabe is the boss, but he does not see the distinction between himself and his boss to the degree that his Japanese co-workers do. For example, Peter undoubtedly feels more free to express disagreement with Mr. Watanabe than do his Japanese co-workers. In the case study, it was mentioned that Mr. Watanabe frowned when Peter came back late from his lunches. Mr. Watanabe feels that this is a message that his subordinate should take seriously. Peter feels that there may be a message in the frown, but that he is free to place it into a category (see Chapter 7) of "less important items." The more important category, from Peter's viewpoint, is the collection of behaviors that contribute to the conclusion that "I am productive." Mr. Watanabe is likely to have a stronger category than Peter consisting of items related to his rights as a boss.

Another way of capturing the distinction between low and high power distance countries is to consider whether superiors and subordinates can become friends. People in low power distance countries will often give a response like, "Sure, I'm on a first-name basis with my boss and we spend free time together coaching a baseball team!" People in a high power distance country are far less likely to entertain the possibility of being on a first-name basis with their boss and of spending voluntary free time together.

UNCERTAINTY AVOIDANCE. The third factor identified by Hofstede (1980) deals with a universal concern. People are concerned about uncertainty in the future (Solomon, Greenberg & Pyszczynski, 1991). Will we have enough money to live comfortably 5 years from now? Will the demand for the products our company sells continue into the future, or should we change our products? If we put pressure on the board of directors to fire the current company president, what are the chances that a new president will be any more capable? If I propose a new policy, how much support am I likely to receive from my co-workers? One way to reduce uncertainty is to adopt rules. If people know that they and others will obey the rules, they will have more confidence concerning the future. Some uncertainty about the future can be reduced through the widespread use of such rules that become, over a number of years, part of one's culture. For example, people are uncertain how much income they will have after they reach 65 years of age and no longer work for a salary. One way of reducing this uncertainty is to establish laws or rules that require people to make contributions to a retirement fund (e.g., social security, and/or a company's pension plan).

Different societies have varying numbers of rules, laws, and norms that deal with uncertainty and become an accepted part of their culture (like the air we breathe, as discussed in Chapter 1). In the United States, for instance, all workers know they will have payroll deductions that represent their contributions to the social security system. Most workers accept the need for such contributions, even though they would often prefer to have the money to spend on today's necessities. Abandonment of the social security system is almost unthinkable—it is part of American culture. Legislators who propose major changes in social security risk not being reelected! If they speak out about aspects of the system that might be improved, legislators run the risk of appearing not to care about America's senior citizens. Because social security is now part of American culture, people who attack it, or even try to make constructive suggestions, can be seen as attacking American culture.

All cultures have guidelines that help in the avoidance of uncertainty, and so differences among cultures refer to the *number and extent* of the rules, laws, norms, and informal guidelines people are expected to know. Countries considered to be high in uncertainty avoidance have large numbers of such rules. People who reside in these countries are socialized to believe that uncertainty about the future is best dealt with if everyone behaves according to widely accepted guidelines. Consider the example of people's employment. Everyone is uncertain about where they will be working 10 years from now. In high uncertainty avoidant countries, we would expect various rules and norms that reduce this uncertainty. For instance, we would expect longer employment with the same company (Brislin & Hui, 1992). If people are working for one company today, they are likely to be working for that same company 10 years from now. Or consider the salaries that people receive. In high uncertainty avoidant countries, we would expect that people will find themselves in jobs where salaries go up slowly each year. People may not become wealthy by working in jobs that yield slow and steady salary increases, but they will not go hungry and they will be able to support a family. There are important links between uncertainty and the stress that people feel and which they know can affect their health. One reason for stress is that people are uncertain about what will happen to them. If they engage in a specific behavior, what exactly will be the result? If they do not know, they may experience stress. If there are many rules in a society that guide people's behavior, stress can be reduced because uncertainty can be reduced. Consider the example of people accepting jobs in a company and showing up for work on the first day. This can be stressful. People will ask themselves, "Will I fit in? Will co-workers accept me?" If people are members of a culture where the strong informal rule is that co-workers will approach the newcomers, talk to them, and express words of welcome, then stress will be reduced.

In low uncertainty avoidance countries, people are noticeably less concerned with unpredictability. They know that they cannot predict exactly what they will be doing in 10 years, but are less willing to deal with the unpredictability by establishing large numbers of rules and regulations. In fact, too many rules and regulations are considered undesirable because they limit freedom of movement in society. If people are expected to stay with the same company for 10 years, for instance, this norm limits the movement of people who want to try a new job, to move to a new community, to seek out better promotion opportunities in another company, and so forth. There is more risk-taking in low uncertainty avoidant countries (Hofstede, 1986). It is easier to take risks (e.g., seek funds for one's own small business venture) if there are *few* rules and regulations that place such limits on the search for funding. People in low uncertainty avoidant countries realize that the future is unpredictable, but don't feel that extensive guidelines for behavior are the way to deal with an uncertain future.

The concept of uncertainty avoidance is at the center of many intercultural encounters. Consider interactions between American businesspeople and their Chinese counterparts as they seek out joint-venture opportunities in China. The United States is considered to be low, and China is considered to be high, on the uncertainty avoidance dimension. One aspect of uncertainty is whether or not one's decisions today will bring praise or reprimands next year. In uncertainty avoidant countries, workers are very hesitant to make decisions, since the decisions may be wrong. Consequently, workers try to avoid making decisions until they have the approval of persons above themselves in the company hierarchy. Then, if the decisions prove wrong, the workers will be spared blame since the higher-level people approved the decision. This desire to avoid making decisions, however, makes it very difficult to find anyone who is willing to approve a new business venture (Holton, 1990). Harry Hui (Brislin & Hui, in press) uses the example of modifications in a product that has proved successful. In China, the general manager of a factory that produced dinnerware refused to change the design of its up-market plates from a round shape to a slightly octagonal shape. He explained his decision: "If the original design was well accepted by consumers in the past, why wouldn't it be in the future. Besides, who else but myself will take the blame if the change flops?" Analyzing similar potential difficulties in American–Chinese business dealings, Baird, Lyles, and Wharton (1990, p. 64) concluded that there is a "need to have clear, specific and detailed rules and procedures governing all aspects of Sino–U.S. joint ventures set down beforehand. Also, the selection of American managers for the venture who can adapt to and understand the Chinese intolerance of uncertainty is important."

To add to the interpretation of the difficulties between Peter Reed and Hirumi Watanabe, we must understand that Japan is higher in uncertainty avoidance than the United States. To deal with uncertainty, such as the flow of future business into a company, the Japanese are more accepting of rules and regulations. These rules extend to such everyday behaviors as the proper time at which work starts, the accepted amount of time for one's lunch hour, the desired way to deal with difficulties that arise in one's work, and so forth. Coming from a country lower in uncertainty avoidance, Peter is not as likely to pay as much attention to these rules. When he comes back late from lunch, it is not a terribly important violation of rules. In contrast, it *is* a significant violation for Mr. Watanabe and his co-workers. If asked, Mr. Watanabe could defend his actions. "If a potential customer wants to talk to Peter Reed, I want to know that Peter will be available at certain times. If Peter respects company rules about such things as lunch hours, I will know exactly when Peter will be back from lunch and I can ask the customer to come by at a certain time." Peter is more likely to feel that spending time and energy learning unimportant rules will interfere with his creativity and productivity.

MASCULINITY–FEMININITY. The fourth factor to be considered in this discussion of work values is known as masculinity–femininity. As will be discussed more fully in Chapter 9, some gender differences are found in all societies. Two are that men are more aggressive and women are more concerned with relationships. When applied to work values "masculinity" leads to assertiveness, competitiveness, and a tough approach to decision making that sometimes downplays the feelings of people affected by the decision. "Femininity" leads to a desire for cooperative and pleasant co-workers, good working conditions, and a more "tender" approach to decision making that takes people's feelings into account. It is important to keep in mind that "masculinity–femininity" represents a continuum rather than a statement about exact opposites. The norm in some societies is that "masculine" approaches are considered more effective, and the norm in other societies is that "feminine" approaches are preferred. Many societies, however, recognize the value of both and consequently have work norms that represent combinations of "masculine" and "feminine" approaches.

As with the other factors under discussion, the distinction between masculinity and femininity refers to the *amount* of attention people give to different values when making decisions about important behaviors in the workplace. Child care provides a good example. Women can bear children—not men. This fact means that all societies have to give some consideration to policies such as women's leave from the workplace for a period of time before and after childbirth. Differences appear in the *amount* and *number* of policies designed to help women. There are differences across countries in the amount of guaranteed leave time, the relative assurance that women have that their jobs will be waiting for them when they return, the amount of government-sponsored child care, and paid leave for husbands so that they can help with the newly arrived baby. Countries with many such policies that recognize the importance of women are considered to be "feminine." Examples are the Scandinavian countries, where government policies ease the burden of leaving one's job, bearing one's child, and returning to work (Yuchtman-Yaar & Gottlieb, 1985). In feminine countries, the many roles that women can play are considered important. Consequently, their special needs (such as the stresses and events surrounding childbirth) will be given attention. Another way of looking at masculinity–femininity is to ask about relative power. In feminine societies, power is more likely to be shared by males and females. Consequently, women will be able to develop an effective political voice and can insist that their concerns be heard by political leaders. As a result, there will be a greater likelihood of policies being established that meet the needs of women. In "masculine" countries, there is less likelihood of such policies given that women have not attained positions that allow their requests to be heard by government officials, executives, and other leaders in society.

In masculine societies, most workers in responsible positions are males, and consequently their preferences concerning what happens in the workplace are given more weight than females. As a result, the goals males have in the workplace are likely to be the goals that are pursued by all workers. Even if some workers would prefer other goals, they learn what goals are preferred by powerholders, what rewards are available, how to obtain those rewards, and so forth. If they are to retain their jobs and/or prosper, they have to adapt to the goals preferred by powerholders. In masculine societies such as Japan, Venezuela, and Italy, worker goals include advancement on the job, earnings, training, and opportunities to remain up-to-date in their specialities. I have called these the traditional goals in a masculine society (Brislin, 1984) since they have long been preferred by males given their role of breadwinner. The use of the word *traditional* reminds us that as more and more women in various countries assume positions of responsibility and assume or share the breadwinner role, these goals will change. Some changes will involve movement toward the "feminine direction." Given the long-term influence of women, and the value placed on their work, societies called "feminine" have a set of work goals that reflect women's traditional preferences. These goals include a friendly work atmosphere, position security, good physical conditions in the workplace, good relations with one's supervisor, and cooperative relations with co-workers. Most of these goals are clearly related to the traditional female concern of good relations with other people.

Japan is a highly masculine country according to the criteria discussed here (Hofstede, 1980)—higher than the United States. This means that predictions can be made about worker preferences in the two countries. Loscocco and Kalleberg (1988) analyzed work values and work commitment in the United States and in Japan. One prediction from an understanding of cultural differences in worker values is that, as workers become older, work will play a more central part in their lives if they live in masculine countries. If the masculine values are advancement, earnings, and being up to date, these are more likely to be achieved by older workers. These older workers (see Chapter 4) will then have the responsibility of socializing younger colleagues into an acceptance of these values. As predicted, older workers in Japan were more committed to their work than were younger workers. The researchers suggested that seniority was a major reason. Promotions are based on seniority, and thus the positions in which one finds the (masculine) rewards will most likely be held by older workers. There was one interesting finding that may have implications for the future. Among the masculine values, younger Japanese workers expressed an interest in greater pay. This may reflect the desire of younger workers to have more everyday comforts (good housing, entertainment, playgrounds for children) than their parents and grandparents expected after the devastation of World War II. Loscocco and Kalleberg (1988, pp. 352–353) speculated on the implications of a concern for greater earnings among younger Japanese workers. "If this trend continues, the frugal and self-sacrificing Japanese employee may disappear entirely, with potentially severe consequences for the Japanese economy." The researchers also found that young Japanese women are desirous of more pay, and this finding suggests that women will become more and more demanding of equal treatment in the businessworld.

While future changes in the treatment of women are likely, Japan today is a highly masculine society with power being held by males. The lack of opportunities for women to achieve high-level leadership positions is a feature of Japanese society that is frequently underdiscussed in books about Japan as a world power and Japan as a major influence on American business (e.g., Katz & Friedman-Lichtschein, 1985; DeMente, 1989). Returning to the case study, Peter tries to arrange luncheon groups composed of both males and females. He is disappointed to find that this is simply not done in the company where he works. Given the strong distinction between males as powerholders and females as subordinates, the Japanese are far more accustomed to forming luncheon groups based on gender. The men will undoubtedly discuss business, and the women would be uncomfortable trying to participate because they do not have access to the same information about current business opportunities that would have been shared among the men. Peter does *not* come from a society in which men and women share power equally, but he is from a country far less "masculine" than Japan. Peter is familiar with the fact that opportunities for women have broadened in the United States over the past 50 years, and he is familiar with luncheon groups composed of both males and females. One of the reasons for his difficulties is that he has not recognized the greater masculinity of the Japanese workplace.

CONFUCIAN DYNAMISM. The fifth factor to be considered is based on research carried out subsequent to the development of the first four factors (Chinese Culture Connection, 1987; Hofstede & Bond, 1988). Called "Confucian dynamism," analysis of this factor emerged from efforts to explain the startling economic growth of some of the Asian nations since about 1970. These countries include Japan, South Korea, Taiwan, Hong Kong, and Singapore (sometimes called the "five dragons"). If readers of this book examine their recent purchases, they will almost surely have acquired products made in one or more of these countries. As guidelines, consider recent purchases of automobiles, clothing, toys, and electronic products. The changes in the quality of products from these countries has been enormous. During my elementary school years (the 1950s), students would give a product "made in Japan" only as a booby prize for the worst performance in a spelling bee, dance contest, or athletic event. The term "made in Japan" was a synonym for something cheap and shabby. Times do change. Now, people look to Japan for high-quality products, such as video recorders and cameras that they expect to *stay out* of the repair shop.

A number of scholars have pointed to the influence of Confucian thought in Asia as one reason for economic development (Kahn, 1979; Bond, 1986). Kong Fu Ze was a high-ranking civil servant in China around the time of 500 BC. Jesuit missionaries later changed the name to Confucius since the syllables in this name were easier for them to pronounce. He was a teacher rather than a religious figure, and he developed a set of practical ethical guidelines to guide everyday behavior. He attracted a large number of pupils, and it was these disciples who recorded his teachings (much like the students of Socrates who recorded his contributions). Some of the key principles of Confucian thought (Hofstede & Bond, 1988) are:

1. Unequal status relationships lead to a stable society. Confucius was not referring to master–slave or tyrant–submissive servant relations. Rather, he was referring to such relations as the ruler–subject, father–son, or older brother–younger brother. In each of these relationships, there are *mutual* obligations. For instance, the younger or less powerful person owes the senior respect and obedience. The older or powerful person owes the junior protection and consideration. A Chinese scholar (Wang Gung Wu) once told me that the senior-to-junior obligation can take interesting and important specific forms in some Chinese families. If a young 25-year-old wants to start a business, the youth can approach elders (father, uncles, older brothers) and ask for investment funds. If the business fails, the youth can expect the elders to bail him or her out and to find money so that a second business can be started. The assumption is that the youth will have learned enough from mistakes so that there will be a far greater chance of success for the second venture. If the second business fails, the elders will not be expected to find money for a third venture, but they *will* try to find a place for the youth somewhere in one of the businesses administered by the family. The important point is that the youth can depend on certain obligations that the seniors have. Especially during the development of the first business venture, it must be very comforting to know that there are people who will put up money for a second venture should the first venture fail.

2. *The family is typical of all social organizations.* A person is not socialized to look upon himself or herself as an individual. Rather, he or she must find identity as a member of a goup, and the first group is the family (recall the discussion of collectivism in Chapter 2). It is important to maintain harmony in the family so that it does not disintegrate into a bickering set of individuals. One way to do this is to maintain one's own and others' *face*; in other words, their dignity, self-respect, and prestige. One does not disagree with an elder in public: That would cause the elder to lose face. A young woman does not date a man who has not earned the approval of her family. That would cause her family to lose face, and it would also cause the woman to lose face in the wider community where the family lives. People "give face" by demonstrating their respect for others.

3. *Virtue in life consists of working hard, acquiring useful skills and as much education as possible, not being a spendthrift, and persevering when faced with difficult tasks.* Acquiring an education, working hard, and developing a reputation for perseverance allows people to take responsible positions in society that can benefit their families. Further, if they are not excessive in their spending, they will have money to invest when *they* are older and are asked to assume the obligations of senior people in their families (point 1, above).

To test the possibility that acceptance of Confucian teachings affects economic growth in a country, a group of scholars led by Michael Bond formed a group called "The Chinese Culture Connection" and published some of the results under that title (Chinese Culture Connection, 1987; see also Hofstede & Bond, 1988; Hofstede, 1991). The researchers began by asking a large number of Chinese scholars to list values that children are expected to learn during their socialization (Chapter 4). This information was collected in the Chinese language and later translated into the English language summaries presented here. The findings of the research are complex, but one of the most important results was that the teachings of Confucius could readily be identified in a set of the values that the researchers identified. Research carried out among respondents in 22 countries demonstrated that people in some countries are more likely to be socialized in these values than are people in other countries. Further, respondents in four Asian countries, where recent economic growth has been achieved, scored at the top of the scale that measured acceptance of the values. These countries were Hong Kong, Taiwan, Japan, and South Korea, with the fifth of the five dragons (Singapore) eighth on the list of 22 countries.

The researchers labeled the set of values "Confucian dynamism." The "Confucian" aspect of the label is due to the fact that all of the values can be identified as the teachings of Confucius. The "dynamic" aspect is due to the fact that there is greater emphasis on some of the teachings as compared to others. The following lists make this distinction. The first includes aspects of Confucianism that people in the economically successful countries were *emphasizing* relative to other aspects. The second list includes those Confucian teachings that people in the economically successful countries were *downplaying* relative to the teachings on the first list. Confucian dynamism, then, is said to place relative emphasis on:

- Persistence and perseverance
- Ordering relationships by status and observing this order
- Thrift
- Having a sense of shame

Confucian dynamism recognizes that the following four values exist, but relatively less emphasis is placed on them:

- Personal steadiness and stability
- Protecting face
- Respect for tradition
- Reciprocation of greetings, favors, and gifts

This important *pattern* of what is emphasized and what is less emphasized needs further discussion. Keep in mind that the Chinese Culture Connection (1987) group chose to use the term *dynamic* when interpreting the pattern.

While there is no interpretation that is perfect in its clarity, most of the pattern can be understood by referring to the importance of "the future" and "hard work." The general interpretation, then, is that countries which have been influenced by the teachings of Confucius emphasize different aspects of those teachings. Those countries which emphasize the dynamic aspects involving the future and the importance of hard work have experienced economic growth in recent years. The first four "emphasized" aspects, above, reveal the concern with the future and with hard work. Persistence and perseverance are important when people face difficulties on the job. Rather than give up, people will continue their efforts. At times, these efforts will involve bringing in the expertise of others. If the status and contributions of others are respected (part of the concept "ordering relationships," above) and if the individuals consulted feel that *they* have obligations to help as much as possible, then the chances of solving problems increases. If people are thrifty, they will have money to invest in new businesses. Examining the amount of capital available for investment, "economists have been struck by the high savings quotas in the Five Dragon countries" (Hofstede & Bond, 1988, p. 18). If people have a sense of shame, they will become upset with themselves if they do not work hard and if they do not contribute to group efforts. They will also be upset at themselves for not developing the expertise and savings that will allow them to fulfill their eventual obligations as elders in their groups.

In countries that have experienced recent economic success, there is relatively less emphasis placed on four aspects of Confucian teachings. The clearest is respect for tradition. An overemphasis on this aspect would preclude dynamic ventures aimed at prosperity in the future. Similarly, personal steadiness and stability can also preclude action that will be useful in the future. For example, people can be steady and stable with their excellent mathematical skills and may be able to demonstrate their competencies with paper and pencils, an abacus, or a small calculator. But this steadiness can prevent them from developing skills useful in a fast-moving economy, such as use of high-speed computers and telecommunications technology. People who are too stable may also be unwilling to take risks, and risks will always be part of any new business venture. If people are occupied with protecting their face, they will be spending time and energy on matters that may be relatively unimportant for future business success. Here it is useful to remember that we are dealing with a dynamic concept. People may become upset if they feel they are losing face, but the best use of their time and energy may be to set their feelings aside and contribute to efforts that will result in group prosperity. The final aspect that is underemphasized involves the reciprocation of greetings, favors, and gifts. The argument that these are not *dynamic* aspects of Confucian thinking is similar to that for saving face. If people put time and effort into reciprocating greetings and gifts, then they may be too concerned with the recent past (e.g., an uncle's gift two weeks ago) and with the present (the way people greet me currently). As Hofstede and Bond (1988, p. 18) put it, the type of reciprocation under discussion here "is a social activity more concerned with good manners than with performance" that can lead to productivity in the workplace.

In everyday terms, Confucian dynamism involves picking and choosing from an array of philosophical principles. This type of selectivity is not uncommon and is not limited to Confucianism. Christians are exposed to a number of principles: "love thy neighbor as thyself," "honor thy father and thy mother," "keep holy the Lord's day," "when insulted, turn the other cheek," "thou shalt not commit adultery," and so forth. Christians are familiar with all these principles, but many choose to emphasize some and to deemphasize others.

Further insights into the case study presented at the beginning of this chapter can be suggested. Japan is higher on the Confucian dynamism factor than is the United States. Peter Reed enjoyed working on a number of problems at the same time. If he had difficulties with one, he would put it aside and work on another. This might have interfered with Mr. Watanabe's preference for persistence and perseverance, which could have been more easily shown if Peter worked on one problem at a time. From Mr. Watanabe's perspective, Peter's workstyle could come across as flippant. In addition, Peter is not "ordering relationships" according to the ideal of Confucian dynamism. From Mr. Watanabe's perspective, Peter should discover the expertise and potential contributions of his co-workers. (He could do this during lunch hours, but he frequently keeps to himself!) Then, he should show respect to the co-workers and ask them to help him solve the problems that he is encountering. Realizing that they are making contributions to a group effort, the co-workers are likely to help as much as they can.

Confucian dynamism is probably the most difficult of the five concepts for most readers to understand. This is not accidental: As discussed in Chapter 2, the emic aspects of complex concepts are the hardest to understand. The other four involve etic or culture-general concepts to which readers can relate. Most have been torn between putting time and effort into their own goals or compromising so that a group effort could take place (individualism–collectivism). Most readers have had a boss who does not participate much in informal activities with co-workers and who would be displeased if attempts were made to establish a close relationship that involved use of first names (power distance). Many readers will be familiar with institutions that have many rules and regulations, and with others that have far fewer (uncertainty avoidance). Perhaps some readers have talked with friends who have gone to different schools. Some schools are noted for their many required courses students *must* take in order to graduate. Other schools are noted for their absence of required courses and their encouragement of students who want to develop their own undergraduate majors. Some readers will be familiar with enough different institutions and organizations to distinguish those where workers value good pay and advancement opportunities in preference to pleasant relations with co-workers ("masculinity–femininity").

Confucian dynamism, on the other hand, will be far more familiar to readers who are from or who have lived extensively in Asia. Among North Americans, for instance, there are not as many links between behaviors with which they are familiar and the teachings of Confucius. This absence of links is often a sign that the concepts involved are emic (Chapter 2) and that they will demand more study until they become familiar. One of the less familiar aspects of Confucian dynamism involves the *obligations* that elders and leaders have to subordinates who show respect. Understanding these obligations is important in the analysis of leadership in the inter-cultural workplace.

LEADERSHIP

Researchers attempt to identify the most important aspects of behavior in the workplace, and there are few topics that have received more attention than leadership (Hollander, 1985; Bass & Stogdill, 1989; Muchinsky, 1990). Leadership has been studied both in highly industri-alized nations and in countries undergoing recent economic development (Ayman & Chemers, 1983; Sullivan, Suzuki, & Kondo, 1986; Ling, 1989). One way to approach the topic is to analyze some basic findings that have been documented in North America and Europe, where there has been a long tradition of research on leadership. Then, we can move into the more recent cross-cultural literature and ask: What *more* needs to be known to understand leadership as it is practiced outside North America and Europe?

Good summaries exist of leadership research that has been carried out in highly industrialized nations (Hollander, 1985; Bass & Stogdill, 1989). Considering the many definitions that have been suggested over a period of 60 years, Hollander (1985) finds that "influence" is one of the most frequently mentioned characteristics. Leadership involves people who influence others to act in certain ways so that goals are attained. Applying this insight to the workplace, Saal and Knight (1988, p. 336) proposed this definition: "Leadership is social influence in an organiza-tional setting, the effects of which are relevant to, or have an impact on, the achievement of organizational goals."

The emphases in this definition are influence, achievement, and goals. Even if they accept this general definition, researchers disagree about which aspects of leadership are most important. Muchinsky (1990) lists six different aspects of leadership, one or more of which could be the focus of a research study. The six, all of which will be discussed, are (1) power and influence; (2) the traits of leaders; (3) the study of people who choose to follow certain leaders; (4) the mutual influence between leaders and subordinates; (5) the influence of the social setting in which leaders and subordinates find themselves; and (6) the emergence of leaders, especially when people are given overseas business assignments in cultures other than their own.

LEADERSHIP AND POWER. The first aspect of leadership identified by Muchinsky (1990) involves power. If leaders can influence others, they must be sensitive to the nature of power. They must decide whether to emphasize the rewards and punishers over which they have control, or whether they should appeal to their good relations with subordinates and put their efforts into persuasion rather than coercion. Leaders must also decide what sort of strategies and tactics to use (Brislin, 1991). In a study comparing Brazilian and American managers, for instance, Rossi and Todd-Mancillas (1987) found differences in how managers tried to settle disputes among company personnel. Brazilian male managers were likely to use the strategy of exercising their power and authority and to give orders. American managers were more likely to use the strategy of engaging in communication with and negotiation among the various parties who had an interest in the dispute. The researchers suggested that the cultural value of "machismo" is more prevalent in Brazil than in the United States and that this value could be influencing the preferred style among Brazilians. If people are socialized into the value of machismo, they learn to engage in traditionally masculine behaviors, such as showing strength, never showing weakness, and never showing doubt about one's decisions.

THE TRAITS OF LEADERS. Another approach to the study of leadership (2) has looked at the traits leaders possess. This is one of the oldest ways of analyzing leadership, and is probably the first approach that comes to mind when people are asked, "What makes a good leader?" *Traits* of the leader come to mind, such as confidence, dominance, ability to analyze problems, and so forth. While attracting extensive attention from researchers, the trait approach has not led to a full understanding of leadership (Bass & Stogdill, 1989). One reason is that too little attention has been given to the context in which leaders behave. Still, the trait approach will always be *part* of leadership research, and that approach will be referred to again later in this chapter when the traits of preferred leaders in India are reviewed.

CONTEXT: SUBORDINATES AND MUTUAL INFLUENCE. Realizing that an emphasis on traits ignored the context in which leaders behave, researchers looked for other approaches that take context into account. One of the important lessons of cross-cultural research has long been, "behavior must be understood in its context." This has been a major theme in this book. In Chapter 5 on formal educational programs, for instance, research was reviewed showing that changing the context led to changes in student achievement. If the context of the classroom was changed to incorporate activities familiar to children (e.g., telling stories to each other), achievement in reading increased. Much of Chapter 7 on intercultural communication dealt with how people might be encouraged to understand the context in which they find themselves. If foreign students from Japan find themselves in a small seminar, this may be an unfamiliar context for them if they are accustomed only to large classes where the professor gives a lecture. There are behaviors that occur in this new context that the foreign students will be wise to rehearse.

Applied to the study of leadership, four approaches (of the six identified by Muchinsky) deal explicitly with context. Current approaches to the study of leadership emphasize (3) that the people who are led are as important as the leader. What do subordinates prefer from their superiors? An example of this concern was reviewed earlier in this chapter (pp. 255–256). British workers, concerned with protecting themselves from the power of managers, were less accepting of direct feedback concerning their work (Earley & Stubblebine, 1989). Another part of the context *in which leaders and subordinates* communicate includes (4) the nature of their interaction and mutual influence. Leaders do not simply communicate their preferences and subordinates do not simply choose to comply with the preferences or to ignore them. Rather, leaders and followers interact, communicate, and negotiate over a long period of time. In some organizations, interaction and communication leads to effectiveness and productivity. In Japan, workers and managers cooperate through participation in "quality circles." All people who have suggestions concerning the betterment of the workplace, and the products that the company manufactures, are encouraged to share their ideas. Workers, over a number of years, learn how to give their suggestions without causing anyone to lose face. When suggestions are made in a respectful manner, managers are neither upset nor threatened. The use of quality control circles is frequently cited as one reason for the reliability of Japanese consumer products (Bocker & Overgaard, 1982; Ferris & Wagner, 1985). Who knows more about making good products than the people "on the line" doing the wiring, assembling, and inspecting? If their suggestions for improvement can be integrated, product quality should improve. Note that an analysis of quality circles is far different from an analysis of "leaders give orders, subordinates follow them." Rather, quality circles are an example of how communication and interaction between leaders and followers can lead to improvements in an organization.

SITUATIONAL DESCRIPTORS. Some researchers have attempted to analyze directly (5) the various situations in which leaders find themselves, testing the general hypothesis that people will be more effective leaders in some situations as compared to others. Consider situations involving time pressures. Readers might consider people whom they know. If there are time pressures to complete a task (say, organizing the efforts of 15 diverse individuals into an effective fund-raising group within a week), do certain potential leaders come to mind? If the situation is changed such that the organizing can take place over a 3-month period, do other potential leaders come to mind? If readers can imagine that some people will perform better under time pressures, and that others will perform better when there is more time for planning and organizing, than they are sensitive to situational differences.

One approach to analyzing situations is to describe their *characteristics*, much like we describe the characteristics of people (Detweiler, Brislin, & McCormack, 1983). When the characteristics of people are described, words such as "aggressive," "dominant," and "friendly" might be used. Although people probably do not think about situations quite as often, key characteristics of situations can be described in similar ways. For example, some situations involve "time pressures" and some do not. Some situations (e.g., small seminars in college) call for "active participation" and others (large lecture) do not. Some situations have lots of rules and others do not. As previously discussed when research on uncertainty avoidance was reviewed (pp. 256–259), the workplace in Japan has more rules that people are expected to follow. What might seem to a casual observer as a similar situation—people designing computer software in an American or Japanese company—is quite different. The distinction involves the number of rules (Henderson & Argyle, 1986). Many company rules are not written down and consequently are difficult for outsiders to learn.

The best-known theory of leadership that has explicitly examined situational variables was designed by Fred Fiedler (Fiedler, 1967; Fiedler & Garcia, 1987). Three situational variables are central to the theory: whether leader–subordinate relations are good or bad, the amount of structure in the group tasks, and the amount of power that the leader has. The most favorable set of situations for the leader are said to be those in which relations among people are good, the task is structured, and the power possessed by the leader is high. Returning to the example of computer software, leaders will find themselves in favorable situations if workers like and can cooperate with one another. The situations leaders face will be even more favorable with high task structure and position power. For example, making corrections to remove the known "bugs" from a word processing program is a more structured task than designing a new program that will compete well in the marketplace. Leaders who have the power to hire and to fire, and to give raises and to assign desirable tasks to selected workers, will find themselves in more favorable situations from their point of view.

It is important to keep in mind that the three factors describe situational favorability for the leader. Subordinates may have other preferences, as cross-cultural research has shown. Workers in various countries have preferences that focus on different *emphases* in their work. While good leader–subordinate relations are undoubtedly welcome in all countries, research has indicated that this situational factor is more important for Americans than for Germans (Friday, 1989). Americans desire work situations in which they can develop good relationships with co-workers so that they become liked by others. Germans are more tolerant of workgroups whose members are efficient and hardworking, but they do not expect friendliness to the degree that Americans do. The desire for Americans to be liked by others has been frequently noted by researchers who study intercultural communication difficulties.

> The American's need to be liked is a primary aspect of his or her motivation to cooperate or not to cooperate with colleagues ... For Americans, the almost immediate and informal use of a

colleague's first name is a recognition that each likes the other. While such informality is common among American business personnel, this custom should probably be avoided with Germans (Friday, 1989, p. 432).

Another situational factor about which workers have different preferences is the amount of power that leaders possess. Within the workgroups, the Japanese prefer a high-status, powerful leader (Nakao, 1987). Americans prefer a leader who is closer in status to the other workers. Americans have long distrusted people who have too much power. The Constitution of the United States was written so that the President would not have excessive power (the possibility of a king was dismissed!), and that any one part of government would have checks and balances on its use of power (Collier & Collier, 1986). When American workers are promoted to positions of leadership, much of the advice they receive consists of how *not* to abuse the power they have been given (Brislin, 1991).

THE EMERGENCE OF LEADERS. The sixth approach to leadership identified by Muchinsky (1990) deals with how people develop their leadership skills and how they become recognized as leaders by others. This dynamic aspect of leadership is especially important in international business ventures (Mendenhall & Oddou, 1985). Many people attempt to establish various cooperative business arrangements in other countries (Tung & Miller, 1990; Adler, 1991). One approach to developing these arrangements is for people from one country to accept long-term employment in another. For example, American managers might accept employment in Japan, Korea, or Sweden. A question centering on the dynamics of leadership is: Who becomes accepted as leaders by co-workers in the host county? In the examples introduced here, the question becomes: Which Americans will emerge as leaders in Japan, Korea, or Sweden from the co-worker point of view in those countries?

A general prediction is that when managers from one country can modify their behavior to meet the expectations of individuals in another country, they are more likely to be treated as leaders. In a study of American managers working in Korea, Lee and Larwood (1983) found that this general prediction was supported. In this study, the more the Americans adopted attitudes and behaviors that are sympathetic toward Korean culture, the more they were accepted by Koreans. Additionally, the job satisfaction of the Americans increased as they adopted respectful attitudes toward Korea. Considering the case of individualists working in a collective country such as Korea, Triandis, Brislin, and Hui (1988) gave recommendations for what these respectful attitudes and behaviors might be. In the workplace, they would include more incorporation of subordinates in the decision-making process, a greater sensitivity to the views of high-level executives, emphasizing cooperation and harmony, and the cultivation of long-term relationships that will exist *after* the individualists return to their own county.

LEADERSHIP CONCERNS
COMMON IN ASIA

The importance of long-term relationships that exist after individuals cease employment with one company and join another is more familiar to people from collectivist cultures. Consequently, people from individualist cultures will have to spend extra time and energy understanding the importance of this concern if they are to succeed on a business assignment in Asia. Another important concern (Weiming Tu, 1989) that is more familiar to people from collective cultures is that the leader has obligations to his or her subordinates. That is, in exchange for respect, subordinates have the right to expect that a leader will look after their interests, will provide opportunities for them to advance, and will help them out in times of difficulty. While people from individualist countries welcome such leaders, they don't necessarily expect to always find them. Take the case of Americans. People from this highly individualist country do not view leaders as having *obligations* to behave in certain ways that benefit subordinates. In one study (summarized by Freiberg, 1991, p. 23), Americans were satisfied if their leaders were merely competent: "It's no secret that bosses are unpopular with their employees. But what hasn't been realized, according to a recent two-year study, is that employees have good reason to dislike them: Most managers are incompetent and are the prime source of job stress."

The concept that superiors have obligations to act as effective leaders is part of many treatments of leadership in Asia (Kumar & Saxena, 1983; Misumi, 1985; Hui, 1990). Kumar and Saxena explain what leaders are expected to do in different contexts, thus exemplifying several of the six approaches to leadership already reviewed (Muchinsky, 1990). Although the explanations of Kumar and Saxena (1983) were developed to explain leadership behavior in India, the descriptions are useful in analyzing superior–subordinates throughout Asia. To understand leadership in India, people must understand superiors' sense of family identification, and their sense of obligation. Most leaders in India are males, and consequently some of the language used to describe leaders (e.g., paternal, authoritative) is masculine rather than feminine or gender neutral. Cultural differences in leadership can be introduced by considering a conversation between a male boss and his female subordinate. The boss calls the subordinate into his office.

> BOSS: I'd like to discuss an issue with you. How long have you been working in my section of the company?
>
> FEMALE SUBORDINATE: About five years.
>
> BOSS: And I've always been happy with your work. However, there is something that is wrong. You're about 28 yers old now, and are not married, and I think that it's time you meet some eligible men. There's a young man in the accounting department who

seems very hardworking. I will arrange a lunch for four people: you, me, him, and his boss.

FEMALE SUBORDINATE: Thank you for your concern.

Could this conversation take place in the United States? Probably not very often. In fact, the boss might face charges based on the "hostile work environment" clause that is part of the sexual harassment codes that many companies have adopted. But the conversation *could* take place in many Asian countries. To understand this conversation (which occurs frequently, since the workplace often provides the meeting place for eligible men and women), we need to understand the viewpoints of leaders and their subordinates. Two concepts (Kumar & Saxena, 1983) are especially important: a sense of family identification, and a sense of obligation.

SENSE OF FAMILY IDENTIFICATION. Some leaders view their subordinates as a group much like their family, and this is called the "own family" identification. With this view, leaders show concern for their subordinates much as a father shows concern for his children. Leaders nurture their followers; exercise their authority in a responsible manner; and behave in a warm, caring manner. So, just as a father is concerned about his daughter's marriage, a boss is concerned that his subordinates marry well. Some contexts, however, prevent this sense of family identification, especially very large organizations where executives cannot even know the names of all people who work for them. Here, the view leaders take is called "other family." The workers are certainly part of the leader's thinking, but there is not the sense of kinship or sense of belonging as there is in the "own family" identification.

SENSE OF OBLIGATION. As previously discussed, once leaders accept their high-status positions, they have obligations toward subordinates. The obligations include looking after the needs of subordinates and taking an interest in their personal lives. The obligations can be either "personal" or "impersonal." With a sense of personal obligation, the leader develops expectations of what specific and known others can offer the organization. For example, the leader learns that specific people, who become well known, can offer their enthusiasm, their skills, and their loyalty (Lincoln, 1985). In return, the leader behaves according to the specific and personalized expectations that subordinates develop during their tenure with the organization. Leaders and subordinates, then, owe debts to each other. "This indebtedness legitimizes a highly personalized [sense of] ethics in relations" (Kumar & Saxena, 1983, p. 357). This acceptance of personal relations with subordinates contrasts sharply with a more impersonal set of obligations that some leaders are forced to accept. One reason, again, is the size of the company, but another is the competitiveness of the industry in which leaders and their subordinates work. In highly competitive, fast-moving industries, such as the development of robots, subordinates have to be shifted quickly from task to task so that any one company maintains its competitive edge. Even though a given set of subordinates may enjoy interacting with members of their current workgroup, the leaders may have to break up this group and reassign the workers to provide on-the-job training for newly hired personnel. The nature of the industry can encourage a more impersonal style if leaders have to keep "industrial competitiveness" foremost in their minds. Rather than internalizing and accepting a set of obligations, leaders who act according to the impersonal orientation behave out of a sense of duty. They learn what tradition dictates (e.g., salary increases, vacation time, job security) and then discharge their duty to lead their subordinates. They do so, however, without a sense of emotional interrelatedness with their subordinates.

EXPECTATIONS ABOUT LEADERSHIP: CULTURAL DIFFERENCES. Another short case study may make some of these concepts clearer. George Jackson is a mid-level manager in the petrochemical industry, and has been assigned a two-year sojourn at the company's branch plant in India. Within his home country, the United States, George has a good reputation as a manager and leader. His subordinates feel that he was fair in his dealings, accepted suggestions well, encouraged a cooperative atmosphere in the workplace, and "knew his stuff" when it came to petrochemicals.

Sudesh Kumar, one of the citizens of India on George Jackson's staff, was an assistant manager for fiscal affairs and reported directly to George. For the first six months of George's sojourn in India, his relations with Sudesh were much like those between a leader and subordinate in the United States. George found Sudesh a competent worker who cooperated well with others and contributed to a pleasant work environment. George was able to accept an invitation from Sudesh and her family to attend a birthday party for her 6 year-old son, and he had a good time at the party. Sudesh's son enjoyed the gift George brought, a large plastic figure of a cartoon hero, since he had seen it on television but had never seen it in the stores.

One day, Sudesh asked George for an appointment to discuss some of her concerns. Since Sudesh had obviously been very busy recently with paperwork related to company finances, George thought that the meeting was to deal with Sudesh's suggestions for handling the workload. But once the meeting started, George realized that all of Sudesh's concerns dealt with her personal life. She told of troubles with her marriage, her suspicions about the faithfulness of her husband, the stress her suspicions were causing her, her concern that she was not being a good mother to her son given the pressures of her job, and other problems involving her extended family. She asked for George's advice concerning exactly what she should do, especially about her husband. George was very uncomfortable with the discussion. He was familiar with giving advice to subordinates about work-related matters, and considered himself quite good at this aspect of his job. He was also familiar with sharing certain types of information that touched on his subordinates' personal lives, such as the names of good schools in the community where parents might send their children, but he never had had discussions of the type that Sudesh desired. He was, in fact, hesitant to discuss issues such as the husband's possible unfaithfulness because company policies with which he was familiar (in his own country) discouraged supervisors' involvement in the personal lives of employees.

After Sudesh finished the discussion of her problems, George tried to express his concern and his sympathy. Since he was not prepared for such a personal conversation, however, he was unable to make any specific suggestions. Recognizing George's discomfort, Sudesh mentioned that they could perhaps meet again at a later date, but she was puzzled at George's unwillingness to make specific recommendations concerning exactly what she should do. What cultural differences might explain the reasons for this unsuccessful meeting?

THE PATERNAL-AUTHORITATIVE LEADER. Sudesh has expectations concerning what leaders should do that are distinctly different from the behaviors with which George is familiar. Following the concepts suggested by Kumar and Saxena (1983), Sudesh prefers a leader who has a sense that workers are part of his "own family," and that his obligations are "personal." Sudesh expects a male leader to behave much like a father, and that he should treat Sudesh in a way that takes her special, personal needs into account. A father should be concerned if his daughter suspects her husband of being unfaithful. The father should take concrete action! And the concern should be personal and should be different from the concern that he would show to *any* subordinate in the workplace. Didn't George enjoy himself at the birthday party and go to the trouble of obtaining a gift that is generally unavailable in India? This demonstrated his personal concern for Sudesh and her family, and consequently she expects a continuation of this personal concern when she has difficulties to discuss with him. Similarly, the woman who learns that she will be attending a luncheon to meet an eligible male appreciates the efforts of her boss. By commenting on her lack of a husband at 28 years of age, the boss is showing his personal interest and concern.

The leadership style that many Indians prefer and expect (Sinha, 1980; Kumar & Saxena, 1983) can be called "paternal authoritativeness." The words are carefully chosen. "Paternal" captures the expectations of concern, nurturance, and the belief that subordinates should be treated like members of the leader's own family. "Authoritativeness" captures that expectations that leaders should know what to do in a wide range of situations. Note that the word is not "authoritarian": that word would have the additional implications that people *must* behave in the way leaders demand or else face negative consequences. "Authoritativeness" recognizes that subordinates are willing to defer to leaders because the leaders are experts and are *obliged* to give good advice. With the expectation that the leader treat workers like family members, there is no sharp distinction between people's personal lives at home and the hours they spend at work. George is much more comfortable with a leadership style that involves expertise in the workplace but respect for the privacy of subordinates' lives once they go home.

THE IMPERSONAL-OTHER FAMILY ORIENTATION. When the two concepts discussed here are combined, the leadership style that contrasts most sharply with paternal authoritativeness might be called the impersonal-other family orientation. The impersonal part of the style means that leaders act according to rules, to guidelines that are written down and widely available, and to laws (e.g., that deal with collective bargaining, harassment in the workplace). As much as possible, the leaders should not behave according to any *personal* relationship that they have with subordinates. Rather, they should treat subordinates equally.

While this style may seem very cold and uncaring, it is meant to serve the needs of as many subordinates as possible. The style is more common in highly industrialized countries where companies are large and where leaders find it difficult to know the personal needs of each subordinate. Readers may be able to appreciate the appropriateness of the impersonal style (in certain contexts) if they consider this example. Assume a professor sets an average score of 92 (out of 100) as the cut-off for a grade of "A." Two students have average scores of 91.5. They visit the professor to see if they can persuade her to grant an "A" grade. If the professor had a personal approach to leadership as discussed here, she would consider her relationships with the two students. Perhaps one of them was a research assistant last semester who worked overtime but did not claim extra hours when submitting her paysheet. Perhaps an "A" grade would be a recognition of his past work. But this can be seen as unfair to the second student who never had a chance to act as a research assistant. This second student will prefer a more impersonal style, based on written guidelines and widely known precedents that ignore any special professor–student relationship. The second student will prefer considerations that focus on the class where the "A" or "B" grade will be given. Such considerations might be class participation, an extra-credit paper, or the regrading of an earlier paper so that a few extra points are granted. If the professor acts according to these more impersonal guidelines, neither student will be the beneficiary of favoritism that is based on a personal relationship.

When the "other family" aspect of this leadership style is added, it indicates that leaders will make sharp distinctions between their own family at home and their colleagues and subordinates in the workplace. Again, this movement away from feelings of closeness will be more common in large companies. Even if they desire to develop a "family atmosphere" in the workplace, leaders with over 100 subordinates find it difficult to do so. If they desire a family atmosphere in a large company, the danger is that some subordinates will be treated as "ingroup" members and some will be treated as "outgroup" members (Hui, 1990; terms also discussed in Chapter 6, this volume). Tensions then arise when some workers feel favored by the leaders compared to others who feel ignored. In the incident involving the two students who desired an "A" grade, both could be treated warmly by the professor if they were attending a small college where small classes were the norm. "We encourage a family-like atmosphere" is a phrase administrators frequently use at small colleges. If the students were at a large state university, on the other hand, the professor is more likely to behave in a cordial but proper manner with both. In large lecture classes, professors have to be careful about favoring some students since they might be accused of ignoring others. Given that the professors have so many students, they cannot become intimate friends with all of them, and consequently they develop a more impersonal style and apply it to virtually all their students.

Returning to the example involving George Jackson and Sudesh Kumar, there is a clash between expectations concerning two quite different leadership styles. Sudesh expects to be treated much like a family member, and she expects that George will take her personal needs into account. George prefers a more impersonal style in which he treats his many subordinates in as equal a manner as possible. Note that one person is not "right" and the other "wrong." Both styles are appropriate in certain cultures and in certain contexts. I have been placed in situations similar to the one described in the example. I work at the East-West Center, an organization that sponsors hundreds of students and mid-career professionals each year as they pursue advanced degrees and/or research projects. When I have worked with graduate students from Nepal, India, Burma, or Thailand, I have been frequently asked about potential marriage partners, directives (not advice!) concerning where to send children to school, precise orders concerning choice of topics for thesis research, and specific recommendations for career development over a 10-year period. I am uncomfortable giving such advice, but I realize that it is part of these students' expectations of what a leader does. If leaders cannot engage in such behaviors, they are considered unworthy of their positions.

Compromises are sometimes possible. I have personally dealt with the request for paternal and authoritative advice by suggesting a *range* of possibilities. I suggest a range of good thesis topics; I introduce students to many members of the opposite sex; young professionals and I discuss various career goals and ways to attain them, and so forth. Since the graduate students and mid-career professionals who work with me are interested in culture and cultural differences, we can relate my recommendations to concepts such as individualism–collectivism and the preference for a paternal–authoritative leader. My work with these people, then, becomes specific examples of concepts they will need to know in their future work in intercultural and cross-cultural studies.

The future. It is always important to consider how people's preferences will change in future years. One of the most impactful influences on change will be the increasing presence of women in the workplace, a trend that may spread from highly industrialized to developing nations (Tung & Miller, 1990; Adler, 1991). As these women assume responsible positions, what will their preferences be? Will they expect a paternal–authoritative style, or will they reject it as contributing to the power base of men? Will they want personalized interventions into their lives, for example, when they receive unwelcome sexual attention at work? Or will they develop an appreciation of very impersonal, formalized rules that specify what is and what is not allowed when men and women interact in the workplace? Will men and women continue to have differing views concerning what is friendly banter and what is harassment (Konrad & Gutek, 1986)? To understand the future, we must understand the importance of gender and gender differences and their relation to people's culture. This is the focus of the next chapter.

CHAPTER SUMMARY

The workplace will increasingly become one of the most important social settings where intercultural interactions take place. People can either (a) tolerate the demands brought on by legal requirements that demand interaction across cultural barriers, or (b) they can look forward to the stimulation that such interactions can provide. When examining cultural differences in the workplace, a good technique is to imagine oneself working in a country other than one's own. Are there new challenges that one will face, or will expectations of workplace behavior be much the same as in one's own country? Given that the answer to the first part of the question will be "yes," and to the second part "no," it is important to examine differences identified by cross-cultural researchers (Hofstede, 1980; Adler, 1991).

Some of the most helpful cross-cultural research is based on ecological correlations, and it is important to understand the difference between this type of correlation and the more common individual-level correlation. When interpreting individual-level correlations, researchers can examine (among other factors) traits and qualities of the individuals involved in the study. If there is a correlation between Americans' fluency in Chinese and their satisfaction with their overseas assignments in China, one set of interpretations can be based on traits of the individuals. Perhaps people who invest time and effort in learning the Chinese language are also very committed to learning a great deal about the Chinese culture. This commitment may assist them in overcoming the inevitable difficulties they will face in China, and consequently their commitment will have a long-term impact on their satisfaction. Note that this interpretation is based on the qualities of people: their language skills, their commitment, their ability to overcome problems, and their eventual satisfaction with life in China.

Ecological correlations are based on measures in which the unit of analysis is larger than an individual. An individual may work hard and earn a great deal of money, and this sum might be included in an analysis of earnings in his or her city, region of the country, or nation. When the results of a research study are based on the analysis of units such as salaries in a city, region, or country, the correlations are said to be "ecological." When interpreting such correlations, *aspects of those units* must become the focus. If ecological correlations are interpreted as if they are individual correlations (an all-too-common practice), then the interpreters are guilty of the "ecological fallacy."

Geert Hofstede (1980, 1986, 1991) and Michael Bond (Chinese Culture Connection, 1987; Hofstede & Bond, 1988) have identified five ecological concepts that assist in understanding intercultural interactions in the workplace. The five are individualism–collectivism; power-distance; masculinity–femininity; uncertainty avoidance; and Confucian dynamism. The unit of analysis for these correlations is the country in which people were socialized: Japan, USA, Sweden, India, Great Britain, and so forth. The most recent treatments of these concepts are based on data from 50 countries (Hofstede, 1991). Given that these are ecological concepts based (in this case) on data from countries, interpretation must focus on aspects of the different countries.

Insights into the masculinity–femininity dimension can be obtained by looking at the people's concerns and preferences in the workplace. In masculine countries, people place an emphasis on salaries, advancement on the job, and opportunities to remain up to date. In countries called "feminine," people prefer a friendly work atmosphere, and cooperative relations with supervisors and co-workers. In the most masculine countries, women will not be found at meetings where decisions are made because they are relatively powerless and are discouraged from offering suggestions regarding important decisions.

Uncertainty avoidance refers to the number of rules and regulations that are commonly found within a country's businesses. One fact about the future is that we don't know exactly what will happen. Countries high in uncertainty avoidance have, over many years, dealt with this fact by imposing many rules and regulations that will hopefully lessen the impact of negative events. Since the start-up of new businesses involves risks, the development of new ventures is often hard in uncertainty-avoidant countries. Would-be businesspeople find many rules and regulations ("red tape"), become frustrated, and take their business elsewhere.

Power distance refers to the distinctions between various groups that are part of a country's status hierarchy. All countries have hierarchies: The important factor here is the degree of difference that separates one hierarchical level from another. A boss has subordinates, but how distant do people feel from their boss? In high power distance countries, people defer to bosses and only rarely disagree with them openly. In low power distance countries (e.g., USA), people do *not* feel that their boss is a great deal more able than they. Further, they enjoy developing cordial relations with their boss and feel it is possible to disagree with their boss.

Individualism–collectivism was discussed as an individual-level variable in Chapter 2. It is also a label for an ecological concept, and this fact admittedly can make interpretations of cross-cultural research difficult to carry out. As an ecological concept, individualism and collectivism refer to the organization of society. To what degree does group membership determine whether or not goals are met? In collectivist societies, the answer is "very much." People have a difficult time achieving their goals unless they are *long-term* members of influential groups, such as a university alumni association, or a well-known company. The phrase "long-term" is important: People must demonstrate loyalty to a group over a number of years. In individualist societies people have an easier time achieving their goals independent of any long-term commitment to a group. For example, people can be members of a company, but within that company can make their contributions working very much by themselves. As long as the people are productive, company executives in individualist countries are far more tolerant of workers who choose to keep to themselves.

Confucian dynamism has been identified as an important factor in Asian countries that have seen economic growth over the past 20 years. The factors refer to the relative influence (high, moderate, low) of philosophical principles formulated by Confucius. The principles that are related to the economic growth of countries involve a concern with the future and with the good that hard work can bring, and consequently this selected list is called "Confucian dynamism." The principles include the importance of persistence and perseverance, the ordering of relationships and attention to the resulting mutual obligations, thrift, and having a sense of shame.

A case study was presented involving difficulties between an American employee and a Japanese boss. All five factors were involved. The American preferred to work alone; the boss preferred contributions through group effort (individualism–collectivism). The American wanted to include women in certain company gatherings; the male boss felt that this was unnecessary (masculinity–femininity). The American was not attentive to company rules, and did not respond to the boss's concern about rule-breaking (uncertainty avoidance and power distance). The American felt that he was most creative when he could work on several tasks at the same time; the boss preferred persistence on one task (Confucian dynamism). As with many intercultural encounters, there is no hero and there is no villain. People's cultures are coming into contact, and there are well-meaning clashes (Chapter 7). Concepts such as the five reviewed here assist in the understanding of such clashes.

Clashes will exist when people exercise the role of "leader" in cultures other than their own. Various approaches to the study of leadership have been adopted by different researchers (Hollander, 1985; Muchinsky, 1990). One centers on power and influence, and another focuses on the traits of successful leaders. A third approach recognizes the fact that in any analysis of leadership, there must be a focus on subordinates as well as leaders. Questions asked by researchers interested in this aspect of leadership include: What are the preferences and expectations of subordinates concerning the behavior of their leaders? A fourth and related approach involves the analysis of the mutual influence that leaders and followers have. The well-known Japanese practice of establishing "quality circles," in which workers make suggestions about the improvement of a company's products, is an example. Leaders are expected to listen carefully to these suggestions, and they often integrate the workers' ideas into company policies. A fifth approach focuses on various situations in which leaders find themselves, and one of its intriguing assumptions is that some people are better leaders in some settings when compared to others. For example, some people are better leaders than others when the task is highly structured. Other people are better leaders when the task is unstructured and when effort has to be put into organizing exactly what different subordinates will do given this relative lack of structure. The sixth approach studies the emergence of leaders. What sorts of people move from modest positions within their organizations to positions of power and influence? This is an especially important question in international business ventures since leaders may be chosen for overseas assignments based on performance in their *own* country. In *another* country, however, they may not be recognized as leaders by host nationals unless they meet the expectations of people in that country.

Americans working in Asia are frequently puzzled by the expectations that subordinates have of their leaders. This discussion is based on research carried out in India (Sinha, 1980; Kumar & Saxena, 1983), and similar expectations concerning what leaders should do can be found in various Asian countries (Misumi, 1985; Hui, 1990). Expectations can be summarized in the phrase, "paternal authoritativeness." Many workers expect their leaders to behave much like concerned fathers. Since fathers know their own children well, the workers prefer to be treated based on the leader's knowledge of their own personal needs. Further, the leaders are expected to know a great deal about many aspects of life, and consequently they are expected to be able to give very authoritative advice on matters involving marriage, the socialization of children, and various activities in the community. These can be very difficult expectations for Americans working in Asia. Many Americans prefer the approach to leadership where they have responsibility to their subordinates during the workday, but that their employees' personal life should be considered just that: personal. Of course, many American employees strongly prefer such leaders: They will accept a leader's directives at work, but feel that leaders have no business intervening into their marriages, dating behavior, community activities, and so forth.

In considering the future of work-related behaviors in various parts of the world, one of the most important factors will be the presence of, and growing influence of, women. As discussed in Chapter 4, women in many countries are dissatisfied if they are limited to the roles of wife, mother, and homemaker. Many women are seeking wage employment, to expand both their own opportunities and the benefits that can accrue to their families. The fact of an increased female presence in the workplace will demand that leaders (many of whom will be female) understand culture's influence on gender and be willing to modify company policies to meet the needs of different workers. Insights gained from the study of culture and gender are covered in the next chapter.

9

CULTURE AND GENDER

As discussed in Chapter 1 and Chapter 4, culture provides people with guidance concerning appropriate thoughts, feelings, and actions. Culture also gives guidance concerning differences in behavior that are expected of persons who hold different roles. One of the most important distinctions occurs for behaviors considered appropriate for "males" compared to "females." An understanding of cultural expectations for males and females is assisted by an examination of how humans process information and form categories.

The amount of information that children must learn to become members of their culture, as well as the amount of information that adults encounter every day of their lives, is so vast that various learning aids are necessary. An extremely important learning aid, with major implications for the way that people from different cultures interact with one another, is the category. As part of their socialization, members of different cultures learn to put specific pieces of information into more general categories, and then react to those categories in making decisions (Gardner, 1985; Chaplin, John, & Goldberg, 1988). Rather than spending time and energy on each piece of information encountered, people can react on the basis of the categories used by well-socialized members of their culture. When encountering an unfamiliar plant, for instance, people are unlikely to spend time considering whether or not it is edible. Rather, they will immediately see that the plant is *not* part of the category that their culture has labelled as "edible foods." If they are searching for food, they will shift their attention immediately to other possibilities. There are advantages and disadvantages to this strategy. If they immediately shift their attention away from the unfamiliar plant, people are protecting themselves if it is poisonous. On the other hand, people may be ignoring a good source of nutrition simply because it is unfamiliar.

If people must draw specific information from their environment so that they will meet their basic physical needs (e.g.: Which water is drinkable? What potential mates are available to me? Are these newcomers to my culture a threat?), then it is certain that there will be categories that deal with this necessary information. If the information deals with aspects of life that must be faced by all people no matter where they reside, then the *existence* of certain categories will be culturally universal. Differences across cultures will be found in the *exact content* of the categories. The category, "edible foods" is a universal. The content of this category varies from culture to culture. Young puppies are a delicacy in some cultures, as are unborn baby birds still in their eggshells; yet neither of these items is considered edible food in other cultures. As might be expected, the difference in the content of categories may cause embarrassments during intercultural encounters. High-status visitors from a country such as the United States find themselves entertained in a rural village in the Philippines. They are served a lavish meal, with puppies and unborn birds as entrées. Even the most well-traveled and interculturally sensitive visitors will have a difficult time at this meal.

It is extremely important to recognize that people categorize all kinds of information. This information does not consist solely of objects, such as potential food and drinkable water. The categorization extends to other people with whom any one individual comes into contact. Again, when there are universal concerns about other people, there will be categories found in all cultures. One concern all people have is mating with someone and producing children. Another is caring and providing for the children, who are completely helpless at birth (Low, 1989). The procreation of children can only be carried out with a member of the opposite sex. Caring for young children demands a division of labor in which some members of a culture (often but not always males) venture out of the place of residence to find food and some members (almost always females) stay with and care for the children. Given that both males and females are needed to produce children, the existence of categories for both men and women will be culturally universal. Just as with physical objects, differences will exist within the content of the categories. What are men expected to do? What behaviors will be seen as desirable by members of the opposite sex? Are behaviors indicative of leadership encouraged in the young women of a certain culture, or are leadership behaviors expected only of men? Again, the cultural differences within the *content* of categories cause difficulties and misunderstandings. Recall the story about Peter Reed in Chapter 8. As an American working in Japan, he tried to involve his female co-workers in the lunch gatherings that he organized. He discovered, however, that females are not frequently included in gatherings where company managers meet and discuss business matters. The category "female" is less likely to include the possibility of "company leader" in Japan compared to the United States.

With the possible exception of the categories "race" and "ethnicity," there is probably more controversy in discussions of males and females than in any other topic that touches upon human behaviors. For every suggestion about possible differences and reasons for these, there are detractors who point to other explanations (Fleming, 1985–1986; Fausto-Sterling, 1985; Hare-Mustin & Marecek, 1988; Hubbard, 1990). One of the most frequently cited *possible* differences (introduced in Chapter 5, and one that will be discussed more fully later in this chapter) is the superior performance of males on tasks involving mathematical computations (e.g., Maccoby & Jacklin, 1974; Bellisari, 1989; Engelhard, 1990). Controversy focuses on both the existence of any difference in mathematical ability and (if a difference is acknowledged) explanations of the research results. Analysts who focus on the importance of socialization ask if parents expect young females to perform as well as young males. Analysts who focus on the schools ask if counselors encourage females to take advanced math courses (and if students say "no" the first time the possibility arises, Do counselors argue more with males than females?). Analysts who focus on power differences within societies (e.g., Hubbard, 1990) argue that men are more likely to encourage other men in mathematics because it is so useful in *retaining* power in complex technological societies. These various arguments provide many perspectives on the admittedly complex study of gender differences, and readers desirous of participation in vigorous debate will have a difficult time finding a more attractive research area.

In my opinion, the study of gender and gender differences has enriched the study of culture and behavior by forcing researchers to consider a broader range of theoretical concepts and practical issues (e.g., issues related to female participation in the workforce). Indeed, I believe that the emphasis on the study of gender is directly reponsible for books such as this one. In the 1960s and 1970s, the percentage of female high school graduates who decided to attend college rose significantly. These females took courses in fields such as psychology, education, communication, and management and *did not find themselves* in their textbooks. Rather, they found that much of the research from which generalizations were drawn was based on experiments, surveys, and behavioral observations of men. They began to demand that their professors include more research about women in their class presentations and to search out texts that integrated research studies that looked directly at the behavior of women. Given the success of these women in influencing their professors, other people began examining their texts and asking the question: Do I find myself in here? For example, this question was asked by members of various ethnically diverse groups, international students, and "nontraditional" students returning to college after several years in the workforce or after years of raising children. These various students demanded that the diversity of the people that they saw every day on campus be reflected in their coursework. Many professors responded positively, began to expand the scope of their research to examine gender and cultural differences, and provided the information that allow books like this one to be written.

The treatment of culture and gender in this chapter will be organized around six themes:

1. The clarification of concepts by attention to terms, such as sex, gender, sex role, and gender role.

2. Differences between males and females that stem from our biological heritage, with special attention to behaviors that led to an evolutionary advantage for our ancestors.

While the study of evolution can lead to some important insights, it cannot explain all male–female differences. People are also strongly influenced by the role models whom they observe during their childhood, and this leads to the necessity of studying the following:

3. The socialization of children to behave according to a culture's norms concerning gender roles.

4. The analysis of sex stereotypes. When many or most members of a sex behave in a certain way, a generalization or stereotype can develop. Some people, on the other hand, do not behave according to the traditional guidelines that their cultures offer. Understanding both stereotypes and individual differences is necessary in the analysis of culture and gender.

5. The concept of relatedness to others. Many researchers have argued that women are more sensitive to, and concerned about, their relations with others in their culture. There are many implications that stem from this difference.

6. The importance of culture change. Cultures change over time, and two reasons are contact with other cultures and the adoption of technological innovations. The changes often have an impact on the behaviors considered acceptable to women. When cultures change, the activities of women often converge with behaviors that have long been observed among men (e.g., greater sexual expressiveness, more political participation).

RECOMMENDATIONS REGARDING TERMS

Confusion can result if terms are inconsistently used. Virginia Prince (1985) offered a set of recommendations that make a great deal of sense. She makes a distinction between sex and gender, and the distinction has been used by other researchers (Unger, 1979; Eagly, 1987). *Sex* refers to a biological fact. Men and women have physiological differences, and the most obvious differences involve their reproductive systems. Men have the ability to produce sperm and females have the ability to produce ova. Members of both sexes are necessary to produce offspring who will be socialized into their culture and who will be responsible for the perpetuation of the culture. The need to produce children to assure a culture's survival is a universal demand all people face. The term *sex roles* includes the activities of men and women necessary for a man's sperm to meet a female's ovum at the time that female is fertile. For women, the sex role also includes behaviors involved in the nursing of children because only women have breasts that provide milk. The male's *sexual identity* includes his awareness that he has the potential to impregnate women and knows the necessary behaviors. Female sexual identity includes the woman's awareness of her reproductive potential and her knowledge about behaviors that lead to pregnancy.

Gender—distinct from sex—refers to people who accept a set of behaviors that a culture defines as proper and acceptable for men and for women. As will be discussed further in the next section, the male gender role includes aggressiveness in behavior, and the female gender role includes the nurturance of others. Other gender roles that many cultures have for males include leaving the home daily to find food or to earn wages, to contribute to the security of the village or town through military means, and to assume positions of leadership. The gender roles that many cultures have for women include raising children, cooking, making clothes, keeping house, and tending small vegetable gardens near the home. The importance of maintaining a distinction between the terms "sex" and "gender" can be seen most clearly in cases where members of the male sex and the female sex want to engage in behaviors that a culture has traditionally deemed inappropriate. The desire to engage in "traditionally inappropriate" behaviors frequently occurs during times of culture change. Many males want to stay home and interact extensively with their children; many females want to earn wages and to assume positions of leadership. The desire to acquire gender roles considered inappropriate for their sex may lead to rejection and discrimination on the part of a culture's members who are familiar and comfortable only with traditional roles.

In the American culture, the distinction between sex and gender can be seen clearly in the women's liberation movement. When Virginia Prince refers to "sociocultural conditions," she is referring to the limits that a culture's norms place on the behaviors in which males and females can engage without formal or informal sanctions from authority figures.

> The women seeking liberation may be female but they are not seeking liberation from their biological state (which would not be possible in any case) but from the sociocultural condition to which the word *woman* refers. In the interest of real equality let me also note that men too need liberation at least as much and probably more than women (Prince, 1985, p. 96).

In this context, the liberation of men refers to behavioral expectations. If both men and women are free to pursue behaviors that were once considered proper for only one gender role, they will have greater chances of finding happiness since their goals are set by themselves, not by the traditional limits of society. Many readers have undoubtedly benefited from the relaxation of traditional limits. I play the harp, for example, and started doing so in the mid 1980s. I hesitate to think of my community's reactions had I started playing this instrument traditionally associated with females when I first began my study of music in the 1950s.

To understand the reasons for traditional limits on gender roles, we need to understand the evolutionary history of our ancestors and the socialization practices of different cultures. These are the topics to be covered in the next two sections.

THE EVOLUTIONARY ADVANTAGE OF SOME SPECIFIC GENDER ROLES

Once males and females fulfill their sex roles (i.e., man impregnates woman, woman gives birth), there are a number of possible gender roles that *could have* become common in various cultures. For example, women could have left the home and could have assumed the responsibility for securing food and for settling arguments with neighbors. By undertaking these activities, women could have acquired community-wide power and status if they were especially skillful. Men could have stayed home and taken care of the children. For a number of reasons, this set of gender roles did not evolve. Rather, a different set of behaviors became common and achieved the status of conferring an evolutionary advantage upon people who adopted them (Chodorow, 1974; Hadiyono & Kahn, 1985; Low, 1989; Buss, 1991). When thinking about human evolution and its implications for human behavior as we experience it and observe it today, we must think of the difficult, dangerous ecologies in which our ancestors lived hundreds of thousands of years ago. An "evolutionary advantage" means that people who adopted certain behaviors were more likely to survive in their difficult environments and consequently were more likely to pass their genes on to future generations. Any genetic tendency that led people to favor engaging in those behaviors, then, would lead to a greater chance of people surviving, producing offspring, and thus passing their genes on to others.

One of the clearest examples is the evolution of language in humans. Our homo sapien ancestors were neither the strongest animals, nor were they the swiftest or the most prolific (having many children so that a few would possibly survive no matter how difficult the environment). However, they evolved into the primates that we now call the most "intelligent," and the major factor in this evolution was the capacity for language. With language, our ancestors could share lessons about survival learned in the recent past, could organize themselves for effective group activity in the present, and could plan for the future (e.g., storing food in anticipation of a possible famine). Our ancestors who did not develop a capacity for language were less likely to have these benefits that encompassed the past, present, and future and were less likely to survive and to pass their genes on to later generations. Presently, humans have the capacity for language and use it for their own benefit, and in so doing they are taking advantage of a capacity that was developed in our evolutionary past.

One of the most important gender distinctions found all over the world (Barry & Child, 1983; Prince, 1985; Low, 1989) is that women stay home and take care of children and men leave the home and acquire food. The food is later brought home and shared with the women. There are several reasons. One is that the behaviors involved in giving birth to children either (at best) take away from the strength and energy of women and (very frequently) actually debilitate women. Consequently, women are simply too weak after giving birth to forage for food. Further, women have a source of food that is extemely beneficial to babies: the milk from breasts. Women who developed the gender role of staying home (to recover from childbirth and to regain their strength) and accepting food supplied by men (to increase their own strength and to increase the supply of breast milk for their babies) were more likely to survive. Men also derived advantages. By supplying food to women, the men were able to help ensure that their children would survive past infancy. The children could later help with work necessary for the culture's survival and (if the parents lived long enough) could provide a form of old-age insurance once the parents could no longer engage in productive work. Another advantage to men was the opportunity for sexual expression. If they developed unions with women for whom they provided food and other of life's necessities, they could expect sexual intercourse in exchange. One implication (admittedly controversial, as will be discussed below) is that the two gender roles led to the development of certain traits that are differently distributed among men and women. If women stay home and take care of their children, they develop the trait that is often called "nurturance," since they become the major caretakers of their offspring. Further, the women may find themselves so weak that they need help taking care of the children (given that the men are off finding food). Consequently, they may develop positive relationships with other women such as sisters, sisters-in-law, and cousins who can help with the children. If the women are sensitive to the importance of developing such relations, they will become better able to care for children. This may lead to the trait called "sensitivity to relationships," or more concisely, "relatedness."

If men leave the home to find food, they may also develop certain traits. For example, the men who are most aggressive may be the best food providers: They may be willing to take more risks when hunting animals, or more willing to enter unfamiliar territories to search for edible plants. They may also develop leadership skills if they organize the efforts of other men to hunt for large animals that would be impossible to kill through the efforts of any one person. Aggressiveness is also an important trait when a community is threatened by hostile forces. Again, since women may be weak from the effects of childbirth and will be responsible for looking after small children who do not have any knowledge about protecting themselves from enemies, the defense of a community will become the responsibility of men. Aggressive men may become the most valued and may achieve the highest status. With a combination of aggressiveness, responsibility for protecting women and children, and community-wide status, men will become comfortable in relationships with women that involve dominance rather than equality.

IMPLICATIONS FOR OBSERVABLE BEHAVIORS TODAY. There are implications (again, that are admittedly controversial: Buss, 1991; Stanislaw, 1991) for the behavior of males and females in today's world. Readers may want to write down their answers to these questions and compare theirs with others. Given that the predicted results will be seen as tendencies that exist only if many people are questioned (e.g., females *more likely* than men to answer in a certain way) any one reader will ideally be able to compare her or his responses with about 20 others. This might be done as part of a class exercise.

1. How old are you? Assume that you are unmarried and unattached to a member of the opposite sex. However, you feel that you might like to begin a relationship that could lead to a serious romance. What is the preferred age range that you have for a person whom you would start dating? (This question is based on the research of David Buss and his colleagues [Buss & Barnes, 1986; Buss, 1989; Buss et al., 1990].)

2. What is your height? Assume that, as in question 1, you are currently unmarried and unattached. What is the height (or range of heights) that you prefer in a person you would start dating? (This question is suggested by the research of Elaine [Hatfield] Walster and her colleagues [1966], also Hatfield & Sprecher [1986].)

3. Think back to your childhood and to your adolescence. With whom did you have more interaction, the relatives on your mother's side or your family, or the relatives on your father's side of your family? (This question was suggested in a personal communication by Herbert Barry, and is based on the findings of several research projects [Barry, Bacon, & Child, 1957; Barry & Child, 1983].)

Questions about mate preference have been asked in 33 countries (located on six continents) by Buss and his colleagues (1990). Several of their findings are consistent with predictions based on the evolutionary advantages that preferences in mate selection can bring. Women are more likely to prefer becoming romantically involved with men who are older than themselves, and men are more likely to prefer women younger than themselves. This prediction stems from the fact that older men are more likely to have stature in their communities and thus more likely to have resources they can share with women. Women look to somewhat older men, then, to take care of them during the times when they cannot provide for themselves (e.g., after childbirth, as discussed previously). Men, in contrast, look to younger women because age is related to the ability to have children. The younger a given woman is, the more likely she is to have child-bearing years ahead of her. A biological fact about sex roles is that older men (in today's world, who are over 50 years old) can impregnate young women, but older women cannot become pregnant.

Arguments about mate preference that involve women's ability to bear children extend beyond attention to age as a factor in men's choices. In the survey of respondents in 33 countries (Buss et al., 1990), men were more likely than women to place importance on physical attractiveness. Women were more likely to place emphasis on factors related to men's "earning potential," again consistent with their sensitivity to choices of men who will be good providers. Focusing on greater male preference for physical attractiveness in potential mates, Buss and Barnes (1986, p. 569) commented:

> Specifically, women's reproductive value and fertility are closely tied to age and health (Symons, 1979). Aspects of physical appearance such as smooth and clear skin, good muscle tone, lively gait, white teeth, and lustrous hair are proximate cues to age and health. Therefore, past selection has favored men who enact a preference for those physical attributes (beauty) that are strong cues for age and health, and hence for reproductive capacity.

My prediction is that prople's answer to question number 2 concerning the height of preferred romantic partners will be consistent with suggestions from evolutionary thinking. When thought about carefully, there is no good reason in today's world (especially one influenced by feminist thinking) why females have a preference for males who are taller than themselves. Yet this preference clearly exists. In a study involving the analysis of why people become attracted to members of the opposite sex, Walster and her colleagues (1966) wanted to randomly pair males and females at an informal dance that they organized as part of their research. They could not proceed in this manner. Women complained that they would simply not become involved in the research project unless they were paired with a male taller than themselves. I doubt that this preference among women has diminished since the mid 1960s. The explanation from evolutionary thinking is that women view height as a sign that a given man is strong and that he can protect them from danger. Another biological fact about men and women is that (when the physical abilities of many people are studied) members of one sex are stronger than the other (Khan & Cataio, 1984). For example, men can lift heavier weights than women, and can lift heavy objects for longer periods of time. If women attach themselves to strong men, they will have an advantage if they are physically threatened by an enemy. My guess is that many female readers will admit that they feel more secure walking across a college campus at 10:00 PM in the company of a man taller, rather than shorter, than themselves.

The answers to the third question about memories of interactions with relatives may reflect another aspect of evolutionary predictions. As previously mentioned, women stayed home with infants while men left home in search of food that they later brought back. Given that women were still weak from childbirth, there was an advantage to involving others who could help with the tasks that needed to be completed in and around the home. Good candidates for members of this support group were the mother's relatives: her sisters, cousins, aunts, and perhaps *her* mother if she was still living. Consequently, women able to integrate others into support group activities had an advantage. As the children grew older, they were likely to interact frequently with members of this support group. Further, women were more responsible than men for introducing children to the norms of their culture while the children were very young (Barry & Child, 1983; Low, 1989). During later childhood and adolescence boys were likely to leave the home to interact with men and to learn gender-appropriate skills such as hunting, but during the early years of childhood members of both sexes were likely to remain home and to learn about their culture. A universal need of every culture is learning the norms concerning the appropriate ways of interacting with various other people: those older, those with more status, and so forth. The mother's relatives provide a readily accessible group of people that can assist in the task of introducing such aspects of their culture. In today's world, women still are more likely to bear the responsibility of introducing children to others in their culture, and consequently responses to question number 3 tend to focus on more memories of interactions with the mother's side of the family. My guess is that if this is a tendency over the responses to which readers have access (e.g., other class members), it will be the weakest tendency of the responses to the three questions. Given that more and more women are entering the workforce, and given that families often move from place to place and have little or no access to relatives on one or either side of the family, the involvement of extended family members as helpers during the child's socialization has diminished in highly industrialized nations.

THE ADVANTAGES OF UNDERSTANDING OUR HUMAN PAST.

Discussions suggesting that people engage in behaviors today, and have certain traits today, because of our evolutionary past are very distasteful to many individuals. They feel that there is a biological fatalism that dictates the opportunities that people can pursue. One response to this reasonable complaint is that a knowledge of our past can suggest directions for our behavior in the present. Bobbi Low (1989, p. 316) explained:

The suggestion of differential paths to reproductive success for the two sexes in humans throughout evolutionary time may seem almost offensive to some. It is important, however, to understand past selective pressures if we wish to understand male–female patterns of behavior toward equality in our own society.

At times, people can take advantage of an evolutionary tendency and turn it to their advantage. As mentioned throughout this book, the future will see more and more intercultural interactions, and success in arenas such as international business negotiations will depend on an understanding of cultural differences. Given their traditional concern with relatedness and with preparing children for membership in their culture, it is quite possible that women will be much more skillful dealing with interactions across cultural boundaries and will be more sensitive to the stresses that people encounter during intercultural interactions. Men, with their natural aggressiveness, may want to forge ahead too quickly during their intercultural interactions, failing to take the time to consider the point of view of people from other cultures.

The differences between males and females that I have discussed thus far are related to the universal demand that adults must produce children who survive so that their culture does not become extinct. The analysis of evolutionary pressures suggests a few reasons for male–female differences. Other reasons can be found only as a result of studying the socialization process during which different behaviors become expected of boys and girls. As discussed in Chapter 4, many socialization experiences involve interactions with various role models from whom children learn behaviors appropriate to their culture.

THE SOCIALIZATION OF BOYS AND GIRLS IN THEIR CULTURES

As discussed in Chapter 4 "socialization" refers to the activities through which children are taught to be acceptable and contributing members of their cultures. Infants know absolutely nothing about the culture into which they were born. Parents and other influential adults in a society have the responsibility to introduce their culture to children and to supervise various activities (consciously and unconsciously) that allow children to learn to behave in culturally appropriate ways.

In the previous section, a case was made that the universal demand that adults produce children has implications for male and female roles. These roles (e.g., males as dominant, females as nurturant and relationship oriented) lead to the procreation, survival, and early caretaking of children. Given the evolutionary selection that favors various genes which may contribute to these role behaviors, it is possible that males are biologically more likely to engage in later behaviors that express dominance, and that women are more likely to engage in nurturant behaviors. These "likelihoods" are reinforced during socialization. That is, males (with a possible biological predilection toward dominance) will be encouraged by adults and other elders to behave in a dominant manner, and females will be encouraged to engage in nurturant behaviors. Various rewards (e.g., approval, attention, extra food) will be distributed by adults based on the behaviors of males and females that are gender-appropriate.

A basic fact about socialization (e.g., Barry & Child, 1983; Block, 1983) is that parents and adults encourage children to engage in behaviors that are necessary for children to integrate themselves into the culture and to make contributions once they become adolescents and later adults. When all cultures have the same goal (e.g., the procreation of children), we can look for possible universal ways of meeting these goals. These can involve the encouragement of the same behaviors in children all over the world, and the examples presented previously centered on male dominance compared to female nurturance. When cultures have somewhat different goals, *or* different ways of meeting universal goals such as procreation, then we can look for different behaviors and different emphases during the socialization of children. Alternatively, we can look for differences within the *relative emphases* that adults in various cultures place on the encouragement of certain behaviors in children. The universal fact of greater male aggressiveness, together with differences in the relative emphasis placed on the encouragement of this aggressiveness in various cultures, provides a good example.

MALE AGGRESSIVENESS. Perhaps the most widely accepted conclusion concerning gender differences is that males are more aggressive than females in all cultures for which documentation exists (Goldstein & Segall, 1983; Block, 1983; Khan & Cataio, 1984). Jeanne Block (1983, p. 1337) summarized a number of studies.

> Research findings surrounding aggression are perhaps the most consistent in the literature and indicate that males are more aggressive than females and from an early age . . . Males engage in more rough-and-tumble play, attempt more often to dominate peers, engage in more physical aggression, exhibit more antisocial behavior, prefer television programs with more aggressive content [where TV exists, of course], and depending upon context, are more competitive than females.

Given this universal observation, there are cultural differences: Males in some cultures are socialized to be more aggressive than males in other cultures. Bobbi Low (1989) has examined male aggressiveness as it relates to competition for the attention of (and eventual possible mating with) females.

An interesting feature of most human societies is that they have polygynous marriage systems. George Murdock (1981) feels that adequate information on marriage systems exists for 1,158 societies, and of these 1,078 are polygynous. In 93 percent of the societies for which we have information, then, men can mate with several females while females can mate with only one male. This means that since some men will have several mates, other men will not have any if the male–female population of a society is roughly equal. Consequently, men have to compete for available mates if they are to produce children and if they are to have opportunities for heterosexual intercourse. Aggressiveness is valued in polygynous societies, and male children are socialized to become aggressive (Low, 1989). If they are more aggressive than others, men have certain advantages. They can fight successfully for available mates. Further, they can compete successfully for various resources in a society (e.g., wealth, status, goods) that will allow them to attract a mate or to attract multiple mates. Aggressiveness will also allow men to compete successfully for resources related to survival (especially food, perhaps medicinal plants) once they produce children and are expected to provide for their families.

FEMALE NURTURANCE AND OBEDIENCE. Looked at in a specific way, the socialization of nurturance and obedience in women is the opposite side of the coin to male aggressiveness. If females are socialized to be nurturant and obedient to others, they may be favored by the most successful, high-status males in a community. Men want women who will bear and nurture their children; women want the highest-status men possible because they will be more likely to secure the resources necessary for survival. Obedience is important to males since women who possess this trait will be more likely to (a) follow orders and thus reinforce the male's dominance and (b) regularly engage in the necessary tasks related to housekeeping and caretaking of children.

OTHER FACTORS HAVING AN INFLUENCE ON AGGRESSIVENESS AND OBEDIENCE. There are differences within various polygynous societies that affect the relative emphasis placed on aggressiveness and obedience (Low, 1989). In some societies, there are strong caste or class structures which place limits on peoples strivings for a better life. In such societies, people are born into a certain class and their opportunities in life are determined by this fact. During their socialization, children would not be rewarded for trying to better their lot in life and to move into a higher class. One of the opportunities that is predetermined for males is the type of mates available to them. If they can choose only from their social class (and do not have to compete with men from higher and lower classes, since they are expected to remain within *their* class), there is not as much need to be aggressive, assertive, and dominant.

Females face an interesting possibility in some societies with strong class or caste structures. In some of these societies, women can "marry up," that is, it is permissible for them to marry males from a higher class.

"A woman who marries up may not have more children than a woman who marries within her class, but her children are likely to be better-invested and survive better. The traits expressed as desirable in wives in [these] societies are chastity and obedience" (Low, 1989, p. 315). Possibly, men from higher classes who marry women from lower classes expect certain features. A chaste wife may be more likely to remain faithful to the high-status male, and consequently the male can assure himself about the parenthood of his offspring. The fact that a man is the only person to have engaged in sexual intercourse with a certain woman may be a status-generating feature for him. The advantages of female obedience have already been mentioned: Obedient women reinforce dominant men, and they will faithfully fulfill their household duties.

These findings may have implication for today's world. Women who marry up may be trading resources: chastity and obedience for the male's higher status and access to society's benefits. This is not unknown today. My guess is that most readers know of women who were from the lower- or workingclass, but they happened to have beauty-queen-level good looks. Some of these women may have traded this resource and married a high-status man with access to money, an exquisite home, and benefits for any eventual children. More speculatively, the fact that most of our ancestors lived in polygynous societies may have an impact. Readers might want to consider this question: If you could act on your own preferences, how many sexual partners would you like to have over the course of a month? Males may answer with a higher number. If our evolutionary background is polygynous, males had the opportunity to seek multiple mates and may have come to prefer such an arrangement. Females were limited to one partner, and may have come to prefer *this* arrangement. Further, females may prefer to have a close relationship with this person rather than a set of interactions limited to the sex act. A number of women have expressed their feelings to me in words similar to the following: "I am more interested in a deep relationship with one person than in superficial relationships with many different people."

ACTIVITY LEVEL. People can behave in quiet, restful ways that are passive and indicate no desire to have an impact on other individuals or the environment. Or, people can engage in activities in which they have to invest energy, which involve a great deal of physical movement, and which lead to impacts on others and on the environments in which they live. The term "high activity level" is used to describe the latter types of behaviors. When the behaviors of males and females are compared, males are more likely to engage in behaviors marked by a high activity level. Jeanne Block (1983, p. 1338) summarized a great deal of literature:

> Males have also been observed to be more curious and to en-
> gage in more exploration, behaviors that may reflect activity
> level (and also may reflect impulsivity and risk taking)....

Boys engage in more manipulation of objects, react more strongly to barriers to attractive goal objects, and play more than girls in outdoor areas. Studies of older boys show that they perceive and describe themselves as more daring and adventurous than females. Consistent with males greater adventurousness is the set of findings (Manheimer, Dewey, Mellinger, & Corsa, 1966) demonstrating, perhaps definitively, in an enormous and representative sample (N = 8,874) that boys have significantly more accidents requiring emergency medical treatment at every age level between 4 and 18 years.

There are several implications that stem from the findings that males are more likely to have a higher activity level. Recall the discussion of socialization in Chapter 4, especially the concept of guided participation suggested by Barbara Rogoff (1990). Children have an important influence on many of their own socialization experiences. They often try out new behaviors (e.g., reading a book beyond their grade level). If they do not do as well as they hoped they would, they may communicate this feeling to adults through either verbal or nonverbal means. The adult can then intervene and offer assistance (the "guidance" in guided participation), perhaps by explaining a few of the longer words or breaking a complex sentence into several shorter phrases. The important point for the present analysis of male–female differences is that the more activities in which children engage, the more opportunities there will be for adults to notice how they might be of assistance. If males engage in more noticeable behaviors that involve high activity levels, then adults will have more opportunities to engage males in guided participation. High activity level, then, leads to noticeability. Noticeability, in turn, leads to opportunities for guided participation during adult–child encounters.

One of the places where boys and girls *might* engage in high levels of noticeable activity is on the playing field or on the playground. Participation in games can bring many benefits (Sutton-Smith & Roberts, 1981). If the games involve large teams, children may have to interact effectively with people from outside their immediate family. If the game is complex, they may have to practice a great deal, thus developing good work habits that may later bring respect in the community once children take on adult tasks. If the game allows participation by people with various skill levels, children can test their limits, gradually setting personal performance goals higher and increasing the risks that they are willing to take. Note that these benefits *could* accrue to both male and female participants. Males, however, are likely to benefit more. As discussed previously, males are more aggressive. This can lead to higher levels of performance in games that have aggressiveness as an element (e.g., American football, basketball, and baseball). If females decide to play games with males, they may drop out because of possible harm to their bodies that can result from aggressive competition. One reason for the common observation of gender differentiation among children after age 6 (Maccoby, 1990) is that females do not like the aggressive play favored by boys. A second and more subtle reason is that when they make suggestions during playtime, boys do not pay much attention to girls. For example, all three of the American team sports mentioned above involve behaviors that will lead to arguments: Was the pass dropped or caught? Was the person fouled while making the basket or not? Was the runner safe or out at second base? Perhaps because of their concern with dominance (discussed previously), boys are more likely to listen to others of the same sex when making decisions about the application of the game's rules. Seeing that they have little influence, girls may drop out and play among members of their own sex. Examining possible distinctions between boys and girls in their attempts to influence others Maccoby (1990, p. 515) also suggested:

> [B]etween the ages of three and a half and five and a half [years of age], children greatly increase the frequency of their attempts to influence their play partners. This indicates that children are learning to integrate their activities with those of others so as to be able to carry out coordinated activities.

However, the means of influence differed. Girls were more likely to make polite suggestions. Boys were more likely to use direct commands. Additionally, boys were not likely to be influenced (in decisions about their own behavior) by polite suggestions from *anyone*. Consequently, the style that girls used was ineffective during their interactions with boys. The girls *were* influential with each other, and they *were* effective in their interactions with teachers and other adults given that the latter prefer suggestions to demands! Still, the positive attention that girls received for their politeness must be irritating to boys, further reinforcing their preference for same-sex playgroups.

As I argued above, the female style will have more use in the long run given that intercultural and international interactions demand mutual respect and will proceed more smoothly if suggestions are offered rather than demands made. Admittedly, however, we are asking young girls to wait a long time (during the seemingly endless period of late childhood and adolescence) before their influence style is useful. Young girls can become upset when they find themselves unable to engage in the high activity level thought appropriate for boys. In a study of satisfaction with gender roles carried out in Australia, Burns and Homel (1986) found that some young girls had a major complaint. While having generally positive self-concepts, 37 percent of the Australian girls from an Anglo background were dissatisfied with the restrictions placed on their participation in sports and games. For example, many wanted to play cricket, but there were far more opportunities for boys to participate in this sport. The other sports mentioned by the girls (and all involving high activity levels) as restricted were soccer, skate-boarding, and tree climbing. One reason for the girls' dissatisfaction was that their expectations were not met. They went to school and heard the claim that Australia offers equal opportunities to males and females. Yet when they tried to participate in some of these opportunities in the form of active sports, they met barriers. Interestingly, other young girls surveyed by Burns and Homel (1986) did not have this dissatisfaction. Young Australian girls from Mediterranean backgrounds (e.g., Greece, Turkey) did not express any sex role dissatisfaction. They did not participate in active sports, but they did not *expect to* and did not *value such participation*. Young girls from Mediterranean backgrounds had internalized other expectations during their earlier socialization. They had learned to value their contribution to family honor through their chastity and preparation for eventual motherhood. The young girls were able to meet these expectations through such activities as helping their mothers at home, and, consequently, they were satisfied with their gender roles.

DEFERENCE DURING INTERACTIONS WITH OTHERS. To prepare for a discussion of people's behaviors during interactions with others, I suggest that readers imagine that they are participants in the two incidents described below. Since some readers are males and some are females, and since the settings involve members of both sexes, people may want to predict typical reactions of same- and opposite-sex participants.

Incident number one: Imagine that a group of six women are discussing political developments in the Middle East. They argue back and forth, occasionally disagree, add ideas to each other's arguments, point out flaws in each other's reasoning, and in general are having a vigorous discussion. An attractive man, who is the same age as the women, enters the room where the discussion is being held. What are some typical reactions that are likely to occur?

Incident number two: Imagine that a group of six men are holding a similar discussion. The give and take between participants is as vigorous (but no more so) as in incident number one. An attractive woman, who is the same age as the men, enters the room. Three of the men know that the woman is particularly well-read about the history and politics of the Middle East. What are some typical reactions that are likely to occur?

A number of research findings suggest that many females are likely to defer to the male and to decrease the vigor of their discussions. Compared to the quality of the ideas that they raise when interacting with members of their own sex, they may bring up less insightful ideas and present them in a quieter manner when a man enters the room (Weisfeld, Weisfeld, & Callaghan, 1982; Maccoby, 1990). In contrast, the men are not likely to decrease the vigor of their arguments and will show no decrease in the quality of the ideas that they offer to the group. In fact, the men may not make any effort to integrate the woman who enters the room, even though three of them know that she is well-read in the area under discussion.

An important fact to keep in mind is that there are no differences in the ability of men and women to make vigorous contributions to the discussion. There is absolutely no claim being made about a *trait* that people possess, that is, an aspect of personality or intellect. Rather, the suggestion is being made that men and women respond differently to a type of *social situation* in which they find themselves. When they find themselves in mixed-sex groups, women become less vigorous and may even show decreases in performance on the tasks called for in the situation (in the examples above, the quality of ideas offered). Men do not show this decline in performance.

Maccoby (1990) suggests that differences in performance in same- and mixed-sex groups can be seen during childhood. In one of her studies she observed the behavior of American children (average age of 33 months) playing with toys with either same-sex or opposite-sex partners. A score for each child was recorded based on his or her social behavior that was directed at another child. This "social behavior" score included both positive (e.g., offering a toy; hugging) and negative (e.g., grabbing a toy; pushing). "Passive behavior," during which the child was simply standing around doing little or nothing, was also recorded. Maccoby (1990, p. 514) summarized some of the findings:

> There was no overall sex difference in the frequency of [passive] behavior, but the behavior of girls was greatly affected by the sex of the partner. With other girls, passive behavior seldom occurred; indeed, in girl–girl pairs it occurred less often than it did in boy–boy pairs. However, when paired with boys, girls frequently stood on the sidelines and let the boys monopolize the toys. Clearly, the little girls in this study were not more passive than the little girls in any overall, trait-like sense. Passivity in these girls could be understood only in relation to the characteristics of their interactive partners.

Additional information on behavior in mixed-sex groups can be found in two interesting studies carried out among Hopi Indian children in Arizona and among Black American children in Chicago (Weisfeld, Weisfeld, & Callaghan, 1982). The researchers recorded the behavior of 12-year-old children during dodgeball games. In dodgeball, a person enters the center of circle. A member of the circle throws a ball at the person in the center. If the individual throwing the ball scores a hit, he or she then enters the middle of the circle. If the person in the center is missed, others in the circle should compete for the ball so that they can make the next throw. The only way to get points is to be the person who scores a hit and subsequently enters the center of the circle. For every thrown ball that is avoided or dodged, the person in the center gets a point. The potential for competitive behavior in this game occurs when children try to get the ball to make the next throw. Children can run into each other when trying to get the ball, and there can be tears if someone falls to the ground.

Weisfeld and her colleagues chose this game because it was equally familiar to boys and girls. They found results that were similar to those reported by Maccoby. When all the players were female, the games proceeded vigorously. Some girls showed themselves to be very skillful players and consistently scored more points than their same-sex peers. However, when boys and girls played dodgeball together, the girls became passive. This reaction took place both among the Hopi in Arizona and among the Black Americans in Chicago. Further, female passivity occurred even when the girls had more ability than many of the boys with whom they were playing in a mixed-sex dodgeball games. The researchers also recorded the exact ways in which the female passivity took place, and the findings are consistent with the discussion of individualism and collectivism that have been presented in several places in this book (e.g., Chapter 2 and Chapter 8). During mixed-sex competition, Hopi girls would not "set" their bodies in a way that would allow them to move quickly if the dodgeball came near them. Rather, they would stand with their legs crossed and their arms folded, "hugging themselves" as if they were seeking protection. The Hopi girls also smiled, perhaps offering this as a sign of appeasement and as a request for harmony as called for in their collective. In contrast, the more individualistic Black American girls engaged in expressive behaviors even though they were clearly not competing. These girls "slipped away to form little cliques alongside the playing circle. In these small groups the girls engaged in extraneous behaviors, eating potato chips, talking, dancing, or teasing the active players" (Weisfeld et al., 1982, p. 39).

In attempting to explain these results, the researchers considered the implications of research on activity level as discussed in the previous section of this chapter. Perhaps the girls felt that the boys were likely to be more physically aggressive in the dodgeball games and they might be hurt when chasing the ball. Or, the girls may have felt that their suggestions for improving the game or for settling disputes (was the person in the center hit or not on a close call?) would be ignored by the more assertive and dominant boys. Examining these possibilities, Weisfeld and her colleagues also studied behavior during spelling bees. As most readers will remember from their own schooling, a teacher or other adult reads words, and the participants try to spell the words. There are usually not as many disputes about applications of the rules in spelling bees compared to athletic events. The researchers reported, "Girls usually spell better than boys, and these [American Indian and Black American participants] were no exceptions. They were matched on spelling ability in this study, and again female inhibition was observed" (Weisfeld et al., 1982, p. 41).

STEREOTYPES AND INDIVIDUAL DIFFERENCES

A point about sex and gender differences that should constantly be kept in mind is that results such as those in both the Maccoby and Weisfeld studies represent trends over *numbers of* males and females. In these studies, a majority of the males and females behaved in the manner reported: Females become passive in mixed-sex competition, and males do not. However, there are exceptions. In the study by Weisfeld and her colleagues, there were individual girls who were just as active and just as assertive in mixed-sex as in same-sex competitions. Currently, we know too little about people who choose to interact in ways that differ from others of their sex. Yet this is a key to understanding the liberation from traditional gender roles for both men and women. My prediction is that the analysis of people who break with tradition and who interact in ways considered atypical in their cultures will be a more common research focus in the future.

With this predicted emphasis on understanding persons who break with traditional gender roles, there will be two sets of research findings that need explanations. One will involve the analysis of individuals who break patterns, and the other will focus on the general trends that can be documented if information is gathered from large numbers of people. Explanations for these latter findings are very useful in the analysis of sex stereotypes, gender stereotypes, and the self-images of men and women from various parts of the world (Williams & Best, 1982, 1990a,b). Images and stereotypes become part of people's thinking after they observe the behavior of many individuals. As discussed in Chapter 6 (and reviewed briefly at the beginning of this chapter), stereotypes and images are types of generalizations that are useful in organizing the massive amounts of information to which people are exposed. As with any generalization, the formation of stereotypes and images *downplays* the behavior of specific individuals in favor of trends across large numbers of people. After many observations of different individuals, people from all over the world are likely to see more aggressive behavior in men, more nurturant behavior in women, more assertion of leadership among men, and more passivity among women in mixed-sex groups. These observations become part of the universal stereotypes and images of men and women (Williams & Best, 1982, 1990b). When drawing their conclusions about men and women, observers do not focus on individual differences. They do not focus their attentions on the individual aggressive woman or the passive man. One of the most important guidelines for professionals (e.g., counselors, clinicians, social workers) who deal with people from different cultures is that to be of assistance, professionals must go beyond stereotypes and images and focus on the individual with whom they are working. Professionals should not begin a counseling session with a woman by imposing the stereotype "nurturant." They should move quickly into assessments of the woman's individual needs, desires, and reasons for seeking assistance.

More information of the work of these professionals will be covered in the next chapter.

Even with the constant reminder to move beyond generalizations about men and women and to focus on individuals, there are good reasons to search for explanations for the generalizations. One is to understand the reasons why gender stereotypes and self-images are formed and why some are worldwide. Another is to help individuals move away from the generalization if that is their goal. For example, an individual woman may want to seek a leadership position in her culture. She may be experiencing stress given that her extended family and friends prefer that she behave in the nurturant manner typical of gender-role expectations. If she understands the reasons for the general expectation about female nurturance (and this can be dealt with in counseling sessions), she may experience a reduction in stress. One of the major reasons for extreme stress is that people feel that "I am the only one having a problem like this, and in addition to the problem, I am weird for feeling the way I do about this." If the counselor can point out that virtually all women who seek leadership positions experience stress given that their cultures expect nurturance, the heavy psychological load stemming from the thought that "I am the only one!" can be lifted.

Let's return to the generalization (keeping in mind that there will be exceptions) that women become more passive in mixed-sex groups compared to all-female groups. The reasons for this are puzzling, and the suggestions presented in this paragraph are the most speculative in the entire chapter. Weisfeld and her colleagues (1982) drew from the analyses of Callan (1970) and suggested that there is a possible explanation that stems from the demands of childrearing. Recall some of the facts about procreation and childrearing reviewed earlier in the chapter. The act of childbirth is often debilitating to the mother, and this must have been more true in the past given the absence of modern medical practices. In addition, children are totally helpless for long periods of time. Children cannot obtain their own food, cannot look after themselves in times of trouble, and need to be instructed concerning proper behavior called for in their cultures. All this attention to children and childrearing takes a great deal of energy. If the mother and father constantly argue about who is to take on what tasks and who will make decisions in certain areas, the time and energy spent on such arguments cannot be invested in the children. In addition, given her weakness after childbirth, the mother does not have much energy to invest in arguments. To ensure that time and energy go into the difficult work of raising children, the culturally universal roles of male dominance and female passivity (in the presence of males) may have arisen. Females who were able to behave in this passive manner were more likely to attract males, mate with them, successfully raise their children, and pass on their genes to future generations.

Williams and Best (1982; 1990b) found that passivity was part of the stereotype of females in 25 cultures. Other parts of the stereotype were that females are deferent, nurturant, and affiliative. In addition to an explanation based on biological differences that lead to responsibilities for child care, Williams and Best (1990a) asserted that additional arguments need to be made about reasons for the stereotype. One argument is that people become comfortable believing that members of each sex either have or can develop the characteristics that are necessary to carry out tasks in a smooth-functioning society.

> If females are to have principal responsibility for the care of the young, it is reassuring to believe that they are—or can become—affectionate, gentle, patient, sympathetic, and so on. If males are to serve as hunters and warriors, it is comforting to believe that they can—or can become—adventurous, aggressive, courageous, energetic, independent, self-confident, and the like.... It may be in this context, the "justification of necessity" with regard to different social roles, that many of the

If men have power over women, they often develop a set of beliefs to justify and maintain their dominance.

sex-trait stereotypes originated. Once established, the beliefs concerning the psychological makeup serve as norms for the behavior of adult men and women and provide models for the socialization of girls and boys toward their assigned [gender] roles (Williams & Best, 1990a, p. 237).

Another needed part of the explanation is consistent with some feminist approaches to the analysis of gender differences (e.g., Stockard & Johnson, 1979; Hare-Mustin & Maracek, 1988). Once men are socialized to act in a dominant manner (part of the male stereotype identified by Williams and Best [1990a]), they become comfortable with their power over women and develop norms that keep women in subservient positions. People who hold power learn to enjoy it (Kipnis, 1976; Brislin, 1991) and are unwilling to relinquish it. When men have power, they often develop beliefs that maintain it (e.g., "We are better able to make tough decisions"). Further, they develop other beliefs that make it difficult for women to gain access to power (e.g., "They are really happier in homemaker roles"). These arguments involving the importance of power are similar to those made in Chapter 6 concerning race relations. One reason for White prejudice toward Blacks in the United States and other parts of the world is that Whites enjoy the power that they possess. By discriminating against Blacks and keeping them in subservient roles, Whites maintain their power.

Returning to the arguments about gender, the tendency for women to become passive in the company of men does not have to dictate behavior among adults in today's world. Knowledge of such research can lead to possible actions, a theme I dealt with in a book on the strategies and tactics for the use of power (Brislin, 1991). With a knowledge of all the research reviewed in this chapter, for instance, one of the female graduate students who works with me has developed a plan. She realizes that there is a tendency for her to defer to men during the give-and-take of arguments about scholarly issues. She has observed, for instance, that when a speaker from another university comes and gives a good presentation, almost all the questions come from the males in the audience. She makes a point, at every presentation she attends, of asking pointed questions. She admits that it was difficult to ask questions at first, but after a few times it became rather matter-of-fact to be an active participant.

We might give a label to behaviors, such as asking pointed questions, in mixed-sex groups and call them examples of "moving beyond" male-female tendencies. As mentioned several times in this chapter, the liberation that stems from moving beyond traditional gender roles can benefit members of both sexes. Men who have a tendency to dominate meetings, for instance, may want to make a point of listening to and respecting the contributions of others. They may find that the meetings will be much more productive. Time and energy will be spent on developing good ideas rather than on sorting out positions in the dominance hierarchy.

What other tendencies should men and women know about so that they can make appropriate decisions about their behavior? One of the most important tendencies, given its widespread implications, is that women are more concerned than men about their relationships with others.

WOMEN'S CONCERN WITH RELATEDNESS

A great deal of research has examined the possibility that women are more concerned about their relationships with others than are men (Prince, 1985; Low, 1989; Maccoby, 1990). As already reviewed, reasons include the universal fact that women bear children and must nurture them. Given their weakness after childbirth and the demands of raising children for many years, women who are able to develop and maintain good relationships can secure assistance in their difficult childrearing demands. Women are responsible for introducing their young children to the norms of their culture, and good relationships with others in one's community are helpful in achieving this goal. Knowing the benefits of good relationships, adults in a culture encourage girls to develop relational skills during socialization. One reason for the frequent observation that girls are more often punished for aggressive behavior than are boys (Barry & Child, 1983; Hendrix & Johnson, 1985) is that aggressiveness among girls may interfere with their ability to develop relationships with others. The "concern with relatedness" has a number of important implications that have been the focus of different research studies.

EXPECTATIONS PEOPLE HAVE OF FRIENDSHIP. When asked the same questions about their expectations concerning friendships with members of the same sex, Morse (1983) provided evidence that women expect more. Interviewing college students in Australia and Brazil about love relationships and friendships, he showed that emotional involvement and dependency distinguished love from friendship in both countries, and that respect and reciprocal communication were important to both types of relationships. In both countries, females expected more of friendships. Both males and females were presented with various characteristics of friendship, and were asked to rate their importance in terms of "what's important for *you* to become good friends with someone of the *same* sex" (Morse, 1983, p. 471). Females rated 10 features of friendship as more important than males, and these included:

- for this person to fulfill your emotional demands;
- for you to feel committed to your relationship with this person;
- to just like to be with this person;
- to be able to confide in this person;
- to feel self-confident when you're with this person;
- to feel secure about your feelings toward this person.

The first implication of the general tendency for females to be more concerned with relationships, then, is that they have more expectations for people with whom they develop close friendships. Further evidence comes from a study of Caucasian Americans and Black Americans attending college in the southern United States (Holland & Eisenhart, 1988). Women's happiness during their college years was strongly affected by the quality of their friendships with peers. Much of what they learned about themselves, and how they learned to evaluate their present behaviors and their likely futures, came from age peers far more than others, such as professors and employers. These findings suggest that if people want to encourage women to expand their thinking beyond the traditional gender roles with which society provides them, it would be wise to work with individual women *and* their peer groups. If the peer group disapproves of any one woman's plans, this can lead to a great deal of stress.

THE IMPORTANCE OF GOOD RELATIONS WITH AUTHORITY FIGURES. The discussion in the previous section should *not* be interpreted as a claim that females are prisoners of their peer group. Rather, the suggestion is being put forward that peer relationships are very important, and that this fact must be kept in mind by those (e.g., teachers, employers) who are are asked to help women achieve their goals. Another implication of their concern for relatedness is that women strongly prefer to have positive feelings about authority figures. Recall from Chapter 8 that this was a feature of societies that Hofstede (1991) labeled "feminine." In feminine societies, where the influence of women has been felt in the workplace, workers rank good relationships with co-workers and bosses as important when considering their job satisfaction. Wise bosses know this and will make a point of maintaining good relationships because they realize that employees will work hard if they think positively about their bosses and their goals, policies, and treatment of workers.

In addition to adults developing their careers, the importance of good relationships with authority figures has also been identified in research among schoolchildren. Buriel (1983) provided evidence that contradicts a piece of common sense. If everyday wisdom suggests that boys seek out more interactions with teachers and volunteer answers to questions more frequently, Buriel showed that this is not always the case. Working with fourth and fifth grade Mexican-American children, Buriel found that girls initiated more work-related contacts with their teachers than did boys. Unfortunately, the teachers whose behavior was recorded did not always follow up on the work-related contacts that their female students initiated. While there was the general finding that teachers who used the most praise (and low amounts of criticism) encouraged the greatest amount of student achievement, there was no reciprocal relationship between student-initiated contact and teacher response. In one of the three classrooms studied, Mexican-American females received more praise; in another classroom, Mexican-American boys received more praise; and in the third,

Anglo-American girls received more praise when they initiated contact with their teachers. Another important finding was that Mexican-American students, possibly because of their more collective socialization with its emphasis on good relationships, responded more positively to teachers who praised good school-related efforts and downplayed any temptations to criticize nonwork activities (e.g., requests to use the bathroom). One practical application of these findings is that teachers should make sure that they encourage and reinforce contacts initiated by all students, and should be especially careful that they are not treating boys and girls differently. Given that the girls initiated more contact in this study, it must have been frustrating when they experienced inconsistent responses to this type of behavior.

SENSITIVITY TO OTHER'S PROBLEMS. If women are more concerned with relationships, they may also be more sensitive to the problems others have that can interfere with smooth and stress-free interactions among people. Doherty and Obani (1986) provided evidence for this possibility in a study of sensitivity to people's handicaps. The researchers provided descriptions of people with various handicaps to adolescents in Great Britain and in Nigeria. In each country, males and females from various age groups were selected so that the influence of both maturity (development of sensitivity over a number of years) and sex could be investigated. The age groups selected were 11, 13, 15, and 17 years of age.

Doherty and Obani (1986) asked a number of direct questions and also presented short case studies to respondents. For example, two of the direct questions were: Which handicap do you think is the worst to have? Why do you say so? One of the case studies involved a young woman named Ida who was a popular teenager with an active social life. However, she developed an illness that caused paralysis in her left leg and arm and that also caused difficulties when she attempted to speak. This caused Ida a great deal of unhappiness. Respondents were asked: Why do you think Ida was unhappy?

The results of the study showed that as the respondents became older, they were more likely to provide insightful answers to the questions. As they matured, their answers became more comprehensive, showed more insight into the problems of the handicapped, and also displayed accurate analyses of the problems faced by the handicapped. In addition, females in both cultures showed more insight and understanding. Their answers were more complete and more likely to reflect thinking that *went beyond* the concepts presented in the questions and the case studies. The results demonstrated that females were more able to recall their personal observations of people in their everyday lives and more likely to apply their insights to the questions asked by the researchers. For example, answering the question about the worst impairment, a British 17-year-old female focused on mental handicaps. Part of her answer included the effects of a handicap on others: "It is the worst one to handle from the family's point of view. To have a child that is unresponsive or at least less than a normal child must be very depressing and frustrating. There are a lot of problems involved and in many cases this is seen to have a destructive influence on the family unit" (Doherty & Obani, 1986, p. 298).

In response to the case study about Ida, a 15-year-old Nigerian female was also aware of the effects of a handicap on other people: "For one who has been the center of attraction for quite a long time, it is quite a hard blow to suddenly find out that you are partially paralyzed and you won't be able to enjoy as much. Also she would have to be dependent and she may think she is a burden on the household" (Doherty & Obani, 1986, p. 301).

If women are more sensitive to people's problems, and to the impacts those problems have on others, this is undoubtedly a reason why women have traditionally entered such fields as nursing, social work, day care, and special education.

THE POSSIBILITY OF BURNOUT. A sensitivity to others that attracts females to the helping professions may have certain negative implications. When people have the responsibility for offering assistance to others, but find that their efforts are hindered, they can experience emotional burnout. The helpers find that they have put a great deal of effort (and a great deal of themselves) into their desire to offer assistance, but find that their efforts do little or no good. There are many reasons why good intentions do not lead to actual assistance being delivered to those needing it: inadequate funds, an overly complex bureaucracy, a legal system that demands evidence "beyond a reasonable doubt" if someone is to be charged with a crime such as spouse abuse, and case loads that offer little time for any one client needing help. Potential helpers find that they cannot cope with "the system," become extremely angry and frustrated, find *themselves* experiencing stress with which they cannot cope, and report that they are simply "burned out" in their attempts to help others.

If women are more concerned with relationships and with the effects of people's problems, they may experience more burnout when frustrated in their attempts to help others. Etzion & Pines (1986) found that this was the case. They interviewed 503 human service professionals in the United States and Israel. In both countries, women reported more frustration and burnout than men. Other results presented information that might assist human service professionals who are experiencing stress. Among women in both countries, the coping strategy of "actively confronting the source of stress" was effective in reducing feelings of burnout. Even though women may *prefer* a less direct strategy (such as avoiding the source of stress), Etzion and Pines demonstrated that when women were more confrontative, they experienced less burnout. If women experiencing burnout develop support groups, discussions and mutual advice-giving about confronting stress directly can be very fruitful. For example, women could share information about how to confront uncaring supervisors, how to lobby more effectively for increased funding, or how to enlist the help of law enforcement officials in spouse- and child-abuse cases. In addition to this direct method for coping with stress, some women benefited from the more indirect approach of getting involved in other community activities. This was more effective among American than Israeli women, and the reason for the difference across the two countries is not entirely clear. One possibility is that there are more community activities in the United States that allow people to "take their minds" off of their troubles: the bridge club, support groups for the opera and symphony, supervision of community activities for children. After the relaxation provided by these activities, people may be able to return to their stressful workplace with a fresher perspective. Given the long-standing conflicts between Arabs and Jews in Israel, there may be far fewer activities that allow Israelis to relax and get their minds off the various stressors in their lives.

INTERPRETING NEGATIVE EMOTIONS. One of the important implications of a greater concern with relationships is that women are sensitive to both the positive and negative aspects of their interactions with others. If relationships are not going well, people often want to intervene and to correct any difficulties. One way they learn about difficulties is through observations of others. If the others are sending out negative signals, people concerned with good relationships should be able to interpret these signals. Given that women are concerned with maintaining good relationships, they should be more responsive to the negative signals others are sending.

Several studies have investigated this possibility, and they have focused on the interpretation of nonverbal behaviors (McAndrew, 1986; Sogon & Izard, 1987). More specifically, researchers have been concerned with the nonverbal communication of emotions such as joy, surprise, fear, sadness, disgust, anger, and contempt. The nonverbal behaviors studied were body posture (Sogon & Izard, 1987) and facial expressions (McAndrew, 1986).

The method chosen by Sogon and Izard was to film Japanese actors and actresses who posed the emotions while facing away from the camera. Viewers, then, had to interpret the emotion that the actors/actresses posed with only a view of the backs of their bodies. The films were shown to American males and females who were asked to guess the emotion that the actors/actresses had in mind. The method chosen by McAndrew was to present photographs that were prepared and published by Ekman and Friesen (1975). McAndrew then showed the pictures for very brief periods of time (less than 1 second, by means of a tachistoscope) to males and females in both the United States and Malaysia. Ekman and Friesen had earlier shown that certain emotions are easier to interpret than others: Happiness seems to be easy for people to display and easy for others to interpret. Other emotions are more "difficult" in the sense that they can be mistaken for others. For example, fear and surprise are frequently confused: A person may think that she or he is communicating surprise, but observers sometimes interpret the emotional display as fear.

Whenever there were sex differences in the two studies, females were more skillful at interpreting nonverbal presentations of emotions. Sogon and Izard (1987) showed that females were more skillful at identifying disgust, fear, and sadness. One interpretation suggested by the researchers is consistent with the arguments presented earlier in this chapter. Females are more sensitive to interpersonal relationships and consequently are more sensitive to difficulties that may be occuring in their relationships. If they are skillful in interpreting such negative emotions as disgust, fear, and sadness, they will be better able to diagnose difficulties in their everyday relationships. Another possibility is that given their lower social status in many societies, women learn to interpret negative emotions so as to avoid powerful people when they are in negative moods. If women learn to diagnose negative emotions and also learn to wait for powerful people to be in good moods, the women may have a higher probability of benefiting from their relationships with the powerful.

McAndrew (1986) found that females in both Malaysia and the United States were better able than males at identifying and distinguishing between facial expressions of fear and surprise. The explanation that stems from the "female concern with relatedness" argument is that females spend more time examining the nonverbal behavior of others so that they can maintain good relationships and intervene in problematic relationships. McAndrew (1986, p. 221) argued:

> Female superiority occurred primarily on the emotions of fear and surprise, which are traditionally the two most readily confused emotions. As one of the reasons for the confusion on fear and surprise is the great similarity in the facial configurations involved in these expressions, it may be that females do better simply because they spend more time looking at other people's faces and are therefore more aware of and sensitive to subtle differences between expressions than are males.

Just as in the arguments about sensitivity to people's problems (burnout if the sensitivity does not lead to positive actions), there is a dilemma that stems from females' ability to interpret negative emotions. People who enforce a culture's norms can take advantage of this ability and place limits on the opportunities allowed to women. Pamela Dorn (1986) argues that the behavior of women can be controlled by gossip, and gossip is not necessarily verbal. A woman who is the subject of gossip, for instance, may not hear what people are saying about her. However, she might observe the facial expressions and body postures of people talking about her, for instance, 20 or 30 meters away from where she is standing. Given her ability to interpret these nonverbal behaviors, she is likely to receive the message that her behavior is under scrutiny. Dorn (1986) studied the behavior of women in a Jewish community in Istanbul, Turkey. Many of the behaviors that would lead to gossip, as well as the nature of gossip itself, were summarized in proverbs. For example, women say to each other, "No one knows what is happening in the pot except for the spoon that turns. Meaning: Everyone talks about what is happening in the house, but only insiders know what is really happening. Thus, gossip can only be speculative and not very dangerous about a woman who stays at home and who keeps the traditional role" (Dorn, 1986, p. 299).

Traditional roles, of course, are exactly what women complain about as they attempt to move about more freely and to pursue the opportunities available in their culture. What happens when women move beyond traditional roles?

THE CONVERGENCE OF BEHAVIORS TYPICAL OF MEN AND WOMEN

As women decide to move into roles that were traditionally denied them, there is a decrease in the number of sharp distinctions that once marked the behaviors of men and women. School-related performance is an example. If there once was a stereotype that women perform less well than men in mathematics and better in language arts, the differences today are either nonexistent or too small to influence decision making about a school's curricula (Maccoby & Jacklin, 1974; Maccoby, 1990; Lummis & Stevenson, 1990). The reason involves access to instruction. Once females are encouraged to take advanced mathematics courses, and once males are encouraged to pursue interests in language and the arts, they are able to take advantage of a school's offerings without the prejudice that "boys do better in math, girls do better in areas involving verbal skills." In an ideal world, once opportunities within a society are opened up to members of both sexes, individuals can pursue various goals based on their abilities and interests. Further, they can pursue their goals without the constant concern that there will eventually be limits placed on them. This ideal world does not yet exist, but there has been research in diverse cultures that has given insights into what a society without unnecessary gender restrictions might look like. Research has focused on the pressures for movements away from traditional restrictions and the results of the changes in the behaviors of males and females. Many of these changes involve a convergence in, rather than a sharp differentiation between, the behaviors of males and females.

PRESSURES FOR CHANGE. One of the most influential factors that has led to changes centers on the roles that women play in their culture. Recall the proverb that Pamela Dorn (1986) discovered in her study of women carried out in Turkey. The lesson to be drawn from the proverb was that women should stay in the home since if they ventured out, they might break a norm and then become the subject of gossip. Yet there are many pressures that encourage women to leave the home. One involves the need to bring in more money to the family, and this leads to the search for wage labor. Another involves the influence of mass media: Women see the greater freedom of the people who are portrayed in television shows and want to experience some of the benefits that freedom appears to bring. Another and related reason involves intercultural contact. With increasing amounts of air travel and with increasing competition for the tourist dollar, places in the world once considered inaccessible are now chosen as vacation spots. Residents of the area where tourists appear observe different behaviors and may decide to try some. Returning to the first argument about jobs, tourism often creates jobs that involve a great deal of face-to-face contact between visitors to and residents of an area. Yet another reason undoubtedly involves the basic human need for growth, development, and stimulation. Many women, seeing the behavior of others on the television or in face-to-face interactions, learn that they are subject to many limits placed on them. Many must want to move beyond these limits simply to exercise their initiative, intelligence, and creativity—features of human beings which differentiate us from other primates (Kenrick, 1987).

Once women make the move away from traditional roles in the home to the increased opportunities found in the community at large, they change their outlook on life. Paguio, Skeen, and Robinson (1987) investigated the ideals that employed and nonemployed mothers have for their children, and they interviewed mothers in both the Philippines and the United States. Compared to their nonemployed counterparts, women with jobs (in both countries) felt more strongly that an ideal female child should be confident, aggressive, and well-adjusted. The employed mothers undoubtedly saw the advantages of these features, given their experiences in the workplace, and they wished them for their daughters. An interesting study by Nevill and Perrotta (1958) showed that preparation to enter the workplace did not necessarily interfere with a commitment to home and family. Adolescents in Australia, Portugal, and the United States were interviewed about various life roles. An unanticipated finding was that, in all three countries, females expressed more commitment to *both* work and the family than did males. The authors explained, "[This] is an unexpected finding given prevailing sex-role stereotypes and shows the effects of the increased role of women in the workplace. However, female high school students did not expect to realize more values through work than did male high school students" (Nevill & Perrotta, 1985, p. 492). One interpretation of these results is that the female adolescents were "hedging their bets." By committing themselves to both work and the home, they may have increased the chances of experiencing a realization of some of their goals. If their efforts in the workplace were thwarted, they could attempt to realize their goals in the home. Given the high divorce rate in highly industrialized nations, the females may also have been preparing themselves for possible disappointments in the home.

With respect to their knowledge of potential problems in the workplace, the female adolescents were unfortunately correct. When a society changes, or when people have to adjust to demands of an unfamiliar society, males seem to be able to adjust more quickly. "Adjustment" is indicated by factors as language acquisition, employment in good-paying jobs, and subjective feelings of happiness. Several studies have been carried out among immigrants and minority groups within the United States. Abramson and Imai-Marquez (1982) worked with Japanese-Americans and Burnam, Telles, Karno, and collegaues (1987) worked with Mexican-Americans. In both studies, males were able to adjust more quickly to the demands of the dominant American mainstream. One reason is that males were allowed more movement outside the home. They could take part-time jobs, join community activities, and travel to other parts of their cities to interact with different kinds of people. Given these experiences, they learned information and participated in experiences that were useful in their adjustment. Given the pressures to maintain at least some allegiance to their traditional roles, females were more likely to spend time in the home. This meant that they could not meet large numbers of people, had fewer chances to practice the language of the dominant culture (English), and had fewer chances to learn about the possibilities that full participation in American society allows.

TYPES OF CHANGES: MALE-FEMALE INTERACTIONS AND AUTONOMY. As mentioned earlier in this chapter, we must always keep in mind the difference between trends (e.g., males faster than females when adjusting to another culture) and individual differences. There *are* individual females who adjust quickly, who accept and benefit from changes, and who begin to behave in ways that move them beyond the guidelines and limits provided for them during their socialization (see Chapter 4). Both trends and the behaviors of individuals will be discussed in this section. One of the most stressful sets of behaviors involves attempts to change traditional expectations concerning interactions between men and women.

In a study investigating the acculturation of immigrants from Hong Kong to either the United States or Australia, Feldman and Rosenthal (1990) found that adjustment to behavioral norms common in the two English-speaking countries was very gradual. Examining various norms, there were differences in the time that teenagers originally from Hong Kong took to press their families for greater personal freedom. In general, males adjusted more quickly than females, probably because of traditional norms to keep females attached to the home. The types of behaviors that changed quickly contrasted to those that changed relatively slowly are interesting to note. The types of behaviors that changed relatively quickly (adolescents from Hong Kong adjusting to the norms of Australia or the

United States) involved attending boy–girl parties, staying home alone at night when parents are out, choosing one's own TV show or movie to watch, choosing one's own friends even in the face of parental disapproval, and staying home alone when one is sick. These behaviors indicate that the adolescents are pressuring their parents for more autonomy and individualism. However, for other behaviors, there was very slow adjustment to the norms in the two English-speaking countries. These behaviors involved preparing one's dinner when home alone, going out on dates, preferring to do things with friends rather than family, and smoking and drinking. A distinction must be made between the relatively quick adjustment involving male–female parties and the slower adjustment to dating norms. The parties do not necessarily involve one-on-one relationships, while dating does. Parents are much more interested in having an influence in the latter area. The behaviors involving preparing one's own meals and interacting with friends rather than family may seem uncontroversial, but meals and family activities are very important in collective cultures (Chapter 2), and parents look at these activities as important for maintaining strong family ties. When gender differences were reported by Feldman and Rosenthal (1990), females were slower to find success in their quest for autonomy. Behaviors involving boy–girl parties at night, no longer telling parents where one is going upon leaving the house, and overnight trips involving both sexes without adult supervision were all approved more slowly for females than for males. One reason is that these behaviors involve the possibility that females might engage in the sex act. I have worked with many students who originally came from cultures where the behaviors of women were carefully monitored. When asked the question, "Why are there more limitations placed on the behaviors of women compared to men?" most of my students have answered, "Because my parents always told me that girls get pregnant and boys don't. And that statement was supposed to end the discussion!"

Once women leave the home and spend large amounts of time in other activities within their communities, several research studies have suggested that the heterosexual behavior of women becomes similar to that of men. Alzate (1989) interviewed unmarried university students in Colombia, and Clement (1989) interviewed unmarried males and females in Germany. In both cases, women reported engaging in as much premarital sexual behavior as men. Both authors indicated that their results suggest that there is a move away from the traditional double standard in which men were expected to have sexual experience prior to marriage whereas women were expected to be chaste. We must be careful, however, not to overinterpret these findings and to declare that the double standard is dead. In the study in Colombia, especially, it must be kept in mind that Alzate (1989) was working with a very select sample of people. Far fewer women attend college in Colombia than in the United States, and so the self-confidence and autonomy of those who do attend college in Colombia is undoubtedly very high. Further, there were indications that men are still expected to have *more* sexual experience than women, and they achieve this through the employment of prostitutes.

Other research suggests that female college students may possess a positive self-concept that allows them to challenge traditional norms. Ezelio (1983) found no difference in the self-concepts of male and female college students in Nigeria. One interpretation is that to be the relatively rare female who strives to pursue a college education in Nigeria, an individual must have a very positive view of herself. Another possibility is that the move away from the traditional confines of the home, and participation in the new opportunities provided in a college, increases the self-concepts of women. Of course, both possibilities can occur for any one woman. A positive self-concept contributes to the decision to attend college, and self-worth increases given successful experiences in this nontraditional environment.

The general point being argued is that once the norms of a society "loosen up" so that unnecessary restrictions are not placed on women, then male–female distinctions often disappear. As another example, Clark and Clark (1987) carried out interviews in Yugoslavia and found that there were no distinctions between male and female participation in the political arena as long as both were part of society's "elite." Here, *elite* refers to the the benefits that membership in society's upper-strata can bring. These include a certain amount of comforts that one can afford, education, and time to think about about political issues. Elite females have as many of these opportunities as elite males, and consequently their political participation is similar. Among the less advantaged, males were more likely to participate in politics than were females. This distinction undoubtedly reflects the fact that among the less advantaged, women have "less" than men: less education, less encouragement to read newspapers, less free time away from the home during which they might develop interests in political issues, and so forth.

SPECULATIONS CONCERNING THE FUTURE

Given a number of pressures experienced by people all over the world, I believe that many traditional practices that place severe limits on the movement of women will weaken over the next 30 to 40 years. These pressures include the worldwide movement toward democracy, increased air travel, the influence of the mass media, greater attention to universal literacy, advances in medical care, and so forth. One way to predict the future is to examine today's research literature and to list activities in which men engage more frequently than women. Most of these will reflect differential emphases during socialization, not differences in innate abilities. The list will include more interest in computers (Sproull, Zubrow, & Kiesler, 1986), the use of power (Davies, 1985; Brislin, 1991), and the demonstration of creativity (Mar'i & Karayanni, 1983). The predictions are that, with the removal of traditional barriers, women will not differ from men in the use of computers, in the responsible use of power, and in creativity. The predictions can also be based on movements in the other direction: With the removal of barriers that limit *their* activities, men will be able to behave in ways traditionally considered unacceptable because of their "femininity." These include sensitivity to the needs of others (Murphy-Berman, et al., 1984), emotional self-disclosure (Snell, Miller, & Belk, 1988), and the distribution of resources within a marriage (Warner, Lee, & Lee, 1986).

These changes may come slowly. In a study of people's perceptions of an ideal member of the opposite sex (Stiles, Gibbons, & de la Garza-Schnellmann, 1990), adolescents from the United States and Mexico drew pictures and also rank-ordered a number of characteristics. Males and females in both cultures valued someone who is fun to be with, kind, honest, and good-looking (with males placing more emphasis on this factor, consistent with the discussion presented earlier in this chapter:

*Gender stereotypes may change as fathers spend more time
taking care of their children.*

pp. 290–291). In Mexico, other values were predictable from a knowledge of long-standing traditions. For example, Mexican adolescents placed a value on family ties, affiliation, and cooperation. However, there were some hints that social changes are having an impact on the values expressed by adolescents. Stiles and her colleagues noted (1990, p. 196), "[W]e saw some evidence of changing [gender] roles in the United States. A few adolescent girls showed the ideal man caring for children. A few adolescent boys drew the ideal woman working at a job." The results are consistant with a finding reported by Williams and Best (1990a) based on a 10-year follow-up study of sex stereotypes in Norway. Comparing results gathered in 1977 and 1987, the traditional male stereotype (e.g., active, dominant, less nurturant than females) was not as familiar among Norwegian 5-year-olds. One reason may be that "in recent years, there has been an increase in participation in child care by Norwegian fathers, which might be expected to soften the more extreme versions of the male stereotype encountered by the children in the popular media and elsewhere" (Williams & Best, 1990a, p. 332).

Not all the changes that might take place in the future will necessarily be positive. If the behavior of men and women is to converge given the movement away from traditional roles, then women may begin to drink as much as men (Gilbert & Cervantes, 1986; Teahan, 1987) and develop problems that lead to suicide attempts (Barraclough, 1987). Men will become more susceptible to depression (Golding & Karno, 1988) and will experience more conflict between their home and their work (Ottaway & Bhatnager, 1988). These possibilities demand that people develop a greater knowledge about threats to their mental and physical health, and this is the subject of the next chapter.

CHAPTER SUMMARY

When organizing the massive amounts of information to which people are exposed, two of the most frequently used categories are "what males do" and "what females do." The sharp distinctions people make about sex and gender stems from one the most basic facts about life: Men impregnate women, and women bear children. These facts have very important implications, as demonstrated in various cross-cultural studies. Childbirth and childrearing involve a great investment of energy. The act of giving birth weakens the mother, and the demands of children (who are virtually helpless for several years) encourages the mother to stay near the home. The father, on the other hand, is far more likely to engage in behaviors outside the home as he secures food and other resources for his family. This division of labor leads to traits that members of the two sexes use in selecting mates.

Especially in societies that have strong norms concerning gender roles, women are likely to seek out competent men in their community who can care for them after childbirth and during the difficult child-rearing years. Men are likely to look for young and nurturant women who have the physical ability to bear children and the psychological readiness to look after them. In a study of mate preference in 33 countries, Buss and his colleagues (1990) found that men and women still keep these traits in mind when thinking about members of the opposite sex. Women were more likely to value men who were well-established in their community because such men could provide resources to a family. Men were more likely to value developing a romantic relationship with younger and attractive women because these two visible "signs" indicate that the women have the capability (e.g., youth and good health) to bear children.

The argument from evolutionary theory (Buss, 1991) is that men and women who had these preferences mated, bore and raised children, and passed their genes on to future generations. These genetic tendencies remain with us today because they had survival value in our ancestral past. This type of analysis is thoroughly distasteful to many who encourage women *and* men to break free from the restrictions of traditional roles. A number of scholars (e.g., Kenrick, 1987; Low, 1989) argue that we must understand the origins of male–female differences if we hope to find ways of achieving equality between the sexes in today's society. It must also be kept in mind that the demands of today's world will encourage the development of various skills and that men will be wise to become more attentive to behaviors that may be more natural for women. The future will see more and more intercultural interaction, and people from other cultures will demand respect when they put their suggestions forward. Females may be much more naturally skillful at listening carefully and integrating the contributions of others. If males have the tendency to dominate the intercultural interactions in which they find themselves, they may miss many opportunities that a softer style would have nurtured.

The analysis of evolutionary theory provides some interesting insights, but many other factors must be considered. Many differences between males and females arise from socialization experiences in their cultures. One the most frequently discussed differences, that is almost certainly a universal, is that boys are more aggressive than girls. Boys engage in more rough-and-tumble play, are punished less frequently for fighting than are girls, and experience more injuries. One explanation is that aggressive boys grow into men who can attract mates. Aggressive men can engage in risk-taking activities such as hunting and exploring unknown areas for possible agricultural use, thus securing resources for their families. Another frequently discussed difference is that women are more nurturant and are more concerned about their relationships with others. One explanation is that nurturant women can attract the most successful men in a community since the men look for women who can provide a home and take care of the children that they father. Given the difficulties of child-rearing, women who are sensitive to their relationships can enlist the help of supportive people such as sisters, sisters-in-law, and other relatives.

Since the woman has the responsibility of introducing very young children to the norms of society, her extended family provides a good core group of people with whom the children can be integrated. Various people in the extended family offer opportunities for learning a culture's norms: Which people deserve respect? Who has important information to share? Why is cooperation more useful in the long run than constant conflict?

One of the most intriguing findings from cross-cultural research is that women often defer to men if the possibility of conflict arises during an interaction. Research by Maccoby (1990) and by Weisfeld and her colleagues (1982) demonstrates that when women interact with members of their own sex, they are vigorous, forthright, and skillful in putting their contributions forward. When men enter a social setting, however, women often become passive and defer to the contributions that men offer. For example, Weisfeld and her colleagues organized dodgeball games and spelling bees for Hopi Indian children in Arizona and for Black American children in Chicago. When playing among members of their own sex, young girls were vigorous and proud of performing well. When young boys entered the dodgeball games or the spelling bees, the young girls engaged in less vigorous activity and performed less skillfully. There is no *overall* difference between the skills of men and women. Rather, there is a differential *performance* of these skills in mixed-sex groups. There is not a thoroughly convincing explanation for these findings. One possibility asks us to return again to the families of our distant ancestors. The time and energy needed to raise children was so extensive that competition between mothers and fathers was unwise. Any time and energy spent on competition would mean that there were fewer resources available for the task of childrearing. Consequently the behavioral tendencies of male assertiveness and female deference (when the mother and father were in the same social setting) became valued and were encouraged during the socialization of children and adolescents.

Research has indicated that there are a number of implications that stem from women's concern with their interpersonal relationships. These include more expectations of others once a friendship has been established (Morse, 1983); greater concern with developing and maintaining positive relationships with authority figures (Buriel, 1983); greater insights into the effects that people's problems will have on themselves and others (Doherty & Obani, 1986); and greater ability to interpret nonverbal expressions of emotions (McAndrew, 1986; Sogon & Izard, 1987). These expectations, insights, and skills can have both positive and negative implications. One positive outcome is that females, more than males, can identify potential problems in interpersonal relationships and intervene quickly before the problems escalate. A negative outcome is that females may experience more burnout when they try to help others. If females are more insightful concerning people's problems and more concerned that (as friends) they offer assistance, they may become frustrated if they experience bureaucratic obstacles and/or uncaring public officials. This frustration can lead to emotional burnout.

Some of the documented differences between men and women are striking. In the Sogon and Izard study (1987), American females were better able to distinguish disgust, fear, and sadness from observations of filmed Japanese actors who had their backs turned toward the camera. There are various explanations for this ability to interpret nonverbal expressions of emotion. One is that, given their greater concern with relatedness, women pay more attention to other people and learn to decode subtle cues that others send out. Another is that, given women's traditionally lower status in societies worldwide, women have had to diagnose the emotions of powerful people so as to increase their chances of receiving favorable attention. If women learn to approach powerful people when they are in good moods, and learn to avoid the powerful when they are experiencing negative moods, then women increase the chances of a favorable hearing for their proposals.

A prediction about the future we can make with absolute certainty is that traditional sanctions limiting the movement of women will decrease in societies all over the world. One result is that, given that they can pursue goals long denied them, women will behave in ways similar to men. For example, the stereotype once existed that women were not as proficient in mathematics as men. Once restrictions concerning the choice of courses disappears, and once women receive as much encouragement as men, current research shows no sex distinction in mathematics (Maccoby, 1990; Lummis & Stevenson, 1990).

There are other types of changes that involve a convergence between the behaviors of men and women once traditional norms change. One of the major pressures for the weakening of behavioral restrictions results from the experiences of women who seek employment outside the home. Once they leave home and have a wider variety of success experiences, women develop nontraditional views of themselves and also develop less-restrictive ideals for their children (Paguio, et al., 1987). Other changes include premarital sexual experiences similar to those of men (Alzate, 1989); self-concepts as positive as those of men (Ezelio, 1983); and increased participation in the political process (Clark & Clark, 1987).

Just because men engage in certain behaviors, of course, is no reason for women to mimic them. A danger in the "convergence of behaviors" possibility is that women will engage in undesirable behaviors that threaten their mental and physical health. In many cultures, men consume more alcohol and engage in more suicide attempts. If men desire greater freedom from the traditional gender roles that have placed limits on the types of goals they set for themselves (Prince, 1985), they should be alert to the undesirable behaviors that are more common among women. These include depressive episodes and stresses emanating from conflicts between home and the workplace. Careful thought must be given to the problem of minimizing the negative effects of the move beyond traditional gender roles while (at the same time) maximizing the benefits. This is a common theme in treatments of the relation between culture and health, and this is the subject of the next chapter.

10

CULTURE AND HEALTH

INTRODUCTION

People's satisfaction with their physical and mental health are two of the most important factors in their overall feelings concerning their happiness and their enjoyment of life (Draguns, 1990; Ilola, 1990). The unique challenge for health professionals sensitive to the concerns covered throughout this book is to deliver services and to encourage healthy lifestyles when the people they might help come from different cultural backgrounds (England, 1986). In many ways, much of the material covered in earlier chapters has relevance to people's health and to intervention efforts when help is needed. The distinction between culture-general concepts and culture-specific concepts (Chapter 3) must be understood when applying labels such as "schizophrenia" or "depression" when clients are from a culture different than that of the diagnostician. People can be socialized (Chapter 4) into everyday practices that can have an impact on the prevention of health problems, such as choices about their diet, alcohol and tobacco use, and the nurturance of potential support groups. Training programs to prepare health care professionals for intercultural encounters (e.g., Westermeyer, 1987; Wade & Bernstein, 1991) make use of the same methods and concepts reviewed in Chapter 6 and Chapter 7 of this volume. The effective use of a country's health services is dependent upon a well-educated citizenry (Chapter 5), a productive economy where job-holders (Chapter 8) are contributing tax dollars for the support of health services, and the use of the talents of all citizens (Chapter 9) in both preventive and intervention activities (Hunter, 1990).

CONCERNS IN THE DELIVERY OF HEALTH SERVICES. Even when health professionals are sensitive to the fact that they may encounter cultural differences, and even when clients are motivated to seek out the help of professionals, the actual delivery of services can be fraught with difficulties. For example, Ahia (1984) pointed to the possibility of two biases. If people behave according to the "limitations bias," they fail to examine important concepts beyond those with which they are already familiar given their socialization in their own culture. Counselors and physicians socialized in an individualistic society, such as the United States, may diagnose accurately that a person is suffering from a depressive episode or has experienced a recent heart attack. If the client or patient is from a collective culture, however, the health care professional may fail to see that the problem will be experienced by the person's extended family. The professional may be unable to move beyond the "limits" of his or her socialization. The limitations bias can also work among people seeking help. If people from a certain culture (e.g., the Japanese) know that they have a healthy diet, they may not move beyond this knowledge and engage in other activities that assist in the maintenance of good health. For example, the Japanese may use tobacco products to excess (Ilola, 1990) and consume excessive amounts of alcohol as part of expectations that they socialize with co-workers (Christopher, 1983).

Another potential problem identified by Ahia (1984) is the "generalization bias." If a health professional discovers that a certain type of intervention or a certain approach to clients works well, then he or she may generalize this to the entire population of which the client is a single member. The generalization bias, of course, is an example of the use of stereotypes that was reviewed in Chapter 6. Health professionals (and all others who engage in extensive intercultural interaction) must realize that not all people behave according to the stereotypes and generalizations that have become attached to their groups. There must be willingness to move beyond generalizations and to consider the unique circumstances of each client. For example, an American physician might discover that a Chinese-American client frequently visits an herbalist for traditional Chinese medicines. The physician might explain the contents of a prescribed drug by linking it to the herbs with which the patient is familiar. This would be a culturally sensitive way of preparing the Chinese-American patient to follow the physician's recommendation. It would be incorrect for the physician, however, to describe medicines in this way to all Chinese-American patients. Many patients will be quite familiar with "Western" medical practice and would feel that a discussion about herbs is patronizing.

As with the limitations bias, the generalization bias can occur with clients. Sue and Zane (1987; see also Lefley, 1989) provided evidence that patients from a number of cultural backgrounds (e.g., Chinese-Americans, Hispanics, and Blacks) expect that health professionals provide something of immediate benefit. That is, members of some minority groups expect to be helped within a very short time after they seek the help of professionals. If they do not experience such benefits, they may generalize from their interactions with one or a few professionals to all potential helpers. People who have good relations with clients might be of assistance by pointing out that, often, improvements in physical and mental health do not always come quickly. Similarly, professionals who expect to have clients from a variety of cultural backgrounds can be told that if they do not provide some sort of benefit quickly (it does not have to be a total cure), then clients may terminate their visits.

MOVING BEYOND POTENTIAL BIASES. One way to deal with these potential biases is to develop collaborative arrangements with people from the cultures whose members are to be served by professionals (Ahia, 1984). The collaborators can check each others' work and share insights to (a) point out potential biases, (b) contribute information on the cultural background of various clients, and (c) to provide a range of professionals with whom clients can consult. The health delivery professionals will also improve their sensitivity to clients by constantly asking these questions (reviewed by Turner, 1990, p. 16):

1. How is this person (client or patient) like all human beings? For example (as will be reviewed below), research has suggested that there is a universal core of symptoms experienced by virtually all schizophrenics.

2. How is this person like some human beings? In answering this question, information about the cultural background of the person can be useful.

3. How is this person like no other human being? If professionals constantly ask this question, they will move away from stereotypes and generalizations and will move toward the person's unique problems, needs, and resources.

THE ORGANIZATION OF THE CHAPTER

No one chapter or even collection of books can cover all the important research on the interrelationships between culture and health. I have attempted to review some highlights that seem to be central to most discussions of health and health delivery, and the five themes I would like to develop are:

1. understanding reasons for differences in health care available to people in different cultural groups;

2. understanding culture-general and culture-specific concepts as they apply to the study of health;

3. analyzing the universal and culture-specific aspects of two important mental disorders—schizophrenia and depression;

4. examining behaviors meant to prevent problems in people's mental and physical health (at times, formal programs can be

introduced that combine traditional treatments with medical practices developed in highly industrialized nations);

5.   developing an awareness of culturally sensitive treatments, with special attention to education and training programs for health professionals

DIFFERENCES IN THE DELIVERY OF HEALTH CARE SERVICES

As discussed in Chapter 4, children must learn a wide variety of behaviors so that they can become respected members of their culture. During their socialization, children learn about various behaviors that the elders of a culture believe will allow them to make contributions to their communities. Some of these behaviors, learned during socialization, are supposed to increase the chances of good mental and physical health. There are clearly differences, however, in people's *expectations* concerning good health, their expectations concerning good health care, and the actual status of people's health as documented in international research studies.

The health of infants is a good example. Many health professionals consider that the infant mortality rate of a country, or the rate among different ethnic groups within a large country, is one of the most sensitive indicators of the health care available to people (Garcia-Coll, 1990; Hunter, 1990). Looking at just the United States, there are differences in infant mortality rates within different ethnic groups. As Garcia-Coll (1990, p. 275) points out:

> Traditionally, disadvantaged ethnic minority populations in the United States have had higher death rates. Despite improvements, infant mortality rates for African-Americans remains high. Moreover, African-American neonatal and infant mortality is elevated at all income levels. . . . Higher rates of prematurity and low birth weight are contributing factors to infant mortality and represent "at risk" factors for poorer developmental outcomes for survivors. Again, differential rates are seen among different minority groups.

The health of infants involves a very complex combination of genetic, economic, cultural, and linguistic factors. There are certain diseases that are more prevalent in certain minority groups, and these involve a genetic component. Examples are sickle cell anemia among African-Americans, cystic fibrosis among Pueblo indians, and lactose intolerance among Asians and Asian-Americans (Overfield, 1985; Garcia-Coll, 1990). Lactose intolerance can lead to diarrhea and dehydration if infants receive too much food containing milk products. With respect to the care given to infants with these and the many other illnesses that children can have, socioeconomic and cultural factors play a major role. In countries without a policy of health insurance for all citizens (such as the United States), the lack of personal insurance or money forces people to stay away from health professionals. When the members of various ethnic minority groups are overrepresented among a nation's poor, then the delivery of health services becomes associated with ethnic status. Given the lack of money or personal insurance, many people call on professionals only after illnesses have advanced to stages where they may be untreatable. Rather than approaching health professionals at the first signs of a problem, poor people may resort to traditional remedies long used in their cultures. These may prove beneficial. If they do not, however, problems may reach a point where no intervention—traditional or modern—can be be effective.

Understanding various cultural barriers to health treatment is difficult because (a) they differ from culture to culture (Qureshi, 1989); (b) they are less visible than factors such as the lack of insurance or money; (c) there are few opportunities for health professionals to learn about them, and (d) even the most culturally sensitive health professionals are sometimes viewed as outsiders who are to be trusted less than fellow members of a culture. In a study of the expectations that mothers have concerning the development of their children, Hopkins and Westra (1989) were interested in the health-care-seeking activities of mothers. They attempted to discover the expectations mothers had for the normal developmental behaviors of their children, and when mothers would seek professional help if children were slow to achieve these behaviors. Examples of the behaviors involved the age at which children would sit by themselves, crawl, walk, and so forth. Working with Jamaican, Indian, and English women in Great Britain, Hopkins and Westra (1989) were surprised to find that mothers did not contact physicians to obtain information about the normal progress of children. Rather, the mothers obtained this information from other women in their communities. The dependence upon others from the same cultural background, incidentally, is a common finding across quite different types of behaviors. For example, Pedersen (1991a) found that foreign students at a large American university are likely to approach same-culture peers when they have a problem, whether it be academic, social, or medical. They prefer contacting peers to consulting with professionals such as highly experienced foreign student advisers employed by the university.

Returning to the work by Hopkins and Westra among mothers of young children, the researchers found that the women's cultural background had an impact on their expectations. Jamaican mothers, for instance, were very sensitive to the age at which their children were able to sit up by themselves. They were not very concerned with the age at which the children learn to crawl, as they considered this "hazardous and non-human" (Hopkins & Westra, 1989, p. 388). Sitting up in a quiet manner

*In some cultures, mothers are attentive to the age at which their children
sit by themselves. In other cultures, mothers are attentive to the age
at which children crawl.*

was considered important to the Jamaican mothers because they used this
milestone as a sign that the children were being successfully trained so
that they would later become polite adults. If the children were not able
to sit up by 6 or 7 months, the mothers would be upset. Knowing these
facts, health care professionals can increase the chances of their recommendations being accepted by linking their suggested actions to mothers'
concerns.

Health care professionals admittedly have a difficult task. They have
a responsibility to deliver the best possible services they can, but must do so
in (a) a culturally sensitive manner to (b) people who do not always
recognize the value of the services. At times, professionals will have to
press forward with their recommendations even at the risk of violating
traditions. Breast-feeding is a good example. Mother's milk has a number
of advantages over bottled milk. It is more easily digested by babies, and
there can be the transfer of immunities to locally common diseases

through mother's milk. However, women in some cultures do not want to breast-feed because they feel their husbands will disapprove (Winikoff & Laukaran, 1989). Professionals will often have to assume the role of educator, explaining the benefits of health practices that are uncommon or frowned upon in a culture.

A number of professionals have made recommendations concerning universal goals in health care, realizing that the actual delivery of such care will be influenced by cultural factors. Broad goals for any nation's health policy (World Health Organization, 1987; Ilola, 1990) include the recommendations that 5 percent or more of a country's gross national product be spent on health, that resources be equitably distributed across social classes, that infant mortality be less than 50 per 1000 live births, that life expectancy at birth be greater than 60 years, and the adult literacy for both sexes be greater than 70 percent. More specifically, the World Health Organization recommends that there be safe water within a 15-minute walking distance, that children and adults receive the basic immunizations, that approximately 20 essential drugs be available in local health care facilities, and that 90 percent of newborns weigh 2500 grams or more at birth.

These recommendations from the World Health Organization are meant to be examples of universal goals and requirements for minimal health care. Understanding the nature of such universals (also called culture-general concepts), together with culture-specific concepts, is one of the central challenges of cross-cultural research and its applications.

CULTURE-GENERAL AND CULTURE-SPECIFIC CONCEPTS

One of the most important guidelines for cross-cultural research (reviewed in Chapter 3) is that investigators should be prepared for the fact that the use of their measuring instruments may be less successful when data are gathered in other cultures. There are many reasons (e.g., translation errors, lack of familiarity among respondents with the responses called for by the instruments), and one of the most important is that complex concepts do not have the exact same meaning in all cultures. For instance, the concept "good health" does not have the same meaning in all cultures. In the United States, the concept would include the absence of harmful bacteria and the absence of chemical imbalances. In China, the concept involves Yin and Yang, which "are the primogenial elements from which the universe was evolved. Health is achieved when Yin and Yang are in harmony. Disharmony or undue prevalence by either would result in ill-health and death" (Cheng & Lee, 1988, p. 208). In addition to these culture-specific components of good health, there are also culture-general components that are important in analyzing good health in all cultures. These include subjective feelings of well-being, adequate energy to go about one's daily tasks, sexual activity appropriate to one's age and position in society (e.g., husband, monk), adequate support from other people who are important in one's life, and feelings that one is able to develop positive emotional ties with others (Nishimoto, 1988; Qureshi, 1989; Draguns, 1990).

The recommendation for people involved in the delivery of health services across cultural boundaries, then, is that they should be prepared to deal with both culture-general and culture-specific components of complex concepts. A research study carried out by Robert Nishimoto (1988) provides a good example. He was interested in the concept of people's ability to meet the everyday challenges of life in an effective way, free of debilitating mental health problems. Realizing that this complex concept would undoubtedly have both culture-general and culture-specific aspects, he designed his research so that he could identify both types of components. As his measuring instrument, he chose the Langer (1962) index of psychiatric symptoms, one of the most frequently used screening instruments health professional use to identify people who are not institutionalized but who have psychological disorders that disrupt their everyday functioning. Nishimoto analyzed data gathered from three groups: Anglo-Americans from Nebraska, Vietnamese-Chinese living in Hong Kong, and Mexicans living either in El Paso, Texas, or Ciudad Juarez, Mexico.

Nishimoto (1988, p. 57) found that 12 of people's reported symptoms were useful in diagnosing mental health difficulties. Health professionals, then could use these 12 indicators in all three cultures to identify people who are in need of health services based on whether they reported these symptoms when thinking about their lives:

- weak all over
- can't get going
- low spirits
- hot all over
- restlessness
- (I'm the) worrying type

- nervousness
- trouble sleeping
- personal worries
- feel apart, alone
- nothing turns out well
- (I can't do) anything worthwhile

In addition to these cultural-general symptoms, Nishimoto also found that there were symptoms useful for diagnostic purposes within each culture. Each set of symptoms would be useful for diagnosis within a specific culture, but not in another. For the Anglo-American respondents, five additional symptoms were reported by people with mental health difficulties:

- heart beating hard
- acid stomach
- shortness of breath

- hands tremble
- headaches

For the Vietnamese-Chinese, there were three additional symptoms:

- heart beating hard
- acid stomach
- fullness in head

And for the Mexican respondents, there were two additional symptoms:

- (problems with my) memory
- headaches

It is probably no accident that the largest number of symptoms were documented as useful for the Anglo-American respondents. The original measuring instrument was developed by an American who had access to large numbers of respondents from his own country. It is only natural that with these two facts, there will be symptoms identified that are meaningful to Americans. An important research step, whenever instruments developed in one country are used, is to actively seek other items that may be diagnostic in the various cultures where the instrument is to be administered (as discussed in the Addendum to Chapter 3). Nishimoto's findings can be interpreted as supporting the general usefulness of the 22-item index developed by Langer (1962), but it also provides us with the reminder that there are undoubtedly other symptoms that could be added to the instrument. These other symptoms may be reported infrequently by Americans but far more often by respondents in other cultures.

As will be discussed more fully later in this chapter, health professionals must be prepared for cultural differences in people's reports about their physical and mental health. A good exercise is to study carefully the reports by researchers such as Nishimoto and to ask: Which of these symptoms are familiar to me, given my own cultural background, and which seem strange? One reason for finding that a symptom is strange, of course, is that people have not encountered it during their socialization. If Americans study the list presented above, I believe that most will find that the core set of 12 symptoms, and the additional culture-specific 5 symptoms, will be familiar. Either they have experienced them from time to time during periods of personal psychological distress, or they have talked with others who have experienced them. Several of the culture-specific symptoms for the Vietnamese-Chinese and the Mexicans, however, may seem unfamiliar as indicators of distress. Many Americans will neither be familiar with the symptom, "fullness in the head," as reported by the Vietnamese-Chinese, nor will they be familiar with the memory problems reported by the Mexicans. This does not mean that Americans do not occasionally experience fullness in the head or memory problems—it means that these two symptoms are not as frequently experienced as part of a more general psychological distress that interferes with everyday functioning.

Looking for symptoms that seem strange is a good exercise, since it can sensitize people to the presence of cultural differences. Further, it can encourage a constant awareness that strangeness is simply a sign that people have not encountered a concept during their own socialization. I told a colleague from India, Dr. Meheroo Jussawala, about Nishimoto's finding that Vietnamese-Chinese did not report headaches as a symptom of distress. She told me that while she was growing up in India, she never had headaches. When she or her Indian friends were upset, they would experience an upset stomach. On moving to the United States, she was surprised to see so many commercials on television that advertise remedies for headaches: aspirin, Tylenol, Ibuprofin, and so forth. Given that she never had headaches (and still does not), she is fascinated by all the fuss that is made about painkillers. But when her students or colleagues complain about headaches, she is able to interpret it as a sign that they are experiencing stress, even though she does not react to stress in the same way.

REASONS FOR CULTURE-SPECIFIC REPORTS OF SYMPTOMS. One of the most interesting concepts in the analysis of culture and health is that people *learn* to express symptoms of distress in ways acceptable to others in the same culture. As part of their socialization, they learn that certain complaints about distress are acceptable and elicit understanding, and that other complaints are unacceptable. Several examples have already been presented in the previous section. When encountering significant distress, Americans learn that they will earn more sympathy when they complain about headaches rather than about memory problems. Mexicans learn that complaints about memory *are* acceptable, and the Vietnamese-Chinese learn that complaints about fullness in the head will be understood by others in their culture. If my colleague is correct, Indians learn that appeals for sympathy about their stomachaches elicit more sympathy than claims about their headaches.

Readers may want to examine their own lives to determine if there were times when they complained about certain symptoms because of their acceptability to others. When I was about 12 years old and playing my first year of little league baseball, my talents kept me sitting on the bench during games. I played before the era of mandatory "two innings of play per player," a policy now common in many if not most American communities. In fairness to my coaches, their choice of where to place me during games was in line with my abilities. Still, I became bored and frustrated with baseball. Before one of the more important games, I reported to my mother that I had a headache and so would not be able to go to the game. In reality, I had an upset stomach because I knew that a certain female classmate would be coming to see her brother play for the opposing team. I didn't want her to see me sitting on the bench for the entire game. Although I did not know about the phrase, "acceptable symptoms within a culture," I felt that my mother would show more sympathy if I told her about my headache rather than my embarrassment stemming from my classmate's presence at the game.

SOMATIZATION. I wish I could remember if I actually had that headache. If so, it would have been an example of somatization. More frequently reported among Asians, Africans, and Latin Americans than among North Americans (Tseng & Hsu, 1980; Lin, Carter, & Kleinman, 1985), somatization refers to the reporting of physical symptoms when people are experiencing psychological distress. For example, Carden and Feicht (1991) studied homesickness among female college students from the United States and Turkey. They found that homesick students reported somatic symptoms as gastrointestinal problems, nausea, tightness in the head/chest, and menstrual irregularities. Further, somatization infers that there are no identifiable organic causes of the physical symptoms, but that they are reported by clients as real and troublesome. One of the major reasons for somatization is that it is socially acceptable in many cultures. People in many cultures are socialized to believe that complaints about anxieties, worries, and depression are signs of weakness. These complaints signal to others that people are somehow sick in the head, and there is far less tolerance for mental illness that there is for physical illness in many cultures. Consequently, when people experience psychological stress due to their inability to meet everyday goals (e.g., good relations with in-laws), they find more acceptance when reporting physical symptoms.

Somatization is so prevalent that it is a frequently used word in programs to prepare professionals who administer various intercultural programs. In a set of materials to be used by these professionals, colleagues and I (Brislin, et al., 1986) described a student from Asia studying at a large American university. He was having problems with both interpersonal relations and with his studies, went to the student health center complaining about pains in various parts of his body, and received a powerful drug from a physician. The underlying reason for his difficulties went unaddressed, and he ran the risk of becoming addicted to the painkiller. Many health care professionals who work with various types of sojourners (foreign students, immigrants, overseas businesspeople and their families) know about the possibility of somatization and examine stress-reducing possibilities rather than prescribing drugs.

In some cultures, somatic complaints are very well established for certain types of health problems. Guarnaccia, Good, and Kleinman (1990) argue that health professionals who work with Puerto Ricans and other Latinos must understand the concepts "nervios" (nerves) and "ataques de nervios" (attacks of nerves). *Nervios* refers to chronic feelings of stress that result from various difficulties in facing life's challenges: a bad marriage, finding employment during a long recession, and so forth. The symptoms include various "psychosomatic experiences, most prominently headaches, heart palpitations, a sense of heat in the chest, generalized body pains, trouble sleeping, and persistent worrying" (Guarnaccia, et al., 1990, p. 1449). An *ataque de nervios* is a well-known response (within the culture) to acute stressful experiences, such as the death of a loved one or a specific and unexpected conflict within a family. The symptoms include "trembling, heart palpitations, a sense of heat in the chest rising into the head, faintness, and seizure-like episodes. A typical attack occurs at a culturally appropriate time, such as during a funeral, at the scene of an accident, or during a family argument or fight" (Guarnaccia, et al., 1990, p. 1450). When people have such an attack, it will be well understood by others, and they will offer what assistance they can.

There are various benefits that stem from a knowledge of culture-specific reactions such as nervios. In comparative studies of symptomatology, researchers will be able to intepret the (common) finding that people from different cultures report differential rates of various symptoms. As Tseng and Hsu (1980, p. 81) reported, for instance, "Latin groups in Europe and America generally tended toward somatization, as did North Africans, while English-speaking populations expressed their distress to a greater extent through anxiety and depression." Professionals in health care delivery will be able to offer more effective services. Assume that English-speaking Americans are working among Latino immigrants in New York City. The least familiar symptom of distress reported by clients (of the list presented above) will probably be "a sense of heat in the chest rising into the head." But with knowledge concerning the culturally appropriate responses to stress known as "nervios" and "ataques de nervios," the professionals can formulate various questions about other symptoms. Realizing that the professionals understand what they are experiencing, clients are likely to feel that they can be helped. Such beliefs in the possibility of positive outcomes are central to the delivery and acceptance of health services (Sue & Zane, 1987; Draguns, 1990).

A FURTHER EXAMPLE: BEHAVIORAL PROBLEMS. Another example of the importance of understanding culture-general and culture-specific components can be introduced through a critical incident. George Andrews and Anna Tanaka were teachers at a preschool in New Mexico. Along with other teachers, they had organized a orientation at their school, to be held a few days before classes were to start, to which parents and students new to the community were invited. The purpose was to familiarize the students with the school and give them an opportunity to meet teachers and some fellow students, prior to the intense activities surrounding the first few weeks of the actual school year.

George was originally from New England and, like the students participating in the orientation, was new to the community. Anna who had worked at the school for 8 years and also enjoyed traveling south to Mexico, had previously participated in two summer-long study tours in Mexico. Both George and Anna interacted with many of the same students during the orientation. One, Robert, was an Anglo originally from the state of Washington. He found it difficult to concentrate during the activities held at the orientation (e.g., games, practice in following school rules, etc). He occasionally became restless, boisterous, and was generally uncooperative in contributing to the success of the orientation program. Another student, Manuel, was originally from Mexico, his parents having moved north to seek out better-paying jobs. Manuel also found it difficult to concentrate, and was often sluggish and inactive during the orientation.

After the orientation, the teachers met to discuss the strong points and the shortcomings of the program, with the goal of improving it in future years. George and Anna happened to get into a conversation about the students they both had met, and their discussion turned to the question: Which students might need special attention and help this year? George felt that Robert would be a disruptive student whose behavioral problems might lead to the need for interventions, such as extra sessions with his parents. While not disagreeing about Robert, Anna also felt that Manuel showed signs that he would have difficulties in school. Robert disagreed, feeling that Manuel was simply a quiet student who might become more active after he became more familiar with the new school. Why did George and Anna have different reactions to the students?

Given her 8 years of experience at the school in New Mexico, and her experiences in Mexico, Anna had learned that the sluggishness and inactivity demonstrated by Manuel can be a culture-specific manifestation of problematic reactions to the challenges of preschool. In a study of behavioral problems among Anglo-American and Mexican-American preschool children, O'Donnell, Stein, Machabanski, and Cress (1982) found one culture-general factor. This was a component of preschool behavioral problems that they labeled "anxiety-withdrawal," and it contained specific behavioral manifestations such as the following: The child . . .

- is self-conscious
- is sad, unhappy, depressed
- is aloof, socially reserved
- is shy, bashful
- doesn't show feelings
- doesn't have fun

There were also culture-specific factors, and one of the most important findings involved the behavior, "is easily distracted." Among the Anglo-Americans, this item was associated with others in a factor called "distractible-hyperactive." Examples of these other behaviors included:

- is restless, fidgety
- is easily excited
- is disruptive
- is boisterous
- is uncooperative
- is impulsive

These are the behaviors that an Anglo teacher like George is likely to have in mind when predicting that a certain student might have problems in school.

In sharp contrast, the item "is easily distracted" was associated with very different behaviors among the Mexican-Americans. O'Donnell and his colleagues labeled the factor, "distractible-hypoactive," with the prefix "hypo" referring to "less than normal level of activity." These other behaviors included:

- lazy in school
- short attention span
- is irresponsible

- is sluggish, inactive
- is passive, suggestible
- daydreams

Given her far greater familiarity with Mexican-American students, these are the behaviors that Anna has in mind when commenting on preschoolers who might face more difficulties than their peers.

O'Donnell and his colleagues (1982, p. 649) summarized their results as "temperamentally distractible Anglo children confronted with the stress of accommodating to the school's demands for concentration react with restless, boisterous behaviors, whereas distractible [Mexican-American] children react to a similar situation with inactive, passive behaviors that suggest daydreaming to their teachers." The researchers caution against overinterpreting this summary statement, pointing out that there will be many individual differences among both Anglo and Mexican-American students and that there will also be differences associated with students' socioeconomic backgrounds, ages, and area of the United States in which the children and parents reside. Still, if teachers and counselors are aware of the *possibility* of cultural differences among students, they will be better able to intervene in the early stages of children's difficulties with their schooling. If difficulties are identified early, problems can be addressed before they become so complex as to defy interventions by professionals.

CULTURE-GENERAL, CULTURE-SPECIFIC ASPECTS OF TWO MAJOR PSYCHOLOGICAL DISORDERS

Two of the major psychological disorders, both of which greatly interfere with people's everyday functioning, are schizophrenia and depression. Both are found in all parts of the world, and both have been analyzed in terms of culture-general and culture-specific concepts.

SCHIZOPHRENIA. The clinical diagnosis most misused by nonspecialists is undoubtedly "schizophrenia." Many people use it to refer to a split personality, and may even use it to describe themselves. For example, if people find themselves behaving quite differently with their parents compared to their age peers, they may call themselves "schizophrenic." This usage is quite different from its use by clinical psychologists and psychiatrists. The word *split* might be used, but the more accurate description is that schizophrenics have a split from reality. Schizophrenics are unable to relate their thoughts, attitudes, and actions to the everyday reality in which they find themselves. That is, they engage in bizarre thinking with frequent delusions about who they are or about the other people in their lives. It is difficult to maintain a conversation with a schizophrenic because there is no relation between one statement and another. Hallucinations are common, with schizophrenics reporting that various unseen speakers are speaking to them. Emotional reactions to others are inconsistent: schizophrenics show anger, happiness, and sorrow with no clear reasons (to the targets of these emotions). Behaviors also do not match the guidelines provided by the social situations in which schizophrenics find themselves. They may laugh at funerals, or remain motionless for hours during family gatherings, sometimes involved only in their own idiosyncratic thoughts.

Of the major psychological disorders, the largest number of culture-general symptoms has been reported for schizophrenia (World Health Organization, 1979; Lin & Kleinman, 1988; Draguns, 1990). The cross-cultural commonality of schizophrenia, together with the sizable number of culture-general symptoms, is one of the major arguments put forward to suggest that there is a biological basis to this major illness. These core symptoms, identified through research carried out in nine research locations in Asia, Africa, Europe, South America, and North America, are:

- restricted affect, or the ability to form emotional ties with others;
- poor insight into the reasons for one's own problems or one's own current thinking;
- thinking aloud;
- poor rapport with others, including professionals who might offer help;
- incoherent speech, in which one phrase or sentence seems to bear no relation to others;
- unrealistic information that would be contradicted by objective facts if the person were able to consider these facts (in the United States, for example, a person cannot buy a new car for $100);
- widespread, bizarre, and/or nihilistic delusions (*nihilism* is marked by feelings that existence is useless and that there is nothing worth living for).

There were also three indicators that demonstrated the possibility of a culture-general core of symptoms that *do not indicate* schizophrenia. That is, if patients demonstrated these symptoms, clinicians would entertain diagnoses other than schizophrenia. Called counterindicators, these three symptoms (Draguns, 1990) are waking up early after sleeping, depressed facial features, and expressions of elation.

Even with this large core of culture-general symptoms, there are many possibilities for the impact of culture-specific factors. For example, culture-specific factors can influence 1) the form that the symptoms of schizophrenia take, 2) the specific reasons for the onset of the illness, and 3) the prognosis concerning outcomes for people afflicted with the disease.

1. The forms in which symptoms appear. The clearest example of culture's effects can be seen in the form that symptoms take. For example, the symptoms of unrealistic information and widespread delusions can be seen in claims that people are hearing voices or that their minds are being invaded by unseen forces. In North America and Europe, these forces keep up to date with technology. In the 1920s, it was voices from the radio; in the 1950s, it was voices from the television; in the 1960s it could be voices from satellites in outer space; and in the 1970s and 1980s it could be spirits transmitted through people's microwave ovens. In cultures where witchcraft is considered common, the voices or spirits would be directed by unseen forces under the control of demons.

Katz and his colleagues (1988) argue that the exact form the symptoms of schizophrenia takes can be understood by looking at predominant cultural values. In Agra, India, schizophrenics separated themselves from others and emphasized the self-centered behavior indicated in the core symptoms, listed previously. This emphasis interfered with the value placed on the collective in India. As Katz and colleagues (1988, p. 351) argue: "In India, in light of the strong emphasis on family and on mystical life, expressions of self-centeredness would clash with societal values. Release of such emotions and egocentric behaviors reflect the breakdown of [reality and control in one's thinking]." In Ibadan, Nigeria, the symptoms shown by schizophrenics emphasized a highly suspicious orientation toward others, with many bizarre fears and thoughts. This set of symptoms is a reflection of how many Nigerians view illnesses. It is normal in Nigeria to view illness as caused by unseen evil forces, and sometimes these forces are directed at a person by enemies and witches. The reactions of schizophenrics are an exaggeration of this normal view, with attributions to enemies, witches, and unseen forces considered bizarre by *other Nigerians* who have a basic belief in the existence of spirits.

To deviate only slightly, this set of findings suggests that some mental illnesses can be seen as exaggerated versions of the values considered normal in a culture (Draguns, 1973). In discussing the Nigerian findings, for instance, Katz and his colleagues (1988, p. 352) argue that "the paranoid aspects of the disorder appear to represent an exaggeration and distortion of the 'normal' state." Juris Draguns (1973) once asked people to consider this argument about "exaggeration of the normal" by imagining a visit to a carnival with a funhouse full of twisted mirrors. People will recognize themselves in funhouse mirrors, but their head, neck, abdomen, or legs will be exaggerated. The metaphor is similar for some mental illnesses. In the United States, for example, hard work is valued. An overemphasis or exaggeration can lead a person to become a workaholic. It is wise to be suspicious of salespeople with offers that sound too good to be true. If this suspicion of strangers is exaggerated and expanded, it can lead to paranoia.

2. The onset of schizophrenia. One theory concerning schizophrenia is that it has a biological basis placing certain people at risk. If these "at risk" people lead relatively stress-free lives, visible symptoms of schizophrenia do not appear. If they are exposed to unanticipated stressful events, however, they may experience the acute onset of schizophrenia (Sanua, 1980;

Draguns, 1990). The distinction between being "at risk" and actually demonstrating obvious symptoms has parallels in other types of health problems. A 12-year-old male may have weak tendons in his right arm, but this might never pose a problem during his everyday physical activities. The weak tendons may lead to obvious problems only with intense activity. For example, if he becomes a baseball pitcher and tries to master both a fastball and a curveball, he might damage his arm severely.

Working in nine research sites in the United States (including Hawaii), Asia, Europe, and South America, Day and his colleagues (1987) presented evidence that acute schizophrenic attacks were associated with stressful events. Further, they argued that these stressful events could be described as external to individuals (not initiated by them), and tended to cluster in a time period two to three weeks before the onset of obvious symptoms. Examples of stressful events include the unexpected death of one's spouse, the loss of one's job, or the divorce of one's parents. Some stressful events were interpretable only if the researchers had considerable information about the cultural background of the people in the various samples. For example, the use of witchcraft as one explanation of disease in Nigeria has already been mentioned. One case study involved a Nigerian man (referred to as T.O.) who was employed as both an electrician and a taxi driver. One day his mother, complaining of an eye condition, went to a religious healer. While receiving treatment, T.O.'s mother announced to the entire congregation that she practiced witchcraft. About six weeks after this episode (somewhat longer than the typical two to three weeks mentioned above), T.O. began to show symptoms of an acute schizophrenia attack. He went into a trance at a religious ceremony, heard voices, saw visions, and continued to behave in an abnormal way after the ceremony. Later, he received "an unexpected bill for his children's education. He threatened to kill his wife and children, became restless, and went without sleep. He developed auditory and visual hallucinations" (Day, et al., 1987, p. 186).

The purpose of the study designed by Day and his colleagues was to document the relation between external events and the acute onset of schizophrenia. In so doing, they were careful to label an event as "external" only if it occurred in people's environment and was not initiated by them. Note that in the case just presented, the facts of the mother's confession of witchcraft and the unexpected bill occurred as "external" to T.O. They had a strong impact on him, but occurred independent of his behavior. In deciding to examine life events in this manner, Day and his colleagues admitted that they may have underestimated the relation between life stress and schizophrenia. For example, the case was presented of a young woman in Colombia who experienced the symptoms of anxiety, insomnia, and a loss of appetite. She feared that she had been bewitched and went to a fortune-teller. The fortune-teller confirmed the young woman's suspicions and recommended a perfume that could protect her. The prescription for the perfume included some of the secretions from the young woman's own body. She became guilty about using this perfume and her condition worsened. She deteriorated rapidly and had to seek treatment at a nearby university health clinic.

Day and his colleagues (1987) did not categorize this story as a piece of information contributing to the proposed link between stressful events and the onset of acute schizophrenia. Even though many people would argue that there were at least two external events (the fortune-teller's confirmation and the use of the perfume), the researchers categorized these as involving activity *initiated by* the young woman. The woman was experiencing some symptoms, and as a result sought out the fortune-teller. This contrasts with the experiences of T.O. presented above, who was not associated with the external events that contributed to his difficulties. Future research activities will undoubtedly examine the relative contributions of (a) external stresses that are unexpected and clearly do not involve the contributions of any individual, and (b) external stresses in which the individual plays a part. For example, the loss of a job (McCormick & Cooper, 1988) during a severe recession can often be considered an example of an external stress as described in category (a). The loss of a job in a recession for a person who had received only mediocre performance ratings during the last three years would be an example of category (b). These two types of categories are admittedly difficult to separate in actual research, but it is an important task to do so because people very frequently contribute to the external events in which they find themselves.

3. The Prognosis for Schizophrenic Patients. Prognosis refers to the anticipation of recovery from illness given the treatments that are available to patients. Lin and Kleinman (1988) have argued that the prognosis for the successful treatment of schizophrenics is better in nonindustrialized societies. At first glance, this is a surprising claim given the availability of drugs, trained psychiatrists, and advanced treatment facilities in highly industrialized nations. The explanation is that to be a functioning member of a "highly industrialized" nation, skills are necessary that are very difficult for schizophrenics to demonstrate. Recall the core symptoms of schizophrenia. Many of them involve relating to others: difficulty forming emotional ties, poor rapport with others, speech that is considered incoherent by listeners, and ignoring facts accepted in one's community. As discussed previously (Chapter 2 and Chapter 8), individualism is valued in most highly industrialized nations. It is up to the *individual* to develop rapport with others and to develop emotional ties. There is no automatic support group available to help with these tasks. In years past there might have been the nuclear family, but its members are often so affected by divorce and intra-familial strife (Sanua, 1980) that it can be a stressor rather than a support. As Lin and Kleinman (1988, p. 561 explain):

> Along with their heavy emphasis of independence, self-reliance, and personal freedom, individualistic value orientations also tend to foster fierce competition, frequent life changes, and

alienation, and they do not usually provide the kind of structured, stable, and predictable environments that allow schizophrenic patients to recuperate at their own pace and to be reintegrated into the society.

In contrast, the slower lifestyle and more integrated collectives commonly found in less industrialized nations may provide a more supportive environment for schizoprenics. There may be a greater likelihood of finding productive work for the afflicted individual, perhaps as part of family agricultural or business activities, leading to a sense of self-worth. On accepting work, the individual is likely to find himself or herself in the company of supportive people who will be more tolerant of mistakes than would employers and co-workers in large, impersonal companies. In collective societies, there are more people who feel that they have the obligation to offer help in times of troubles. These people are not just one's mother, father, and brothers: They also include cousins, uncles, and long-time family friends who have various honorary types of collective membership (e.g., godparents). If one member of a collective cannot communicate with a schizophrenic, there is a chance that someone else in the collective can. The extended family, in contrast to the smaller and often troubled nuclear family found in individualistic societies, may have more resources to offer help to their schizophrenic member. The results of the analysis by Lin and Kleinman (1988) remind us of the importance of social support in one's life, and this is a concept to which we will return several times in this chapter.

DEPRESSION. An understanding of depression is as necessary in today's world as an understanding of inoculations against diseases, dietary habits that increase the chances of good health, and the dangers of alcohol abuse. In a study designed to predict the chances of a severe depressive episode during a person's life, Sturt, Kumakura, and Der (1984) estimated that the chances are 11.9 percent for men and 20.2 percent for women in England. These estimates are similar to those calculated independently for residents of Denmark, Iceland, and the United States (Wing & Bebbington, 1985). This means that the majority of this book's readers will either experience a depressive episode in their lives, or they will have strong relationships with relatives or friends who will have a depressive episode.

The evidence for a culture-general core of depressive symptoms is not as strong as for the core schizophrenic symptoms already reviewed. There are more differences in the manner in which depression is expressed compared to the manner in which schizophrenia is expressed. Based on research in four countries—Iran, Japan, Canada, and Switzerland (World Health Organization, 1983)—and combining this research with a study carried out in Colombia and the United States (Escobar, Gomez, & Tuason, 1983), the best evidence to date suggests the possibility of this culture-general core:

- *Sad Affect*: Everyone feels the emotion of sadness from time to time. When the emotion is frequent, intense, and occurs for long periods of time, it becomes a symptom of depression. In the study by Escobar and his colleagues, patients in the United States and Colombia were able to point to the fact that they were depressed.
- *Loss of Enjoyment*: People seem to take no pleasure in life, and fail to find enjoyment in activities in which they once participated with enthusiasm.
- *Anxiety*: People experience anxiety about their lives, and/or apprehension concerning forthcoming events.
- *Concentration*: People experience difficulties concentrating on tasks necessary for everyday functioning.
- *Energy Level*: The energy necessary for setting simple goals and working toward their accomplishment is lacking.

In addition to this culture-general core, there are other symptoms that are commonly found, though with less frequency than the core. These symptoms are frequently included in diagnostic instruments intended to identify people with depressive disorders (Escobar, et al., 1983; Draguns, 1990):

- loss of sexual interest;
- loss of appetite;
- weight reduction;
- feelings of hopelessness concerning doing anything positive to improve one's own mental health;
- self-accusatory ideas that focus on the self as the cause of the difficulties that have led to one's depressive state.

Important research has also been carried out on culture-specific symptoms, the greater frequency of depression among women, and the types of thinking in which depressives engage.

1. Culture-specific symptoms. Depression manifests itself in various ways in different parts of the world. In North America and Europe, feelings of guilt are more common than in other parts of the world. Research carried out in Nigeria, for instance, has identified many depressives who do not show evidence of guilt (Marsella, 1980). In fact, cross-cultural research has provided a corrective to the analysis of depression (Draguns, 1990) since guilt was once thought to be central to its existence as a psychological disorder. In China, Kleinman (1982) argued that somatization was more frequent than in other parts of the world. As Draguns (1990, p. 311) summarized, "In China, as well as in many other cultures, somatization serves as the channel of communication for the experience of helplessness and even despair, as a culturally sanctioned and generally understood cry for help." Depression is often associated with suicidal behavior (Diekstra,

1989), but suicidal intentions are not part of the core because there are exceptions. Chiles and his colleagues (1989) present arguments comparing reactions to suicidal threats among depressives in the United States and China. In the United States, if a person threatens suicide, members of his or her support group are likely to bring the depressive to a hospital. There, the patient is well treated and, perhaps, is taken out of a stressful environment in the home and in the workplace. The suicidal threats, then, are reinforced—they led to positive outcomes, and one of the most basic concepts in psychology is that behaviors that are reinforced are likely to be repeated. In China, on the other hand, suicidal intentions do not elicit sympathy from one's support group.

> [In China], suicidal behavior tends to be seen less as a symptom of illness or psychological distress and more as a condition that brings embarrassment and shame to one's family and, to a lesser extent, to one's work group. . . . The immediate consequence of a suicide attempt is likely to be stern discussions with the support group, with the emphasis on, "You must stop this," rather than, "Now that we recognize your pain, how can we help you?" (Chiles, et al., 1989, p. 344).

Finding that suicidal behaviors do not bring reinforcement, the depressive is less likely to repeat them.

2. *Depression among women.* The finding that women are more likely to express depressive symptoms than men has been documented so frequently, in different parts of the world, that it is one of the most widely accepted conclusions in the analysis of mental illnesses (Fugita & Crittenden, 1990). This finding calls for the analysis of possible reasons. There is no widely accepted single reason for the difference (which can be on the order of two depressive women for every one depressive man [Boyd & Weissman, 1981]), and the eventual conclusion will undoubtedly be that there are a number of factors that work in combination. Research to date has dealt both with biological and social factors. For example, hypothyroidism is higher in women, leading to behavior marked by low energy, which is one symptom of depression. Hormonal changes associated with different stages of women's menstrual cycle, which often lead to observable changes in mood, have also been investigated (Thase, Frank, & Kupfer, 1985).

Social factors include the relative powerlessness of women in almost all societies and the subsequent frustrations stemming from the inability of women to achieve the goals they set for themselves. Recall the discussion in Chapter 9: Boys are frequently allowed more freedom of movement outside the home. Analyzing data from a longitudinal study in the United States, Block, Gjerde, and Block (1991, p. 735), pointed to the difficulties that bright young girls can face:

Over time, bright girls, with their greater emergent awareness of their self and of the world in which they are allowed to function, may build up a sense of stultification and depression about the way their life is being shaped and the criteria on which they are evaluated.

Depression, then, can be a response to societal norms that place limits on the movement of women.

Another discussion in Chapter 9 centered on the greater amount of aggressive behavior found in boys, and this was suggested as a cultural universal. One explanation for the lower amount of depression among males is that they act out their problems in more active, vigorous behaviors. Thase and his colleagues (1985, p. 871) argue: "it is assumed that the lower rate of depression in males results, in part, from expression of the depressive disorder in the form of alcoholism or antisocial behavior." In

Women who have personal problems often turn inward and become depressed. Men with similar problems often "act out" and abuse alcohol and/or engage in antisocial behaviors.

support of this possibility, Egeland and Hostetter (1983) worked among the Amish, a culture in which there are very strong norms against alcohol abuse and antisocial behavior. Among the Amish, males and females have equal rates of depression as expressed in the types of symptoms previously reviewed (low energy, loss of enjoyment, and so forth).

3. *The thinking of depressives.* The thought processes of depressives are marked by large numbers of negative thoughts involving the acceptance of blame for any difficulties they encounter (Seligman, 1989). Assume that a person does not receive a job offer after an interview. A healthy response would be, "Well, I just have to keep trying. Perhaps I should look over my résumé and make sure that it describes my qualifications clearly." A response indicative of depression would be, "This shows that I am not qualified, and that the employer was wise to reject me." In particular, depressives have three features in their thinking. Their thinking is *internal*, meaning that they take the blame for problems, even when there are external factors (e.g., a very competitive job market) on which their thinking could focus. Their thinking focuses on *stable* factors, such as a permanent unsuitability for the world of work, which is self-defeating because it allows little opportunity for positive change. Thinking that focuses on unstable factors is more healthy because it allows for positive change. "If a factor is unstable, it may change so that it favors me!" Thinking of depressives is also *universal*: Not only do they feel unsuitable for the job market, they also feel unsuitable for any role in life. Therapists who work with depressives frequently focus on their patients' thinking, encouraging them to avoid excessive amounts of self-blame, to examine aspects of their lives that can be changed in postive directions, and to avoid generalizing from a specific (and potentially modifiable) difficulty to conclusions about their entire lives (Seligman, 1989).

This analysis of how depressives think was developed in the United States, and it has been tested in other cultures. Crittenden and Lamug (1988) tested the model in the Philippines and found that Filipino depressives thought in similar ways. There were important additional findings in the Philippines that can be interpreted as culture-specific additions to the general core of internal, stable, and universal thinking among depressives. For example, the depressive pattern of thinking predicted somatic symptoms among respondents in the Philippines, but not among the Americans interviewed in the study. This may reflect the fact that Filipinos, as part of their socialization, learn that somatic symptoms such as a sleep disturbance, decreased libido, decreased weight, and constipation are part of the depressive state. Americans learn to focus more on psychological symptoms such as indecisiveness, emptiness, and hopelessness. Filipinos are also more likely to express depression through psychomotor agitation (Fugita & Crittenden, 1990), in contrast to the more listless behavior shown by Americans. These findings provide other examples of a point argued in several places throughout this chapter: As part of their socialization, people learn to express psychological disturbances in ways that are acceptable within their culture, in ways that will be understood, and in ways that will evoke sympathy from others.

THE PREVENTION OF HEALTH PROBLEMS

In the discussion of schizophrenia and depression, a number of factors were mentioned as *lessening* the chances that people would be debilitated by these illnesses. These factors included the avoidance of stress, the nurturance of a group of supportive individuals, creating opportunities to engage in positive thoughts about one's life, and others. A great deal of research has been carried out in recent years on various behaviors, in which people can engage, that will increase their chances for good health and decrease their chances for illness. The shorthand term "preventive health" has often been used to identify these types of behaviors. Given that people are concerned about their health, summaries of this research have been given extensive coverage in the mass media (e.g., "Feeding frenzy," 1991; "Health guide," 1991). Cross-cultural research has played a solid role in the development of various recommendations people can consider when making decisions about their behaviors. For example, recommendations have been made about diet, about alcohol use, and about sex education for teenagers. One way to determine the probable effects of such recommendations is to examine the health of people in various countries who engage in different behaviors related to these factors. With diet, for example, people in other countries typically obtain fewer of their calories from fat than do people in the United States (Ilola, 1990). With respect to alcohol, people in some countries (e.g., France, Portugal) typically consume more than do citizens in others (e.g., Norway, South Africa [Smart, 1989]). By examining data such as mortality figures due to heart disease in these countries, the effects of behaviors such as adopting a low-fat diet or moderating one's alcohol consumption can be estimated.

Space limitations prevent extension discussions of all the relevant literature. I will summarize key research findings by listing the recommended behaviors, briefly discussing some cross-cultural research that has contributed to the recommendations, and indicating where sensitivity to culture and cultural differences can play a part in the development of preventive health programs.

DIET, WITH SPECIAL ATTENTION TO THE NUMBER OF CALORIES FROM ANIMAL FATS. In Hawaii, native Hawaiians have the shortest life expectancy of any ethnic group. Threats to the health of native Hawaiians include high cholesterol, obesity, high blood pressure, and diabetes. One possible reason is that, in adjusting to the pressures of modernity introduced by Americans of European descent, Hawaiians have adopted the high-fat diet typical of Caucasian Americans. In contrast, the native diet was much healthier, with its emphasis (in today's terms) on low fat, an abundance of complex carbohydrates, and a great deal of bulk. An intervention project was recently established that encouraged Hawaiians to move back to their more traditional diet (Shintani, Hughes, Beckham, & O'Connor, 1991). The contents of the diet included large amounts of sweet potatoes and poi, the latter a vegetable product produced from the taro plant. Other acceptable items were breadfruit, a variety of vegetables, seaweed, fruit, fish, and chicken. Note the *absence* of animal fats in products such as red meat, eggs, milk, and cheese. Results of a 21-day program indicated that participants lost an average of 17.1 pounds, lowered their serum cholesterol by an average of 14 percent, and also significantly lowered both their systolic (7.8 percent) and diastolic (11.5 percent) blood pressure.

WEIGHT. Recommendations regarding diet, of course, will have an impact on people's weight. With the possible exception of avoiding the smoking habit, there are few preventive health recommendations suggested more frequently than keeping one's weight at levels appropriate to gender, age, and height. In examining the health of people from the Amish culture within the United States, Fuchs and his colleagues (1990) concluded that the relative infrequency of obesity is a positive feature of their lifestyle and an important contributor to their good health.

EXERCISE. In addition to its role in assisting people to maintain their weight at desired levels, regular exercise has a positive impact on people's cardiovascular fitness, their muscle tone, and their stamina. In contrast to diet, where the influence of Westernization has often led to increases in the intake of animal fats (discussed above), people with modern outlooks on life appear to make a point of adding regular exercise to their lives. Among Chinese living in Malaysia, Quah (1985, p. 355) found that "young, educated, and well-informed [from the mass media and from public health campaigns] Chinese are more likely to exercise regularly than their older, less-educated, and less-informed counterparts." Recalling the discussion in Chapter 8 concerning the convergence of behaviors once traditional restrictions are lifted, differences in exercise behavior among males and females were small when comparisons were made among the young and well educated. Among the less well educated, males were more likely to exercise, perhaps because they had more opportunities for activities outside the home.

DRUGS AND ALCOHOL. Discussions of problems brought on by the use of drugs and alcohol are often covered under discussions of "substance abuse." Among Native Americans, a number of alcohol-related health problems are more prevalent than in any other ethnic group in the United States. These include cirrhoses, diabetes, fetal abnormalities, accident fatalities, and homicides. The use of substances, such as marijuana, inhalants (e.g., glue), and other illicit drugs contribute to educational difficulties when children attend school, criminal acts among adults, and severe pressures on a family's economic resources. After reviewing these and other difficulties, Moncher, Holden, and Trimble (1990) attempted to identify youth who were at risk for substance abuse. More specifically, they attempted to predict the abuse of tobacco, smokeless tobacco, alcohol, inhalants, cannabis, and cocaine/crack. They identified a number of predictors that could identify Native American youth who (a) were at risk and who (b) might become participants in educational and health delivery programs aimed at preventing problems before they occurred.

The various risk factors included the fact that members of an individual person's family smoked and/or used smokeless tobacco; the presence of peers who smoked; the presence of peers who used alcohol; the quality of one's family life; school adjustment; deviant behaviors that were not directly related to substance abuse; religiosity; and cultural identification. This last factor—cultural identification—refers to an individual's feelings about his or her status as a Native American, and it also refers to the individual's ability to function effectively in the dominant Anglo–American culture. Skills for functioning in the dominant culture are important since it is often the source of advanced educational opportunities, employment, and health delivery services. The goals of many intervention programs include biculturalism, or the ability to be comfortable in one's interactions whether they take place among Native Americans or among members of any other ethnic group. As LaFromboise (1982, p. 12) noted, bicultural skills allow young people to "blend the adaptive values and roles of both the culture in which they were raised and the culture by which they are surrounded." Frustrations in one's ability to maneuver effectively can be one reason for escape through the use of various health-threatening substances.

TAKING ACTIONS TO PREVENT HEALTH DIFFICULTIES. Whenever there is a discussion of such activities as the avoidance of harmful substances or the development of skills useful in a society, there has to be attention given to individual initiative. At some point, *individuals* have to monitor their diet, watch their weight, set time aside for exercise, make decisions about their sexual activity, avoid the use of drugs, develop certain skills, and so forth. If programs are to be established in which these activities are recommended, people have to attend and carry out the recommended activities after the program ends.

The presence of various health-delivery programs is more common in some countries than in others. Many countries (not the United States) have national health insurance programs in which people can consult physicians without the worry of a financial drain. The number of visits to physicians varies across countries. In Germany (Payer, 1988), for example, people consult a physician an average of 12 times a year, compared to an average of 4.7 visits for Americans and 5.2 for the French. Germans (specifically, West Germany before reunification) also receive large numbers of prescription items: 11.2 prescriptions per year compared to the 6.5 prescriptions received by the average patient in Great Britain. The interesting question arises: Does all this attention from physicians, and easy access to health professionals, interfere with people's own initiative in looking after their health? After investigating health care in the United States and West Germany, Cockerham, Kunz, and Lueschen (1988) answer "no." This answer has important implications for social policy since proponents of a national health insurance program can argue that people still take the initiative to look after their own health even if far more government services become available to them. Cockerham and his colleagues (1988, p. 117) describe the German system:

> [T]he state provides comprehensive health insurance, featuring free medical and dental treatment, drugs, and hospitalization for an indefinite period of time. Sick or injured workers also receive full wages from their employers for six weeks; they receive their approximate take-home pay from public health benefits for 78 weeks thereafter. . . . Extensive maternity and death benefits also are paid through public health insurance.

In addition to actually receiving these benefits, Germans have adopted the philosophy that they are *entitled* to these types of services from their government. Many Americans are more distrustful of having too many government programs that might affect their lives.

With the possible exception that they consume greater quantities of alcohol (beer being the most common drink), Germans were as concerned as Americans with preventive health behaviors. Germans were more likely to be careful about the food they eat and to seek time for relaxation; Americans were more likely to be careful about their alcohol consumption and to be concerned about their appearance (e.g., good complexion, good posture). Both Americans and Germans gave attention to exercise and were making attempts to quit if they had the smoking habit. Overall, the respondents were equally attentive to maintaining a healthy lifestyle, even though they gave more emphasis to some factors relative to others. Cockerham and his colleagues (1988, p. 125) conclude: "West Germans, with their more extensive state-sponsored health benefits, appear to work just as hard to stay fit as do Americans, who have more individual responsibility for obtaining and maintaining coverage for health services." Government programs do not necessarily interfere with personal incentives to engage in a healthy lifestyle.

AVOIDING STRESS. One of the factors in a healthy lifestyle emphasized by Germans more than Americans was time for relaxation. This emphasis is part of the more general advice to avoid stress whenever possible and to seek out relaxing activities in the form of hobbies, time with one's family and friends, vacations, and so forth. People in individualist countries, such as the United States and Canada, appear to suffer more stress-related illnesses than people in collectivist countries, such as China, Thailand, and India (Bond, 1991). One reason is that individualists have to do so much on their own: find a job, work effectively at the job, find a spouse, raise children, provide for the financial security of the nuclear families, and so forth. In collectivist cultures, there are others who help in major ways with these tasks (as discussed in Chapter 2) and so there is less stress on any one person. The stress-related illnesses to which individualists are more prone include ulcers, heart disease, stroke; and cancer of the stomach, colon, and rectum (Bond, 1991). Stress has impacts on other health problems. As previously discussed, people in various parts of the world who are at risk for schizophrenia are more likely to have acute attacks after stressful episodes in their lives (Day, et al., 1987). Summarizing research carried out in seven countries, McCormick and Cooper (1988) argue that job loss and family conflicts are two of the most stressful life events. The stress resulting from job loss may be less (a) in countries where companies have a tradition of never laying off employees or doing so only under the most extreme circumstances or (b) countries where unemployment is so low that people can find jobs easily. Stress resulting from conflicts within the nuclear family can be lessened in collectivist cultures if there are supportive members of the extended family or organization who can offer various forms of assistance (Golding & Baezconde-Garbanati, 1990).

NURTURING A SUPPORT GROUP. This discussion of the relationship between collectivism and the lower frequency of stress-related diseases leads to another piece of advice for a healthy lifestyle. If people do not naturally have a supportive group in the form of an extended family or employment in a paternal organization (as discussed in Chapter 8), they should strongly consider developing a network of people who can offer assistance in times of difficulty. In many types of jobs at which people work, stress cannot be *eliminated*. However, stress can be *managed* in ways that decrease the chances of negative impacts on one's health. One of the ways in which stress can be decreased is to have supportive others in one's life who can act as buffers between stressful events and harmful effects on one's health (Kelley & Kelley, 1985; Harari, Jones, & Sek, 1988).

Examples of jobs in which stress cannot be totally eliminated include air traffic controllers at busy airports who are working when the weather is bad, retail sales workers just before the major holidays during which gifts are exchanged, or social workers dealing with clients who are unwilling to accept bureaucratic procedures for receiving public assistance. The presence of people who care about the difficulties in one's life can have major impacts. In a discussion of suicide attempts in 19 European countries, with special emphasis on information from the Netherlands, Diekstra (1989) presented an argument that is consistent with the discussion of gender in

Chapter 9 of this book. Females, compared to males, expect more from their friends (Morse, 1983). These expectations can include listening to discussions about the stresses in one's life. Males are either less likely to expect that friends will want to hear about their stresses, or are less comfortable discussing their emotions. When females experience depression and/or thoughts of suicide, the fact that they discuss their emotions with others has a number of benefits. The others may offer various types of support, or at least they may not allow the troubled individual to find herself alone. It is very difficult to commit suicide when others are present. Diekstra (1989, p. 205) summarizes:

> . . . although women may indeed more often experience [depressive] feelings, they also seem more inclined to admit and communicate such feelings to others (even in the form of nonfatal suicide attempts), while men are less inclined to do so and more often cope with them by substance abuse. . . . [This increases] the probability of not only worsening such feelings but also of more severe social, interpersonal and physical disruption, that in turn increases their risk for . . . suicide attempts and completed suicides.

Intervention programs aimed at males often include the recommendation that they learn to discuss their emotions more openly with members of their support groups (Kelley & Kelley, 1985).

ENGAGING IN A VARIETY OF ACTIVITIES. Support groups often develop out of the activities in which any one person engages. Interactions take place with colleagues in the workplace, with other community-minded people during volunteer activities, and with friends who share activities associated with a variety of hobbies. Engaging in a variety of activities is associated with good health. In an 8-year longitudinal study of Mexican- and Anglo-Americans age 60 and older, Markides and Lee (1990) investigated the relation between health and activities, such as going to the movies, a dance, a picnic, the museum, the zoo, or a sporting event; going hunting or fishing; going to parades or fiestas; meeting with friends or neighbors; and going sight-seeing. Activity level decreased with age, suggesting "the importance of targeting activity programs at the very old" (Markides & Lee, 1990, p. S72). The model presented by the researchers suggests a relationship between health and activity level. The exact nature of the relationship is admittedly ambiguous: Good health allows people to engage in more activities, and poor health (for reasons unassociated with an active lifestyle) can force people to decrease their activities. As with many complex analyses of behavior, the relationship between health and activity can exist for a number of reasons. In addition to activity affecting health, and vice versa, a third variable can affect both. Socioeconomic status (Palmore, Nowlin, & Wang, 1985) can affect access to a healthy diet;

A good diet can affect one's energy level, one's energy level can affect the number of activities in which a person engages, and the number of activities can affect a person's health.

People often obtain approval from others if they are engaged in work-related activities that are considered important in a culture. Lin and Kleinman (1988) suggest that people at risk for schizophrenia are less likely to have acute attacks if they participate in a culture's workforce. If they can successfully carry out tasks that benefit a society (e.g., agricultural work, construction work), they receive approval, social support, and a sense of meaning in their lives. Schizophrenics who are members of collective cultures sometimes fit well into the workforce because supportive members of their groups (a) see that they obtain jobs that are not beyond their abilities and (b) "keep an eye" on them so that as many problems as possible can be avoided.

PARTICIPATING IN INTERVENTION PROGRAMS. At times, the activities in which people should engage are either formal programs designed to prevent health problems or programs to deal with problems should they arise. Preventive programs are often the most cost-effective. The treatment of certain diseases, such as alcoholism, can be very expensive, and the expenses multiply if a disease is especially prevalent in a culture. Programs to prevent problems before they occur are often far less expensive and, of course, can have additional positive impacts on family members who do not participate directly (see Chapter 5). People can reap benefits if illness does *not* strike a spouse, son, or daughter who is an active program participant.

Adolescents worldwide are exposed to temptations to abuse alcohol. Whenever adolescents congregate for social purposes, alcohol consumption often becomes one of the possible activities. Perry and her colleagues (1989) introduced school-based alcohol education programs in four countries: Australia, Chile, Norway, and Swaziland. The target population was 13- and 14-year-olds in these countries, and the goal was to encourage the adolescents to minimize the use of alcohol. A group of age peer leaders was carefully trained to be comfortable with the content of the educational program, which included presenting information about alcohol's effects, organizing small group discussions, role-playing, and synthesizing information generated by program materials combined with participant suggestions. Special attention was given to developing skills, such as examining the promises made in advertisements for alcohol, analyzing peer influences to use alcohol at parties, and refusing invitations to use alcohol in a way that does not alienate friends. The effectiveness of peer-led programs was compared to teacher-led programs, and (perhaps surprisingly), the peer-led programs were more effective in all four countries. Reasons for this finding include the possibility that participants view peers as more knowledgeable about the pressures that adolescents face when they are confronted with invitations to use alcohol. Perry and her colleagues (1989,

p. 1167) further suggest that "teachers are often viewed as authority figures and [are] not seen as 'experts' on adolescent social decisions. . . . Peer leaders may be more credible role models since they employ the social language of their classmates. They also carry the message with them into the social environment outside the school or classroom." There remains, of course, some major tasks for adults if they decide to use peer-led education programs. Adults can give attention to selecting the most influential adolescents, can prepare materials for training, can organize the training programs for peer leaders, and can evaluate the entire set of intervention efforts so that improvements can be made. Yao (1990) made similar recommendations for AIDS awareness workshops among youth in Africa, where AIDS has been transmitted through heterosexual contact more frequently than in other parts of the world (Krieger & Margo, 1991). On the one hand, youths may be more willing to listen to each other make recommendations about sexual activity. On the other hand, adults have much to do in the preparation of workshops, selection of youth leaders, and follow-up activities such as evaluations months and years after young people participate in the workshops. It is important to note that this statement about more transmission through heterosexual contact in Africa is based on data gathered through 1990. Many analysts (e.g., Erlanger, 1991) fear that AIDS will spread in countries such as Thailand, where prostitution is common, extramarital sex is tolerated, and where public health education programs are underfinanced.

At times, intervention programs will involve detailed knowledge of a culture. Bastien (1987) described a program he developed for physicians working in Andean communities (to speakers of the Aymara and Quechua languages) in Bolivia. Recommended medical practices could sometimes be communicated to Andeans through the use of myths and stories with which they were already familiar. Physicians often found themselves trying to communicate the seriousness of diarrhea. People (especially young children) with diarrhea can become dehydrated, and cases of death from dehydration are not uncommon. The physicians' recommendation that people with diarrhea drink fluids was communicated by appealing to the story about Sajima, which is well known to Andeans. Sajima was a mountain that lost all its water because gophers drilled so many holes in it. Sajima was dying because of water loss, and a condor had to fly to neighboring mountains to bring back a special type of water. Because of the water, Sajima was saved. In presenting this story to Andeans, physicians added details about the special water. They said that to make a liter of water special so that it could be used in a way similar to saving Sajima, people should add two soup spoons of sugar, and small amounts of salt and bicarbonate of soda. A child who has lost water, like Sajima, should receive small amounts of this special liquid every 5 minutes. Given that the physicians recommendations were linked to a story they already knew, the Andeans were more likely to consider diarrhea and dehydration as serious problems and to take appropriate action.

DEVELOPING CULTURAL SENSITIVITY IN THE DELIVERY OF HEALTH CARE

When physicians modify their behaviors so that their recommendations are placed into frameworks familiar to patients (as in the example of Sajima), they are demonstrating a sensitivity to culture and to cultural differences. Many researchers and practitioners have made recommendations and/or have developed programs to encourage the development of cultural sensitivity among health care workers (e.g., Draguns, 1975, 1990; Ahia, 1984; Ponterotto & Benesch, 1988; Weiss & Parish, 1989; Lefley, 1990; Pedersen, 1991b). Many people concerned with the development of cultural sensitivity feel that a good starting point is to analyze universal aspects of health care delivery. If universal aspects can be identified, people have a convenient framework to think about health care delivery in their own culture. In addition, they have a framework to examine other cultures so that they can identify the manner in which the universal aspects operate.

UNIVERSALS IN THE DELIVERY OF HEALTH CARE. A number of scholars have examined interactions between health care professionals and people seeking help in various parts of the world. While the emphasis has been services for people with psychological complaints, I believe that the universal aspects identified by these scholars (Torrey, 1986; Draguns, 1975, 1990; Ponterotto & Benesch, 1988) are applicable to interactions between professionals and clients concerning any type of health problem. It is important to note that the word *professionals* is meant to be very broad. It includes people with advanced degrees in highly industrialized nations to whom citizens give the label "physician," "psychiatrist," "public health worker," and so forth. It also includes people in less industrialized nations, such as native healers, shamans, and herbalists.

Six universal aspects will be reviewed here. Health care specialists (1) *apply a name to a problem.* When clients learn that their problem has a name, it seems to be a positive step toward identifying solutions that might solve the problem. I remember when one of my children, then about 18 months, was constantly fussy. My wife and I went to the doctor and learned that an appropriate label (in the United States) was that the baby suffered from colic. Even though I knew that the label "colic" says little more about our baby than the symptom of fussiness that we already knew, realizing that the problem had a label was comforting. Perhaps one reason for the comfort is learning that we are not unique (and perhaps inadequate) as parents. Other parents have colicky babies. In the example of Sajima previously presented, when babies suffer diarrhea the label "water loss" is given, and this label is familiar to Andean parents.

The second universal aspect is that (2) *qualities of the health care professional are important* (Sue & Zane, 1987). They must be seen by clients as caring, competent, approachable, and concerned with identifying and finding solutions to problems. These qualities contribute to the client's belief that a solution can be found and that the physical or psychological pain that led to the search for help will be relieved. In discussing interventions with minority groups in the United States, Sue and Zane (1987) emphasized that professionals must communicate a sense of credibility that they can be of help. Further, they should give attention to offering benefits of some kind as soon as they can. If professionals do not offer benefits, there is the risk that clients will terminate contact, for instance, by not keeping appointments. "Offering benefits" does not mean total cure. It can entail smaller contributions: offering a helpful piece of advice, a concrete suggestion regarding some aspect of the patient's life (such as developing a good résumé for a job search), or introductions to people from the same cultural background who might become part of a support group (e.g., Alcoholics Anonymous for a person with a drinking problem).

The (3) *establishment of credibility* can be assisted through the use of symbols and trappings of status that are familiar in a culture. In highly industrialized nations, people are put at ease if they seek help from a professional who works out of an attractive office, has diplomas on the wall, and dresses in a certain way. Among professionals known as native healers, credibility would be established if clients knew that the healer had served many years as an apprentice to a person enshrined in the oral legends of a culture. In all cultures, professionals can increase their credibility by good "word of mouth," that is, testimonials from former patients who speak highly of the professionals' abilities. Credibility is also related to the fourth universal, (4) *the placing of the client's problems in a familiar framework*. If long-held beliefs in a culture center on witchcraft as the cause of certain problems, healers are likely to present their exact diagnoses in terms of evil spirits rather than bacteria. On the other hand, physicians in industrialized nations are far more likely to appeal to bacteria, diet, unsafe sex, or the smoking habit as the cause of medical problems because these are familiar to patients. One reason why people choose one psychotherapist over another involves the frameworks that different mental health specialists offer. If a person seeking help had a difficult childhood and accepts the possibility that parent–child relations have major impacts 20 years later, he or she may be attracted to a therapist trained in Freudian analysis. People who do not find explanations based on childhood appealing, and want to focus on very specific problems, such as hostility or depression in their *current* lives, may experience much more success with a clinician trained in behavioral or cognitive therapies.

After the problem is identified, a professional then (5) applies *a set of techniques meant to bring relief*. These techniques should also fit into the patients' worldview concerning the problems that brought them to seek professional help. If patients are familiar with the work of psychiatrists, for example, they will not be surprised when they are asked to talk a great deal about themselves. If they are familiar with the germ theory of disease, they will accept injections meant to either kill bacteria or to stimulate the body's own immune system. If they are familiar with the presence of spirits, they will look forward to rituals that rid the body of demons. Within industrialized nations, there are differences within psychotherapies based on the source of advice that will lead to relief. In some therapies, patients are expected to gradually become aware of possible solutions, and the clinician is expected to encourage this process. In other therapies, the clinician is expected to give very direct advice that the client is expected to follow. Members of minority groups in the United States often expect direct advice (Sue & Zane, 1987; Sue, 1988), and clinicians unwilling to offer it often find that patients fail to keep appointments.

Interactions between professionals and clients occur at (6) *a special time and place* (Draguns, 1975, 1990). The special places vary across cultures, of course, and take the form of doctor's offices, hospitals, ceremonial huts, and areas that are taboo to anyone but healers and people they designate as acceptable visitors. Professional–client interactions often take the form of an acceptable period of "time out" from the problems that caused the clients to seek help. But within this limited time frame, professionals and their clients engage in intense, concentrated, and emotionally charged activities that have the goals of diagnosis and recommended solutions to problems. Given that they are interacting with a credible professional who they believe will offer help, and given that they are focusing solely on their problem and are setting aside their other life concerns, clients experience intense emotions. "The opportunity to behave, think, and feel differently from one's day-to-day experience is another common denominator of many very different therapeutic procedures" (Draguns, 1975, p. 286).

MORE ON THE CHARACTERISTICS OF HELPERS: CULTURAL SENSITIVITY. Other issues in the delivery of health services can be introduced in a short critical incident. Jane McKenna is an Anglo-American from a small city in the American Midwest. She was active in community organizations during her high school years. She became interested in the helping professions during the two years she spent as a volunteer at a social services agency. On entering college, she took a number of psychology courses and eventually attended graduate school with the aim of becoming a counseling psychologist. She did well in her coursework and accepted an internship at a mental health clinic in Chicago. On her first day there, she learned that she would be working with a number of Black American clients from the inner city. Jane wondered if she could be of assistance. She feared that since she was White and some of her clients were Black, there might be a lack of effective communication and client acceptance of their counselor. Can Jane be an effective counselor in a mental health clinic?

The answer is, "yes" and the key issue is Jane's sensitivity to culture and to cultural differences. When making recommendations regarding the selection and training of professionals who *could* offer help to clients from other cultural backgrounds, the term *cultural sensitivity* is used repeatedly (Ponterotto & Benesch, 1988; Lefley, 1990; Newhill, 1990; Gim, Atkinson, & Kim, 1991). It is important to understand this concept since a number of research studies (Campion, 1982; Sue, 1988; Hess & Street, 1991; Wade & Bernstein, 1991) indicate that professionals can interact effectively with clients from other cultural groups, and can offer help, as long as they possess "cultural sensitivity." This term refers to a professional's knowledge of culture and cultural differences, examples of which can be found throughout this book. But knowledge is not enough. Sensitivity also includes the willingness to bring one's knowledge to interactions with different clients, and the ability to take culture into account during discussions of important topics such as recommendations regarding the alleviation of pain and stress.

Training programs have been established to encourage the development of intercultural sensitivity among health care professionals. Often, programs use a variety of approaches so that the various aspects of sensitivity are addressed: knowledge about culture, willingness to incorporate this knowledge into health care delivery, and actual practice in doing so. One training method can be borrowed from the efforts of Gim and her colleagues (1991) who developed audiotapes that presented examples of culturally sensitive counseling. Trainees can listen to these tapes and identify examples of good counselor–client interactions. In this exercise, an important distinction is between empathy and cultural sensitivity. All of the counselor's comments in the examples presented below show empathy, or clear attempts to understand and share the feelings of clients, and this characteristic of counselors is considered essential in all types of interventions. But not all show cultural sensitivity, the characteristic considered necessary when counselors and clients are from different cultural backgrounds. In this conversation taken from the audiotapes prepared by Gim and her colleagues (1991, p. 58), the material in brackets provides examples of cultural sensitivity that go beyond empathy. The client is an Asian-American female.

CLIENT: But, you know, more than anything else, I feel really different from everybody. I grew up in a big city with a lot of Asians and other minority groups. My high school was pretty mixed; but here, I feel out of place, I miss my friends a lot.

COUNSELOR: Yes, it's hard to leave behind a familiar place and start all over in a new place. [But it also sounds like you're feeling alienated because there aren't many people who share your cultural background.]

CLIENT: Yeah, it's really hard on me sometimes. I wish there were more Asians here.

COUNSELOR: I can see that this situation is affecting you a great deal. [In addition to the usual difficulties of adjusting to a new place you also feel culturally isolated.]

Other culturally sensitive remarks could focus on the client's relation with her family (Chapter 4), communication difficulties when making friends that might be based on styles familiar in different cultures (Chapter 7), and expectations that different cultures place on females (Chapter 9).

Another method of developing sensitivity is for trainees to engage in role playing, as introduced in Chapter 7. Paul Pedersen (1988) has developed a unique version of role playing called the triad model, in which three people engage in simulated counseling sessions. Two of the people play the well-known roles of client and counselor, and a third person acts in a variety of ways meant to assist or to challenge the counselor and client. For example, the third person can act as a very knowledgeable person who knows a great deal about the client's culture. Or, the third person can act as *the problem* and can try to maintain its existence. If the client brings the problem of alcohol use to the counseling session, the third person would make comments such as the following: "But you're so much fun when you've had a couple of drinks. It's nice to look forward to a couple of relaxing drinks when you are having a stressful day at work. Keep in mind how frequently alcohol is served at social gatherings in your culture." The person role-playing the counselor has to deal with these comments in various ways and keep the client focused on the reason that she or he sought help.

The purpose of the triad model is to encourage trainees to (1) describe and explain the client's problem so that cultural factors are clearly identified, (2) deal with client resistance (for instance, resistances stemming from the fact that client and counselor might be from different cultural backgrounds), (3) recognize and deal with any defensiveness that people may be expressing *as counselors*, and (4) recover from any mistakes made during counseling sessions. Wade and Bernstein (1991) evaluated the effects of a cultural sensitivity training program that included the triad model. The clients in the evaluation study were Black American females. Some clients were assigned to experienced counselors who had not participated in the training program, and other clients were assigned to graduates of the program. Clients rated trained counselors higher on a number of important dimensions: expertise, trustworthiness, ability to show positive regard, and empathy. Further, clients expressed greater satisfaction with their experience in counseling and returned for more follow-up sessions if they were assigned to the program graduates. One conclusion of this evaluation study is that cultural sensitivity is a characteristic of good counseling that can be developed in well-thought-out programs.

Another conclusion is that well-prepared counselors can work across cultural barriers. Both Black and White counselors participated in the study, but the Black clients did not prefer a given counselor just because she or he was from the same race. As Wade and Bernstein (1991, p. 13) concluded, "Black female clients' perceptions of counselors and the counseling process were affected more by cultural sensitivity training of the counselors than by counselor race." I believe that this finding, which is consistent with other evidence reviewed by Sue (1988), shows that health delivery professionals can increase their knowledge of culture and cultural differences and become more effective as a result. It also supports one of the themes presented throughout this book. People, whether they are teachers, businessmen and businesswomen, deliverers of health care, government officials, or members of other professions, can work effectively with individuals who happen to come from a different cultural background. The culture in which people were socialized does not necessarily place an insurmountable barrier on their ability to carry out the goals of their professions. Instead, a knowledge of culture may provide guidelines for achieving the goals (the best education possible, good health care, respect for contributions in the workplace) more effectively. If they put time and effort into understanding culture's influence on their own behavior and the behavior of others, people may even look forward to the challenges and stimulation that intercultural interactions can bring.

CHAPTER SUMMARY

As more and more people move across cultural boundaries, the people from whom they seek health care will be from very different backgrounds. The importance of culture and cultural differences in the delivery of health care services will become an essential part of training programs in the health professions. Various biases will have to be overcome, such as the difficulty of moving beyond the guidelines for behavior that people learn in their own culture (the limitations bias); or the tendency to repeat new behaviors if they have been successful with *one person* from another culture (the generalization bias). A good basic guideline for dealing with cultural differences is to nurture professional relationships with colleagues from different backgrounds. Collaborators in the delivery of health care services can then identify potential biases that their colleagues may be carrying, contribute information about the different cultures from which the professionals are drawing clients, and provide a number of helpers among whom clients can choose.

The task of integrating cultural knowledge into health care delivery is not easy. Cultural influences vary greatly from culture to culture, demanding very specific knowledge. For instance, Jamaican mothers living in Great Britain were sensitive to the age at which their children learned to sit up by themselves, but were not concerned with the age at which crawling started (Hopkins & Westra, 1989). Pediatricians have to know this fact if they are to encourage mothers to secure professional assistance if their babies develop slowly. Another difficulty is that people frequently seek medical advice from friends and family members rather than from professionals. By the time they finally see professionals, the problems may have becomes so severe that any form of intervention will be unsuccessful (Pedersen, 1991a). At times, professionals will have to make recommendations that go against cultural norms. Mothers in some cultures are hesitant to breast-feed their infants because their husbands disapprove. Given the benefits of breast milk, such as the transfer of immunities from mother to babies, professionals may have to risk the charge of "cultural insensitivity" if they are to deliver the best health care possible.

IDENTIFYING THE IMPACT OF CULTURE. Many health problems have both culture-common and culture-specific components. Analyzing an instrument meant to identify people who are at risk for mental health difficulties, Nishimoto (1988) worked with Anglo-Americans, Vietnamese-Chinese, and Mexicans. A number of indicators of mental health difficulties were common to all three cultures, and these included nervousness, trouble sleeping, and feeling weak all over. There were additional symptoms useful in one of the cultures but not the others. For instance, shortness of breath was an identifying symptom among Anglo-Americans; fullness in the head was a symptom among Vietnamese-Chinese, and problems with memory was a symptom among Mexicans. People from one cultural background will naturally feel a sense of strangeness when considering the symptoms that are specific to other cultures. This sense of strangeness should be taken as a reminder that culture plays a role in the diagnosis and treatment of health problems, and that professionals should be constantly alert to discover culturally influenced factors that can improve health care services. One factor occurs so often that professionals will surely encounter it. People from many cultures somatize their psychological problems. Rather then describe symptoms, such as an inability to carry out their daily routines, people describe their problems in physical terms such as headaches and back pains. If they are unaware of the frequency with which some people somatize, physicians are likely to prescribe drugs that address the reported symptoms but not the underlying problems.

The distinction between culture-common and culture-specific symptoms has been very helpful in the study of schizophrenia and depression. Schizophrenics are unable to relate their thoughts, attitudes, and actions to the reality in which they find themselves. "Reality" includes the expectations that people have of appropriate behavior in a culture: A funeral is not a wedding, and an informal chat with a close friend is not a confrontation with a total stranger. Schizophrenics make so many responses that are inconsistent with expectations of appropriate behavior (getting angry at a friend for no apparent reason) that they have severe difficulties meeting the demands that society places on people. Culture-common symptoms of schizophrenia include difficulties forming emotional ties with others, poor self-insight, thinking aloud, poor rapport with others, incoherent speech, and widespread delusions. Culture-specific factors deal with the *form* that these general symptoms take, the reasons for the onset of illness, and the prognosis for people afflicted with the disease. In Ibadan, Nigeria, the symptoms of schizophrenia emphasize an intense suspicion of others, with many bizarre fears and thoughts (Katz, et al., 1988). Many Nigerians believe that illness is caused by evil forces, but schizophrenics move beyond this belief into bizarre suspicions about unseen forces. These suspicions become so intense that they interfere with people's everyday functioning as judged by other Nigerians.

Acute schizophrenic attacks tend to be associated with stressful events in people lives that occur approximately two to three weeks before onset of the disease. Some of these events are interpretable only with cultural knowledge. The common belief in evil forces among Nigerians has already been mentioned. One Nigerian male experienced an acute attack of schizophrenia after his mother confessed to the practice of witchcraft in an open forum within their community. Evil forces may exist for the Nigerian male, but the sudden realization that his mother practiced witchcraft became too overwhelming for his coping resources. Interestingly, the possibility exists that this individual, like other people in less industrialized nations, may have a better prognosis for improvement than schizophrenics in highly industrialized nations (Lin & Kleinman, 1988). Schizophrenics in less industrialized nations may have a more active support group and may be able to find work (e.g., a simple but important agricultural job) that is valued in the culture. Recall from Chapter 2 and Chapter 8 that industrialization is associated with individualism. In individualistic societies, people have greater responsibilities for taking care of themselves. Schizophrenics, with their delusional thoughts and problems establishing rapport with others, are going to have difficulties in such necessary efforts as finding and retaining a job, developing and maintaining a support group, keeping appointments with health care professionals, and so forth.

With depression, research evidence suggests this common core: frequent and intense sad affect, loss of enjoyment, anxiety, difficulties when concentrating, and lack of energy. There are also culture-specific components. Feelings of guilt are found more often in North America and Europe than in other parts of the world. Somatic complaints are often heard among depressives in China. Women may be twice as likely to have a depressive episode in their lives compared to men. Many reasons have been suggested, including the relative powerlessness of women. Another is that men have as many problems, but (given that they are more aggressive, see Chapter 9) are more likely to act out their negative feelings in antisocial behaviors, such as alcohol abuse. Women are more likely to turn their negative feelings inward. Intervention efforts aimed at helping depressives often focus on their thinking. Depressives can be encouraged to intercept their negative thoughts and to avoid overgeneralizing from the discouragements that everyone experiences in their day-to-day lives. For example, depressives may interpret an unsuccessful job interview as a total rejection of their suitability for employment. People not suffering from depression are more likely to view an unsuccessful job interview as a learning experience and to identify ways in which to make themselves more attractive for the next potential employer.

PREVENTIVE HEALTH-CARE MEASURES. Cross-cultural research has been a major contributor to lists of recommended actions that people can undertake to prevent threats to their health. For example, people in some cultures consume diets far lower in fat than people in other cultures. If one type of diet leads to fewer health problems than another, this can lead to recommendations for intervention programs. For example, Shintani and his colleagues (1991) documented that if Native Hawaiians returned to their traditional diet, as compared to the diet that many have adopted since European contact, then their health improved.

There is a sense of familiarity to many of the preventive health-care recommendations because of coverage in the mass media. These recommendations include (1) adopting a low-fat diet that is high in bulk and complex carbohydrates; (2) keeping one's weight at levels appropriate to gender, age, and body size; (3) maintaining a regular program of exercise; (4) avoiding drugs (including tobacco) and using alcohol in moderation; (5) adopting the general outlook that people can have a positive impact on their own health if they take the initiative and adopt a healthy lifestyle; (6) avoiding stress as much as possible; (7) contributing to and drawing from the resources of a support group; and (8) engaging in a variety of activities and nurturing a variety of interests.

People can also be encouraged to participate in various intervention programs designed to either promote a healthy lifestyle or to cope with problems that currently threaten their health. In a program designed to prevent alcohol abuse among teenagers, Perry and her colleagues (1989) worked in Australia, Chile, Norway, and Swaziland. They found that programs led by trained adolescents were more effective than programs led by teachers. One possible reason is that program participants viewed peers as more knowledgeable about the pressures faced by teenagers when they are handed a drink at a social gathering. Even though adults may not be the most effective leaders once a program starts, there are many roles for them. Adults can select the most influential adolescents, train *them* in the skills necessary for effective program leadership, prepare impactful materials for use in the program, and evaluate the program to identify points where improvements are possible. Intervention programs often demand a detailed knowledge of the culture in which health professionals are working. Bastien (1987) found, for example, that recommendations to take diarrhea seriously could be communicated to Andeans in Bolivia if links were made to stories and legends with which the Andeans were familiar.

DELIVERING HEALTH CARE. Whenever health care professionals interact with clients for the purposes of offering assistance, there are a number of universal elements. Professionals (1) give the client's problem a name, (2) present themselves as caring, competent and concerned, and (3) establish credibility through the use of symbols respected in the client's culture. (4) They place the client's problem in a familiar framework and (5) apply a set of techniques meant to bring relief. Especially in contrast to times when people seek help from friends and family members, help from professionals (6) occurs at a special time and place. Further, the help takes place as a sort of "time out" from the daily hassles that contributed to the client's problems.

Culturally sensitive professionals have a characteristic that goes beyond the (very necessary) qualities of concern, empathy, and credibility. Sensitive professionals have the knowledge, willingness, and ability to take the cultural background of clients into account during help-giving interactions. If they wish to do so, health care professionals can develop this quality. Wade and Bernstein (1991) evaluated a program for training counselors who had clients seeking help with their personal problems. Black American female clients preferred graduates of the training program. Further, they were more satisfied with the counseling process and more likely to keep later appointments than were age peers who interacted with untrained counselors. An important additional finding was that the Black female clients did not have an automatic preference for counselors of their own race. Rather, they preferred trained counselors, regardless of race.

This finding is consistent with other research evidence (Sue, 1988) that people from one cultural background can offer assistance to people from another as long as they are well prepared. Cultural barriers can be overcome in the delivery of health care. As more and more people engage in extensive intercultural interactions, "culture" will hopefully become seen as more than a hurdle to overcome. Culture and cultural differences will ideally be viewed as important and stimulating challenges that, at times, will provide insights about health that people can apply in their own lives.

11

Some Predictions
Some Predictions
FOR THE FUTURE

A prediction about the future that can be made with certainty is that people will engage in extensive intercultural contact. People attending college will interact with students from other countries; managers in businesses and industries will be interviewing immigrants or their sons and daughters; people will find employment in companies owned by foreign nationals; tourism will be adopted as an industry in more and more countries; schoolchildren will interact with peers from different ethnic and cultural backgrounds; legal decisions will assist people who want to live in certain neighborhoods that once may have been denied them because of race. Even if people would prefer to interact with others who have the same cultural background, same skin color, same accent, and same general interests, they will find themselves in the company of extremely diverse individuals. This contact will not automatically lead to positive relationships (Allport, 1954; Stephan, 1985). Many people will continue to hold their prejudicial attitudes (Chapter 6), but others will accept the challenge of developing positive intercultural relationships (Chapter 7).

THE EFFECTS OF EXTENSIVE INTERCULTURAL CONTACT

The frequency of intercultural interaction will have a number of specific effects that I would like to discuss in this final chapter:

1. There will be challenges to people's ethnocentric viewpoints, and this will force them to expand their thinking.

2. Women will be more concerned about their abilities to make choices concerning their lives.

3. People will be able to analyze the role that culture and cultural differences play as they think about their own lives and about policies in their own societies.

4. As people become involved in new research ventures, either as investigators, participants, funders, or as gatekeepers who can approve or disapprove proposals, the importance of practical applications will become paramount.

5. Basic information concerning the benefits and potential pitfalls of intercultural interaction will be widely discussed among people, just as they discuss preventive health behaviors today.

CHALLENGES TO ETHNOCENTRISM. Part of everyone's socialization is that there is a right and wrong way to go about everyday tasks, such as eating, sleeping, working, and interacting with others. *Ethnocentrism* refers to the universal feeling that members of certain cultures not only have found the right and wrong ways, but that other cultures have *not*. Further, people who engage in ethnocentric thinking judge the behavior of others with their own standards of "right" and "wrong" in mind. One guaranteed outcome of extensive intercultural interaction is that the ethnocentric tendencies of people will be challenged. They *will* observe behaviors that they find irritating, incorrect, or boorish based on their own standards. But instead of immediately thinking of a negative label for the behaviors and applying it, people can look at the challenge as an opportunity to learn more about culture and cultural differences.

Consider this incident, very frequently reported by North Americans and Europeans working in Japan (Sakamoto & Naotsuka, 1982, p. 1).

> JAPANESE MALE: I just got married and I would like you to come to our house for dinner next Saturday.
>
> AMERICAN FEMALE: That's wonderful! Congratulations! Thank you, I'd love to. I'm looking forward to meeting your wife.
>
> JAPANESE MALE: She's not beautiful, and she can't cook very well. But I hope you'll come.

The American female will have the clear temptation to dismiss the Japanese male's behavior as rude and unkind. But she might also consider the possibility that such a conclusion would be ethnocentric, and instead might explore the incident to determine if there are cultural factors involved.

There are several. One is that a Japanese male considers his wife part of his collective identity (Chapter 2). He should be modest about himself, and since his wife is part of his identity he should also be modest about her. The wife, incidentally, might use similarly negative terms when discussing *him* among her friends: "He is not very good looking and rather lazy." Another cultural difference is that people are more likely to be considered a permanent part of one's collective among the Japanese. Americans have an easier time than Japanese when asked the question: "Could you please give me the names of people with whom you were once very close, but with whom you currently do not interact?" One implication is that the Japanese do not give a great deal of attention to special, personalized acts that help to develop or maintain a marriage. The marriage *is*: There is no emphasis on consciously thinking about behaviors that might be pleasing to one's spouse so that the marriage bond is strengthened. In the United States, on the other hand, many people make a point of engaging in behaviors that will keep a marriage fresh. Men buy flowers for their wives; wives discover their husband's favorite aftershave lotion and purchase it; either marriage member surprises the other with breakfast in bed. Since the marital bond is not treated as something permanent and indissolvable (50 percent of marriages in the United States end in divorce), people have to take steps to keep a marriage successful.

Examining intercultural incidents in this manner (a) allows people to explore the influence of culture in people's lives, and (b) allows them to develop fresh insights into their own behavior. It also allows (c) interventions into difficulties. I have counseled many American women married to Japanese men who complain of their husband's cavalier treatment of them in public. American women do not like working in their kitchens for 6 hours, only to hear husbands make apologies to friends once the first course is served. Seeing his American wife's reaction, a Japanese husband becomes upset about her inappropriate behavior in front of his friends. When the cultural background for the husband's behavior and the wife's irritation are discussed openly, the people are less likely to interpret the behaviors as personal attacks on them as individuals. If they can learn to identify some of their own and their spouses' behaviors as the results of their cultural backgrounds, they will be more able to develop compromises that will increase the chances of marital harmony.

WOMEN AND CHOICES. When considering this incident and my recommendation to look for cultural influences, many readers may have experienced the same reaction as some of the women whom I have counseled. "I can understand why criticizing me in public can be seen as part of his cultural background and why I should not take it personally. But I am still extremely irritated!" This is a common reaction, and it will continue to be so in the future. People enjoy being treated well, having nice things said about them, being verbally reinforced at work when they put in extra effort, and consulted about decisions that will affect them. If the norms of a culture do not include the recommendations that people be praised, recognized, and consulted, the pressures of culture contact, industrialization, and modernization will encourage the adoption of these behaviors. One of my colleagues is a Japanese woman who received one of her college degrees in Japan and a second degree in the United States. She reports, "It's a lot more enjoyable to receive flowers and compliments from my American boyfriend than to be told how fat I am by my [former] Japanese boyfriend."

Given various technological innovations, women in all parts of the world will be exposed to differences and many will be attracted to them. These innovations include air travel and development in the tourist industry, leading to face-to-face interactions among women raised in traditional and highly industrialized societies. The entertainment industry also has its impact: People in all parts of the world view movies and television shows that depict alternative ways of behaving in a variety of social situations. Many women raised according to very traditional norms will become attracted to these alternatives, whether they include treatment by men, greater opportunities in the job market, and/or decisions concerning the number of children to bear. Other women will not be attracted to such changes and will have a greater chance of finding happiness by behaving according to traditional norms. The key is that many women will want to make their own choices and will resist having their actions controlled by traditional authority figures. This will lead to changes in their cultures and to stresses in their lives. Both of these topics will be important areas of research well into the twenty-first century.

The increasing opportunity for women to make choices will have important impacts on many social issues. Bassett and Mhloyi (1991) predicted possible implications of women's choices on the transmission of AIDS in Zimbabwe, Africa. As discussed in Chapter 10, AIDS has been spread through heterosexual contact in Africa. One reason is that traditions of male dominance and limited job opportunities for women in Zimbabwe have forced many females into subservient positions within their society. Further, males traditionally have left their wives home and have accepted work as migrant laborers, leading to transmission of the HIV virus through extramarital sex. Since women have less power, they are inexperienced in asserting themselves and requesting that their partners use condoms. Given the limited opportunities women have for wage employment, some must enter the sex industry to survive. If women acquire the freedom to make more of their own choices, then the number of AIDS cases may diminish given women's demands for protection during sexual intercourse and their ability to find employment outside the sex industry.

The movement from traditional roles to roles based on choice is not a simple one. Moghaddam, Ditto, and Taylor (1990) interviewed immigrant women from India who were living in Montreal, Canada. The more changes from traditional expectations that the women desired, the more distress they experienced. The changes desired by the most distressed women included movement away from the traditional role of homemaker, greater opportunities in the job market, unwillingness to pass on traditional gender roles to their children, and the desire for an egalitarian relationship with their husbands. The desire (and movement toward) these changes led to stress, however, and resulted in the same sorts of symptoms discussed in Chapter 10: psychosomatic complaints, trouble sleeping, feelings of depression, anxiety, and so forth. Reasons for the distress include a lack of familiarity with the behaviors necessary to achieve the newly formulated goals, lack of support from husbands and extended family members, and prejudicial reactions from members of the dominant society. Research on the most effective content and structure of various intervention programs to assist people to deal with these stresses will continue as a high-priority need (Berry, Poortinga, Segall, & Dasen, 1992).

One of the driving forces behind societal changes is the desire for freedom in making choices about one's own life. In recent years, this desire has been part of political movements all over the world as people have expressed their demands for elected governments that will replace traditional and authoritarian ruling bodies. These demands have been seen in the former U.S.S.R. republics, South Africa, East Germany before reunification with the West, Nepal, Romania, China, the Philippines, Cuba, and other countries. One of the graduate students with whom I worked closely recently returned to one of these countries after two years in the United States. I asked him what he would miss most about his two-year sojourn, and he said simply "freedom." I believe that he meant the ability to make his own choices concerning where he would work, the manner in which he could criticize authority figures, the places to which he could travel, the right to vote in honest and open elections, and so forth. He went home and almost immediately joined the democracy movement in his country. Bullets flew over his head during a demonstration, and he spent time in jail. The movement was successful, his country has an elected legislative body, and he and others are struggling to make democracy work. The desire for freedom is extremely strong, and I believe that we will continue to see its impact in various parts of the world.

CULTURAL FACTORS IN MAJOR POLICY CHANGES. As people move toward more democratic forms of government, cultural factors will have an impact on how quickly the move will take place as well as the stresses that people will experience. Democracy, with its emphasis on the participation of citizens in decision making, sounds fine as an ideal. It is very hard to put into practice. One reason is that people in some cultures are socialized to be much more respectful of, and deferent to, authority than are people in other cultures (Chapter 8). Such people will be uncomfortable when they actually have to *make decisions* themselves in contrast to *talking about their desire* to make decisions. Further, people who have been socialized to respect authority will be uncomfortable when asked to vote someone out of office who is from a respected family but who has been engaging in graft.

Further, people in newly developing democracies will have to develop ways of making choices among various proposals for scarce resources. Again, the distinction between the ideal and the real is involved. Ideally, people in democracies can speak freely and make demands on their governments. In reality, government representatives have to make choices among these demands since there are not enough resources (especially money) to satisfy everyone. In a book that analyzed people's acquisition and use of power, I discussed the worldwide movement toward democracy (Brislin, 1991, p. xiv):

> In a democracy, people can speak their minds, can dis-agree with authority figures, and can assume leadership roles as long as they can persuade others to follow them. . . . Given the movement toward democratic government today in various parts of the world, more and more people will be able to put their ideas forward and to pursue their goals without concern of reprisals from traditional authority figures. These ideas will not be put forward only by people concerned with their countries' formal political systems. New ideas will also be introduced by people concerned with education, social welfare, religion, the status of women and minority groups, expansion of businesses, international relations, and so forth. But who will be successful in putting their ideas forward and who will be ignored?

Important research will be carried out on the development of leaders, the creation of various mechanisms that allow choices to be made among competing proposals, and the treatment of proposals put forward by various ethnic groups who are competing for their governments' resources.

Understanding cultural differences can sometimes bring insights into arguments about governments in one's own country. The United States, in sharp contrast to European countries, does not have a policy of universal health insurance funded by the government. It is possible that the cultural norm of individualism in the United States is having an impact. It is possible, when decisions are made among competing pro-posals for government funding (education, transportation, social security), that many Americans believe that people should take care of their own health insurance. Further, the American desire for individualism leads people to distrust programs that allow government agencies to tell them what they can and cannot do. Under a national health insurance policy, a government agency would become involved in decisions about health care, especially elective surgery. Government officials would have to interpret policies and tell people what medical care they can and cannot receive. Many individualists are very unhappy when they have to deal with government agencies that can place limits on their behavior.

Cultural differences also have an impact on the acceptance of inter-vention programs that are meant to address major social problems. Ilola (1990) analyzed the efforts of the Finnish government to encourage its citizens to adopt healthier lifestyles. In 1972, after seeing figures that Finland had one of the highest mortality rates due to cardiovascular diseases, leaders in the government instituted a number of programs.

There were programs established to treat hypertension, to discourage the consumption of foods high in fat (such as butter and cream), to reduce the number of people with the smoking habit, and to reduce alcohol consumption. For example, the government prevented the tobacco industry from advertising in the mass media or on billboards, and it established luxury taxes on cigarettes that made their use prohibitively expensive for many. The consumption of alcohol was discouraged through strict controls on sales and severe penalties for driving under the influence (DUI), including jail time and automatic loss of drivers' licenses. The key is that, in Finland compared to the United States, people are more likely to respect and to defer to the decisions of government leaders. In the United States, decisions about tobacco advertising can (and have) brought lawsuits concerned with restrictions on the freedom of speech. Decisions about the suspension of drivers' licenses will surely bring lawsuits concerned with the violation of people's constitutional rights. As Ilola (1990, p. 291) summarizes: "It is clear that health education efforts will be more successful in a culture such as Finland, where institutional intervention and support is viewed as positive and not a violation of individual rights or responsibilities." Research on how best to develop culturally appropriate intervention programs into problem areas, such as health, education, and worker productivity, will become a necessity rather than an academic luxury.

THE POTENTIAL FOR THE APPLICATION OF RESEARCH FINDINGS. This discussion of scarce resources and academic luxuries is closely related to an issue that is frequently discussed by researchers from less industrialized nations (e.g., Zaidi, 1979; Sinha, 1983). To be acceptable, research projects will have to be concerned with topics that have clear potential applications for the alleviation of social problems (Blowers & Turtle, 1987). There are simply not enough resources, such as money and the time of research collaborators from various cultures, to allow the pursuit of inquiry into theoretically interesting but practically unimportant topics. Given these statements, my purpose is not to draw a sharp distinction between theoretical and applied topics. Many times, researchers can investigate theoretically important topics as long as they link them to potential applications in which practitioners may be interested. In Chapter 4, for instance, the theoretically important work of Barbara Rogoff (1990) on guided participation was reviewed. This is an important concept for teachers as they develop tasks that build upon students' existing abilities. Further, knowledge of guided participation allows teachers to encourage students to improve their skills so that they can take on more difficult tasks as they move toward mastery of topics areas in which they are especially interested.

The need for attention to applied topics has also been recommended for researchers who are themselves citizens of less industrialized nations. Sinha (1983, p. 13) argues that there is a "need for certain attitudes and sensitivity, if [s]he is to be engaged in cross-cultural research. Apart from [his or her] general competence in the subject, [the investigator] has to be highly sensitive to the country's problems so that the research effort has some relevance to the national needs." In choosing research results for review in this book, I have leaned in the direction of studies that have potential for applications in such areas of education, work, health, culture change, and programs to encourage positive intercultural contact. I believe that such studies have many benefits. A knowledge of theory can guide the selection of concepts that can form the basis of intervention programs. In turn, theoretical advances are made if a concept can survive the test of application in the "real world" of scarce resources, competition for people's attention, and the presence of *other* concepts that can work against an intervention into social problems. Further, theoretical concepts can be sharpened when results based on their application are carefully examined. For example, the work of Kagitcibasi on home based schooling was reviewed in Chapter 5. Some of the concepts that guided the interventions were based on a knowledge of collectivism, which included mothers' concerns that success in Turkey's schools could lead to a distancing between children and parents. Despite scarce resources to put family programs into practice and the busy schedules of mothers and schoolchildren, the researchers found that programs to involve mothers had a number of benefits, including the mothers' realization that autonomy and family loyalty are not incompatible. The theoretical understanding of collectivism was also increased as researchers noted unexpected results, such as learning of new knowledge by the target children's younger siblings. This knowledge was learned as the younger children listened while on the fringes of sessions between researchers, mothers, and older children; and as part of post-session activities during which older children took the role of teacher and passed on what they had learned to their younger siblings.

WIDESPREAD DISCUSSIONS OF INTERCULTURAL INTERACTIONS.
If contact across cultural boundaries is to become commonplace, as predicted throughout this book, then people will discuss the benefits and difficulties of intercultural interactions among themselves. I hope that they will use a sophisticated set of concepts when so doing. I once asked a well-known physician, "What do you think is the major advance in medicine that has helped people over the last thirty years?" His response was, "the concept of blood pressure." In discussing his answer, he referred to people's knowledge about and use of this concept. Blood pressure is a concept that people can understand, can discuss, and can monitor in their own lives. If their blood pressure is too high, they can take steps to reduce it (e.g., reducing stress in their lives, modifying their diet). Developing a goal for blood pressure reduction also gives people a target to work toward over a period of time. Further, once people develop

an interest in their blood pressure, other targets for preventative health care, such as exercise, smoking cessation, and a low-fat diet, can be added to their changing lifestyles.

Cross-cultural research has led to insights that can assist people's discussions as they analyze the intercultural interactions in their lives. Covered throughout this book, and especially in Chapter 6 and Chapter 7, these concepts can help people put puzzling and difficult interactions into a clearer perspective. For example, people will always have a very difficult time avoiding the temptation to stereotype (Chapter 6). There are so many individuals that any one person meets and/or observes that it is necessary to form categories that capture a few key features of these individuals: all the conservatives, all the young women, all the Blacks, all the immigrants, and so forth. However, it is not necessary for people *to make decisions* about these individuals based on the stereotyped groupings into which they are placed (Fiske, et al., 1991). People can quite consciously stop themselves when they are tempted to make decisions based on stereotypes and can remind themselves that they should keep individuals in mind. For example, high school counselors can say, "I should not withhold recommendations concerning advanced math classes just because I am dealing with a young woman. I should examine her individual record, preparation, and goals to determine if advanced math is an option she should consider." Similarly, students can learn to avoid decision making based on stereotypes and look to individual interests and abilities as they invite classmates to join various academic, athletic, and social activities.

These goals are based on the assumption that people can learn about such concepts as "stereotypes" and "individual differences." I believe that this is a realistic possibility. Concepts, such as stereotypes, prejudice, and interaction style (Chapter 7) are no more difficult and complex than concepts such as blood pressure, cholesterol, and the fat content of one's diet. Concepts to help people analyze their intercultural interactions can be presented in the same places as concepts related to their health: in the mass media (e.g., Goleman, 1991), in high school and university level coursework, and in public outreach programs sponsored by colleges, government agencies, and community volunteer groups. As concepts dealing with intercultural interactions are discussed widely, a general tone of tolerance, understanding, and mutual enrichment will hopefully become the norm that people accept and disseminate. Again, there are parallels with health. In many parts of the United States today, smoking in public areas is no longer acceptable. Nonsmokers, concerned about *their* health, have been successful in setting the norm that smokers have to modify their behavior. Similarly, people concerned with positive intercultural interactions can set the norm that understanding and enrichment are reasonable goals and that intolerance will not be socially acceptable.

THE IMPORTANCE OF CULTURE IN THE STUDY OF HUMAN BEHAVIOR

As I mentioned in Chapter 9, I am delighted that various groups have insisted that more research attention be given to such issues as gender, ethnicity, and culture. In the past, different people have examined textbooks and have found that their authors describe the behavior of Caucasian males in an adequate manner, but that females, members of other ethnic groups, and people from different cultural backgrounds seem absent. A final prediction is that when authors contemplate writing a text, they will automatically be inclined to give attention to human diversity brought on by cultural, ethnic, and gender differences. The importance of these concepts will become so widely accepted that authors will not have to stop and make a point to integrate them into their writings. Terms such as "cross-cultural psychology" and "intercultural interactions" will become less commonly used since the analysis of human behavior will, of necessity, consider cultural influences.

REFERENCES

Aberle, D., Cohen, A., Davis, A., Levy, M., & Sutton, F. (1950). The functional prerequisites of a society. *Ethics*, 60, 100–111.

Abramson, P., & Imai-Marquez, J. (1982). The Japanese-American: A cross-cultural, cross-sectional study of sex guilt. *Journal of Research in Personality*, 16, 227–237.

Adler, N.A. (1991). *International dimensions of organization behavior* (2d ed.). Boston: PWS-Kent.

Ahia, C. (1984). Cross-cultural counseling concerns. *Personnel and Guidance Journal*, 62, 339–341.

Allport, G. (1954). *The nature of prejudice*. Reading, MA: Addison-Wesley.

Althen, G. (1984). *The handbook of foreign student advising*. Yarmouth, ME: Intercultural Press.

Altman, I., & Chemers, M.M. (1980). Cultural aspects of environment-behavior relationships. In H.C. Triandis & R.W. Brislin (Eds.), *Handbook of cross-cultural psychology* (Vol. 5, pp. 355–393). Boston: Allyn & Bacon.

Alzate, H. (1989). Sexual behavior of unmarried Colombian university students: A follow-up. *Archives of Sexual Behavior*, 18, 239–250.

Amir, Y. (1969). Contact hypothesis in ethnic relations. *Psychological Bulletin*, 71, 319–343.

Anastasi, A. (1988). *Psychological testing* (6th ed.). New York: Macmillan.

Anderson, C., & Bowman, M. (1965). *Education and economic development*. London: Frank Cass.

Arbeiter, S. (1984). *Profiles, college-bound seniors, 1984*. New York: College Entrance Examination Board.

Argyle, M., Furnham, A., & Graham, J. (1981). *Social situations*. Cambridge: Cambridge University Press.

Aronson, E., & Osherow, N. (1980). Cooperation, prosocial behavior, and academic performance: Experiments in the desegregated classroom. In L. Bickman (Ed.), *Applied social psychology annual*. Beverly Hills, CA: Sage.

Arsenault, R. (1989). Air-conditioning. In C.R. Wilson & W. Ferris (Eds.), *Encyclopedia of Southern culture* (pp. 321–323). Chapel Hill, NC: University of North Carolina Press.

Ashmore, R. (1970). Prejudice: Causes and cures. In B. Collins, *Social psychology* (pp. 245–296). Reading, MA: Addison-Wesley.

Atkinson, D., Morten, G., & Sue, D. (1989). Minority group counseling: An overview. In D. Atkinson, G. Morten & D. Sue (Eds.), *Counseling American minorities: A cross-cultural perspective* (pp. 11–34). Dubuque, IA: William C. Brown.

Ayman, R., & Chemers, M. (1983). Relationship of supervisory behavior ratings to work group effectiveness and subordinate satisfaction among Iranian managers. *Journal of Applied Psychology*, 68, 388–341.

Baird, I., Lyles, M., & Wharton, R. (1990). Attitudinal differences between American and Chinese managers regarding joint ventures management. *Management International Review*, 30(special issue), 53–68.

Bandura, A. (1986). *Social foundations of thought and action: A social-cognitive view*. Englewood Cliffs, NJ: Prentice-Hall.

Bandura, A. (1989). Human agency in social cognitive theory. *American Psychologist*, 44, 1175–1184.

Barna, L. (1983). The stress factor in intercultural relations. In D. Landis & R. Brislin (Eds.), *Handbook of intercultural training, vol. 2: Issues in training methodology* (pp. 19–49). Elmsford, NY: Pergamon.

Barraclough, B. (1987). Sex ratio of juvenile suicide. *Journal of the American Academy of Child and Adolescent Psychology*, 26, 434–435.

Barry, H., Bacon, M., & Child, I. (1957). A cross-cultural survey of some sex differences in socialization. *Journal of Abnormal and Social Psychology*, 55, 327–332.

Barry, H., & Child, I. (1983). Cultural variations in motivational satisfactions for men and women. *Behavior Science Research*, 18, 306–322.

Bass, B., & Stogdill, R. (1989). *The handbook of leadership* (3d ed.). New York: Free Press.

Bassett, M., & Mhloyi, M. (1991). Women & AIDS in Zimbabwe: The making of an epidemic. *International Journal of Health Services*, 21, 143–156.

Basso, K. (1970). "To give up on words": Silence in Western Apache culture. *Southwestern Journal of Anthropology*, 26, 213–230.

Bastien, J. (1987). Cross-cultural communication between doctors and peasants in Bolivia. *Social Science and Medicine*, 24, 1109–1118.

Befus, C. (1988). A multilevel treatment approach for culture shock experienced by sojourners. *International Journal of Intercultural Relations*, 12, 381–400.

Belle, D. (1990). Poverty and women's health. *American Psychologist*, 45, 385–439.

Bellisari, A. (1989). Male superiority in mathematical aptitude: An artifact. *Human Organization*, 48, 273–279.

Berry, J. (1969). On cross-cultural comparability. *International Journal of Psychology*, 4, 119–128.

Berry, J. (1979). A cultural ecology of social behavior. In L. Berkowitz (Ed.), *Advances in experimental social psychology* (Vol. 12, pp. 177–207). New York: Academic Press.

Berry, J. (1984). Towards a universal psychology of cognitive competence. *International Journal of Psychology*, 19, 335–361.

Berry, J. (1990). Psychology of acculturation: Understanding individuals moving between cultures. In R. Brislin (Ed.), *Applied cross-cultural psychology* (pp. 232–253). Newbury Park, CA: Sage.

Berry, J., Poortinga, Y., Segall, M., & Dasen, P. (1992). *Cross-cultural psychology: Research and applications*. Cambridge and New York: Cambridge University Press.

Bhawuk, D.P.S. (1989). Cross-cultural sensitivity and its relation to individualism and collectivism. Unpublished master's thesis, College of Business Administration, University of Hawaii, Honolulu, Hawaii.

Bhawuk, D.P.S. (1990). Cross-cultural orientation programs. In R. Brislin (Ed.), *Applied cross-cultural psychology* (pp. 325–346). Newbury Park, CA: Sage.

Biernat, M. (1991). Gender stereotypes and the relationship between masculinity and femininity: A developmental analysis. *Journal of Personality and Social Psychology*, 61, 351–365.

Biernat, M., & Wortman, C. (1991). Sharing of home responsibilities between professionally employed women and their husbands. *Journal of Personality and Social Psychology*, 60, 844–860.

Black, J. (1990). The relationship of personal characteristics with the adjustment of Japanese expatriate managers. *Management International Review*, 30, 119–134.

Block, J. (1983). Differential premises arising from differential socialization of the sexes: Some conjectures. *Child Development*, 54, 1335–1354.

Block, J., Gjerde, P., & Block, J. (1991). Personality antecedents of depressive tendencies in 18-year-olds: A prospective study. *Journal of Personality and Social Psychology*, 60, 726–738.

Blowers, G., & Turtle, A. (Eds.). (1987). *Psychology moving East*. Sydney, NSW, Australia: Sydney University Press.

Bobo, L. (1983). Whites' opposition to busing: Symbolic racism or realistic group conflict? *Journal of Personality and Social Psychology*, 45, 1196–1210.

Bock, P. (Ed.). (1970). *Culture shock: A reader in modern cultural anthropology*. New York: Knopf.

Bocker, H., & Overgaard, H. (1982). Structuring quality circles: A management challenge to combat ailing productivity. *Leadership and Organization Development Journal*, 3(5), 17–29.

Bond, M. (Ed.). (1986). *The psychology of the Chinese people*. New York: Oxford.

Bond, M. (1991). Chinese values and health: A cultural level examination. *Psychology and Health*, 5, 137–152.

Bond, M., Wan, K., Leung, K., & Giacalone, R. (1985). How are responses to verbal insults related to cultural collectivism and power distance? *Journal of Cross-Cultural Psychology*, 16, 111–127.

Boyd, J.H., & Weissman, M.M. (1981). Epidemiology of affective disorders. A reexamination and future directions. *Archives of General Psychiatry*, 38, 1039–1046.

Braithwaite, C. (1990). Communicative silence: A cross-cultural study of Basso's hypothesis. In D. Carbaugh (Ed.), *Cultural communication and intercultural contact* (pp. 321–327). Hillsdale, NJ: Lawrence Erlbaum.

Braunwald, S., & Brislin, R. (1979a). The diary method updated. In E. Ochs & B. Schieffelin (Eds.), *Developmental pragmatics* (pp. 21–42). New York: Academic Press.

Braunwald, S., & Brislin, R. (1979b). On being understood: The listener's contribution to the toddler's ability to communicate. In P. French (Ed.), *The development of meaning* (pp. 71–113). Hiroshima Japan: Bunka Hyoran Publishing Co.

Brewer, M. (1979). Ingroup bias in the minimal intergroup situation: A cognitive-motivational analysis. *Psychological Bulletin*, 86, 307–324.

Brewer, M., & Miller, N. (1984). Beyond the contact hypothesis: Theoretical perspective on desegregation. In N. Miller & M. Brewer (Eds.), *Groups in contact: The psychology of desegregation* (pp. 281–302). Orlando, FL: Academic Press.

Brislin, R. (1970). Back-translation for cross-cultural research. *Journal of Cross-Cultural Psychology*, 1, 185–216.

Brislin, R. (1978). Structured approaches to dealing with prejudice and intercultural misunderstanding. *International Journal of Group Tensions*, 8, 33–48.

Brislin, R. (1980). Translation and content analysis of oral and written materials. In H. Triandis & J. Berry (Eds.), *Handbook of cross-cultural psychology, vol. 2: Methodology* (pp. 389–444). Boston: Allyn & Bacon.

Brislin, R. (1981). *Cross-cultural encounters: Face-to-face interaction*. Elmsford, NY: Pergamon.

Brislin, R. (1984). Cross-cultural psychology. In R. Corsini (Ed.), *Encyclopedia of psychology*, Vol. 1 (pp. 319–327). New York: John Wiley.

Brislin, R. (1986). The wording and translation of research instruments. In W. Lonner & J. Berry (Eds.), *Field methods in cross-cultural research* (pp. 137–164). Newbury Park, CA: Sage.

Brislin, R. (1986). Prejudice and intergroup communication. In W. Gudykunst (Ed.), *Intergroup communication* (pp. 74–85). London & Baltimore: Edward Arnold.

Brislin, R. (1988). Increasing awareness of class, ethnicity, culture, and race by expanding on students' own experiences. In I. Cohen (Ed.), *The G. Stanley Hall Lecture Series*, Vol. 8 (pp. 137–180). Washington, DC: American Psychological Association.

Brislin, R. (1989). Intercultural communication training. In M. Asante & W. Gudykunst (Eds.), *Handbook of international and intercultural communication* (pp. 441–457). Newbury Park, CA: Sage.

Brislin, R. (1991). *The art of getting things done: A practical guide to the use of power*. New York: Praeger.

Brislin, R., Cushner, C., Cherrie, C., & Yong, M. (1986). *Intercultural interactions: A practical guide*. Newbury Park, CA: Sage.

Brislin, R., & Hui, C.H. (1992, forthcoming). The preparation of managers for overseas assignments: The case of China. In O. Shenkar & N.L. Kelley (Eds.), *International business in China*. London: Routledge.

Brislin, R., & Keating, C. (1976). Cultural differences in the perception of a three-dimensional Ponzo illusion. *Journal of Cross-Cultural Psychology*, 7, 397–411.

Brislin, R., Landis, D., & Brandt, E. (1983). Conceptualizations of intercultural behavior and training. In D. Landis & R. Brislin (Eds.), *Handbook of intercultural training, vol. 1: Issues in theory and design* (pp. 1–35). Elmsford, NY: Pergamon.

Brislin, R., Lonner, W., & Thorndike, R. (1973). *Cross-cultural research methods*. New York: Wiley.

Brislin, R., & Pedersen, P. (1976). *Cross-cultural orientation programs*. New York: Wiley/Halsted.

Broaddus, D. (1986). Use of a culture-general assimilator in intercultural training. Unpublished doctoral dissertation, Indiana State University, Terre Haute, Indiana.

Brophy, W. (1989). Defense of segregation. In C.R. Wilson & W. Ferris (Eds.), *Encyclopedia of Southern Culture* (pp. 1176–1178). Chapel Hill, NC: University of North Carolina Press.

Burg, B., & Belmont, I. (1990). Mental abilities of children from different cultural backgrounds in Israel. *Journal of Cross-Cultural Psychology*, 21, 90–108.

Buriel, R. (1983). Teacher–student interactions and their relationship to student achievement: A comparison of Mexican-American and Anglo-American children. *Journal of Educational Psychology*, 75, 889–897.

Burnam, M.A., Telles, C.A., Karno, M., Hough, R., et al. (1987). Measurement of acculturation in a community population of Mexican Americans. *Hispanic Journal of Behavioral Sciences*, 9, 105–139.

Burns, A., & Homel, R. (1986). Sex role satisfaction among Australian children: Some sex, age, and cultural group comparisons. *Psychology of Women Quarterly*, 10, 285–296.

Buss, D. (1989). Sex differences in human mate preference: Evolutionary hypotheses tested in 37 cultures. *Behavior and Brain Sciences*, 12, 1–49.

Buss, D. (1991). Evolutionary personality psychology. *Annual Review of Psychology*, 42, 459–491.

Buss, D., Abbot, M., Angeleitner, A., Asherian, A., et al. (1990). International preferences in selecting mates: A study of 37 cultures. *Journal of Cross-Cultural Psychology*, 21, 5–47.

Buss, D.M., & Barnes, M.F. (1986). Preferences in human mate selection. *Journal of Personality and Social Psychology*, 50, 559–570.

Callan, H. (1970). *Ethology and society: Toward an anthropological view*. Oxford: Clarendon Press.

Campbell, D. (1964). Distinguishing differences in perception failures of communication in cross-cultural studies. In F. Northrop & H. Livingston (Eds.), *Cross-cultural understanding: Epistemology in anthropology*. New York: Harper & Row.

Campion, J. (1982). Young Asian children with learning and behaviour problems: A family therapy approach. *Journal of Family Therapy*, 4, 153–163.

Carbaugh, D. (Ed.). (1990a). *Cultural communication and intercultural contact*. Hillsdale, NJ: Erlbaum.

Carbaugh, D. (1990b). Toward a perspective on cultural communication and intercultural contact. *Semiotica*, 80, 15–35.

Carden, A., & Feicht, R. (1991). Homesickness among American and Turkish college students. *Journal of Cross-Cultural Psychology*, 22, 418–428.

Carson, R. (1989). Personality. *Annual Review of Psychology*, 40, 227–248.

Cashmore, J.A., & Goodnow, J.L. (1986). Influence of Australian parents' values: Ethnicity versus socioeconomic status. *Journal of Cross-Cultural Psychology*, 17, 441–454.

Chaika, E. (1989). *Language: The social mirror*. New York: Newbury House.

Chang, D. (1989). "Heaven is high, and the emperor is far away." *Harvard Business Review*, 67(6), 33–36.

Chaplin, W., John, O., & Goldberg, L. (1988). Conceptions of states and traits: Dimensional attributes with ideals as prototypes. *Journal of Personality and Social Psychology*, 54, 541–547.

Cheng, Y., & Lee, P. (1988). Illness behaviour in Chinese medical students. *Psychologia: An International Journal of Psychology in the Orient*, 31, 207–216.

Chernin, D. (1990). An American learns to work in Japan. *World Monitor*, 3(7), 50–56.

Chesanow, N. (1985). *The world-class executive*. New York: Rawson.

Chick, J. (1990). The interactional accomplishments of discrimination in South Africa. In D. Carbaugh (Ed.), *Cultural communication and intercultural contact* (pp. 225–252). Hillsdale, NJ: Erlbaum.

Child, I.L. (1954). Socialization. In G. Lindzey (Ed.), *Handbook of social psychology* (Vol. 2) (pp. 665–692). Cambridge, MA: Addison-Wesley.

Chiles, J., Strosahl, K., Ping, Z., Michael, M., et al. (1989). Depression, hopelessness, and suicidal behavior in Chinese and American psychiatric patients. *The American Journal of Psychiatry*, 146, 339–344.

Chinese Culture Connection. (1987). Chinese values and the search for culture-free dimensions of culture. *Journal of Cross-Cultural Psychology*, 18, 143–164.

Chodorow, N. (1974). Family structure and feminine personality. In M.Z. Rosaldo & L. Lamphere (Eds.), *Women, culture and society*. Stanford, CA: Stanford University Press.

Christopher, R. (1983). *The Japanese mind*. New York: Fawcett Columbine.

Cialdini, R. (1990). Personal communication. Arizona State University, Tempe, AZ.

Clark, C., & Clark, J. (1987). The gender gap in Yugoslavia: Elite versus mass levels. *Political Psychology*, 8, 411–426.

Clement, U. (1989). Profile analysis as a method of comparing inter-generational differences in sexual behavior. *Archives of Sexual Behavior*, 18, 229–237.

Cockerham, W., Kunz, G., & Lueschen, G. (1988). Social stratification and health lifestyle in two systems of health care delivery: A comparison of the United States and West Germany. *Journal of Health and Social Behavior*, 29, 113–126.

Cole, M., Gay, J., Glick, J.A., & Sharp, D.W. (1971). *The cultural context of learning and thinking*. New York: Basic Books.

Cole, M., & Scribner, S. (1974). *Culture and thought: A psychological introduction*. New York: John Wiley.

Collier, C., & Collier, J. (1986). *Decision in Philadelphia: The Constitutional Convention of 1787*. New York: Random House.

Cook, S.W. (1969). Motives in a conceptual analysis of attitude-related behavior. In W.J. Arnold & D. Levine (Eds.), *Nebraska symposium on motivation*. Lincoln: University of Nebraska Press.

Crick, B. (1982). *In defense of politics* (2d ed.). New York: Penguin.

Crittenden, K., & Lamug, C. (1988). Causal attribution and depression: A friendly refinement based on Philippine data. *Journal of Cross-Cultural Psychology*, 19, 216–231.

Crosby, F., Bromley, S., & Saxe, L. (1980). Recent unobtrusive studies of black and white discrimination and prejudice: A literature review. *Psychological Bulletin*, 87, 546–563.

Crowne, D., & Marlowe, D. (1964). *The approval motive*. New York: Wiley.

Cui, G., & Van Den Berg, S. (1991). Testing the construct validity of intercultural effectiveness. *International Journal of Intercultural Relations*, 15, 227–241.

Cummins, J. (1976). The influence of bilingualism on cognitive growth: A synthesis of research findings and explanatory hypothesis. *Working Papers on Bilingualism*, 9, 1–43.

Cushner, K. (1989). Assessing the impact of a culture-general assimilator. *International Journal of Intercultural Relations*, 13, 125–146.

Cushner, K. (1990). Cross-cultural psychology and the formal classroom. In R. Brislin (Ed.), *Applied cross-cultural psychology* (pp. 98–120). Newbury Park, CA: Sage.

Cushner, K., McClelland, A., & Safford, P. (1992). *Human diversity in education: An integrative approach*. New York: McGraw-Hill.

Damen, L. (1987). *Culture learning: The fifth dimension in the language classroom*. Reading, MA: Addison-Wesley.

Dane, F. (1990). *Research methods*. Pacific Grove, CA: Brooks/Cole.

Dasen, P. (1984). The cross-cultural study of intelligence: Piaget and the Baoule. *International Journal of Psychology*, 19, 407–434.

Dasen, P., & Heron, A. (1981). Cross-cultural tests of Piaget's theory. In H.C. Triandis & A. Heron (Eds.), *Handbook of cross-cultural psychology: Vol. 4: Developmental psychology* (pp. 295–342). Boston: Allyn & Bacon.

Davies, J. (1985). Why are women not where the power is? An examination of the maintenance of power elites. *Management Education and Development*, 16, 278–288.

Daws, G. (1977). Looking at islanders: European ways of thinking about Polynesians in the eighteenth and nineteenth centuries. In R. Brislin (Ed.), *Culture learning: Concepts, applications, and research* (pp. 176–181). Honolulu, HI: University of Hawaii Press.

Day, R., Nielsen, J., Korten, A., Ernberg, G., et al. (1987). Stressful life events preceding the onset of schizophrenia: A cross-national study from the World Health Organization. *Culture, Medicine, and Psychiatry*, 11, 123–205.

DeMente, B. (1989). *The Japanese influence on America*. Lincolnwood, IL: Passport Books.

Deregowski, J.B. (1980). Perception. In H.C. Triandis & W.J. Lonner (Eds.), *Handbook of cross-cultural psychology: Vol. 3: Basic processes* (pp. 21–115). Boston: Allyn & Bacon.

Detweiler, R., Brislin, R., & McCormack, W. (1983). Situational analysis. In D. Landis & R. Brislin (Eds.), *Handbook of intercultural training, vol. 2: Issues in training methodology* (pp. 100–123). Elmsford, NY: Pergamon.

Deutsch, M., & Collins, M. (1951). *Interracial housing: A psychological evaluation of a social experiment*. Minneapolis: University of Minnesota Press.

Devine, P., Monteith, M., Zuwerink, J., & Elliot, A. (1991). Prejudice with and without compunction. *Journal of Personality and Social Psychology*, 60, 817–830.

Dichtl, E., Koeglmayr, H.G., & Mueller, S. (1990). International orientation as a precondition for export success. *Journal of International Business Studies*, 21, 23–40.

Diekstra, R. (1989). Suicidal behavior and depressive disorders in adolescents and young adults. *Neuropsychobiology*, 22, 194–207.

Doherty, J., & Obani, T. (1986). The development of concepts of handicap in adolescence: A cross-cultural study: III. *Educational Studies*, 12, 291–311.

Dorn, P. (1986). Gender and person level: Turkish Jewish proverbs and the politics of reputation. *Women's Studies International Forum*, 9, 295–301.

Draguns, J. (1973). Comparison of psychopathology across cultures: Issues, findings, directions. *Journal of Cross-Cultural Psychology*, 4, 9–47.

Draguns, J. (1975). Resocialization into culture: The complexities of taking a worldwide view of psychotherapy. In R. Brislin, S.

Bochner, & W. Lonner (Eds.), *Cross-cultural perspective on learning* (pp. 273–289). Beverly Hills, CA: Sage.

Draguns, J. (1990). Applications of cross-cultural psychology in the field of mental health. In R. Brislin (Ed.), *Applied cross-cultural psychology* (pp. 302–324). Newbury Park, CA: Sage.

Dutton, D. (1976). Tokenism, reverse discrimination, and egalitarianism in interracial behavior. *Journal of Social Issues*, 32(2), 93–107.

Eagly, A. (1987). *Sex differences in social behavior: A social role interpretation.* Hillsdale, NJ: Erlbaum.

Earley, P. (1980). Social loafing and collectivism: A comparison of the United States and the People's Republic of China. *Administrative Science Quarterly*, 34, 565–581.

Earley, P., & Stubblebine, P. (1989). Intercultural assessment of performance feedback. *Group and Organizational Studies*, 14, 161–181.

Egeland, J.A., & Hostetter, A.M. (1983). Amish study: I. Affective disorders among the Amish. *American Journal of Psychiatry*, 140, 56–61.

Ehrenhaus, P. (1983). Culture and the attribution process. In W. Gudykunst (Ed.), *Intercultural communication theory*. Newbury Park, CA: Sage.

Ekman, P., & Friesen, W.V. (1975). *Unmasking the face: A guide to recognizing emotions from facial clues*. Englewood Cliffs, NJ: Prentice-Hall.

Elms, A. (1972). *Social psychology and social relevance*. Boston: Little, Brown.

Engelhard, G. (1990). Gender differences in performance on mathematics items: Evidence from the United States and Thailand. *Contemporary Educational Psychology*, 15, 13–26.

England, J. (1986). Cross-cultural health care. *Canada's Mental Health*, 34(4), 13–15.

Erlanger, S. (1991). A plague awaits. *New York Times Magazine* (July 14), pp. 24–26, 49–53.

Escobar, J., Gomez, J., & Tuason, V. (1983). Depressive phenomenology in North and South American patients. *American Journal of Psychiatry*, 140, 47–51.

Etzion, D., & Pines, A. (1986). Sex and culture in burnout and coping among human service professionals: A social psychological perspective. *Journal of Cross-Cultural Psychology*, 17, 191–209.

Ezelio, B. (1983). Age, sex, and self concepts in a Nigerian population. *International Journal of Behavioral Development*, 6, 497–502.

Fausto-Sterling, A. (1985). *Myths of gender: Biological theories about men and women*. New York: Basic Books.

"Feeding frenzy." (1991). *Newsweek*, Vol 117(21), May 27, 46–53.

Feldman, S., & Rosenthal, D. (1990). The acculturation of autonomy expectations in Chinese high schoolers residing in two Western nations. *International Journal of Psychology*, 25, 259–281.

Ferris, G., & Wagner, J. (1985). Quality circles in the United States: A conceptual reevaluation. *Journal of Applied Behavioral Science*, 21, 155–167.

Fiedler, F.E. (1967). *A theory of leadership effectiveness*. New York: McGraw-Hill.

Fiedler, F.E., & Garcia, J.E. (1987). *New approaches to leadership: Cognitive resources and organizational performance*. New York: Wiley.

Fiske, A. (1991). *Structures of social life*. New York: Free Press.

Fiske, S., Bersoff, D., Borgida, E., Deaux, K., & Heilman, M. (1991). Social science research on trial: Use of sex stereotyping research in *Price Waterhouse v. Hopkins*. *American Psychologist*, 46, 1049–1060.

Flavell, J.H. (1963). *The developmental psychology of Jean Piaget*. Princeton, NJ: Van Nostrand.

Fleming, A. (1985–1986). Sex differences and cross-cultural studies. *Women and Therapy*, 4, 23–32.

Foa, U., & Chemers, M. (1967). The significance of role behavior for cross-cultural interaction training. *International Journal of Psychology*, 2, 45–57.

Fontaine, G. (1990). Cultural diversity in intimate intercultural relationships. In D. Cahn (Ed.), *Intimates in conflict: A communication perspective* (pp. 209–224). Hillsdale, NJ: Lawrence Erlbaum.

Freed, R., & Freed, S. (1981). Enculturation and education in Shanti Nagar. *Anthropological papers of the American Museum of Natural History*, Vol 57, Part 2. New York: American Museum of Natural History.

Freiberg, P. (1991). Surprise: Most bosses are incompetent. *The American Psychological Association Monitor*, 22(1 January), 23.

Friday, R. (1989). Contrasts in discussion behaviors of German and American managers. *International Journal of Intercultural Relations*, 13, 429–446.

Fuchs, J., Levinson, R., Stoddard, R., Mullet, M., & Jones, D. (1990). Health risk factors among the Amish: Results of a survey. *Health Education Quarterly*, 17, 197–211.

Fugita, S., & Crittenden, K. (1990). Towards culture- and population-specific norms for self-reported depressive symptomatology (Korea, the Philippines, Taiwan, and the United States). *The International Journal of Social Psychiatry*, 36, 83–92.

Funder, D., & Colvin, C.R. (1991). Explorations in behavioral consistency: Properties of persons, situations, and behaviors. *Journal of Personality and Social Psychology*, 60, 773–794.

Furnham, A., & Bochnner, S. (1986). *Culture shock: Psychological reaction to unfamiliar environments*. London & New York: Methuen.

Gabrenya, W., Wang, Y., & Latane, B. (1985). Social loafing on an optimizing task: Cross-cultural differences among Chinese and Americans. *Journal of Cross-Cultural Psychology*, 16, 223–242.

Gaertner, S., & Dovidio, J. (1986). The aversive form of racism. In J. Dovidio & S. Gaertner (Eds.), *Prejudice, discrimination, and racism* (pp. 61–89). San Diego: Academic Press.

Garber, H.L. (1988). *The Milwaukee Project: Preventing mental retardation in children at risk*. Washington, DC: American Association on Mental Retardation.

Garcia-Coll, C. (1990). Developmental outcome of minority infants: A process-oriented look at our beginnings. *Child Development*, 61, 270–289.

Gardner, H. (1985). *The mind's new science: The history of the cognitive revolution*. New York: Basic Books.

Gaskins, S., & Lucy, J. (1987). The role of children in the production of adult culture. A Yucatec case. Paper presented at the meetings of the American Ethnological Society, San Antonio, Texas.

Gaylord-Ross, R. (1987). Vocational integration for persons with mental handicaps: A cross-cultural perspective. *Research in Development Disabilities*, 8, 531–548.

Georgie-Hyde, D.M. (1970). *Piaget and conceptual development*. London: Holt, Rinehart and Winston.

Gerver, D., & Sinaiko, H.W. (Eds.). (1978). *Language interpretation and communication*. New York: Plenum.

Gilbert, D., & Kahl, J.A. (1982). *The American class structure: A new synthesis*. Homewood, IL: Dorsey.

Gilbert, M.J., & Cervantes, R. (1986). Patterns and practices of alcohol use among Mexican Americans: A comprehensive review. *Hispanic Journal of Behavioral Sciences*, 8, 1–60.

Gim, R., Atkinson, D., & Kim, S. (1991). Asian–American acculturation, counselor ethnicity and cultural sensitivity, and ratings of counselors. *Journal of Counseling Psychology*, 38, 57–62.

Ginsburg, H.P., & Opper, S. (1969). *Piaget's theory of intellectual development: An introduction*. Englewood Cliffs, NJ: Prentice-Hall.

Glaser, W. (1978). *The brain drain*. New York: Pergamon.

Glickman, H. (1983). *Basic psychology*. New York: Norton.

Golding, J., & Baezconde-Garbanati, L. (1990). Ethnicity, culture, and social resources. *American Journal of Community Psychology*, 18, 465–486.

Golding, J., & Karno, M. (1988). Gender differences in depressive symptoms among Mexican Americans and non-Hispanic whites. *Hispanic Journal of Behavioral Sciences*, 10, 1–19.

Golding, J., Karno, M., & Rutter, C. (1990). Symptoms of major depression among Mexican–American and non–Hispanic whites. *American Journal of Psychiatry*, 147, 861–866.

Goldstein, M., & Segall, M. (1983). *Aggression in global perspective*. Elmsford, NY: Pergamon.

Goleman, D. (1991). "New way to battle bias: Fight acts, not feeling." *New York Times*, July 16, pp. B1, B9.

Gough, H.G. (1969). *California Psychological Inventory*. Palo Alto, CA: Consulting Psychologists Press.

Greenfield, P.M. (1984). A theory of the teacher in the learning activities of everyday life. In B. Rogoff & J. Lave (Eds.), *Everyday cognition* (pp. 117–138). Cambridge: Harvard University Press.

Greenfield, P.M., & Lave, J. (1982). Cognitive aspects of formal education. In D.A. Wagner & H.W. Stevenson (Eds.), *Cultural perspectives on child development* (pp. 181–207). San Francisco: W.H. Freeman.

Guarnaccia, P., Good, B., & Kleinman, A. (1990). A critical review of epidemiological studies of Puerto Rican mental health. *American Journal of Psychiatry*, 147, 1449–1456.

Gudykunst, W., & Hammer, M. (1983). Basic training design: Approaches to intercultural training. In D. Landis & R. Brislin (Eds.), *Handbook of intercultural training, Vol. 1: Issues in theory and design* (pp. 118–154). Elmsford, NY: Pergamon.

Gudykunst, W., & Hammer, M. (1988). Strangers and hosts. In Y.Y. Kim & W. Gudykunst (Eds.), *Cross-cultural adaptation* (pp. 106–139). Newbury Park, CA: Sage.

Gudykunst, W., & Kim, Y. (1984). *Communicating with strangers: An approach to intercultural communication*. Reading, MA: Addison-Wesley.

Gudykunst, W., & Nishida, T. (1989). Theoretical perspectives for studying intercultural communication. In M. Asante & W. Gudykunst (Eds.), *Handbook of international and intercultural communication* (pp. 17–46). Newbury Park, CA: Sage.

Guthrie, G., & Lonner, W. (1986). Assessment of personality and psychopathology. In W. Lonner & J. Berry (Eds.), *Field methods in cross-cultural research* (pp. 231–264). Newbury Park, CA: Sage.

Hadiyono, J., & Kahn, M. (1985). Personality differences and sex similarities in American and Indonesian college students. *Journal of Social Psychology*, 125, 703–708.

Hakuta, K. (1986). *Mirror of language: The debate on bilingualism*. New York: Basic Books.

Hall, E. (1959). *The silent language*. Garden City, NY: Doubleday.

Hall, E. (1966). *The hidden dimension*. Garden City, NY: Doubleday.

Hall, E. (1976). *Beyond culture*. Garden City, NY: Anchor.

Hamilton, V. L., Blumenfeld, P., Akoh, H., & Miura, K. (1991). Group and gender in Japanese and American elementary classrooms. *Journal of Cross-Cultural Psychology*, 22, 317–346.

Hammer, M. (1989). Intercultural communication competence. In M. Asante & W. Gudykunst (Eds.), *Handbook of international and intercultural communication* (pp. 247–260). Newbury Park, CA: Sage.

Hammer, M.R., Gudykunst, W.B., & Wiseman, R.L. (1978). Dimensions of intercultural effectiveness: An exploratory study. *International Journal of Intercultural Relations*, 2, 382–392.

Harari, H., Jones, C., & Sek, H. (1988). Stress syndromes and stress predictors in American and Polish college students. *Journal of Cross-Cultural Psychology*, 19, 243–255.

Hare-Mustin, R., & Marecek, J. (1988). The meaning of differences: Gender theory, postmodernism, and psychology. *American Psychologist*, 43, 455–464.

Harris, J.G. (1973). A science of the South Pacific: An analysis of the character structure of the Peace Corp volunteer. *American Psychologist*, 28, 232–247.

Hatfield, E., & Sprecher, S. (1986). *Mirror, mirror... The importance of looks in everyday life*. Albany: State University of New York Press.

Hawes, F., & Kealey, D.J. (1981). An empirical study of Canadian technical assistance. *International Journal of Intercultural Relations*, 5, 239–258.

Headland, T., Pike, K., & Harris, M. (Eds.). (1990). *Emics and etics: The insider/outsider debate*. Newbury Park, CA: Sage.

"Health guide." (1991). *U.S. News and World Report*, vol. 110(19), May 20, 68–99.

Heath, S. (1983). *Ways with words: Language, life, and work in communities and classroom*. Cambridge: Cambridge University Press.

Heber, R., & Garber, H. (1975). The Milwaukee Project: A study of the use of family intervention to prevent cultural-familial mental retardation. In B.Z. Friedlander, G.M. Sterrit, and G.E. Kirk (Eds.), *Exceptional infant: Vol. 3: Assessment and intervention*. New York: Brunner/Mazel.

Henderson, M., & Argyle, M. (1986). The informal rules of working relationships. *Journal of Occupational Behaviour*, 7, 259–275.

Hendrix, L., & Johnson, G.D. (1985). Instrumental and expressive socialization: A false dichotomy. *Sex Roles*, 13, 581–595.

Herskovits, M. (1948). *Man and his works*. New York: Knopf.

Hess, R., Azuma, H., Kashiwaga, K., Dickson, W., Nagano, S., Holloway, S., Miyake, K., Price, G., Hatano, G., & McDevitt, T. (1986). Family influence on school readiness and achievement in Japan and the United States: An overview of a longitudinal study. In H. Stevenson, H. Azuma, & K. Hakuta (Eds.), *Child development and education in Japan*. New York: Freeman.

Hess, R., & Street, E. (1991). The effect of acculturation on the relationship of counselor ethnicity and client ratings. *Journal of Counseling Psychology*, 38, 71–75.

Hess, R.D., Chang, C.M., & McDevitt, T.M. (1987). Cultural variations in family beliefs about children's performance in mathematics: Comparisons among People's Republic of China, Chinese-American, and Caucasian-American families. *Journal of Educational Psychology*, 79, 179–188.

Higgins, E.T., & Bargh, J. (1987). Social cognition and social perception. *Annual Review of Psychology*, 38, 369–425.

Hijirida, K., & Yoshikawa, M. (1987). *Japanese language and culture for business and travel*. Honolulu: University of Hawaii Press.

Hilton, J., & von Hippel, W. (1990). The role of consistency in the judgment of stereotype-relevant behaviors. *Personality and Social Psychology Bulletin*, 16, 430–448.

Hofstede, G. (1980). *Culture's consequences: International differences in work-related values*. Newbury Park, CA: Sage.

Hofstede, G. (1986). Cultural differences in teaching and learning. *International Journal of Intercultural Relations*, 10, 301–320.

Hofstede, G. (1991). *Cultures and organizations: Software of the mind*. London: McGraw-Hill.

Hofstede, G., & Bond, M.H. (1988). Confucius & economic growth: New trends in culture's consequences. *Organizational Dynamics*, 16(4), 4–21.

Holland, D., & Eisenhart, M. (1988). Moments of discontent: University women and the gender status quo. *Anthropology and Education Quarterly*, 19, 115–138.

Hollander, E. (1985). Leadership and power. In G. Lindzey & E. Aronson (Eds.), *The handbook of social psychology*, 3d ed., vol. 2 (pp. 485–537). New York: Random House.

Holton, R. (1990). Human resource management in the People's Republic of China. *Management International Review*, 30(Special Issue), 121–136.

Hopkins, B., & Westra, T. (1989). Material expectations of their infants' development: Some cultural differences. *Developmental Medicine and Child Neurology*, 31, 384–390.

Howard, G. (1991). Culture tales: A narrative approach to thinking, cross-cultural psychology, and psychotherapy. *American Psychologist*, 46, 187–197.

Hsia, J. (1988). Limits on affirmative action: Asian American access to higher education. *Educational Policy*, 2, 117–136.

Hsu, F.L.K. (1981). *American and Chinese: Passage to differences* (3d ed.). Honolulu, HI: University of Hawaii Press.

Hubbard, R. (1990). *The politics of women's biology*. New Brunswick: Rutgers University Press.

Hudson, R. (1981). Some issues on which linguists can agree. *Journal of Linguistics*, 17, 333–343.

Hui, C.H. (1990). Work attitudes, leadership styles, and managerial behaviors in different cultures. In R. Brislin (Ed.), *Applied cross-cultural psychology* (pp. 186–208). Newbury Park, CA: Sage.

Hui, C.H., & Triandis, H. (1985). Measurement in cross-cultural psychology: A review and comparison of strategies. *Journal of Cross-Cultural Psychology*, 16(2), 131–152.

Hunter, S. (1990). Levels of health development: A new tool for comparative research and policy formulation. *Social Science and Medicine*, 31, 433–444.

Hyde, J., Fennema, E., & Lamon, S. (1990). Gender differences in mathematics performance: A meta-analysis. *Psychological Bulletin*, 107, 139–155.

Ilola, L. (1990). Culture and health. In R. Brislin (Ed.), *Applied cross-cultural psychology* (pp. 278–301). Newbury Park, CA: Sage.

Irvine, S., & Berry, J. (Eds.). (1988). *Human abilities in cultural context*. Cambridge: Cambridge University Press.

James, W. (1890). *Principles of psychology*. New York: Henry Holt.

Johnson, D., & Johnson R. (1987). *Learning together and alone: Cooperative, competitive, and individualistic learning* (2d ed.). Englewood Cliffs, NJ: Prentice-Hall.

Johnson, J.D., & Tuttle, F. (1989). Problems in intercultural research. In M. Asante & W. Gudykunst (Eds.), *Handbook of international and intercultural communication* (pp. 461–483). Newbury Park, CA: Sage.

Jones, E. (1979). The rocky road from acts to dispositions. *American Psychologist*, 34, 107–117.

Jordan, C., & Tharp, R. (1979). Culture and education. In A. Marsella, R. Tharp, & T. Ciborowski (Eds.), *Perspectives on cross-cultural psychology* (pp. 265–285). New York: Academic Press.

Jordan, W. (1989). Racial attitudes. In C. Wilson & W. Ferris (Eds.), *Encyclopedia of Southern culture* (pp. 1118–1120). Chapel Hill, NC: University of North Carolina Press.

Kagan, S. (1990). The structural approach to cooperative learning. *Educational Leadership*, 47(4), 12–15.

Kagitcibasi, C. (1988). Diversity of socialization and social change. In P. Dasen, J. Berry, & N. Sartorius (Eds.), *Health and cross-cultural psychology: Toward applications* (pp. 25–47). Newbury Park, CA: Sage.

Kagitcibasi, C. (1990). Family and home based intervention. In R. Brislin (Ed.), *Applied cross-cultural psychology* (pp. 121–141). Newbury Park, CA: Sage.

Kagitcibasi, C., & Berry, J. (1989). Cross-cultural psychology: Current research and trends. *Annual Review of Psychology*, 40, 493–531.

Kagitcibasi, C., Sunar, D., & Bekman, S. (1989). *Preschool education project*. Ottawa: IDRC Final Report.

Kahn, H. (1979). *World economic development: 1979 and beyond*. Boulder, CO: Westview.

Kahneman, D., & Tversky, A. (1972). On the psychology of prediction. *Psychological Review*, 80, 237–251.

Kahneman, D., & Tversky, A. (1984). Choices, values, and frames. *American Psychologist*, 39, 341–350.

Kakkar, S. (1970). Family conflict and scholastic achievement. *Indian Journal of Psychology*, 45, 159–164.

Kapur, P. (1970). *Marriage and the working women in India*. New Delhi: Vikas.

Katriel, T. (1990). "Griping" as a verbal ritual in some Israeli discourse. In D. Carbaugh (Ed.), *Cultural communication and intercultural contact* (pp. 99–113). Hillsdale, NJ: Lawrence Erlbaum.

Katriel, T., & Philipsen, G. (1981). What we need is communication: "Communication" as a cultural category in some American talk. *Communication Monographs*, 48, 301–317.

Katz, D. (1960). The functional approach to the study of attitudes. *Public Opinion Quarterly*, 24, 164–204.

Katz, J. (1977). The effects of a systematic training program on the attitudes and behaviors of white people. *International Journal of Intercultural Relations*, 1, 77–89.

Katz, J., & Friedman-Lichtschein, T. (Eds.). (1985). *Japan's new world role*. Boulder, CO: Westview.

Katz, M., Marsella, A., Dube, K., Olatawura, M., et al. (1988). On the expression of psychosis in different cultures: Schizophrenia in an Indian and in a Nigerian community (A report from the World Health Organization Project on Determinants of Outcome of Severe Mental Health Disorders). *Culture, Medicine, and Psychiatry*, 12, 331–355.

Kealey, D. (1988). *Explaining and predicting cross-cultural adjustment and effectiveness: A study of Canadian technical advisors overseas*. Hull, Quebec: Canadian International Development Agency.

Kealey, D. (1989). A study of cross-cultural effectiveness: Theoretical issues, practical applications. *International Journal of Intercultural Relations*, 13, 387–428.

Kealey, D.J., & Ruben, B.D. (1983). Cross-cultural personnel selection: Criteria, issues and methods. In D. Landis & R. Brislin (Eds.), *Handbook of intercultural training Vol. 1: Issues in theory and design* (pp. 155–175). New York: Pergamon.

Kelley, P., & Kelley, V. (1985). Supporting natural helpers: A cross-cultural study. *Social Casework*, 66, 358–366.

Kenrick, D. (1987). Gender, genes, and the social environment: A biosocial interactionist perspective. In P. Shaver & C. Hendrick (Eds.), *Sex and gender* (Review of Personality & Social Psychology, vol. 7, pp. 14–43). Newbury Park, CA: Sage.

Khan, A., & Cataio, J. (1984). *Men and women in biological perspective*. New York: Praeger.

Kim, K., Park, H.J., & Suzuki, N. (1990). Reward allocations in the United States, Japan, and Korea: A comparison of individualistic and collectivistic cultures. *Academy of Management Journal*, 33, 188–198.

Kim, U. (1990). Indigenous psychology: Science and applications. In R. Brislin (Ed.), *Applied cross-cultural psychology* (pp. 142–160). Newbury Park, CA: Sage.

Kinder, D. (1986). The continuing American dilemma: White resistance to racial change 40 years after Myrdal. *Journal of Social Issues*, 42, 151–171.

Kipnis, D. (1976). *The powerholders*. Chicago: University of Chicago Press.

Kipnis, D. (1984). The use of power in organizations and in interpersonal settings. In S. Oskamp (Ed.), *Applied Social Psychology Annual*, Vol. 5 (pp. 179–210). Newbury Park, CA: Sage.

Kleinhesselink, R., & Rosa, E. (1991). Cognitive representation of risk perceptions: A comparison Japan and the United States. *Journal of Cross-Cultural Psychology*, 22, 11–28.

Kleinman, A. (1982). Neurasthenia and depression: A study of somatization and culture in China. *Culture, Medicine, and Psychiatry*, 6, 117–190.

Klineberg, O., & Hull, F. (1979). *At a foreign university*. New York: Praeger.

Kochman, T. (1981). *Black and White style in conflict and communication*. Chicago: University of Chicago Press.

Kochman, T. (1990). Force field in Black and White communication. In D. Carbaugh (Ed.), *Cultural communication and intercultural contact* (pp. 193–217). Hillsdale, NJ: Lawrence Erlbaum.

Kohn, M.L. (1977). *Class and conformity* (2d ed.). Chicago: University of Chicago Press.

Konrad, A.M., & Gutek, B.A. (1986). Impact of work experiences on attitudes toward sexual harassment. *Administrative Science Quarterly*, 31, 422–438.

Krieger, N., & Margo, G. (1991). Women and AIDS: Introduction. *International Journal of Health Services*, 21, 127–130.

Kroeber, A.L., & Kluckhohn, C. (1952). *Culture: A critical review of concepts and definitions*. Peabody Museum Papers, vol. 47, no. 1. Cambridge, MA: Harvard University.

Kumar, U., & Saxena, S. (1983). Interpersonal construct system and work styles of Indian managers. In J. Deregowski, S. Dziurawiec, & R. Annis (Eds.), *Expications in cross-cultural psychology* (pp. 356–370). Lisse, Netherlands: Swets & Zeitlinger.

Laboratory of Comparative Human Cognition. (1986). Contribution of cross-cultural research to educational practice. *American Psychologist*, 41(10), 1049–1058.

LaFromboise, T. (1982). *Assertion training with American Indians: Cultural/ behavioral issue for trainers*. Las Cruces: New Mexico State University Press.

Lambert, W.E., Hamers, J.F., & Frasure-Smith, N. (1979). *Child-rearing values: A cross-national study*. New York: Praeger.

Lambert, W.E., & Tucker, G.R. (1972). *Bilingual education of children: The St. Lambert experiment*. Rowley, MA: Newbury House.

Landis, D., & Brislin, R. (Eds.). (1983). *Handbook of intercultural training* (3 vols.). Elmsford, NY: Pergamon.

Landis, D., Brislin, R., & Hulgus, J. (1985). Attributional training versus contact in acculturative learning: A laboratory study. *Journal of Applied Social Psychology*, 15, 466–482.

Landy, F. (1989). *Psychology of work behavior* (4th ed.). Belmont, CA: Brooks/Cole.

Langer, T. (1962). A twenty-two item screening score of psychiatric symptoms indicating impairment. *Journal of Health and Human Behavior*, 3, 269–276.

Latane, B., Williams, K., & Harkins, S. (1979). Many hands make light the work: Causes and consequences of social loafing. *Journal of Personality and Social Psychology*, 37, 822–832.

Lebra, T. (1976). *Japanese patterns of behavior*. Honolulu: University of Hawaii Press.

Lee, Y., & Larwood, L. (1983). The socialization of expatriate managers in multinational firms. *Academy of Management Journal*, 26, 657–665.

Lefley, H. (1989). Empirical support for credibility and giving in cross-cultural psychotherapy. *American Psychologist*, 44, 1163.

Lefley, H. (1990). Culture and chronic mental illness. *Hospital and Community Psychiatry*, 41, 277–286.

Leibowitz, H.W., Brislin, R., Perlmutter, L., & Hennessey, R. (1969). Ponzo perspective illusion as a manifestation of space perception. *Science*, 166, 1174–1176.

Leong, F., & Kim, H. (1991). Going beyond cultural sensitivity on the road to multiculturalism: Using the Intercultural Sensitizer as a counselor training tool. *Journal of Counseling and Development*, 70, 112–118.

Leung, K., & Iwawaki, S. (1988). Cultural collectivism and distributive behavior. *Journal of Cross-Cultural Psychology*, 19, 35–49.

Leung, K., & Wu, P.G. (1990). Dispute processing: A cross-cultural analysis. In R. Brislin (Ed.), *Applied cross-cultural psychology* (pp. 209–231). Newbury Park, CA: Sage.

LeVine, R., & Campbell, D. (1972). *Ethnocentrism*. New York: Wiley.

Lin, E., Carter, W., & Kleinman, A. (1985). An exploration of somatization among Asian refugees and immigrants in primary care. *American Journal of Public Health*, 75, 1080–1084.

Lin, E., & Kleinman, A. (1988). Psychopathology and clinical course of schizophrenia: A cross-cultural perspective. *Schizophrenia Bulletin*, 14, 555–567.

Lincoln, J. (1985). Work organization and workforce commitment: A study of plants and employees in the U.S. and Japan. *American Sociological Review*, 50, 738–760.

Lindgren, H.C., & Suter, W.N. (1985). *Educational psychology in the classroom* (7th ed.). Monterey, CA: Brooks/Cole.

Ling, W. (1989). Pattern of leadership behavior assessment in China. *Psychologia: An International Journal of Psychology in the Orient*, 32, 129–134.

Lonner, W. (1980). The search for psychological universals. In H. Triandis & W. Lonner (Eds.), *Handbook of cross-cultural psychology, vol. 1: Perspectives* (pp. 143–204). Boston: Allyn & Bacon.

Lonner, W. (1985). Television in the developing world. *Journal of Cross-Cultural Psychology*, special issue, 16(3), 259–397.

Lonner, W. (1990). An overview of cross-cultural testing and assessment. In R. Brislin (Ed.), *Applied cross-cultural psychology* (pp. 56–76). Newbury Park, CA: Sage.

Lonner, W., & Berry, J. (Eds.). (1986). *Field methods in cross-cultural research*. Newbury Park, CA: Sage.

Loscocco, K., & Kalleberg, A. (1988). Age and the meaning of work in the United States and Japan. *Social Forces*, 67, 337–356.

Low, B. (1989). Cross-cultural patterns in the training of children: An evolutionary perspective. *Journal of Comparative Psychology*, 103, 311–319.

Lummis, M., & Stevenson, H. (1990). Gender differences in beliefs and achievement: A cross-cultural study. *Developmental Psychology*, 26, 254–263.

Maccoby, E. (1990). Gender and relationships: A developmental account. *American Psychologist*, 45, 513–520.

Maccoby, E.E., & Jacklin, C.N. (1974). *The psychology of sex differences*. Stanford, CA: Stanford University Press.

Mackey, W.F., & Beebe, V.N. (1977). *Bilingual schools for a bicultural community: Miami's adaptation to the Cuban refugees*. Rowley, MA: Newbury House.

Magnusson, D., & Endler, N. (Eds.). (1977). *Personality at the crossroads*. New York: Wiley.

Malinowski, B. (1927). *Sex and repression in savage society*. London: Kegan Paul.

Malpass, R., & Poortinga, Y. (1986). Strategies for design and analysis. In W. Lonner & J. Berry (Eds.), *Field methods in cross-cultural research* (pp. 47–83). Newbury Park, CA: Sage.

Manheimer, D.L., Dewey, J., Mellinger, G.D., & Corsa, L. (1966). 50,000 child-years of accident injuries. *Pacific Health Reports*, 81, 519–533.

Mar'i, S., & Karayanni, M. (1983). Creativity in Arab culture: Two decades of research. *Journal of Creative Behavior*, 16, 227–238.

Marin, G., & Marin, B.V. (1991). *Research with Hispanic populations*. Beverly Hills, CA: Sage.

Markides, K., & Lee, D. (1990). Predictors of well-being and functioning in older Mexican Americans and Anglos: An eight-year follow-up. *Journal of Gerontology* (Special Issue), 45, S69–S73.

Markus, H., & Kitayama, S. (1991). Culture and the self: Implications for cognition, emotion, and motivation. *Psychological Review*, 98, 224–253.

Markus, H., & Zajonc, R. (1985). The cognitive perspective in social psychology. In G. Lindzey & E. Aronson (Eds.), *Handbook of social psychology*, 3d ed., Vol. 1 (*Theory and method*) (pp. 137–230). New York: Random House.

Marsella, A. (1980). Depressive experiences and disorder across cultures. In H. Triandis & J. Draguns (Eds.), *Handbook of cross-cultural psychology, Vol. 6: Psychopathology* (pp. 237–289). Boston: Allyn & Bacon.

Martin, J. (Ed.). (1986). Theories and methods in cross-cultural orientation. *International Journal of Intercultural Relations*, 10(2), Special issue, pp. 103–254.

Martin, J. (Ed.). (1989). Intercultural communication competence. *International Journal of Intercultural Relations*, 13(3), 227–428, special issue.

McAndrew, F. (1986). A cross-cultural study of recognition thresholds for facial expressions of emotion. *Journal of Cross-Cultural Psychology*, 17, 211–224.

McCafferey, J. (1991). Role plays: A powerful but difficult training tool. In S. Fowler & M. Mumford (Eds.), *Intercultural sourcebook: Cross-cultural training methodologies*. Yarmouth, ME: Intercultural Press.

McConahay, J., & Hough, J. (1976). Symbolic racism. *Journal of Social Issues*, 32(2), 23–45.

McCormick, I., & Cooper, C. (1988). Executive stress: Extending the international comparison. *Human Relations*, 41, 65–72.

Meichenbaum, D. (1977). *Cognitive behavior modification: An integrative approach*. New York: Plenum.

Mendenhall, M., & Oddou, G. (1985). The dimensions of expatriate acculturation. *Academy of Management Review*, 10, 39–47.

Messick, D., & Mackie, D. (1989). Intergroup relations. *Annual Review of Psychology*, 40, 45–81.

Miller, D. (Ed.). (1991). *Handbook of research design and social measurement*. Newbury Park, CA: Sage.

Miller, J. (1984). Culture and the development of everyday social explanation. *Journal of Personality and Social Psychology*, 46, 961–978.

Miller, J., & Kilpatrick, J. (1987). *Issues for managers: An international perspective*. Homewood, IL: Irwin.

Miller, N., & Brewer, M. (Eds.). (1984). *Groups in contact: The psychology of desegregation*. Orlando, FL: Academic Press.

Misumi, J. (1985). *The behavioral science of leadership: An interdisciplinary Japanese research program*. Ann Arbor, MI: University of Michigan Press.

Mizokawa, D., & Rychman, D. (1990). Attributions of academic success and failure: A comparison of six Asian–American ethnic groups. *Journal of Cross-Cultural Psychology*, 21, 434–451.

Moghaddam, F, Ditto, B., & Taylor, D. (1990). Attitudes and attributions related to psychological symptomatology in Indian immigrant women. *Journal of Cross-Cultural Psychology*, 21, 335–350.

Moncher, M., Holden, G., & Trimble, J. (1990). Substance abuse among Native-American youth. *Journal of Consulting and Clinical Psychology*, 58, 408–415.

Morrison, A., & Von Glinow, M. (1990). Women and minorities in management. *American Psychologist*, 45, 200–208.

Morse, S. (1983). Requirements for love and friendship in Australia and Brazil. *Australian Journal of Psychology*, 35, 469–476.

Muchinsky, P. (1990). *Psychology applied to work* (3d ed.). Pacific Grove, CA: Brooks/Cole.

Murdock, G.P. (1981). *Atlas of world cultures*. Pittsburgh: University of Pittsburgh Press.

Murphy-Berman, V., et al. (1984). Factors affecting allocation to needy and meritorious recipients: A cross-cultural comparison. *Journal of Personality and Social Psychology*, 46, 1267–1272.

Nachmias, D., & Nachmias, C. (1987). *Research methods in the social sciences*. New York: St. Martin's Press.

Nagar, D., & Paulus, P. (1988). *Residential crowding experience scale: Assessment and validation*. Arlington, TX: University of Texas at Arlington.

Nakao, K. (1987). Analyzing sociometric preferences: An example of Japanese and U.S. business groups. *Journal of Social Behavior and Personality*, 2, 523–534.

Nath, R. (Ed.). (1988). *Comparative management*. Cambridge, MA: Ballinger.

Neal, A., & Turner, S. (1991). Anxiety disorders research with African Americans: Current status. *Psychological Bulletin*, 109, 400–410.

Nevill, D., & Perrotta, J. (1985). Adolescent perceptions of work and home: Australia, Portugal, and the United States. *Journal of Cross-Cultural Psychology*, 16, 483–495.

"The new whiz kids." (1987, August 31). *Time Magazine*, pp. 42–51.

Newhill, C. (1990). The role of culture in the development of paranoid symptomatology. *American Journal of Orthopsychiatry*, 60, 176–185.

Nishimoto, R. (1988). A cross-cultural analysis of psychiatric symptom expression using Langer's twenty-two item index. *Journal of Sociology and Social Welfare*, 15(4), 45–62.

Oberg, K. (1958). *Culture shock and the problem of adjustment to new cultural environments*. Washington, DC: Dept. of State, Foreign Service Institute.

O'Brien, G., Fiedler, F., & Hewlett, T. (1971). The effects of programmed culture training upon the performance of volunteer medical teams in Central America. *Human Relations*, 24, 209–231.

O'Brien, G., & Plooj, D. (1977). Development of culture training manuals for medical workers with Pitjantiatjara aboriginals: The relative effects of critical incident and prose training upon knowledge, attitudes, and motivation. In G. Kearney & D. McElwain (Eds.), *Aboriginal cognition: Retrospect and prospect* (pp. 383–396). Canberra: Australian Institute of Aboriginal Studies.

O'Donnell, J., Stein, M., Machabanski, H., & Cress, J. (1982). Dimensions of behavior problems in Anglo–American and Mexican–American preschool children: A comparative study. *Journal of Consulting and Clinical Psychology*, 50, 643–651.

Offermann, L., & Gowing, M. (1990). Organizations of the future: Changes and challenges. *American Psychologist*, 45, 95–108.

Ottaway, R., & Bhatnagar, D. (1988). Personality and biographical differences between male and female managers in the United States and India. *Applied Psychology: An International Review*, 37, 201–212.

Overfield, T. (1985). *Biological variation in health and illness*. Reading, MA: Addison-Wesley.

Padila, A., Lindholm, K., Chen, A., Duran, R., et al. (1991). The English-only movement: Myths, reality, and implications for psychology. *American Psychologist*, 46, 120–130.

Paguio, L.P., Skeen, P., & Robinson, B. (1987). Perceptions of the ideal child among employed and nonemployed American and Filipino mothers. *Perceptual and Motor Skills*, 65, 707–711.

Paige, M. (1990). International students: Cross-cultural psychological perspectives. In R. Brislin (Ed.), *Applied cross-cultural psychology* (pp. 161–185). Beverly Hills, CA: Sage.

Paige, R.M. (1986). *Cross-cultural orientation: New conceptualizations and applications*. Lanham, MD: University Press of America.

Palmore, E., Nowlin, J., & Wang, H. (1985). Prediction of function among the old-old: A ten-year follow-up. *Journal of Gerontology*, 40, 244–250.

Pandey, J. (1990). The environment, culture, and behavior. In R. Brislin (Ed.), *Applied cross-cultural psychology* (pp. 254–277). Newbury Park, CA: Sage.

Pascale, R., & Athos, A. (1981). *The art of Japanese management: Applications for American executives*. New York: Simon & Schuster.

Paulston, C.B. (1980). *Bilingual education: Theories and issues*. Rowley, MA: Newbury House.

Payer, L. (1988). *Medicine and culture*. New York: Holt.

Pedersen, P. (1988). *A handbook for developing multicultural awareness*. Alexandria, VA: American Association for Counseling and Development.

Pedersen, P. (1991a). Counseling international students. *The Counseling Psychologist*, 19(1), 10–58.

Pedersen, P. (Ed.). (1991b). Multiculturalism as a fourth force in counseling. *Journal of Counseling and Development* (Vol. 70, No. 1: Special Issue).

Peeters, R. (1986). Health and illness of Moroccan immigrants in the city of Antwerp, Belgium. *Social Science and Medicine*, 22, 679–685.

Pepitone, A. (1987). The role of culture in theories of social psychology. In C. Kagitcibasi (Ed.), *Growth and progress in cross-cultural psychology* (pp. 12–21). Lisse: Swetz & Zeitlinger.

Perry, C., Grant, M., Ernberg, G., Florenzano, R., et al. (1989). WHO collaborative study on alcohol education and young people: Outcome of a four-country pilot study. *International Journal of the Addictions*, 24, 1145–1171.

Pettengill, S., & Rohner, R. (1985). Korean–American adolescents' perceptions of parental control, parental acceptance-rejection, and parent-adolescent conflict. In I. Reyes Lagunes & Y. Poortinga (Eds.), *From a different perspective: Studies of behavior across cultures* (pp. 241–249). Lisse, Netherlands: Swets & Zeitlinger.

Philipsen, G. (1975). Speaking "like a man" in Teamsterville: Cultural patterns of role enactment in an urban neighborhood. *Quarterly Journal of Speech*, 62, 15–25.

Philipsen, G. (1990a). Reflections on "communication" as a cultural category of some American speech. In D. Carbaugh (Ed.), *Cultural communication and intercultural contact* (pp. 95–97). Hillsdale, NJ: Lawrence Erlbaum.

Philipsen, G. (1990b). Reflections on speaking "like a man" in Teamsterville. In D. Carbaugh (Ed.), *Cultural communication and intercultural contact* (pp. 21–26). Hillsdale, NJ: Lawrence Erlbaum.

Phillips, H. (1960). Problems of meaning and translation in field work. *Human Organization*, 18, 184–192.

Piaget, J. (1966). Nécessité et signification des recherches comparatives en psychologie génétique. *Journal International de Psychologie*, 1, 3–13. Need and significance of cross-cultural studies in genetic psychology (C. Dasen, Trans.). In J.W. Berry & P.R. Dasen (Eds.), (1974), *Culture and cognition* (pp. 299–309). London: Metheun.

Piaget, J. (1970). Piaget's theory. In P.H. Mussen (Ed.), *Carmichael's manual of child psychology* (Vol. 1, 3d ed.) (pp. 703–732). New York: John Wiley.

Ponterotto, J., & Benesch, K. (1988). An organizational framework for understanding the role of culture in counseling. *Journal of Counseling & Development*, 66, 237–241.

Poortinga, Y., & Malpass, R. (1986). Making inferences from cross-cultural data. In W. Lonner & J. Berry (Eds.), *Field methods in cross-cultural research* (pp. 17–46). Newbury Park, CA: Sage.

Prasse, D., & McBride, J. (1991, August). The Milwaukee Project: Follow-up through high school. Paper presented at the Annual Meeting of the American Psychological Association, San Francisco.

Price-Williams, D.R., Gordon, W., & Ramirez, M. (1969). Skill and conservation. *Developmental Psychology*, 1, 769.

Prince, V. (1985). Sex, gender, and semantics. *Journal of Sex Research*, 21, 92–96.

Quah, S. (1985). The health, belief model and preventive health behavior in Singapore. *Social Science and Medicine*, 21, 351–363.

Qureshi, B. (1989). *Transcultural medicine: Dealing with patients from different cultures*. Dordrecht, Netherlands: Kluwer Academic Publishers.

Ramsey, S., & Birk, J. (1983). Preparation of North Americans for interaction with Japanese: Considerations of language and communication style. In D. Landis & R. Brislin (Eds.), *Handbook of intercultural training, vol. 3: Area studies in intercultural training* (pp. 227–259). Newbury Park, CA: Sage.

Randolph, G., Landis, D., & Tseng, O. (1977). The effects of time and practice upon culture assimilator training. *International Journal of Intercultural Relations*, 1(4), 105–119.

Reed, D., McGee, D., Cohen, J., Yano, K., Syme, S., & Feinlab, M.

(1982). Acculturation and coronary heart disease among Japanese men in Hawaii. *American Journal of Epidemiology*, 115(6), 894–905.

Reitsberger, W., & Daniel, S. (1990). Japan vs. Silicon Valley: Quality-cost trade-off philosophies. *Journal of International Business Studies*, 21, 289–300.

Rigby, J.M. (1987). The challenge of multinational team development. (Special Issue: multicultural management development.) *Journal of Management Development*, 6, 65–72.

Riordan, C. (1978). Equal-status interracial contact: A review and revision of the concept. *International Journal of Intercultural Relations*, 2(2), 161–185.

Ritter, P.L., & Dornbusch, S.M. (1989, March). Ethnic variation in family influences on academic achievement. Paper presented at the American Educational Research Association Meetings, San Francisco.

Robinson, W. (1950). Ecological correlations and the behavior of individuals. *American Sociological Review*, 15, 351–357.

Rogers, E. (1989). Inquiry in development communication. In M. Asante & W. Gudykunst (Eds.), *Handbook of international and intercultural communication* (pp. 67–86). Newbury Park, CA: Sage.

Rogoff, B. (1981). Schooling and the development of cognitive skills. In H.C. Triandis & A. Heron (Eds.), *Handbook of cross-cultural psychology. Vol. 4: Developmental psychology* (pp. 233–294). Boston: Allyn & Bacon.

Rogoff, B. (1990). *Apprenticeship in thinking: Cognitive development in social context*. New York: Oxford University Press.

Rohner, R. (1986). *The warmth dimension*. Newbury Park, CA: Sage.

Rohner, R., & Pettengill, S. (1985). Perceived parental acceptance-rejection and parental control among Korean adolescents. *Child Development*, 56, 524–528.

Romano, D. (1988). *Intercultural marriage*. Yarmouth, ME: Intercultural Press.

Rossi, A., & Todd-Mancillas, W. (1987). Machismo as a factor affecting the use of power and communication in the managing of personnel disputes: Brazilian versus American male managers. *Journal of Social Behavior and Personality*, 2(1), 93–104.

Saal, F., & Knight, P. (1988). *Industrial/organizational psychology: Science and practice*. Pacific Grove, CA: Brooks/Cole.

Sakamoto, N., & Naotsuka, R. (1982). *Polite fictions: Why Japanese and Americans seem rude to each other*. Tokyo: Kinseido.

Sanua, V. (1980). Familial and sociocultural antecedents of psychopathology. In H. Triandis & J. Draguns (Eds.), *Handbook of cross-cultural psychology, Vol. 6: Psychopathology* (pp. 175–236). Boston: Allyn & Bacon.

Saraswathi, T., & Dutta, R. (1988). Current trends in developmental psychology: A life-span perspective. In J. Pandey (Ed.), *Psychology in India: The state of the art. Vol. 1: Personality & mental processes* (pp. 93–152). New Delhi, India: Sage.

Schneider, D. (1991). Social cognition. *Annual Review of Psychology*, 42, 527–561.

Scribner, S., & Cole, M. (1981). *The psychology of literacy*. Cambridge: Harvard University Press.

Sears, D., & Funk, C. (1991). The role of self-interest in social and political attitudes. In M. Zanna (Ed.), *Advance in experimental social psychology*, Vol. 24 (pp. 1–91). San Diego: Academic Press.

Segall, M., Dasen, P., Berry, J., & Poortinga, Y. (1990). *Human behavior in global perspective*. Elmsford, NY: Pergamon.

Segall, M.H., Campbell, D.T., & Herskovits, M.J. (1966). *The influence of culture on visual perception*. Indianapolis: Bobbs-Merrill.

Seligman, M. (1989). Research in clinical psychology: Why is there so much depression today? In I. Cohen (Ed.), *The G. Stanley Hall Lecture Series*, vol. 9. Washington, DC: American Psychological Association.

Serpell, R. (1982). Measures of perception, skills, and intelligence: The growth of a new perspective on children in a Third World country. In W. Hartrup (Ed.), *Review of child development research* (Vol. 6). Chicago: University of Chicago Press.

Sherif, M. (1966). *In common predicament: Social psychology of intergroup conflict and cooperation*. New York: Houghton Mifflin.

Sherman, S., Judd, C., & Park, B. (1989). Social cognition. *Annual Review of Psychology*, 40, 281–326.

Shintani, T., Hughes, C., Beckham, S., & O'Connor, H. (1991). Obesity and cardiovascular risk intervention through the *ad libitum* feeding of traditional Hawaiian diet. *American Journal of Clinical Nutrition*, 53, 1647S–1651S.

Shweder, R. (1991). *Thinking through cultures: Expeditions in cultural psychology*. Cambridge: Harvard University Press.

Shweder, R., & Bourne, E. (1984). Does the concept of the person vary cross-culturally? In R. Shweder & R. Levine (Eds.), *Culture theory* (pp. 158–199). New York: Cambridge University Press.

Singleton, W., Spurgeon, P., & Stammers, R. (Eds.). (1980). *The analysis of social skills*. New York: Plenum.

Sinha, D. (1983). Cross-cultural psychology: A view from the Third World. In J.B. Deregowski, S. Dziurawiec, & R.C. Annis (Eds.), *Expiscations in cross-cultural psychology* (pp. 3–17). Lisse: Swets and Zeitlinger.

Sinha, D. (1988). The family scenario in a developing country and its implications for mental health: The case of India. In P. Dasen, J. Berry, & N. Sartorius (Eds.), *Health and cross-cultural psychology: Toward applications* (pp. 48–70). Newbury Park, CA: Sage.

Sinha, D. (1989). Personal communication, Honolulu, Hawaii.

Sinha, D. (1990). Interventions for development out of poverty. In R. Brislin (Ed.), *Applied cross-cultural psychology* (pp. 77–97). Newbury Park, CA: Sage.

Sinha, J. (1980). *The nurturant task leader*. New Delhi: Sage.

Slovic, P., Fischhoff, B., & Lichtenstein, S. (1985). Characterizing perceived risk. In R. Kates, C. Hohenemser, & R. Kasperson (Eds.), *Perilous progress: Managing the hazards of technology* (pp. 91–125). Boulder, CO: Westview.

Smart, R. (1989). Is the postwar drinking binge ending? Cross-national trends in per capita alcohol consumption. *British Journal of Addiction*, 84, 743–748.

Smith, H. (1988). *The power game: How Washington works*. New York: Random House.

Snell, W., Miller, R., & Belk, S. (1988). Development of the emotional self-disclosure scale. *Sex Roles*, 18, 59–73.

Snell, W., Miller, R., Belk, S., & Garcia-Falconi, R., et al. (1989). Men's and women's emotional disclosures: The impact of disclosure recipient, culture, and the masculine role. *Sex Roles*, 21, 467–486.

Sogon, S., & Izard, C. (1987). Sex differences in emotion recognition by observing body movements: A case of American students. *Japanese Psychological Research*, 29, 89–93.

Solomon, S., Greenberg, J., & Pyszczynski, T. (1991). A terror management theory of social behavior: The psychological functions of self-esteem and cultural worldviews. In M. Zanna (Ed.), *Advances in experimental social psychology* (pp. 93–159). San Diego: Academic Press.

Spitzberg, B. (1989). Issues in the development of a theory of interpersonal competence in the intercultural context. *International Journal of Intercultural Relations*, 13, 241–268.

Sproull, L., Zubrow, D., & Kiesler, S. (1986). Cultural socialization to computing in college. *Computers in Human Behavior*, 2, 257–275.

Stanislaw, H. (1991). Why aren't we all Darwinians? *American Psychologist*, 46, 248.

Stephan, W. (1985). Intergroup relations. In G. Lindzey & E. Aronson (Eds.), *The handbook of social psychology*, vol. 2 (pp. 599–658). New York: Random House.

Stephan, W.G., & Stephan, C.W. (1984). The role of ignorance in intergroup relations. In N. Miller & M.B. Brewer (Eds.), *Groups in contact: The psychology of desegregation* (pp. 229–255). Orlando, FL: Academic Press.

Stevenson, H., Azuma, H., & Hakuta, K. (Eds.). (1986). *Child development and education in Japan*. New York: Freedman.

Stiles, D., Gibbons, J., & de la Garza-Schnellmann, J. (1990). Opposite sex ideal in the U.S.A. and Mexico as perceived by young adolescents. *Journal of Cross-Cultural Psychology*, 21, 180–199.

Stockard, J., & Johnson, M. (1979). The social origins of male dominance. *Sex Roles*, 5, 199–218.

Sturt, E.S., Kamakura, N., & Der, G. (1984). How depressing life is: Lifelong risk of depression in the general population. *Journal of Affective Disorders*, 7, 109–122.

Sue, S. (1988). Psychotherapeutic services for ethnic minorities: Two decades of research findings. *American Psychologist*, 43, 301–308.

Sue, S., & Okazaki, S. (1990). Asian-American educational achievements: A phenomenon in search of an explanation. *American Psychologist*, 45, 913–920.

Sue, S., & Zane, N. (1987). The role of culture and cultural techniques in psychotherapy: A critique and reformulation. *American Psychologist*, 42, 37–45.

Sue, S., Zane, N., & Ito, J. (1979). Alcohol drinking patterns among Asian and Caucasian Americans. *Journal of Cross-Cultural Psychology*, 10, 41–56.

Sullivan, J., Suzuki, T., & Kondo, Y. (1986). Managerial perceptions of performance: A comparison of Japanese American work groups. *Journal of Cross-Cultural Psychology*, 17, 379–398.

Super, C., & Harkness, S. (1986). The developmental niche: A conceptualization at the interface of society and the individual. *International Journal of Behavioral Development*, Vol. 9(4), 545–570.

Sutton-Smith, B., & Roberts, J. (1981). Play, toys, games, and sports. In H. Triandis & A. Heron (Eds.), *Handbook of cross-cultural psychology, Vol. 4: Developmental psychology* (pp. 425–471). Boston: Allyn & Bacon.

Symons, D. (1979). *The evolution of human sexuality*. New York: Oxford University Press.

Talbot, L. (1972). Ecological consequences of rangeland development in Masailand, East Africa. In M. Farvar & J. Milton (Eds.), *The careless technology: Ecology and international development* (pp. 694–711). Garden City, NY: Natural History Press.

Taylor, D., Dube, L., & Bellerose, J. (1986). Intergroup contact in Quebec. In M. Hewstone & R. Brown (Eds.), *Contact and conflict in intergroup encounters* (pp. 107–118). Oxford and New York: Basil Blackwell.

Teahan, J. (1987). Alcohol expectancies, values, and drinking of Irish and U.S. collegians. *International Journal of the Addictions*, 22, 621–638.

Thacore, V. (1973). *Mental illness in an urban community*. Allahabad, India: United Publishers.

Thase, M., Frank, E., & Kupfer, D. (1985). Biological processes in major depression. In E. Beckman & W. Leber (Eds.), *Handbook of depression: Treatment, assessment, and research* (pp. 816–913). Homewood, IL: Dorsey Press.

Thurow, L.M. (1987). A surge in inequality. *Scientific American*, 256(3), 30–37.

Tobin, J., Wu, D., & Davidson, D. (1989a, April). How three key countries shape their children. *World Monitor*, pp. 36–45.

Tobin, J., Wu, D., & Davidson, D. (1989b). *Preschool in three cultures: Japan, China, & the United States*. New Haven: Yale University Press.

Torbiorn, I. (1988). Culture barriers as a social psychological construct: An empirical validation. In Y. Kim & W. Gudykunst (Eds.), *Cross-cultural adaption: Current approaches* (pp. 168–190). Newbury Park, CA: Sage.

Torrey, E. (1986). *Witchdoctors and psychiatrists: The common roots of psychotherapy and its future*. New York: Harper & Row.

Toupin, E., & Son, L. (1991). Preliminary findings on Asian Americans: The "model minority" in a small private East Coast college. *Journal of Cross-Cultural Psychology*, 22, 403–417.

Tran, T. (1990). Language acculturation among older Vietnamese refugee adults. *Gerontologist*, 30, 94–99.

Triandis, H. (1972). *The analysis of subjective culture*. New York: Wiley.

Triandis, H. (1977). *Interpersonal behavior*. Monterey, CA: Brooks/Cole.

Triandis, H. (1989). The self and social behavior in differing cultural contexts. *Psychological Review*, 96, 506–520.

Triandis, H. (1990). Theoretical concepts that are applicable to the analysis of ethnocentrism. In R. Brislin (Ed.), *Applied cross-cultural psychology* (pp. 34–55). Newbury Park, CA: Sage.

Triandis, H., & Berry, J. (Eds.). (1980). *Handbook of cross-cultural psychology, vol. 2: Methodology*. Boston: Allyn & Bacon.

Triandis, H., Brislin, R., & Hui, C.H. (1988). Cross-cultural training across the individualism–collective divide. *International Journal of Intercultural Relations*, 12, 269–289.

Triandis, H., & Davis, E. (1965). Race and belief as determinants of behavioral intentions. *Journal of Personality and Social Psychology*, 2, 715–725.

Triandis, H., Lambert, W., Berry, J., Lonner, W., Heron, A., Brislin, R., & Draguns, J. (Eds.). (1980). *Handbook of cross-cultural psychology* (six volumes). Boston: Allyn & Bacon.

Trifonovitch, G. (1977). On cross-cultural orientation techniques. In R. Brislin (Ed.), *Culture learning: Concepts, applications, and research* (pp. 213–222). Honolulu: University of Hawaii Press.

Tseng, W., & Hsu, J. (1980). Minor psychological disturbances of everyday life. In H.C. Triandis & J. Draguns (Eds.), *Handbook of cross-cultural psychology: Vol. 6: Psychopathology* (pp. 61–97). Boston: Allyn & Bacon.

Tu, Weiming (1989). *The way, learning, and politics: Essays on the Confucian intellectual*. Singapore: Institute of East Asian Philosophies.

Tung, R. (1984). *Business negotiations with the Japanese*. Lexington, MA: Lexington Books.

Tung, R., & Miller, E. (1990). Managing in the twenty-first century: The need for global orientation. *Management International Review*, 30, 5–18.

Turner, F. (1990). Social work practice theory: A trans-cultural resource for health care. *Social Science and Medicine*, 31, 13–17.

Unger, R. (1979). *Female and male: Psychological perspectives*. New York: Harper & Row.

Veilleux, F., & Tougas, F. (1989). Male acceptance of affirmative action programs for women: The results of altruistic or egotistical motives. *International Journal of Psychology*, 24, 485–496.

Vitz, P. (1990). The use of stories in moral development: New psychological reasons for an old education method. *American Psychologist*, 45, 709–720.

Vogt, L., Jordan, C., & Tharp, R. (1987). Explaining school failure, producing school success: Two cases. *Anthropology and Education Quarterly*, 18, 276–286.

Vygotsky, L. (1987). Thinking and speech. In R. Bieber & A. Carton (Eds.), *The collected works of L.S. Vygotsky* (N. Minick, Trans.). New York: Plenum.

Wade, P., & Bernstein, B. (1991). Culture sensitivity training and counselor's race: Effects on Black female clients. *Journal of Counseling Psychology*, 38, 9–15.

Wagner, D. (1988). "Appropriate education" and literacy in the Third World. In P. Dasen, J. Berry, & N. Santorious (Eds.), *Health and cross-cultural psychology: Toward applications* (pp. 93–111). Newbury Park, CA: Sage.

Wagner, D.A. (1977). Ontogeny of the Ponzo illusion: Effects of age, schooling, and environment. *International Journal of Psychology*, 12, 161–176.

Walster, E., Aronson, V., Abrahams, D., & Rottmann, L. (1966). Importance of physical attractiveness in dating behavior. *Journal of Personality and Social Psychology*, 4, 508–516.

Ward, M.C. (1971). *Them children: A study in language learning*. New York: Holt, Rinehart, and Winston.

Warner, M.G. (1990). Hired guns for Hungary. *Newsweek*, 115, (Jan. 29), 48.

Warner, R., Lee, G., & Lee, J. (1986). Social organization, spousal resources, and marital power: A cross-cultural study. *Journal of Marriage and the Family*, 48, 121–128.

Weisfeld, C., Weisfeld, G., & Callaghan, J. (1982). Female inhibition in mixed-sex competition among young adolescents. *Ethology and Sociobiology*, 3, 29–42.

Weiss, B., & Parish, B. (1989). Culturally appropriate crisis counseling: Adapting an American method for use with Indochinese refugees. *Social Work*, 34, 252–254.

Weldon, D., Carlston, D., Rissman, A., Slobodin, L., & Triandis, H. (1975). A laboratory test of the effects of culture assimilator training. *Journal of Personality and Social Psychology*, 32, 300–310.

Westermeyer, J. (1987). Cultural factors in clinical assessment. *Journal of Consulting and Clinical Psychology*, 55, 471–478.

Whiting, D.B. (1980). Culture and social behavior: A model for the development of social behavior. *Ethos*, 8, 95–116.

Whiting, R. (1989). *You gotta have wa*. New York: Macmillan.

Williams, J. (1987). *Eyes on the prize: America's civil rights years, 1954–1965)*. New York: Penguin.

Williams, J., & Best, D. (1982). *Measuring sex stereotypes: A thirty-nation study*. Beverly Hills, CA: Sage.

Williams, J., & Best D. (1990a). *Measuring sex stereotypes: A multination study* (rev. ed.). Newbury Park, CA: Sage.

Williams, J., & Best, D. (1990b). *Sex and psyche: Gender and self viewed cross-culturally*. Newbury Park, CA: Sage.

Wing, J., & Bebbington, P. (1985). Epidemiology of depression. In E. Beckman & W. Leber (Eds.), *Handbook of depression: Treatment, assessment, and research* (pp. 765–794). Homewood, IL: Dorsey Press.

Winikoff, B., & Laukaran, V. (1989). Breastfeeding and bottle feeding controversies in the developing world: Evidence from a study in four countries. *Social Science and Medicine*, 29, 859–868.

Witkin, H. (1967). A cognitive-style approach to cross-cultural research. *International Journal of Psychology*, 2, 233–250.

Witkin, H., Dyk, R.B., Faterson, H.F., Goodenough, D.R., & Karp, S.A. (1962). *Psychological differentiation*. New York: John Wiley.

Wober, M. (1974). Towards an understanding of the Kiganda concept of intelligence. In J. Berry & P. Dasen (Eds.), *Culture and cognition*. London: Methuen.

World Health Organization. (1979). *Schizophrenia: An international follow-up study*. New York: John Wiley.

World Health Organization. (1983). *Depressive disorders in different cultures: Report of the WHO collaborative study of standardized assessment of depressive disorders*. Geneva: Author.

World Health Organization. (1987). *World health statistics annual*. Geneva: Author.

Yando, R., Seitz, V., & Zigler, E. (1979). *Intellectual and personality characteristics of children: Social-class and ethnic-group differences*. Hillsdale, NJ: Erlbaum.

Yang, K.S. (1988). Will societal modernization eventually eliminate cross-cultural psychological differences? In M. Bond (Ed.), *The cross-cultural challenge to social psychology* (pp. 67–85). Newbury Park, CA: Sage.

Yao, F.K. (1990). The prevention of AIDS among African youths: Cultural constraints. *Hygie*, 9(4), 18–21.

Yuchtman-Yaar, E., & Gottlieb, A. (1985). Technological development and the meaning of work: A cross-cultural perspective. *Human Relations*, 38, 603–621.

Zaidi, S.M.H. (1979). Applied cross-cultural psychology: Submission of a cross-cultural psychologist from the Third World. In L. Eckensberger, W.J. Lonner, & Y.H. Poortinga (Eds.), *Cross-cultural contributions to psychology* (pp. 236–243). Amsterdam: Swets and Zeitlinger.

INDEX

AUTHOR INDEX

SUBJECT INDEX